# New Technology-Based Firms in the New Millennium

**New Technology-Based Firms at the Turn of the Century**

*New Technology-Based Firms at the Turn of the Century (2000)*
Edited by Ray Oakey, Wim During and Michelle Kipling

**New Technology-Based Firms in the 1990s**

*New Technology-Based Firms in the 1990s Volume VI (1999)*
Edited by Ray Oakey, Wim During and Syeda-Masooda
Mukhtar

Previous titles in this series published by Paul Chapman
Publishing

*New Technology-Based Firms in the 1990s Volume I (1994)*
Edited by Ray Oakey

*New Technology-Based Firms in the 1990s Volume II (1996)*
Edited by Ray Oakey

*New Technology-Based Firms in the 1990s Volume III (1997)*
Edited by Ray Oakey and Syeda-Masooda Mukhtar

*New Technology-Based Firms in the 1990s Volume IV (1998)*
Edited by Wim During and Ray Oakey

*New Technology-Based Firms in the 1990s Volume V (1998)*
Edited by Ray Oakey and Wim During

**Other titles of interest from Elsevier Science**

*Management of Technology, Sustainable Development and
Eco-Efficiency*
Edited by Louis A. Lefebvre, Robert M. Mason and Tarek
Khalil

**Related journals – sample copies available on request**

*Journal of Engineering and Technology Management*
*Journal of High Technology Management Research*
*Technological Forecasting and Social Change*
*Technovation*

# New Technology-Based Firms in the New Millennium

Edited by

**WIM DURING**
**RAY OAKEY**
and
**SALEEMA KAUSER**

2001

PERGAMON
An Imprint of Elsevier Science
Amsterdam – London – New York – Oxford – Paris – Shannon – Tokyo

ELSEVIER SCIENCE Ltd
The Boulevard, Langford Lane
Kidlington, Oxford OX5 1GB, UK

First edition 2001

Library of Congress Cataloging in Publication Data:
New technology-based firms in the new millennium/edited by Wim During, Ray Oakey, and Saleema Kauser. — 1st ed.
    p. cm.
  ISBN 0-08-043976-4
    1. High technology industries. 2. Small business — Technological innovations. 3. New business enterprises — Effect of technological innovations on. 4. Technological innovations — Economic aspects. 5. Strategic alliances (Business) I. During, W.E. II. Oakey, R.P. (Raymond P.) III. Kauser, Saleema.
HC79.H53 N496 2001
338'.064 — dc21

                                                                                          2001020795

British Library Cataloguing in Publication Data:
  1. High technology industries
  I. During, Wim II. Oakey, R.P. (Raymond P.) III. Kauser, Saleema
  658.5'14
  ISBN 0080439764

ISBN: 0 08 043976 4

∞ The paper used in this publication meets the requirements of ANSI/NISO Z39.48-1992 (Permanence of Paper).

Printed in The Netherlands.

# Contents

*List of Contributors*     vii

PART I    INTRODUCTION

1. The Development of High-Technology Small Firms: Is it a Matter
   of Growth Management and Networking?     1
   WIM DURING, RAY OAKEY AND SALEEMA KAUSER

PART II    DEVELOPMENT AND GROWTH

2. Fighting for Survival and Legitimacy: Growth Trajectories of High
   Technology Firms in the Netherlands     4
   TOM ELFRING AND WILLEM HULSINK

3. Impact of the Product Characteristics on the Internationalisation
   Processes of the Born Globals – The Case of the Finnish
   Telecommunication and Information Technology Software
   Suppliers and Content Providers as an Example     26
   OLLI KUIVALAINEN

4. Developing Strategies for Growth in HTSFs: Looking Beyond
   Survival in an Increasingly Competitive Marketplace     42
   WILLIAM KEOGH, VICTORIA STEWART AND JOHN TAYLOR

5. Internet Usage in Small Irish Firms     57
   JAMES GRIFFIN

6. The Barriers to the Deployment of Strategic Planning in
   High Technology Small Firms – an Empirical Assessment     71
   NICHOLAS O'REGAN, ABBY GHOBADIAN AND JONATHAN LIU

7. Equity Gaps in Depleted Communities: An Entrepreneurial Response     84
   HARVEY JOHNSTONE

8. Modelling Returns to R&D: An Analysis of Size Effects     95
   PETER BROUWER AND HENRY NIEUWENHUIJSEN

9. Managing Training in SMEs for Holistic High Performance     108
   ZULF KHAN AND MARK COOPER

PART III    CO-OPERATION, NETWORKING AND CLUSTERING

10. Barriers in Co-operation between Small and Large Technology-Based
    Firms: A Swedish Case Study     114
    MAGNUS KLOFSTEN AND CARINA SCHÄRBERG

11. Local Skills and Knowledge as Critical Contributions to the Growth
    of Industry Clusters in Biotechnology                                    127
    CHRIS HENDRY AND JAMES BROWN

12. Entrepreneurial Networking in the Dutch Manufacturing Sector:
    The Role of Key Decision Leaders in SME-Based Alliances                  141
    WIM DURING AND AARD J. GROEN

13. New Product Development (NPD) Alliances between Research
    Institutes and SMEs: The Development, Technology Transfer
    and Spin-Off of Advanced Material Burners                                157
    PETRA C. DE WEERD-NEDERHOF AND AARD J. GROEN

14. Academic Spin-Off Ventures: A Resource Opportunity Approach             175
    CÉLINE DRUILHE AND ELIZABETH GARNSEY

15. Commercialisation and Regional Economic Development: Universities
    and their Role in the Emergence of New Technologies                     191
    SARAH Y. COOPER

# Contributors

PETER BROUWER, EIM Small Business Research and Consultancy, Italiëlaan 33, PO Box 7001, 2701 AA Zoetermeer, The Netherlands

JAMES BROWN, City University Business School, Frobisher Crescent, Barbican Centre, London EC2Y 8HB, England

MARK COOPER, Engineering Business Support Unit (Rm T309), School of Engineering, Coventry University, Priory Street, Coventry CV1 5FB, England

SARAH Y. COOPER, School of Management, Heriot-Watt University, Riccarton, Edinburgh, Scotland

PETRA C. DE WEERD-NEDERHOOF, University of Twente, PO Box 217, 7500 AE Enschede, The Netherlands

CÉLINE DRUILHE, Judge Institute of Management Studies, Trumpington Street, Cambridge CB2 1AG, England

WIM DURING, University of Twente, Faculty of Technology & Management, PO Box 217, 7500 AE Enschede, The Netherlands

TOM ELFRING, Erasmus University Rotterdam, Faculty of Business Administration, Rotterdam School of Management, Department of Strategic Management and Business Environment, PO Box 1738, 3000 DR Rotterdam, The Netherlands

ELIZABETH GARNSEY, University of Cambridge, The Judge Institute of Management Studies, Mill Lane, Cambridge CB2 1RX, England

ABBY GHOBADIAN, Middlesex University Business School, The Burroughs, London NW4 4BT, England

JAMES GRIFFIN, Centre for Entrepreneurial Studies, University of Limerick, Limerick, Ireland

AARD J. GROEN, University of Twente, Faculty of Technology & Management, PO Box 217, 7500 AE Enschede, The Netherlands

CHRIS HENDRY, Frobisher Crescent, Barbican Centre, London EC27 8HB, England

WILLEM HULSINK, Erasmus University Rotterdam, Faculty of Business Administration, Rotterdam School of Management, Department of Strategic Management and Business Environment, PO Box 1738, 3000 DR Rotterdam, The Netherlands

HARVEY JOHNSTONE, Director SME Institute, University College of Cape Breton, PO Box 5300, B1P 6L2, Canada

ZULF KHAN, Engineering Business Support Unit (Rm T309), School of Engineering, Coventry University, Priory Street, Coventry CV1 5FB, England

SALEEMA KAUSER, Manchester Business School, Booth Street West, Manchester M15 6PB, England

WILLIAM KEOGH, Aberdeen Business School, The Robert Gordon University, Aberdeen AB15 7AW, Scotland

MAGNUS KLOFSTEN, Linköping University, Centre for Innovation and Entrepreneurship, Teknikringen 7, 581 83 Linköping, Sweden

OLLI KUIVALAINEN, Researcher, Lappeenranta University of Technology, Telecom Business Research Center Lappeenranta, PO Box 20, FIN-53851, Lappeenranta, Finland

JONATHAN LIU, Middlesex University Business School, The Burroughs, London NW4 4BT, England

HENRY NIEUWENHUIJSEN, EIM Small Business Research and Consultancy, Italiëlaan 33, PO Box 7001, 2701 AA Zoetermeer, The Netherlands

RAY OAKEY, Professor of Business Development, Manchester Business School, Booth Street West, Manchester M15 6PB, England

NICHOLAS O'REGAN, Middlesex University Business School, The Burroughs, London NW4 4BT, England

CARINA SCHÄRBERG, Linköping University, Centre for Innovation and Entrepreneurship, Teknikringen 7, 581 83 Linköping, Sweden

VICTORIA STEWART, Aberdeen Business School, The Robert Gordon University, Aberdeen AB15 7AW, Scotland

JOHN TAYLOR, Department of Economics, University of Lancaster, Bailrigg, Lancaster LA1 4YX, England

PART I  Introduction

CHAPTER 1

# The Development of High-Technology Small Firms: Is it a Matter of Growth Management and Networking?

WIM DURING, RAY OAKEY AND SALEEMA KAUSER

## INTRODUCTION

The focus of the first High Technology Small Firms (HTSF) Conference in this new millennium was more on organizational rather than policy-related issues. The papers in this eighth and latest volume in the book series emanating from the above conference confirm how the external environment for the birth and growth of new technology-based firms is constantly changing. Recent prominent examples can be found in the technical fields of Information Technology (IT) and developments in the Life Sciences. Under the influence of developments as far apart, technologically, as the explosive birth and sudden death of 'dot-com' firms, uncertainties created by the 'mad cow disease' disaster, new opportunities have been created, while others have disappeared. However, a solid understanding of processes of strategic management, the management of growth, professional development, technology cooperation, and internationalization can be instrumental in helping to create and sustain successful new HTSFs. The main conference contributions on these themes, presented in this volume, are thus important for all entrepreneurs, consulting bodies and policy makers involved in HTSF developments. In an earlier volume of this series (6), we expressed the expectation that development and growth processes, together with the study of cooperation and networking, would remain on the of HTSF research agenda for some years to come. These are precisely the major themes that have emerged from this year's conference, and comprise key conceptual areas into which individual chapters of this volume are grouped.

## THE PAPERS

### Development and growth (Part II)

In Chapter 2 Elfring and Hulsink present evidence of two different growth trajectories within HTSFs, one Schumpeterian (i.e. creative destruction), the other Kirznerian in view (i.e. opportunity seeking). They use four case studies of Dutch high technology start-up companies to examine these approaches. Early internationalization is increasingly recognized as a special trait of HTSF start-up companies. In Chapter 3 Kuivalainen contributes a paper, based on an exploratory study of 171 Finnish telecommunications and information technology SMEs firms, in which he examines the impacts of product characteristics on the internationalization processes within these 'born global' enterprises. In Chapter 4, the internationalization theme is continued in a Scottish context through continuing research provided by Keogh et al., who explore the national and international strategic behavior of oil industry related firms in the local Aberdeen area.

Another recent development issue of key relevance to HTSF growth is Internet usage, and its impact on strategy and innovation management within these already technology based firms. In Chapter 5 results from a survey of Irish HTSFs is presented by Griffin. These Irish firms show a high usage of the Internet compared to small firms in Canada and Australia. Irish firms appear to have a higher acceptance of the importance of the Internet, and are more ready to incorporate the use of the Internet in their strategic planning. O'Regan et al. in Chapter 6 explore the subject of the deployment of strategic planning within HTSFs in the United Kingdom. Their results show that firms activating strategic planning are better equipped to succeed than firms with no planning approach, regardless of the local external environments in which they exist. None the less Johnstone, in Chapter 7, through a study of venture capital provision in the Cape Breton region of Canada, provides evidence that the variable regional availability of investment capital may frustrate the strategic objectives of HTSF entrepreneurs.

The mastering of technology development and innovation is a necessary condition for success in HTSFs. A key issue in this process is the monitoring of the value of R&D inputs in terms of returns on such investments. Brouwer and Nieuwenhuijsen in Chapter 8 investigate the impact of firm size on the efficiency of R&D in Dutch manufacturing firms. However, successful R&D depends on key individuals who are often the causal driving force behind the rather 'cold' statistical effects represented by R&D outputs. Thus, the authors argue that developing and sustaining sophisticated professional competencies in the workforce should command a high priority in such firms. In Chapter 9 Khan and Cooper show the importance of training in relation to a process of continuous improvement. Based on a literature survey, they discuss why British SMEs provide less job-related training than large companies.

### Cooperation, networking and clustering (Part III)

Strategic alliances, cooperation, networking and clustering continue to take a prominent place in HTSF research agendas. Thus, in this Volume, several papers deal explicitly with this important topic. In Chapter 10, Klofsten and Scharberg describe and analyze different barriers to cooperation between small and large technology-based firms by using the case of a 'spin-off' firm from Linkoping University in Sweden. Similarly, Hendry and Brown in Chapter 11 examine the role of local skills and knowledge in the development of biotechnology clusters in the United Kingdom. In Chapter 12 During ad Groen report from continuing research on strategic alliances between SMEs in the Netherlands, as part of wider international research. For four types of alliances the opinions of key decision leaders are presented with respect to the strategic rationale relating to each alliance, and the organizational conditions necessary for successful cooperation. In terms of economic theory, the forming of alliances is often expressed through the establishment of markets and hierarchies as a result of human interactions. In Chapter 13, in order to better analyze and understand new product development alliances, De Weerd-Nederhof and Groen use a social systems view, when analyzing a case study of cooperation between a Dutch research organization and a small 'spin-off' company. This example provides general lessons for the establishment of this type of alliance.

By cooperating and forming alliances with local firms, universities play a role in local and regional economic development. However Druilhe and Garnsey, in Chapter 14, remind us that the process of incubation from a university into the business world at the local level is never faultless. Finally in Chapter 15 Cooper explores the role that universities can play in fostering HTSF formation and growth at the regional level. In particular, the paper considers the approach adopted by Heriot-Watt University in Edinburgh, aimed at encouraging innovation and commercialization.

CHAPTER 2

# Fighting for Survival and Legitimacy: Growth Trajectories of High Technology Firms in the Netherlands

TOM ELFRING AND WILLEM HULSINK

## INTRODUCTION

New technology-based firms often have ambitious growth targets of achieving substantial sales, obtaining crucial patents, or preparing for a stock market listing within 5–10 years after their formation. They are characterised by massive R&D efforts and experimentation and a high percentage of highly-educated employees with university or postgraduate degrees, working in corporate laboratories and in new product development units (Martin, 1994; Bolland and Hofer, 1998). New technology-based firms are often established by college-educated engineers and scientists with prior business experience, who focus on the production and commercialisation of new technological knowledge and innovations. University 'spin-offs' and new technology-based firms try to keep, or establish, a link with the science and business communities by carrying out joint research, while relying upon licensing agreements and various alliances in order to commercialise their new technologies.

New high technology firms face a number of hurdles on their path towards commercial success. In order to reach a relatively secure position in a market segment, the high-technology start-up firm needs to acquire the resources, and find internal and external partners. A high technology start-up firm faces the difficult task of exploiting its initial innovation before it is challenged by stronger and more experienced rivals, while simultaneously establishing the technological capability for a continuing stream of 'follow-up' innovations. Some of the bottlenecks young firms have to overcome are related to the scientific and technological uncertainties, which may hamper product development, regulatory approval and a market launch. Also the lack of financial and organisation resources may threaten the start-up firm's survival and constrain its growth. New high-growth companies are rarely in a position to finance themselves; often their expansion can only be realised with the assistance of powerful professional investors (e.g. business angels and venture capitalists) and other specialists (e.g. lawyers, recruiters, leasing companies).

New organisations have a high propensity to fail, partly due to the absence of entrepreneurial drive and key resources, but also due to a lack of legitimacy. Aldrich and Fiol (1994: 645) have characterised the process of entrepreneurs mobilising resources and building up legitimacy in a new industry as both ambitious and ambiguous: 'founders of new ventures appear to be fools, for they are navigating, at best, in an institutional vacuum of indifferent munificence and, at worst, in a hostile environment impervious to individual action.' We will argue in this paper that gaining legitimacy is necessary for the continued growth and survival of the vulnerable technology-based firm. Furthermore by actions aimed at informing, furthering and justifying its goals to key external stakeholders and the general public, the young firm also seeks to achieve advance socio-political legitimacy.

A weakness of new technology-based entrepreneurs is that they do not have a track record in terms of service delivery, product quality, solvency and ties with customers. Besides developing skills and securing tangible and intangible assets, new technology-based firms should also become known in the wider community and acquire knowledge on sectoral competition rules, regulations, conventions and rituals. Other ways to increase credibility is to have contractual relationships with larger firms, establish a (symbolic) foreign presence or prepare flotation. For instance, in the present electronic commerce and ICT market, all the 'dotcom' companies suffer from a lack of legitimacy. In order to embed their economic activities effectively, new high-tech entrepreneurs must take a number measures to reduce the risks of professional investors through, for example, hiring experienced law firms, senior managers, and by involving established customers.

Recently, research has been carried out to investigate how 'so-called' incubator and accelerator centres, such as St John's Innovation Centre (Cambridge), Twinning (the Netherlands), Idealab and Garage.com (both from the USA) can help young innovative firms by offering them access to a number of facilities (e.g. housing, finance, contacts, access to business networks) (Reid and Garnsey, 1998; Elfring and Hulsink, 2000; Elfring et al., 2000). The objective of these centres is to improve the survival rate of new technology-based small companies during their start-up phase, and to speed up the growth process by offering them specialised services and intangible assets (often in exchange for shares in the company's stock). Probably their biggest intangible asset is that they confer cognitive and institutional legitimacy on all the 'start-up' firms with which they deal.

## THE STRUCTURE OF THIS PAPER

In our paper we will examine high technology start-up firms in the Netherlands. Our focus is on their strategies in pursuit of growth and the normative support and recognition of other significant parties and individuals. Before discussing the particular evolution of high-technology firms, and the critical phases through which they pass, we will discuss entrepreneurship theory in general, and high-tech entrepreneurship in particular. In our integrative process approach, the relevant dimensions are time, the entrepreneur and the context of the venture. One of our key theoretical challenges is to synthesise the personal trait perspective and the network perspective. These two perspectives may be seen as complementary since each of them appears to have clear limitations. The psychological characteristic perspective cannot fully explain why certain persons become successful entrepreneurs in high-tech ventures. In this type of research, insufficient attention is paid to the role of particular external circumstances. Furthermore, the network approach to entrepreneurship has resulted in an impressive list of stakeholders, who help determine the fortunes of the entrepreneur. Although networks certainly are useful to entrepreneurs in reducing uncertainty through the acquiring or exchange of resources, and by rendering legitimacy, the role of network relationships varies over time and depends on the type of entrepreneur involved.

Both the personal traits and network perspective approaches are the 'building blocks' of growth trajectories. New organisations have a high propensity to fail, partly due to a lack of assets and capabilities (e.g. premises, finance, staff, and products) and partly due to problems associated with initial legitimacy (e.g. credibility, track record for the founding team, support network). We intend to make a distinction between problems related to fighting for survival by seeking to get the required resources on the one hand, and gaining legitimacy by acquiring the right knowledge, knowing the right people and developing contractual relationships with larger firms on the other hand. In short, the leading research question for our paper is the following: how do high-technology companies fight for survival and seek to gain legitimacy?

In this exploratory study, we will analyse the growth patterns of new high technology firms from the Netherlands, and the cognitive and the socio-political networks in which they exist. Issues such as why are entrepreneurs acting to pursue opportunities and how do they secure resources and legitimacy are addressed. In this paper we distinguish between two dominant growth trajectories, Schumpeterian and Kirznerian, and the key characteristics of these two growth paths. In the Schumpeterian trajectory the concept for the start-up is radically new and the issue of cognitive and socio-political legitimacy might hamper its development. In the Kirznerian case the start-up pursues a clear market opportunity, where the issue of accessing to crucial resources in a timely fashion is the main concern for entrepreneurs.

After a discussion of our conceptual approach, four case studies of Dutch ICT and biotechnology companies are presented, which all had to overcome the liabilities of newness. They faced a number of hurdles, which needed to be overcome in order to survive. Some of the impediments were merely of a technological nature, while others included the financial and organisational bottlenecks that threaten the start-up firm's early growth (e.g. lack of capital, customers and business partners). In addition, all four companies faced the difficulty of gaining cognitive and/or socio-political legitimacy: varying from promising technologies in search of markets (Synoptics), persuading both customers and banks of the commercial potential of new methods of payment (Digicash), lobbying for the support of farmers and patients and overcoming massive protestations from animal rights activists and others against cloning (Pharming), and selling an innovative software package to several industries (Noldus).

## THE BUILDING BLOCKS OF A PROCESS APPROACH IN HIGH-TECHNOLOGY ENTREPRENEURSHIP

Entrepreneurship can be described in many different ways, ranging from purposeful innovative behaviour (Drucker, 1985) to risk taking (McGrath, 1999) and from 'creative destruction' (Schumpeter, 1934) to 'opportunity seeking' (Kirzner, 1973). Each of these descriptions stress particular aspects of entrepreneurship and can be related to particular research traditions. To be innovative, or to bring new products to the market, is seen as an important competitive advantage. Entrepreneurship is the ability or competence of an individual or firm (Bird, 1995) to develop innovative products or create new markets. Why are entrepreneurs willing to take the risks associated with start-ups and what are the characteristics of entrepreneurs? The third perspective on entrepreneurship focuses on the results or consequences of entrepreneurship when it disrupts existing economic conditions. Schumpeter perceived the entrepreneur to be an extraordinary person, a visionary who is able to change the rules of the game in a particular industry. Thus, the entrepreneur plays an important role in capitalism, according to Schumpeter, as he or she is able to revitalise and stimulate economic development. The fourth and last perspective on entrepreneurship stresses the alertness of the entrepreneur to pursue opportunities. It is seen as a discovery process (Kirzner, 1997), driven by market imperfections.

The above two perspectives both originate in economics, but have different conceptions of entrepreneurship and its consequences. Schumpeterian entrepreneurship promotes dis-equilibrium through new combinations, which disrupt existing conditions. Entrepreneurial 'start-ups' cause radical innovations and change the rules of the game in an industry. In contrast, Austrian entrepreneurship is a process *towards* equilibrium. 'Entrepreneurial discovery is seen as gradually, but systematically, pushing back the boundaries of sheer ignorance, and in this way, increasing mutual awareness among market participants and thus, driving prices, output and input quantities, toward the values consistent with equilibrium' (Kirzner, 1997, p. 62). In the Austrian conception of entrepreneurship, the alert entrepreneur discovers the existence of profitable discrepancies, gaps, and mismatches in knowledge and information that others have not yet perceived or exploited. The discovery process provides knowledge about the market through market interaction. In this action driven process, information about flawed plans becomes available. However, such failures might reveal new opportunities to alert and imaginative entrepreneurs. The discovery process increases knowledge about a given situation (see also McGrath, 1999), and reduces the level of uncertainty.

Others treat these opposing views as complementary. In a situation of high uncertainty, the scope for the equilibrium promoting activities of the Austrian entrepreneurial type are large. As the level of certainty rises, as a result of processes towards equilibrium set in motion by Austrian oriented entrepreneurs, the scope for Schumpeterian entrepreneurship also rises. Theories about entrepreneurship should be able to give insight and explain both Schumpeterian and Austrian entrepreneurship.

Contributions to an understanding of the entrepreneurial processes originate in different disciplines and focus on different units of analysis. For example, the risk taking perspective builds on psychological insights where the unit of analysis is the individual. In the innovation perspective of Drucker, the firm is the unit of analysis, and in the last two perspectives, it is the interaction between the firm and its environment, which dominates his analysis. In these perspectives economics has made a substantial contribution, but also sociology left its mark through the concepts of embeddedness (Granovetter, 1985) and the role of social networks (Aldrich and Zimmer, 1986).

## WHY DO ENTREPRENEURS ACT?

In studies addressing the 'why' issue, the entrepreneur and his or her traits is the object of analysis. The person who provides entrepreneurship plays an important, and in some studies, a crucial role in the process of pursuing opportunities. Schumpeter, for example, pictures the entrepreneur as a heroic personality who can set revolutionary changes into motion. The major accomplishments of some entrepreneurs lead to a need to examine whether these individuals are somehow different, since it is argued that the special psychological characteristics of some individuals make them prone to behaving and succeeding as entrepreneurs. This psychological characteristic approach has been extensively tested through experimentation studies. Literature reviews of this large body of work have identified the following four personality traits of entrepreneurs (Brockhaus and Horwitz, 1985): need for achievement, internal locus of control, high-risk propensity and tolerance for ambiguity.

However, this approach lacks strong empirical evidence. One of the problems is that of selection bias (Aldrich and Zimmer, 1986). The traits of successful entrepreneurs are examined in detail, but they are not sufficiently compared to the traits of persons whose ventures fail, and/or a representative control group. For example, it is argued that the 'need for achievement' characteristic is common to many individuals and does not predict an entrepreneurial tendency. And the 'internal locus of control' trait has also been identified in successful managers (Amit et al., 1993). Therefore one should be careful; at the most one can speak of antecedents of particular entrepreneurial behavior. Indeed no causal link can be established between any of the above-mentioned traits and entrepreneurship. There is for example the possibility that the observed characteristics are actually the *product* of entrepreneurial experience. In addition, there is evidence that the importance of certain characteristics depend on particular situations. The ethno-entrepreneurship literature shows that immigrants prior to immigration are mostly very similar to the others around them, but in their new surroundings they take on entrepreneurial characteristics (Aldrich and Zimmer, 1986).

## NETWORKS AND INCENTIVES

The psychological characteristic approach clearly has its limitations in dealing with the issue of why entrepreneurs act. Combining the psychology approach with insights from sociology and economics expands our understanding of the reasons why entrepreneurs act to seize opportunities. Both disciplines take the environment into account. The social network perspective is a contribution by sociological studies (Granovetter, 1985), and the role of the structure of payoffs and incentives has been put forward by economists to explain the incidence of entrepreneurship (Baumol, 1993).

Opportunities are irrelevant unless they are taken advantage of, and networks offer a number of ways of improving the ability of entrepreneurs to seize opportunities. First, networks, and in particular, weak ties within the network, provide access to information about a diverse set of topics, ranging from potential markets for goods and services to innovations and promising new business practices. In the network literature, a distinction is made between weak and strong ties. Strong ties are built on a history of past dealings and in these relationships a degree of trust can play a role (Aldrich and Zimmer, 1986). Weak ties refer to a diverse group of persons with whom one has some form of business connection. When strong ties can be associated with close friends, weak ties can be connected to acquaintances (Gravenotter, 1973). Weak ties can lead to a more varied set of information and resources than the strong ties can (Bloodgood et al., 1995), and consequently weak ties enhance the ability of entrepreneurs to discover opportunities. Kirzner (1997) has stressed the importance of alertness, and weak ties may raise the alertness of entrepreneurs.

Secondly, networks, and in particular strong ties, are important in getting the required resources to exploit the identified opportunities. Network members, representing strong ties, are more motivated to help the entrepreneur than the network members with whom the entrepreneur has weak ties. Potential entrepreneurs assess their ability to get hold of the required resources at relatively low cost on the basis of their strong ties. Thus a network with sufficient strong ties raises the chances that a potential entrepreneur will act as it reduces the perception of uncertainty about the returns of investment in certain opportunities. The way they actually assemble the required resources will be discussed in more detail below.

Understanding why entrepreneurs act is affected by the incentive structure. Baumol (1993) argued that the rules regarding the allocation of gains and losses influence the degree to which potential entrepreneurs will act to seize observed opportunities. To increase the gains, and to limit the losses of entrepreneurial activities, creates an incentive for the entrepreneur to take action. McGrath (1999) shows how, in some countries, entrepreneurial activities have been depressed by limiting the upside gains. Comparable material can be found in studies of internal corporate venturing. Inadequate compensation of successful venture champions relative to external opportunities is likely to lead to an exodus of intrapreneurs.

## HOW TO SECURE RESOURCES AND TO GAIN LEGITIMACY

When we have understood why entrepreneurs act, it becomes important to assess *how* they act in order to achieve success. One of the crucial tasks of an entrepreneur is to assemble the resources that are needed. This is quite a difficult task as in the initial stages of a start-up the financial resources are limited, and given the uncertainty about the growth of the venture, it is not very clear which resources are required. One of the key survival strategies is 'asset parsimony' (Bhide, 1994; Hambrick and MacMillan, 1984). The required resources need to be secured at minimum cost. Paying the market price for resources, such as labour, materials, advice and commitment is often too expensive. Social transactions play a critical role in the acquisition of venture resources. These resources can be acquired below the market price when entrepreneurs (and also intrapreneurs) employ social assets such as friendship, trust, and obligation (Starr and MacMillan, 1990, p. 84).

While networks improve the ability of entrepreneurs to acquire resources, they may also provide legitimacy to a new venture, important in starting something innovative (DiMaggio, 1992). Novel ways of combining resources, or entering new markets, create conditions of high uncertainty. This uncertainty rises as the new venture breaks with established norms or the industry ways of doing business. In such a case of Schumpeterian entrepreneurship, it is crucial to gain legitimacy in order to proceed.

## LIABILITY OF NEWNESS AND LACK OF LEGITIMACY

In a seminal text on the relationship between the development of organisations, Stinchcombe (1965: 148–150) has introduced the notion of the 'liability of newness'. Simply stated, while established organisations have a set of institutional roles and stable customer ties which contribute to an effective provision of their services, novel organisational forms are more likely to fail because they struggle to develop and acquire such prerequisites. The reasons for the higher mortality rates of new firms include the creation and learning of new roles (without role models), and the development of new links with users and clients.

Organisation ecologists (Freeman et al., 1983; Carroll, 1997) have elaborated Stinchcombe's argument about the higher propensities of young(er) organisations to fail by relating his 'liability of newness' to their concepts of 'social legitimisation' and 'diffuse competition' levels in particular populations of organisations. In the early phases of the development of a population or industry, density levels are normally low and social contact is also low or even absent: competition is diffuse, capital and employees may be hard to find, suppliers and customers need to be educated, and many institutional rules (hampering the evolution of the new firms and industries) must be changed.

## THE DEFINITION OF LEGITIMACY

Although often referred to as key to organisational evolution, a proper definition and use of the concept legitimacy in theoretical and empirical organisational research is hard to find. This may be due to the fact that it is an elusive and multi-faceted concept, which may refer to, pragmatic, normative, and cognitive forces that constrain, construct and empower actors. However, legitimacy includes a number of dynamic processes, such as the built-up, maintenance and repair stages, which are often dealt with differently and/or selectively by researchers. Searching for, and trying to gain, legitimacy by organisations is paradoxical: on the one hand organisations seek to make their actions, outputs and corporate goals fit with certain societal variables and values, while ultimately legitimacy is beyond their calculative and purposive control. Pfeffer and Salancik (1978: 194) have made the point that legitimacy is intangible and non-proprietary; it is 'conferred status and, therefore, always controlled by those outside the organisation.' Suchman (1995: 574) has defined legitimacy in a broad sense as 'a generalised perception or assumption that the actions of an entity are desirable, proper, or appropriate within some socially constructed system of norms, values, beliefs, and definitions.' In his overview article, Suchman (1995) makes a useful distinction between strategic and institutional legitimacy. In the first approach legitimacy is being treated as a kind of commodity or a special resource, which is not only embedded in a web of stakeholders relations but also being traded and exchanged by them (e.g. Pfeffer and Salancik, 1978). The second approach refers to legitimacy as moral and cognitive pressures acting upon the structure of firms and organisational fields towards consonance with relevant rules or laws, cultural conformity and alignment, and normative support (Scott, 1995).

Achieving sociopolitical legitimacy is particularly difficult when the new venture is very novel and challenges the existing industry boundaries. In such cases, changes in the institutional framework are often required. Entrepreneurial ventures, which require changes in institutional regulations in order to accommodate their development, have a strong incentive to organise legitimacy. In the study by Aldrich and Fiol (1994) a number of strategies on the part of the founding entrepreneurs to overcome existing legitimacy barriers are discussed. Concerning cognitive legitimacy, network actors, such as competitors, distributors and universities, should be mobilised to create partnerships in order to achieve a wider understanding of new concepts. Organising sociopolitical legitimacy involves collective action, negotiations with other industries, and joint marketing and lobbying efforts.

## COMPLEMENTARY RESOURCES AND SEARCH

The issues of legitimacy and getting the required resources are closely linked to the discovery process of finding information about the project, relevant persons and the context of the project. A good deal of the activities are related to searching, monitoring, scouting, evaluating, testing, and the confirming of information. The 128 Venture Group case on high technology ventures provides evidence of the importance of these high technology activities to entrepreneurs. This 128 Venture Group was founded in 1983 and it established a meeting ground for young start-up entrepreneurs, venture capitalists and consultants in order to realise their complementary interests. This group facilitated the process of discovering and learning about trends and opportunities in general, and it has been helpful in getting 'leads' and exchanging 'tacit' knowledge and it cleared the ground for action such as realising 'deals'.

The action orientation in entrepreneurship is prevalent in a number of studies concerned with the search process for information about the feasibility of a venture (Kirzner, 1997; Bhide, 1994; McGrath, 1999). In the entrepreneurial discovery process new information is discovered through interaction. It is not only 'imperfect information' which might be unraveled by the innovation process, but also information which has been termed by the Austrians as 'previously unthought-of knowledge' (Kirzner, 1997, p. 65). An element of surprise is involved in this notion of 'discovering new information'. For some new products and services the only way to learn how they might meet the needs of future customers is to put a product on the market and see how customers react (McGrath, 1999). In order to profit from such a trial-and-error approach a proactive analysis of failure might be helpful. One of the first lessons from the analysis by McGrath is to correct an anti-failure bias. This bias discourages entrepreneurial action by penalising those who try (and fail) and holding blameless those who do not. A second step is to learn from failure. Failures provide information, which can be used to re-conceptualise the product of a venture. Understanding the failure helps to reduce uncertainty about the potential of the new product, and new efforts can benefit from the analysis of positive and negative outcomes. Thus integration of this knowledge into the design of the next set-up improves its survival rate. There are a number of cases from the literature, which show how this combinative process of putting together a new venture has resulted in successful new products (Maidique and Zirger, 1985). These successes are based on intelligent failures, defined by Sitkin (1992) as failures from which something useful is learned.

## LIMITATIONS OF THE NETWORK PERSPECTIVE

The role of the network in organising required resources and providing legitimacy has its limitations. It was shown in the previous section that the success of a 'start-up' could not be explained outside the context of the entrepreneur. The entrepreneur is embedded and the network is used for various purposes. However, the importance of external factors seems to vary from one situation to another (Bloodgood et al., 1995). The network may play a crucial role in organizing legitimacy, while in other contexts networks do not play a significant role at all. In addition, the importance of particular network relationships varies over time. Bloodgood et al., (1995) suggest that family and social ties have a major impact in the initiation stages of an entrepreneurial venture, while economic ties, such as customers, employees and suppliers play a central role in the development stage. However, these variations over time have yet to be fitted to a satisfactory explanatory framework.

## GROWTH TRAJECTORIES AS PROCESSES IN THE DEVELOPMENT OF A VENTURE

In the previous two sections we have discussed the personal traits perspective and the network approach. Both perspectives have some limitations and in a way they complement each other. The development of a venture can be conceptualised as a process in which the characteristics of the entrepreneur and the network play roles. Thus the process perspective may be used as a vehicle to synthesise the personal traits perspective and the network approach, since these two sets of factors influence the development of a venture over time. A way to capture the dynamic nature of the entrepreneurial process is to distinguish a number of stages. In this section we will examine this process perspective and propose two typical growth trajectories. The two distinctive trajectories are based on three factors, which have shown to be of importance:

- the type of entrepreneur;
- the context and in particular, the stakeholders in the network and the role of the network in providing resources and legitimacy;
- the third factor is time and, in particular, the notion that a 'start-up' has to go through a number of stages.

The type of entrepreneur and his/her preference for certain initiatives has an impact on the entrepreneurial processes. The heroic characterisation of the entrepreneur by Schumpeter, and the 'creative destruction' resulting from entrepreneurial activities, is associated with quite different processes than the alert opportunity seeker who is able to react swiftly to a niche in the market. These two ideal types positioned at opposing ends of a continuum may be used to distinguish two distinctive trajectories for 'starting up' and developing a venture.

The context, or network or embeddedness of entrepreneurial activities has resulted in an impressive list of factors affecting the success of a venture. These factors are, however, independent from time and content. We will try to link these factors to time by introducing stages in the analysis and to the content by recognising two different types of entrepreneurs. In this explorative work four case studies on high-tech ventures will be used.

The entrepreneurial process can be seen as a sequence of stages that entrepreneurs undergo from 'initiative' to 'successful development'. The stage approach is a way of capturing the element of time in the analysis. Each stage can be characterised by certain challenges to the entrepreneur and the key environmental factors affecting the development of a venture. In a number of stage models the evolution of small business growth has been described. Most famous are the stage models by Greiner (1972) and Churchill and Lewis (1983). They distinguish the following phases: inception, success, take-off, growth and resource maturity.

## GROWTH TRAJECTORIES IN HIGH TECHNOLOGY

The traditional stage models have been developed to describe small business evolution, but seem to inadequately explain the high-tech start-up (Hulsink et al., 1999). The search and discovery process involves various iterations in order to establish a fit between the technological possibilities and the demands of particular 'niche markets'. During this lengthy process it is difficult to earn money, and the substantial financial requirements of this stage can be partly explained by this period of minimal earnings. High-tech ventures require more capital and hence the role of the venture capitalist is much larger. In addition, the venture capitalist may not only provide capital, but also advice counseling, and in some cases, complementary capabilities, such as managerial experience. This experience is needed to deal with the high uncertainties in emerging high-tech markets. Another way to manage this uncertainty is by teams instead of a single entrepreneur. Team-based ventures appear to be relatively successful in the first stages (Roberts, 1991). The high-tech focus of the founder needs to be complemented by management knowledge.

The effort to conceptualise and develop a commercially viable product is relatively long and substantial (Bolland and Hofer, 1998). In the early phase, the orientation of most of the high-tech start-ups changes gradually. Initially, the large majority of enterprises have a knowledge focus in which they sell their highly specialised knowledge. They may be characterised as research consultancies. This knowledge orientation is replaced by most of them by an increasing focus on the development of a product although, for some of these high-tech 'start-ups', it takes many years before they actually have a sellable product (Roberts, 1991). And usually it takes more time to complement this product focus with a clear perspective on the market and ways to carve out a particular niche. The degree of planning in this first stage is not very sophisticated. Bolland and Hofer (1998) found that in their sample of high-tech ventures the use of planning techniques varied considerably.

The environment of the high-tech firm is found to have an important impact on the number of successful ventures. The ideas for high-tech ventures often originate from work the entrepreneur is performing for another employer, usually a big company or a university. The network of the entrepreneur and his/her founding team plays a crucial role in the 'start-up' phase of the venture. A long list of network relationships to potential suppliers, consultants, venture capitalists, families and friends are found to enhance the survival rate. However it is not very clear when, to which extent and how, these ties are utilised.

The fight for resources in the initial stages of a high-tech firm's growth trajectory appears to be more complex than portrayed in traditional stage models. In addition to the resource problem we want to add the legitimacy gap. High-tech firms are often based on novel technologies and an innovative business model. There is an absence of objective information and evidence about the new activity. As a result these high-tech firms lack legitimacy. Founding entrepreneurs have to develop strategies to gain legitimacy. The discussed distinction between cognitive and sociopolitical legitimacy is relevant here, because these two types of legitimacy require different approaches. Gaining cognitive legitimacy implies strategies to improve the understanding of others regarding the new concepts. The founding entrepreneur has to build trust and reliability to convince others of the potential of the new activities. Convincing future employees, business partners and leading customers are crucial steps to the spreading of knowledge about the new activities. Ultimately when the activity is taken for granted, it has achieved cognitive legitimacy. The issue of sociopolitical legitimacy is strongly related to the extent to which a new activity conforms to the accepted norms and rules of society. The founding entrepreneur has to gain public acceptance by convincing key stakeholders as opinion leaders and government officials that the new activity is appropriate and in line with existing norms.

Thus, the role of planning, the impact of teams and the role of the network in assembling both the required resources and the strategies necessary to gain legitimacy are not recognised in traditional stage models. In addition, these new aspects appear to have a different role in the growth trajectories of high-tech ventures. We will try to distinguish between two dominant growth trajectories for high-tech firms: Schumpeterian and Kirznerian trajectories. In the Schumpeterian trajectory the concept for the 'start-up' is radically new, while the issue of cognitive and socio-political legitimacy might hamper its development. In the Kirznerian case, the 'start-up' is pursuing a clear market opportunity, and issues of getting access to crucial resources in a timely fashion are the main concern of entrepreneurs.

## CASES OF HIGH TECHNOLOGY START-UPS

The growth trajectories of four high-tech start-ups are compared below. The four companies are Noldus, Synoptics, Pharming and Digicash.

### *Noldus*

The main products of Noldus are standard software packages, such as *The Observer, EthoVision* and *UltraVox*, which enable the collection and analysis of data on human and animal behaviour. The company's mission states that these products help scientists, engineers and practitioners to study behavioural processes, automate measurements, improve the quality of their data, and increase their productivity. In addition to the standard software packages, they offer integrated data acquisition and data analysis systems, including PCs and audiovisual equipment. Furthermore, custom software development, training and consulting services can be also part of the package.

Applications to study human and animal behaviour can be found in a large number of disciplines, such as neuroscience, pharmacology, ethnology, veterinary sciences, ergonomics, industrial engineering, and sports research. These disciplines are found in many companies, government agencies and universities and Noldus has over 1500 clients in over 65 countries. The main office is in Wageningen, and Noldus has subsidiaries in Sterling, USA and Freiburg, Germany. In the ten years of its operations it has grown from a one-person company to a high-tech firm of around 40 employees and sales of about 5 million guilders. Important clients are Bayer, Glaxo and Organon from the pharmaceutical industry; Microsoft, Oracle and SAP from the software industry; Ericcson and Deutsche Telekom from the telecommunication industry; DaimlerChrysler and Volvo from the car industry; Lockheed Martin and NASA from the aerospace industry.

Lucas Noldus, following a Ph.D. from Wageningen University in 1989, founded the company. In the last stages of his Ph.D., Lucas Noldus started to develop, in his spare time, a software application called The Observer. The university was supportive, in the sense that they agreed that he could use the university facilities outside office hours to work on his new software package. In that case the university would not claim any intellectual property rights or royalties. The decision for Mr. Noldus to become an entrepreneur was simplified by the fact that in his field of entomology the university could not offer him any job openings. The university, however, was his first client. The change from a research culture to an entrepreneurial environment was relatively small for Mr. Noldus, because his father was an entrepreneur. In addition, the financial risks of his venture were moderated, as the family income was stable since his wife was expected to finish her studies soon and look for a job.

Mr. Noldus started his firm in an incubator building. Although he did not use some of the additional services available to advise start-up companies in these types of buildings, Mr. Noldus benefited from the discussion with other entrepreneurs from other start-up companies in that building.

Investments in product development and distribution in the first years were funded internally and externally. Senter provided some technical subsidies and internally he reinvested as much as possible in the development of new software. His parsimonious policy for example went as far as allocating only a minimal salary to himself and all he could save went into product development.

Most of the marketing efforts of Noldus are directed at conferences of the relevant research fields to make contact with researchers, engineers and practitioners who might use the software products to study behavioral processes. The marketing strategy can also be characterised as a 'stepping stone' approach. From a strengthening position in the pharmaceutical industry Noldus contacted researchers in the psychology and neuroscience field. Visiting conferences in these latter disciplines gave them leads to new customers. An example of a recent client, Volvo, illustrates the dynamics involved. This client uses the Noldus software in their ergonomics group. Ergonomics is an important discipline in the design of cars.

Growth engendered by this 'stepping stone' strategy has been substantial. However, it is a rather labour-intensive marketing strategy, and consequently, it is difficult to grow very fast. In fact, an ambition of Mr. Noldus is balanced growth, since he is clearly aware of the dangers of fast growth. Growth is also constrained by his strategy of financing new product development and new distribution channels by internal means. As a result he does not need venture capital in order to finance the growth of the company. This conservative growth strategy has resulted in a stable growth path, with annual growth figures between 15 and 50 per cent in the last 7 years, a reasonable profit margin, and a healthy balance sheet.

## Synoptics

Synoptics provides expertise in the application of remote sensing techniques in Geographical Information Systems (GIS). These techniques and systems provide data on the processes that occur on the earth surface which are important for clients who map and/or monitor land use, growth of crops and watercourses.

Synoptics was founded as a partnership in 1993 in Wageningen. A team of four Ph.D. graduates started this company in anticipation of a growing demand for remote sensing techniques. Initial financing came from a number of sources including the university, the Ministry of Economic Affairs (from the BCRSV – Beleids Commissie Remote Sensing) and the European Community Human Capital and Mobility Program. In 1995 the winning of larger projects led to the creation of a privately owned company. By 1999, the company had grown to estimated sales of 1.5 million guilders and 15 employees. Of the four founders, two have left for more secure jobs, and the two remaining, Jos Bakker and Hans van Leeuwen, manage the company. One of the directors has a particular responsibility for the technical development, while the other focuses on financial and managerial tasks.

Presently about 80 per cent of the work can be characterised as research and development. As each project is unique, there is hardly any standardisation of approaches or methodology. To cope with this burden, a project-management structure has been implemented and five project-leaders share the task with the management team to acquire new projects. A strategic challenge has been to develop applications, which can be repeated for a number of different clients, in order to have a more steady and secure stream of income. The development of this type of product requires an extension of activities by Synoptics in order to cover the complete 'value chain'. Presently, core activities are data modelling and analysis and integration of the remote sensing and GIS data. Others currently provide data acquisition and data distribution. When Synoptics can provide these activities, they will be able to sell a 'complete' product to a final customer. It is for this reason that since January 1999 Synoptics has become part of Synoptics Holdings BV.

The strategy to develop a product seems to be tempting, because presently there is a danger of an increasing presence of competitors. In particular the increasing commercial orientation of some of the DLO institutes poses a potential threat. In addition, these developments create some difficulty in developing cooperative relationships with knowledge centres at and around the university. The move towards 'standard' applications for niche markets creates, however, a financial problem. It might be necessary to get access to external financial resources, such as venture capitalists. The entrepreneurs appreciate their autonomy and they would welcome the advice of a venture capitalist, however, they are presently not willing to hand over some of their decision powers to an outside party.

### Pharming

Together with the American biotechnology company Genzyme and the Roslin Institute's 'spin-offs' PPL and Geron Biomed (both from Scotland), the Dutch firm Pharming is one of the leading players in the field of genetic manipulation, cloning and successfully transferring genetic material from one life-form to another. In common with Dolly, the first sheep that was cloned, Pharming has been heavily involved in the generating and breeding of Herman, the first transgenic bull in the world, in the face of massive protests and regulatory hurdles. Today, Pharming is a listed medium-sized company with a workforce of approximately 150 people and annual revenues of 13 million Euros (1999).

After the Ministry of Economic Affairs had granted the RijksUniversiteit Leiden (RUL) an R&D subsidy to investigate the possible production of biopharmaceutical proteins by transgenic cattle (i.e. approximately 1.5 million Euros) in 1988, the idea for an academic 'spin-off' emerged. As a consequence, the biotechnology company Genfarm (the forerunner of Pharming) was founded. The company was co-founded by Professor Herman De Boer, a biology professor at the RUL, who had previously worked at Genentech (the biotechnology pioneer from San Francisco) between 1980 and 1987, and Mr. Otto Postma, an industrial liaison officer at the Centre for Bio-Pharmaceutical Sciences of the RUL. The ties between the start-up company and the university were close from the beginning. Genfarm located its corporate offices and laboratories on the premises of the university's Science Park and RUL participated in the stock of the company (in exchange for the facilities and intellectual property rights). Due to a lack of venture capital in the Netherlands at the end of the 1980s, the founders came up with the suggestion for a two-tier structure in which a Dutch/European subsidiary would be part of a larger American holding company. In April 1989, the company was renamed as GenPharm Europe BV, and became a subsidiary of GenPharm International (GPI) of Mountain View (California, USA). While the GenPharm was (GPE) owned by GPI and a partnership of the founders and the RUL, GPI, in turn, had Genencore (a daughter company of Genentech) and Chimera Biotech as major shareholders.

Although very often in the spotlight, the company was struggling and the American shareholders put GenPharm under increasing pressure. In 1993, a new CEO was appointed to streamline the firm's activities and, due to an internal conflict, co-founder Professor De Boer, then Director of R&D, left GenPharm. Two years later, GenPharm was separated from GPI through a sort of (Dutch) management buy-out and received new investments from ABN-AMRO, NPM Capital, GIMV/ Biotech Fund, RUL and the American Red Cross. The company renamed itself Pharming NV. In the same year, Pharming acquired FinnGene Ltd, a small and specialised Finnish biotechnology company, active in the field of transgenic technology (e.g. a producer of EPO and human lactoferin). Initially, a spin-off from the University of Kuopio, FinnGene became fully integrated into the Dutch biotechnology company and was renamed Pharming Oy.

The year 1998 was key in the corporate evolution of Pharming with expanding moves and impediments happening almost simultaneously. On the one hand, Pharming set up a subsidiary in the USA (Rockville, Maryland), close to its contract research partner, the American Red Cross, and furthermore signed an agreement with the Genzyme Corporation to develop and commercialise worldwide the enzyme human alpha-glycosides for treatment of Pompe's disease (a lethal hereditary muscle disease, also known as acid maltase deficiency). In the same year Pharming became a public company, when it became listed on the Pan-European Stock Exchange EASDAQ (a year later the company became also listed at the Amsterdam Stock Exchange). On the other hand, in 1998, Pharming was also forced, due a final ban of the Dutch Ministry of Agriculture on animal cloning, to relocate its dairy farm operations from the Netherlands and transfer them to Finland, Belgium and the USA.

In the 1990s, Pharming was in the process of transforming itself from a technology-driven into a (more) market and product driven company. Its objective has been to find niche markets for unmet medical needs (e.g. an 'orphan drug' for Pompe's disease) and to expand the sales and marketing efforts of its proprietary treatments (e.g. drugs for genetic disorders, infectious diseases, tissue/bone damage, and cardiovascular diseases). Pharming has developed an excellent science and technology base by carrying out solid in-house and contract research activities. Over the years, the company has built up a strong worldwide patent position, consisting of about 10 patents filed in Europe and in the USA, which churn out a steady stream of royalties. Pharming is still very much dependent on subsidies and contract research, without any products on the market place yet, in order to speed up R&D and the testing and production of drugs and also leverage their intellectual property portfolios.

## Digicash

As expressed in its mission statement, and throughout its corporate activities from 1990 to 1999, Digicash has sought to offer 'solutions for security and privacy'. The firm's primary activity was to develop and commercialise safe and secure payment technology products. Digicash's new money systems were widely praised by leading experts in the field, as being innovative, safe and guaranteeing 100 per cent anonymity. The company's micro-payment technology based on small money transfers over the Internet with 'electronic coins' (varying between 25 cents and $10), provided users with the familiar attributes of real cash: finality, consumer privacy and person-to-person payment.

In April 1990, Digicash was set up as a 'spin-off' of the Amsterdam-based CWI, the Centre for Research in Mathematics and Computer Science of the University of Amsterdam. The newly established high technology company located itself at the Amsterdam Science Park WTCW. The founder of the company Dr. David Chaum, then head of the Cryptography Group at CWI, is a world-leading expert in the field of cryptography. Initially, most of Digicash products and applications were based on Chaum's patents in public key cryptography. The main reason to establish a company was the plan by the Dutch Government to develop a road pricing system. Initially, Digicash had a family capital of 2.5 million NLG to set up the company. In order to survive and to grow, the start-up firm had to rely upon the revenues generated by consultancy projects and contract research in the field of smart card technologies and electronic payment systems. As a world-leading pioneer and early developer of advanced cryptography, Digicash participated in a number of technology promotion projects sponsored by the Dutch government and the European Commission (as part of its ESPRIT and ACTS programmes). In 1995, Digicash was acknowledged as a successful high-technology start-up in Europe and a potential winner in a business area thus far dominated by American companies: the company was awarded the European Information Society Technologies' (IST) prize in 1995 by the European Union for its outstanding contribution to technology and innovation.

In its formative years the company did not have any informal investors and/or venture capitalists on board and did not have any tangible products, that could be sold. The first years of the company were very much project-oriented, characterised by a kind of self-management being relatively chaotic and ill structured. It was only after more than five years of *ad hoc* organising that a strong tendency towards professionalisation emerged. The further development and growth of Digicash was very much technology-driven and inspired by the firm's participation in several technology promotion projects. This pioneering firm in the development of electronic payment systems was determined to bring secure and safe electronic cash into the main stream. The company started to bind some larger clients to its (proprietary) technology. Digicash considered itself a front runner. It was sure it would carve out a major share of the market (for instance, when teaming up with a major bank or an alliance with another business partner). Digicash issued a number of licenses to banks all over the world to experiment with and use its e-cash technology. The scope of Digicash's business, however, was not completely restricted to the financial services sector. AMTECH, world-leader in automatic road toll collection and key supplier of microwave tagging for transport networks, and CRYPTO, an international manufacturer and distributor of cryptographic devices, were non-exclusive licensees of Digicash's digital payment technologies. By the mid-1990s, things were going fine for the Dutch-American company. Digicash employed about 50 people and started to give the company an international outlook. In addition to its Amsterdam-based headquarters, Digicash established subsidiaries in the USA and in Australia. The company, however, relied very much on public funding and sales were very marginal.

In the early 1990s, the market for small-scale and micro-payments was still relatively open and fragmented, containing only a few small-scale providers, such as Mondex, Cybercash and First Virtual. In the mid-1990s, however, larger competitors from neighbouring industries moved in. By then, Digicash had not found the leading edge customers and/or strategic partners it was aiming for. In the US, Citibank and Wells Fargo had started experimenting with chipcards. Microsoft and a rivalling consortium including Netscape, Intuit, Quicken and RSA Data Security pushed for electronic money as an add-on to Internet browsers. More importantly, the credit card companies MasterCard and VISA, together with a number of software companies, were working hard on the effective promotion of the Secure

Electronic Transaction (SET) standard. In Digicash's home base, the Dutch banks were also working together through their co-operative clearing house Interpay on a system which was designed for bigger financial transactions and for a broader range of applications. Initially, the banks had approached Digicash, but Digicash asked too much money for its involvement. For their I-pay system, the Dutch banks eventually adopted the SET standard, which had by then become the *de facto* standard, supported by VISA, MasterCard and the major software companies.

Although Digicash was profitable until 1997, the company wanted to break into the US market. As a consequence, the headquarters and research laboratory were moved to Silicon Valley (Palo Alto) to get more input and feedback on technological and commercial developments in Internet-based payments and electronic commerce. The decision to move the company's headquarters to Silicon Valley was strongly promoted by a group of American and Dutch venture capitalists, who announced in April/May 1997 they were investing between US$10 and 15 million in the still pioneering digital commerce company. For the first time, after having relied on subsidies and retained earnings (consultancy fees, patent/license royalties) to finance its expansion, Digicash strengthened its capital base through venture capital. One of the investors' demands was that management needed to be replaced, because major business experience was lacking. Founder Chaum stepped down as president and CEO of Digicash (as largest shareholder, he stayed on as member of the Supervisory Board), and took up the post of Chief Technology Officer. Mr. Nash, a smart card veteran (previously at Amdahl and VISA), was hired as the new CEO.

More than a year later, Digicash's situation looked much worse. In August 1998, another new CEO was appointed, Mr. Loftesness (a former First Data Corporation executive), bringing the total count to three CEOs within a year. Furthermore, the firm had to negotiate a stand-by-credit with its investors. At more or less the same time (September 1998), when Digicash was also nominated for the Dutch Broos van Erp prize for successfully promoting innovative ICT technologies and applications, its Dutch subsidiary ran into financial difficulties and went bankrupt. Furthermore, in October 1998, Digicash lost its toehold in the US as the only American bank testing its system, the Mark Twain bank in Missouri, abruptly closed the three-year trial with anonymous electronic cash. A month after closing their European offices, the Digicash holding company, with a debt of US$4 million, had to ask for a Chapter 11 filing: by then, the number of employees had already been scaled back from more than 50 employees during its peak to six employees. Less than a year later, a suitor was found to buy Digicash's intellectual assets. The Seattle-based company, e-Cash Technologies, in August 1999 announced the acquisition of the firm's technologies, including the patented blind signature encryption scheme.

## ANALYSIS OF CASES

### Noldus

Noldus fits with the notion of Austrian entrepreneurship. A search for a successful product has been limited. In addition, there has been only a slight legitimacy problem. The founder of Noldus once remarked that: 'I never told my first corporate clients that the software was developed on basis of observations of wasps, that might have damaged the credibility of the software'. In the initial stage the emphasis was on exploitation, and to sell this successful software package to as many new clients as possible and develop software for different application as efficiently as possible. An alert entrepreneur discovered the niche in the market. The degree of uncertainty and the level of ambiguity concerning the purpose and strategy of the venture were limited. The means to accomplish the development of the software package and to sell this package to the targeted group of clients was, however, highly uncertain. In the initial period of the venture trial and error is an important mode for learning about the development and planning of new products and markets. The network of the Wageningen University has been used purposefully, for example to get qualified employees and to get access to scientific networks, which may be used for the marketing of the software product.

Achieving legitimacy has not been a major hurdle for Noldus. Sociopolitical legitimacy was not a problem, largely because the standard software industry is well established. However, the type of software developed by Noldus was new and achieving cognitive legitimacy was important in order to convince clients to buy the software, to become a reliable partner for suppliers and other parties and to become an attractive employer. Noldus was able to describe his software package in rather broad terms, the collection and analysis of data on human and animal behaviour, encompassing existing knowledge (Aldrich and Fiol, 1994). In addition, his collaboration with some research fields and the close ties with the university have helped him to achieve cognitive legitimacy.

### Synoptics

For Synoptics, the search for a more or less standardised product remains the main activity three years after the firm was started. Exploration is dominant, although some elements of exploitation have been introduced. Research grants help to improve the legitimacy of the venture. The purpose and the strategy of the venture are still uncertain. The entrepreneurs foresee the development of remote sensing technologies and the potential of this technology for a range of potential customers. At this initial stage they act as consultants and explore the opportunities to develop a product. Information gathered concerns a wide variety of knowledge backgrounds, ranging from highly technical knowledge to client preferences and the costs of operating in international markets. In this type of ventures an entrepreneurial team has been of crucial importance as it enhances the capacity to deal with a wide variety of knowledge requirements.

The Schumpeterian trajectory, as illustrated by Synoptics, is dependent on network ties for a number of reasons. The primary concern for Synoptics has been the issue of legitimacy. The understanding of the business concept by the relevant stakeholders is at stake: the cognitive legitimacy. In addition, institutional support to gain sociopolitical legitimacy has to be acquired. This is of particular importance, as the novel technology of Synoptics is to some extent a solution in search of a problem to be recognised by major stakeholders. Concerning cognitive legitimacy the network may be helpful in involving other parties in developing and distributing the new product. Also linkages with established educational curricula are not difficult to design, as the university is more or less the knowledge centre of the network. The Wageningen Life Sciences network is, however, not sufficiently developed to assist Synoptics in their efforts to gain sociopolitical legitimacy.

### Pharming

The case of Pharming's organisational evolution from the perspective of legitimacy is an interesting one. The company's goals and activities became very controversial with a selective spread of knowledge, depending on the interests of the group of internal and/or external stakeholders. The University of Leyden was keen to have a successful and prestigious 'spin-off' that would furthermore be located at its newly created Technology Park.

Pharming was able to play off the various stakeholders against each other. To farmers and the Ministry of Agriculture, Pharming justified the genetic manipulation of the bull Herman, because this would eventually allow for a treatment of the cow disease 'mastitis'. To patients suffering from all kinds of hereditary diseases, Pharming found an ideal partner willing to stand up against the animal liberation front lobby and defend its biotechnological experiments. Pharming's communications policy was not always coherent over time: on a couple of occasions key information was manipulated, in which the truth became economised or hidden. This may have had something to do with the secretive character of the young biotechnology industry in which patent building and appropriating exclusive knowledge is everything.

Although the company performed well in having acquired a small number of important patents, sales remained negligible and the long-term financial situation continues to be vulnerable. Probably, Pharming is one of the most famous biotechnology companies in the Netherlands, but sadly enough, not because of its patent or product portfolio, but simply because of all the (inter) national media hype around Herman the bull. In its strategy of being the 'lone ranger' in the developing biotechnology industry, Pharming could not rely upon a trade association which could inform the general public and hold seminars to explain various institutionalised practices within Pharming and its competitors.

## Digicash

The market for micro-payments remains something of a non-starter, or to paraphrase the words of Aldrich and Fiol: it is an industry in creation where fools like Digicash and other pioneers in-on-line payment systems first rushed and then ran into trouble. The problem for struggling Digicash was whether there really is a market for the micro-payment solutions in which the company sought to specialise. Furthermore, the disappointing results of various testbeds and roll-outs of smartcards, initiated to boost confidence in on-line payments and credibility of the new electronic banks, could not prevent prevailing scepticism from both shopkeepers and customers (e.g. the disappointing smartcard experiment in New York). In the Netherlands, the massive launch of two rivalling smartcards, namely *chipknip* supported by the incumbent banks and *chipper,* has so far failed to contribute to a substantial increase in electronic payments in shops and retail outlets.

In the early to mid-1990s, when a number of trials with on-line payments via electronic cash and smart cards were carried out, expectations and initial legitimacy of these 'new' financial systems were high. Over the years with the proliferation of the Internet, electronic commerce services and credit cards (especially in western Europe), however, this fear seems to have subsided and most consumers prefer to use credit cards for arranging secure transactions. Compared to the potential of revolutionary Digicash-like systems, consumers instead preferred an evolutionary change towards adjusting the already established credit card system for secure on-line payments on the basis of the widely accepted SET-standard (e.g. VISA, MasterCard, Microsoft, IBM and Netscape). As an insurgent into the market for facilitating financial transactions, Digicash could not cope with the 'gradual conservatism' of the credit card companies and the banking community.

As a consequence of its structural dependence on grants and technology subsidies in the Dutch and European setting, Digicash became very sceptical about government support. In the first place, this was because it had a destructive effect on the company management structure. Instead of having a market-driven and product-based organisational structure, the management system and leadership style of the company was still very much *ad hoc* and organic, reflecting the execution of various government-sponsored projects. Second, despite its high involvement in those technology projects and pilots, Digicash's activities continued to focus primarily on innovation and exploration (for which the overhead was by then far too high) without raising revenues from selling products and licenses. Third, government support made it necessary to develop capabilities one normally does not need in a competitive market place (e.g. tendering for subsidies and projects): the entrepreneurial spirit was driven to the background in western Europe while at the same time in the US critical developments in the (micro-) payments market were taking place (notably with the credit card companies and the larger software companies involved). Digicash's cognitive legitimacy was very much targeted towards its R&D contractor (e.g. government) and their R&D partners, with limited attention to the large business users  (e.g. banks) and the general audience.

Also Digicash's socio-political legitimacy was low: the firm did not put a lot of effort in making itself known in the policy arena and was more concerned with further experiments.

### Implications for growth trajectories

The above four cases shed light on the relevance of traditional stage models (Greiner, 1972) and the growth trajectories (Schumpeterian and Kirznerian), as conceptualised in this paper. The traditional growth stage models do not fully accommodate the dynamic aspects of the evolution of new technology-based firms since such theories do not take the efforts of management in gaining legitimacy into account. The two growth trajectories, as devised in this paper, are different in terms of getting access to key resources on the one hand, and strategies to strive and maintain legitimacy on the other. The main characteristics of the Schumpeterian trajectory include: a high level of uncertainty, the importance of team(s) for obtaining complementary capabilities, exploitative search (shifting focus, from knowledge to product to market), network used to achieve cognitive and sociopolitical legitimacy, and persuasive leadership from the founding entrepreneur(s) (i.e. convincing others in order to gain legitimacy). Evidence of this Schumpeterian path can be found in the case studies of Pharming and Synoptics. In both cases, the companies experienced difficulties in gaining cognitive and socio-political legitimacy because of the high level uncertainty of the market potential of their novel technologies. The main characteristics of the Kirznerian growth trajectory include limited uncertainty, clear goals, emphasis on exploitation, the network used to assemble resources (mainly cognitive legitimacy problems), and 'alert' leadership directed at spotting and exploiting opportunities. Evidence of this Kirznerian path can be found in the Noldus case, where the entrepreneur captured niche market opportunities quickly by mobilizing the required resources and actively working on the cognitive legitimisation of his software package. In addition, the new technology firm being unable to choose one of the available trajectories can explain the Digicash failure. As such, the company was not alert enough and, hence, could not pursue a well-defined niche market strategy (e.g. collaborating with/subcontracting to the major players in on-line payments), hereby fitting the requirements of the Kirznerian approach. Also, the company was slow in product and market development and in mobilising key partners and networks in the field. As such, Digicash, having ignored the development of socio-political legitimacy through lobbying and partnering, missed out on the market place, and was not involved in setting the global SET standard. As such, the company did not fulfill the requirements of the Schumpeterian approach.

## CONCLUSIONS

In this paper we have reviewed a number of perspectives in the entrepreneurship literature. A process approach has been used to synthesise some of the existing perspectives. The complementary insights of the personal trait perspective and the network approach have been the building blocks of our process model and the growth trajectories we have introduced. In most of the traditional stage models, the pivotal role of the network and the concept of entrepreneurial teams has been undervalued. Furthermore, in some of the research on high-tech entrepreneurship, the network-effects on the performance of the venture and the importance of teams were inconclusive. By making a distinction between Schumpeterian and Kirznerian growth trajectories, these inconclusive results could be put in perspective. Schumpeterian trajectories involve a large degree of uncertainty, and one of the mechanisms to reduce uncertainty is the formation of an entrepreneurial team. The complementary capabilities in a team are required to explore the various opportunities in order to develop and refine a new business model. In a Kirznerian trajectory the purpose of the venture and the business model are more or less clear; in this case the main challenge is to assemble the resources and exploit the opportunity. In such situations a single leadership structure is helpful in that it is able to react swiftly to a window of opportunity. Major differences in the two trajectories have been observed concerning the way the network can be used by the entrepreneurs to attain legitimacy. The strategic challenges to be addressed by the entrepreneur in the Schumpeterian trajectory involve both cognitive and sociopolitical legitimacy. In the Kirznerian trajectory the entrepreneurial concern regarding legitimacy is largely restricted to achieving cognitive legitimacy.

Despite the fact that Kirzner and Schumpeter's theories seem to be complementary, they have their shortcomings too, when put into use in the area of high technology entrepreneurship. Both theories basically focus on the self-employed entrepreneur who targets mainly local markets with a strong bias towards dynamic competition, promoting creative destruction and innovation. However, technology-based companies can also be established by teams of entrepreneurs (i.e. an intra-corporate network of complementary specialists, which have stake in the company). Other alternative forms include a quasi-hierarchical relationship with established international producers acting as sponsors for the new company (e.g. licensing, original equipment manufacturing (OEM)), and co-development in local/regional techno-industrial clusters. Another shortcoming of the Kirzner and Schumpeter approaches is that technology is 'taken for granted', waiting to be marketed and traded. Processes such as invention, R&D and the systematic integration of various components into a larger techno-economic system, are often treated as a 'black box'. Instead, some sociologists (e.g. the actor-network theorists MacKenzie, Latour, and Callon) have exactly addressed this issue and referred to the social construction and the more or less deliberate shaping of technology. In his empirical studies of great technology entrepreneurs such as Edison, Sperry, and Rathenau, and the engineering companies they founded, General Electric & Thomson-Houston, Sperry Gyroscope/Rand, and AEG, the historical sociologist Hughes (1989) has introduced the concept of *systems builders*. Those engineers/ entrepreneurs were involved in systematic research and invention, and subsequently in the construction of durable links that tied together human and non-human entities in techno-organisational networks in order to solve managerial, financial and legitimacy problems before bringing their 'solution' into use. Whether these insights from the social shaping of technology and the building of techno-economic systems and organisational/institutional webs, are small, but intriguing, subdivisions of the Schumpeterian trajectory, or may contain the ingredients for a new 'Hughesian' growth trajectory, remains to be seen. As always in limited academic exercises, more cognitive research and socio-political argumentation is needed.

## REFERENCES

Aldrich, H.E. and Fiol, C.M. (1994) 'Fools Rush In? The Institutional Context of Industry Creation', *Academy of Management Review*, Vol. 19, pp. 645–670.

Aldrich, H.E. and Zimmer, C. (1986) 'Entrepreneurship through Social Networks', in: D. Sexton and J. Kasarda (eds) *The Art and Science of Entrepreneurship*, Ballinger, Cambridge, MA.

Amit, R., Glosten, L. and Muller, E. (1993) 'Challenges to Theory Development in Entrepreneurship Research', *Journal of Management Studies*, Vol. 30, pp. 815–834.

Bahrami, H. and Evans, S. (1995), 'Flexible Re-Cycling and High-Technology Entrepreneurship', *California Management Review*, Vol. 37, pp. 52–89.

Baumol, W.J. (1993) *Entrepreneurship, Management and the Structure of Payoffs*, MIT Press, Cambridge, MA.

Bhave, M.P. (1994) 'A Process Model of Entrepreneurial Venture Creation', *Journal of Business Venturing*, Vol. 9, pp. 223–242.

Bhide, A. (1994) 'How Entrepreneurs Craft Strategies that Work', *Harvard Business Review*, March-April, pp. 150–163.

Bird, B. (1995) 'Towards a theory of entrepreneurial competency', in: J.A. Katz and R.H. Brockhaus (eds), *Advances in Entrepreneurship, Firm Emergence and Growth*, JAI Press, Greenwich, Conn.

Bloodgood, J.M., Sapienza, H.J. and Carsrud, A.L. (1995) 'The Dynamics of New Business Start-ups: Person, Context, and Process' in: J.A. Katz and R.H. Brockhaus (eds), *Advances in Entrepreneurship, Firm Emergence, and Growth*, JAI Press, Greenwich, Conn.

Bolland, E.J. and Hofer, C.W. (1998) *Future Firms; How America's High Technology Companies Work*, Oxford University Press, Oxford.

Brockhaus, R.H. and Horwitz, P.S. (1986) 'The psychology of the entrepreneur', in: D. Sexton and J. Kasarda (eds), *The Art and Science of Entrepreneurship*, Ballinger, Cambridge, MA.

Cable, D.M. and Shane, S. (1997) 'A Prisoner's Dilemma Approach to Entrepreneur-Venture Capitalist Relationships', *Academy of Management Review*, Vol. 22, pp. 142–176.

Carrol, G.R. (1997) 'Long-term evolutionary change in organisational populations: Theory, Models and Empirical Findings in Industrial Demography.' *Industrial and Corporate Change*, 6 (1), 119–143.

Churchill, N.C. and Lewis, V.L. (1983) 'Growing Concerns; The Five Stages of Small Business Growth', *Harvard Business Review*, May–June, pp. 30–50.

DiMaggio, P. (1992), 'Nadel's Paradox Revisited: Relational and Cultural Aspects of Organizational Structures', in: N. Nohria and R.G. Eccles (eds) *Networks and Organizations; Structure, Form, and Action*, Harvard Business School Press, Harvard, Cambridge, MA.

Drucker, P. (1985) *Innovation and Entrepreneurship*, Harper and Row, New York.

Elfring, T. and Hulsink, W. (2000) 'Laat duizend nieuwe bedrijven bloeien (in Dutch: Let a thousand new firms bloom). *Economisch-Statistische Berichten* 14-4-2000: 312–315.

Elfring, T., Hulsink, W., Busink, N. and Rijnders, D. (2000) *Onderzoek naar Incubatoren en Participatiew-erken in de Nieuwe Economie (in opdracht van Twinning)* (in Dutch: Research into incubators and participation networks in the New Economy). Universiteit Wageningen/EUR-FBK/RSM.

Freeman, J.H., Carroll, G.R. and Hannan, M.T. (1983) The Liability of Newness: Age dependence in organizational death rates.' *American Sociological Review*, 48: 692–710.

Garvin, D.A. (1983) 'Spin-offs and the new Firm Formation Process', *California Management Review*, Vol. 25.

Gimeno, J., Folta, T.B., Cooper, A.C. and Woo, C.Y. (1997) 'Survival of the Fittest? Entrepreneurial Human Capital and the Persistence of Underperforming Firms', *Administrative Science Quarterly*, Vol. 42, pp. 750–783.

Granovetter, M. (1985) 'Economic Action and Social Structure: A Theory of Embeddedness', *American Journal of Sociology*, Vol. 82, pp. 929–964.

Greiner, L.E. (1972) 'Evolution and Revolution as Organizations Grow', *Harvard Business Review*, July–August, pp. 55–64.

Hambrick, D. and I.C. MacMillan (1984) 'Asset Parsimony – Managing Assets to Manage Profits', *Sloan Management Review*, Winter, pp. 67–74.

Hughes, T.P. (1989) *American Genesis; A Century of Invention and Technological Enthusiasm 1870–1970*, Penguin Books, London.

Hulsink, W., van der Meer, B. and Meeusen-Henniger, E. (1999) *High-Tech Entrepreneurship in the Low Countries?* Management Report No. 01-99, Rotterdam School of Management, Rotterdam.

Kazanjian, R.K. and Drazin, R. (1990) 'A Stage-Contingent Model of Design and Growth for Technology Based New Ventures', *Journal of Business Venturing*, Vol. 5, pp. 137–150.

Kirzner, I.M. (1973) *Competition and Entrepreneurship*, University of Chicago Press, Chicago.

Kirzner, I.M. (1997) 'Entrepreneurial Discovery and the Competitive Market Process: An Austrian Approach', *Journal of Economic Literature*, Vol. 19, pp. 60–85.

Maidique, M.A. and Zirger, B.J. (1985) 'The new product learning cycle', *Research Policy*, 14, pp. 299–313.

Martin, M.J.C. (1994) *Managing Innovation and Entrepreneurship in Technology-based Firms*. New York: John Wiley & Sons.

McGrath, R.G. (1999) 'Falling Forward: Real Options Reasoning and Entrepreneurial Failure, *Academy of Management Review*, Vol. 24, pp. 13–30.

Parhankangas, A. (1999) *Disintegration of Technological Competences; An Empirical Study of Divestments through Spin-off Arrangements*, Acta Polytechnica Scandinavica; Mathematics, Computing and Management in Engineering Series, No. 99, Finnish Academy of Technology, Helsinki.

Pfeffer, J. and Salancik, G.R. (1978) *The External Control of Organizations. A Resource Dependence Perspective*. New York: Harper & Row.

Portes, A. (1995) *The Sociology of Immigration. Essays on Networks, Ethnicity and Entrepreneurship*, Russell Sage Foundation, New York.

Reid, S. and Garnsey, E. (1998) 'Incubation policy and resource provision: Meeting the Needs of Young, Innovative Firms.' In: R. Oakey and W. During (eds), *New Technology-based Firms in the 1990s, Volume V*. London: Paul Chapman.

Roberts, E.B. (1991) *Entrepreneurs in High Technology; Lessons from MIT and Beyond*, Oxford University Press, New York.

Schumpeter, J.A. (1934) *The Theory of Economic Development*. Harvard University Press, Cambridge, MA.

Scott, W.R. (1995) *Institutions and Organizations*. Thousand Oaks: Sage.

Sitkin, S.B. (1992) 'Learning through failure: The strategy of small losses', In B.M. Staw and L.L. Cummings (eds), *Research in Organizational Behavior*, Vol. 14. JAI Press, Greenwich, CT.

Starr, A.S. and I.C. MacMillan (1990) 'Resource Cooptation via Social Contracting: Resource Acquisition Strategies for New Resources', *Strategic Management Journal*, Vol. 11, pp. 79–92.

Stinchcombe, A.L. (1965) 'Social structure and organisations.' In: J.G. March (ed.), *Handbook of Organizations*. Chicago: Rand McNally & Company.

Suchman, M.C. (1995) 'Managing legitimacy: Strategic and institutional Approaches.' *Academy of Management Review*, 20 (3): 571–610.

CHAPTER 3

# Impact of the Product Characteristics on the Internationalisation Processes of the Born Globals – The Case of the Finnish Telecommunication and Information Technology Software Suppliers and Content Providers as an Example

OLLI KUIVALAINEN

## INTRODUCTION

Internationalisation has been the focus of considerable research interest during the last few decades. Historically, research on the internationalisation process research has tended to focus on the challenges and problems related to large enterprises (see e.g. Johanson and Wiedersheim-Paul, 1975; Johanson and Vahlne, 1977; Buckley and Casson, 1979). However, more recent research is concentrating on small and medium sized firms (SMEs), especially small high technology firms (see e.g. Coviello and McAuley, 1999; Coviello and Munro, 1997; Bell, 1995). It has been argued those traditional models, and in particular, the stages theory of internationalisation processes (also called the Uppsala model) is not applicable to firms of this kind. Moreover this model is not capable of explaining 'leap-frogging' or the speeding up of the internationalisation process by not following the normal market entry patterns (Madsen and Servais, 1997; Bell, 1995; Andersen, 1993).

Firms that have become international almost immediately after being established are often called 'born global' or 'international new ventures' (Madsen and Servais, 1997; Oviatt and McDougall, 1994). In this paper the term 'born global' will be used. This term implies that firms and their products should become international rapidly after their establishment, i.e. they take a 'fast track' in their internationalisation process. This development is often enabled by modern technology as advancement of communication and transportation technologies facilitate global connections.

Many high technology firms, especially information technology (IT) firms, the so-called 'dot-coms' and new media firms are categorised under the 'born global' term. There are several reasons that necessitate the faster internationalisation of these firms; e.g. shorter product life cycles (SPLC) as a result of technological developments, and globalisation of markets and technologies. Furthermore, telecommunication and information technology products extend beyond the boundaries of a single country because of the homogenisation of consumers' wants and needs and can thus be sold in a number of national markets that vary widely in economic, cultural and competitive characteristics. This has led to such products being suitable for global marketing strategies, i.e. for standardised marketing strategies. The desirability of pursuing a strategy of standardisation of marketing mix across national boundaries is well founded in the international marketing literature (see e.g. Hout et al., 1982; Terpstra, 1987). Standardisation clearly offers certain advantages for the firms such as cost savings and economies of scale.

There are many researchers, however, who believe that the advantages of product adaptation to individual national markets are more fundamental (e.g. Hill and Still, 1984) and that adaptation in general can strengthen the product's position in a number of markets. It has been argued that the idea of a continuum between the two spectrums could be advantageous and the degree of standardisation or adaptation is dependent upon various internal and external factors. Cavusgil and Zou (1993) state that '... recently, researchers have proposed that neither complete standardisation nor complete adaptation of marketing program is conceivable'. There are also other important questions related to the characteristics of products:

- Are they components of another product or can they be sold alone?
- How does the place in the value chain affect the market entry strategy?
- How do tailor-made or modified products differ from standardised ones in their internationalisation? etc.

## BACKGROUND FOR THE STUDY

Product and product strategies were chosen as the focal point for the study because information technology products are challenging and complex entities which clearly have an effect on the process of internationalisation. As a matter of fact, the product forms the basis for defining the whole IT-sector. The aim of this paper is to consider the international product strategies of telecommunications and high technology firms (the infocom sector), specifically software producers, and relate them to specific product features, which may have an effect on the internationalisation of product strategies. The research question is first analysed through a theoretical discussion about the process of internationalisation and the characteristics of telecommunication and information technology products. Subsequently, the review develops testable propositions in order to address the patterns that impact on foreign market operation mode and on the supporting activities of the internationalisation process of high technology firms.

The empirical part of the work aims to test the propositions developed. The empirical data for this investigation is derived from Finnish information technology and telecommunications SMEs through an Internet survey. Finally, the research findings and their implications for the management and future research are discussed.

Although considerable progress is being made to determine the nature and cause of internationalisation in this industry, much remains to be accomplished. The literature on the internationalisation initiatives of high technology firms is quite limited. The current research will expand on previous findings and endeavor to offer new insights into the international product strategies of telecommunication and information technology firms. More specifically, the main objective of this research is to examine the internationalisation patterns of Finnish high technology SMEs.

## INTERNATIONALISATION PROCESS AND FOREIGN MARKET ENTRY MODE

In the field of international business, the question of international entry mode has been one of the main concerns. There are many reasons for this, one of which is that an entry mode is the main vehicle for internationalisation. Buckley and Ghauri (1999) note that the relationship between internationalisation and forms of foreign market servicing is a close one, i.e.: '... the conditions under which a firm will choose exporting, licensing or foreign direct investment interact with internationalisation.' Despite the existence of relevant evidence, the literature contains many seemingly unrelated considerations with no identification of key frameworks and constructs that address the question of entry mode choice. Still, new models are being put forward to explain the choice of entry modes (see e.g. Andersen, 1997; Buckley and Casson, 1998). Root (1994) categorised factors affecting the entry mode choice as internal and external factors. External factors include target country market factors, environmental factors, production factors and home country factors. Internal factors consist of product factors and the company's resource/commitment factors.

Most previous research has focused on the choice between general modes of foreign market servicing: exporting, licensing/other contractual modes, and foreign direct investments (see e.g. Erramilli, 1990; Root, 1994; Clark et al., 1997; Buckley and Casson, 1998). Some view the entry mode choice as an incremental and cumulative process (see e.g. Johanson and Wiedersheim-Paul, 1975; Johanson and Vahlne, 1977, 1990), while others (e.g. Dunning, 1988) have examined the choice as a more static process, in which decisions are taken when certain issues change.

Dunning's eclectic theory (or OLI paradigm) of the multinational enterprise is based on the idea that the firm's market entry choice decision is influenced by three types of factors, i.e. 'if a firm has certain ownership based (O), location based (L) or internalisation (I) based advantages, the firm has a tendency to make a foreign direct investment (FDI)' (Dunning, 1993, p. 83). The whole paradigm is based on ideas from international trade theory, resource-based theory and transaction cost theory (Andersen, 1997). It states that a company has ownership-based advantages if it can profitably produce services or products in relation to its current or potential competitors. Ownership-based advantages are a basic requirement for all international activities. Locational advantages vary depending on how ownership-based advantages are combined with advantages based on the production factors in a certain market. Internalisation advantages can shape the choice of entry mode. Dunning argues that the most beneficial development is for the firm to internalise all three by extending its own activities. Foreign markets would then be served entirely by exports and home markets by home production (Dunning, 1993; Erramilli, 1990).

## INTERNATIONALISATION OF THE SMALL TELECOMMUNICATIONS AND INFORMATION TECHNOLOGY FIRMS

The majority of studies concerning SMEs and their internationalization have dealt with manufacturing firms. Their internationalization patterns tend to follow traditional internationalization processes better than their service counterparts do (see Coviello and McAuley, 1999). Quite often firms that have been characterized as high technology, knowledge-based and service intensive, are seen as networkers who have internationalised through their business networks. Previous findings have indicated that exporting is not always the preferred initial entry mode for high technology firms. They have been shown to follow routes other than the export development mode prescribed by much of the internationalisation literature (see e.g. Bell, 1995; Coviello and Munro, 1997; Erramilli and D'Souza, 1995; Sharma and Johanson, 1987).

In many SME studies software firms have been categorised as services (Bell, 1995; Coviello and Munro, 1995, 1997). However, to classify information technology or telecommunications firms into a particular group is more difficult. These industries include many different types of firms and products. Moreover, the rapid ongoing development of technologies together with the increasing convergence of the media industry and the telecommunication industry makes this more problematic.

Majkgård and Sharma (1998) argue that in the case of service firms the fundamental process underlying the choice of foreign market entry mode is the accumulation of experimental knowledge. The 'born global' view of internationalisation, however, suggests that this knowledge can be achieved before the firm starts to internationalise. Experienced personnel and good connections within the firm's network mean that a firm may gain the needed skills without a learning process of its own. In this context, synthesising both the stage theory and the network theory can advance our understanding of certain aspects of internationalisation.

There are few studies available on content providers for telecommunication and information technology sectors. The industry is young and has emerged fairly recently as the Internet, and mobile technologies and applications initiated their revolutions. However, they are closely linked with software producers as this makes it possible to add new services quickly and cheaply into the information technology and telecommunications sector (Persson et al., 1999). At the same time software is gaining ground from hardware as the open global standards start to emerge.

There are many motives behind the process of internationalisation that impact the choice of entry mode (e.g. see Bell, 1995). According to Erramilli (1990) software firms choose from a variety of entry modes. However, Bell (1995), found that SME software producers in Finland, Ireland and Norway have a propensity to export. The majority of SME software firms are owned or led by technical specialists who develop the software. Accordingly these firms may have a need to cooperate in other areas (e.g. marketing). The choice of a distribution channel depends on how much support or service a product needs (Coviello and Munro, 1997). If a software product is tailor-made it may require more interaction with the end-user and an active presence in the market place. Packaged software on the other hand, can be sold more easily without the support of the producer. Embedded or integrated software generally requires substantial support and service to add value. In addition, digital products can be transferred to the customer through the Internet or other electronic commerce solutions and there may not be any need for the traditional incremental internationalisation process at all.

The question of resources and the window of opportunity are also worth mentioning. In many cases, as transaction cost theory suggests, a subsidiary is the most preferred mode of entry for a firm. However, there may not be enough resources or time for this, as in most cases the advantages of technology or product are lost if market entry is delayed. The two factors, scarcity of resources and short time-window, are particularly important for the 'born global' firms in the high-technology sector. It must be noted that a scarcity of resources does not only mean a shortage of money as in many cases there is also a shortage of skilled professionals in international operations.

## PRODUCT, SERVICE OR WHAT: THE PRODUCT CHARACTERISTICS

In 1998 the world market for information and communication technology (ICT) products and services was about 1,445 billion Ecu of which Europe holds 30 per cent (European Information Technology Observatory, EITO, 1998). The industry itself is truly global and is growing fast. In Europe the growth rate of the ICT sector was estimated to be 10 per cent in 1999–2000 (EITO, 1999). However, it is often difficult to define the boundaries of the industry.

One way to explore software products and new media content and the factors that may influence the choice of entry modes is to examine their characteristics through a service-marketing framework (Zeithaml et al., 1985). Services are *intangible* (cannot be seen, touched smelt tasted or heard before purchase); *perishable* (must be created fresh for each customer); *heterogeneous* (hard to standardise because the product varies each time it is delivered); and *inseparable* (involve both the service provider and the customer in the production of the service). In addition Bradley (1991) has identified ownership as being another significant characteristic. For example the intangibility of both software and content means that it is hard for a customer to consider the quality of the product. Customer interaction in developing the product may help the consumer to understand and provide some clarity of the augmented product. The majority of software is purchased by the customer and stored. Thus perishability in the software business will be an issue in the future as the application service provider market starts to boom. Durlacher Research (1999) estimated that by the end of the year 2000, the European market would have grown from US$14 million in 1999 to US$100 million. Heterogeneity is not a problem for packaged software programs. While there may be issues concerning tailor-made software and content services, it would be difficult to provide guidelines because of the different characteristics of the potential offerings in these groups. Erramilli (1990) states that inseparability is important when considering the mode of entry. This is due to the fact that in the service sector production and consumption must occur simultaneously, e.g. getting a new haircut at the hairdresser's. A distinction between hard and soft services should also be made. The entry mode choices of hard services will be different from those of soft services. In hard services production and consumption can be separated and thus exported. Examples of hard services (which can often be seen as offerings, combinations between physical good and services) are packaged software products and engineering designs. In soft services the service provider and receiver need to be physically near each other, and thus exporting is often not possible or cost-effective (Erramilli, 1990). Examples of these include tailor-made software and certain new media solutions.

The digital economy may create both opportunities and threats for media firms and software producers. The copying of software and digital content is relatively easy and copyright laws often lag behind the actual development. Patents are also easy to break as it is not easy to patent knowledge. Table 3.1 illustrates the different types of software and new media content services and the differences between them.

In addition to the characteristics related to the service side of the telecommunications and IT products, there are some other important aspects that should be

**Table 3.1:**  *Comparison of IT and telecommunication products and their characteristics*

|  | Tailor-made software | Packaged software | Media content |
|---|---|---|---|
| **Intangibility** | Needs more presence to make product tangible. | More tangible than tailor-made product. | Intangibility varies depending on the type of product and distribution channel. |
| **Perishability** | Normally not perishable, except for certain services (database runs etc. which) are perishable. | Currently not an issue, but application services are the future. | Often perishable, but digital copying possible in many cases. |
| **Heterogeneity** | As implied by the term tailor-made. | Standardized. | ? |
| **Inseparability** | Needs communication, the amount varies depending on the task, often hard to export economically (depends on the size of the project). | Hard service, can be exported and production and consumption can be separated. No need for physical interaction. | New technologies enable inseparability.<br><br>Can be culturally sensitive, though. |
| **Ownership** | Can be transferred. | Can be transferred, potential threat of piracy. | Patent protection can be problematic. How is the billing done? |

considered. The first is the length of the product life cycle before a new technology, substitute products or competitors capture the market. Secondly, how tacit the knowledge related to the product is and how idiosyncratic the product is must also be considered (see e.g. Kogut and Zander, 1993). The third notion concerns the degree of autonomy in the product. This is related to the standardisation-adaptation issue, i.e. how packaged or tailor-made the product is. Even a packaged software product can be integrated into another software product or be embedded into a totally different environment. Both the position related to the end-user and the need of market information is connected to the product characteristics.

The overall objective of the research was to investigate the internationalisation behaviour of Finnish telecommunication and information technology SMEs. More, specifically, we aim to identify differences in the internationalisation patterns of the firms in terms of the product and/or service offerings, the product life cycle and product related market factors and to classify the firms into specific groups.

## THE PROPOSITIONS

Based on a review of the literature a number of research propositions were developed. It is proposed that since FDIs lead to higher commitment and risk, firms that establish FDIs need to have sufficient resources for investment, enough experience and a highly asset-specific/idiosyncratic product, which needs internalisation. This suggests that small 'born global' firms that set up FDIs are more likely to have standardised products and greater experience. Given that hard (i.e. more tangible and inseparable) services are also easier to export it can be hypothesised that firms with standardised and packaged products are more likely to be international. Thus, we propose that:

P1    *Firms with standardised products are more likely to have international customers.*
P2    *Firms with standardised products are more likely to become international faster.*
P3    *Firms with standardised products are more likely to have target markets in which they can operate.*
P4    *Firms with standardised products are more likely to export compared to other firms.*
P5    *Firms with standardised products are more likely to set up FDIs, as they are more experienced in their internationalisation.*

The new distribution channels, specifically the Internet, developments in transportation and communication technologies have made internationalisation faster, even for softer services. In each case, there may be a need for product adaptation. Tailor-made software especially media content can also be culturally sensitive. To overcome potential problems associated with this market, knowledge and experience are needed. Many small 'born global' firms may acquire this through cooperative agreements. Furthermore, tailor-made products, especially if they are integrated with other products (i.e. systemic) require cooperation between participants in the transaction process. Thus, it can be proposed that:

P6    *Firms whose products need modification/tailoring are more likely co-operate with other firms.*
P7    *Firms whose product is systemic are more likely to sell through collaborative agreements.*
P8    *Firms whose product is autonomous are more likely to sell through exporting.*

The Internet has enabled firms with scarce resources to globalise. As an international distribution channel it is especially attractive for firms with digital products. These include both software and media content applications for which this is a great opportunity to become international. However, selling software through the Internet is easier with standardised products because it requires limited interaction with the customer. There may also be problems with selling culturally sensitive media content through the Internet because of the lack of knowledge of the target market. Thus, we propose that:

P9    *Firms with standardized products are more likely to sell through the Internet.*
P10   *Firms that sell more through the Internet have become international more rapidly.*

The type of product and characteristics the firm believes its competitive advantage is based on may have an effect on internationalisation. Often competitive advantage is based on tacit knowledge that is not easily transferable. In such cases firms are more likely to use sales branches and subsidiaries. In other instances, firms that base their products' competitive advantage on patents or similar legal arrangements can guard their interests through cooperative arrangements. Hence:

P11   *Firms whose competitive advantage is based on tacit knowledge are more likely to internalise their international operations.*
P12   *Firms that have a patent, trademark or copyright are more likely to have contractual arrangements in their international operations.*

Firms that operate in the home market (e.g. in the case of Finland) can grow through international market development to achieve sales growth and economies of scale. It can be proposed that firms need to internationalize faster to increase their sales. Hence:

P13   *Firms that operate in a niche market are more likely to be international.*

IT and telecommunications products have shorter product life cycles than most other products. It has been argued that shorter PLCs push firms to internationalise faster because of the need to make as much profit as possible in a short time. Hence:

P14   *Firms that have products with shorter product life cycle are more likely to become international faster.*

## METHODOLOGY

The data for this study were collected by a survey of 405 Finnish information technology and telecommunications SMEs through an Internet survey. The sample represented both software producers and content providers. A comprehensive survey of the Internet and a number of commercial databases was carried out to locate the names and addresses of the companies. The sample size was considered to be representative of the population, as it has been estimated that there were more than 300 companies operating in the new media business sector in Finland in 1999 (TAIK/Mediastudio, 1999). The companies were first contacted by telephone to request their participation in the study. The assumption was that this would increase the response rate. Furthermore, it was necessary to establish whether the firms actually belonged to the focus group. On the basis of this process a few firms were eliminated from the sample. Following this questionnaires and instructions were e-mailed to the remaining firms.

A total of 171 usable questionnaires were received, giving a response rate of 42.2 per cent. In light of previous research, this can be said to be a good response rate and was likely to have been influenced by the initial enquiry by telephone to each firm to inform respondents that they would receive a questionnaire. Moreover, the validity of the data was considered to be satisfactory as no differences were found between early and late responses (see Armstrong and Overton, 1977). The extent of international involvement was not used as a selection criterion. The sample included firms with international activities as well as firms operating only in Finland. Of the total 171 firms, 73 were operating internationally and the remaining 98 companies were firms operating only in Finland. Therefore, only international firms answered questions relating to internationalisation.

The data analyses for testing the propositions proposed in this study were carried out in two stages. In the first stage, the firms were grouped according to specific product characteristics using a hierarchical cluster analysis. Hierarchical cluster analysis was conducted using nine product type measures as the clustering variables. The clustering variables were determined by the following factors:

1. Focus on information content within the firm's strategy as indicated by the firm,
2. Focus on service platform products and/or services,
3. Focus on control management system products and/or services,
4. The share of subcontracting in the firm's business,
5. The share of tailor-made software products in the firm's business,
6. The share of packaged software in the firm's business,
7. The share of technical consultancy in the firm's business,
8. The length of the product life-cycle with the firm's products on average and
9. The length of the upgrading period of the firm's products.

The relationship between cases was measured by squared Euclidean distance and clusters were formed using the Ward method. The number of clusters was determined by the change in the agglomeration coefficient. The four distinct clusters identified are shown in Table 3.2 together with the factors used to determine them. The clusters have been labelled as 'packaged software producers', 'tailor-made software producers', 'content providers' and 'subcontractors'. The clusters are similar to each other in terms of size with the exception of 'subcontractors', a group we had not identified prior to the analysis. The use of the quick cluster procedure with cluster centroids from the hierarchical solution as initial seeds validated the cluster solution. It was found that the solution derived from quick clustering did not differ significantly from the results of hierarchical clustering made. In the second stage the propositions were tested using the sample of international firms to identify differences and similarities between the clusters. The tests included Mann-Whitney U and Kruskal-Wallis tests for multi-scale variables and crosstabulation with Chi-square test for bi-variate analysis. Internationalisation measures analysed included the speed of internationalisation (from the establishment of the firm), the percentage of the foreign customers from the turnover, different operation modes, the amount of countries in which the firm operates, the results of internationalisation, the anticipated share of foreign operations of the turnover in 2000 and 2002 and the firms' views on resources available for internationalisation.

To further assess the validity of the clusters identified additional product variables were analysed. These included autonomy of the product and specific questions related to the firm's market position. These were importance of tacit knowledge, importance of patents, copyrights and trademarks, importance of the first mover's advantage, importance of the ability to copy cost-effectively ideas from the others, and ability to exploit niches. These variables were all tested in relation to the internationalisation variables.

## SURVEY FINDINGS

Table 3.3 shows the impact of the international variables on the market position and competitive advantage of Finnish IT and telecommunications SMEs. The results indicate that there are few differences between the market position related factors and internationalisation. No significance was found between effects on profitability, know-how, image and internationalisation. It would appear that because firms are small and inexperienced it is difficult for them to evaluate the impact of these variables.

The market position-related variables were also tested with different operation modes. The results revealed few significant differences. In the case of firms with sales subsidiaries, tacit knowledge was found to be less important with a significance level of $p < 0.05$. This was contradictory to our expectations and thus proposition 11 was not supported. One explanation is that there were only eight respondents to validate this proposition. However, for firms using joint ventures, patents proved to be more significant and thus proposition 12 was supported. There were no significant differences found for other operation modes.

The results indicated a number of differences between the clusters. The four clusters illustrated that content providers were smaller, had fewer international activities and were less profitable than the other groups. In addition packaged software producers were depicted to have the most international operations. Thus

**Table 3.2:** *Clusters and clustering variables*

| Variables | Clusters | | | | |
| --- | --- | --- | --- | --- | --- |
| | Tailor-made software | Content | Packaged software | Sub-contractors | Total |
| **Mean** | | | | | |
| Content production and/or products and services related to this | 2.63 | 4.47 | 2.67 | 2.13 | 3.20 |
| Service platform products and/or services | 3.71 | 1.87 | 2.46 | 3.69 | 2.83 |
| Control and management system products and/or services | 3.71 | 1.60 | 3.71 | 2.67 | 2.93 |
| Share of subcontracting from the turnover (%) | 11.2 | 33.3 | 5.53 | 53.1 | 21.2 |
| Share of tailor-made products from the turnover (%) | 49.3 | 21.4 | 16.7 | 20.3 | 30.3 |
| Share of packaged software from the turnover (%) | 16.0 | 6.52 | 68.5 | 13.1 | 23.9 |
| Share of technical consultancy from the turnover (%) | 10.6 | 11.9 | 4.18 | 6.25 | 9.19 |
| Product life-cycle (months) | 27.4 | 20.2 | 61.4 | 40.5 | 33.1 |
| Upgrading period of the product (months) | 7.26 | 4.78 | 8.77 | 21.4 | 7.92 |
| **N** | | | | | |
| Content production and/or products and services related to this | 59 | 55 | 36 | 16 | 166 |
| Service platform products and/or services | 56 | 53 | 35 | 16 | 160 |
| Control and management system products and/or services | 59 | 52 | 34 | 15 | 160 |
| Share of subcontracting from the turnover | 58 | 50 | 34 | 16 | 158 |
| Share of tailor-made products from the turnover (%) | 56 | 50 | 33 | 16 | 155 |
| Share of packaged software from the turnover | 55 | 50 | 33 | 16 | 154 |
| Share of technical consultancy from the turnover (%) | 56 | 50 | 33 | 16 | 155 |
| Product life-cycle (months) | 55 | 48 | 30 | 11 | 144 |
| Upgrading period of the product (months) | 46 | 41 | 29 | 10 | 126 |

**Table 3.2:** *Continued*

| | | | Clusters | | |
|---|---|---|---|---|---|
| **Variables** | **Tailor-made software** | **Content** | **Packaged software** | **Sub-contractors** | **Total** |
| **Std. Deviation** | | | | | |
| Content production and/or products and services related to this | 1.17 | .716 | 1.29 | .885 | 1.38 |
| Service platform products and/or services | 1.06 | .941 | 1.24 | 1.08 | 1.34 |
| Control and management system products and/or services | .984 | .891 | 1.22 | .899 | 1.39 |
| Share of subcontracting from the turnover | 13.2 | 29.2 | 9.57 | 22.4 | 25.2 |
| Share of tailor-made products from the turnover (%) | 24.6 | 27.5 | 17.5 | 14.8 | 27.4 |
| Share of packaged software from the turnover (%) | 16.9 | 14.4 | 23.3 | 18.2 | 29.6 |
| Share of technical consultancy from the turnover (%) | 11.7 | 13.8 | 4.17 | 6.71 | 11.3 |
| Product life-cycle (months) | 16.8 | 14.0 | 37.8 | 32.1 | 27.8 |
| Upgrading period of the product (months) | 3.93 | 3.62 | 4.57 | 20.1 | 7.85 |

*Please note that the scale in the first three items is a 5-point scale.*
*N = 73 Correlation coefficients are presented in the cells when they are significant.*
*\* Correlation is significant at the 0.1 level.*
*\*\* Correlation is significant at the 0.05 level.*

**Table 3.3:** *Correlations between market position related factors and internationalisation*

| Variables related to internationalisation | Tacit knowledge | Patents, trademarks etc. | First mover advantage | Cost-effective follower | Niche |
|---|---|---|---|---|---|
| Customers abroad, % | | | | | 0.157* |
| Speed of internationalisation | | | | | |
| Number of countries | | 0.194** | | | |
| Turnover at the int'l markets '00, % | | 0.254** | 0.174** | | 0.206* |
| Turnover at the int'l markets '02, % | | 0.280** | 0.283** | | 0.234** |
| Effect on turnover | | | | | |
| Effect on image | | | | | 0.061* |

both proposition 1 and proposition 3 were supported which suggests that standardized packaged software producers are more likely to have international customers and more target markets in which to operate compared to firms with less standardized products. However, no differences were found concerning the speed at which internationalisation occurred and thus proposition 2 was not supported. It may be that because the majority of firms within the sample intended to internationalise, differences in time were difficult to realise.

In terms of proposition 4 inconclusive support was found. This may be due to the classification of exporting into indirect, direct and own exporting. While exporting has been shown to be the most widely used mode of entry by all firms, differences were found between the type of exporting used. Firms with systemic products used more indirect exporting (i.e. they may have a customer already that operates as a system integrator) while firms with autonomous products used more direct export sales.

In the case of the type of distribution channels used the results provided mixed support for propositions 6, 7, 8, 9 and 10. There were no differences between the clusters for proposition 6 and proposition 9. This suggests that firms with systemic products do not necessarily use cooperative agreements and firms with standardised products are less likely to sell through the Internet. However, the results indicated that firms with systemic products were more likely to contract through licensing and cooperative agreements compared to firms with autonomous products. Thus proposition 7 was supported. There was some support for proposition 8. The results indicated that while firms with autonomous products were more likely to sell via exporting, firms with systemic products were more likely to use indirect exporting. The results supported proposition 10, which suggested that if the Internet was used there was a tendency to become international more rapidly.

Proposition 5, which states that firms with standardised products are more likely to operate through FDIs, was supported. The results found significant differences in the use of own greenfield FDIs. However, the number of firms using this mode of operation was found to be insignificant (N = 5) and thus the validity of this finding is questionable. The most commonly used mode of operation was found to be exporting (46 per cent of all international firms). In addition partnerships and/or strategic alliances were also shown to be commonly used (42 per cent of all the firms). However, few significant differences were

**Table 3.4:** *Clusters and internationalisation*

| Internationalisation variables | | Clusters | | | | |
| --- | --- | --- | --- | --- | --- | --- |
| | | Tailor-made software | Content providers | Packaged software | Sub-contractors | Total |
| Customers abroad, %** | Mean | 6.86 | 11.2217 | 21.0000 | 9.3750 | 12.1232 |
| | N | 29 | 23 | 22 | 8 | 82 |
| | Std. Deviation | 10.6326 | 20.3801 | 26.1880 | 14.2522 | 19.4817 |
| Number of countries ** | Mean | 2.8462 | 5.1579 | 7.7619 | 4.1250 | 4.9730 |
| | N | 26 | 19 | 21 | 8 | 74 |
| | Std. Deviation | 1.5670 | 11.1069 | 9.7566 | 6.4683 | 8.0800 |

*** significant differences in the chi-square tests at $p < 0.05$ level*

found between the firm classes. Operation modes and their differences within the groups are highlighted in Table 3.5.

Firms pursuing niche strategies had more international customers and a greater turnover from being international. These firms also postulated that international operations enhanced their image. Thus proposition 13 was supported. The average PLC was estimated to be approximately 20 months for cluster firms and 61 months for content providers. However, no correlation was shown between the speed of internationalisation and PLCs. Proposition 14 was not supported and thus shorter PLCs do not suggest faster internationalisation.

## DISCUSSION AND CONCLUDING REMARKS

The primary objective of this paper was to increase our understanding of the effects of product characteristics on the internationalisation processes of Finnish IT and telecommunications SMEs. More importantly, since the whole industry is developing rapidly, there is a greater need to understand the patterns of internationalisation for these firms. Given the weak findings of this research, the above results have provided new evidence regarding the potential of the 'born globals'. According to our survey 90 per cent of the respondents indicated that they hoped to become international within two years. Furthermore, one third of the respondents believed that half of their turnover would come from foreign operations in 2002.

A major limitation of this study is the lack of empirical evidence available that addresses the convergence of the media industry, information and telecommunication technologies. The majority of firms are young and small, and are operating as 'department stores' for potential customers. This makes it is difficult to categorise the firms into different classes and examine the differences in the process of internationalisation. There is also scope for standardised products. These findings complement existing research and provide a greater contribution to our understanding of the process of internationalisation. Further research is needed to understand the importance and development of internationalisation theories.

Overall our findings have indicated that 'born global' firms tend to use exporting and partnerships as their international mode of operation. This was the case for both hard and soft services. However, it must be noted a number of important issues were excluded from the study. For instance cultural differences were not accounted for and it was assumed that our focal products (i.e. new

**Table 3.5:** *Entry modes and product characteristics*

| Entry/operation mode | Differences/important notions |
| --- | --- |
| 1. Sales through the Internet | Subcontractors were using the Internet most, though between the clusters there were no significant differences in the usage of the Internet. It is a fast way to become international and there was also significant correlation between fast-track internationalisation and Internet use. As expected, the systemic–autonomous scale did not prove to have any significant difference. Use of the Internet is going to increase in the future according to estimates. |
| 2. Exporting | Exporting proved to be the most popular operation mode at the moment. This supported the 'born global' thinking. There was significant correlation between indirect exporting and the importance of the first mover advantage. Chi-square was 0.011. There were no significant differences between the clusters. |
| 3. Licensing | Licensing and systemic products correlate with each other significantly. 40% of the firms that have systemic products use licensing, in comparison to 13% of those firms with autonomous product. There were no significant differences between the clusters. |
| 4. Joint ventures, strategic alliances | Systemic products and alliances correlate with each other. 60% of the firms who produce systemic products use alliances as an entry mode. In general partnerships, alliances and joint ventures are estimated to gain even more importance. There were no significant differences between the clusters. |
| 5. FDI (sales or manufacturing subsidiary) | From the clusters the packaged software firms had a tendency to have more FDIs. This is statistically significant (Pearson chi-square, p = 0.050). However, N is small. Packaged software firms received more turnover from the foreign operations and operated in a larger market area. |

high-technology products) could easily be standardised. In particular media content providers are sensitive to cultural differences and their products often require modifications and/or adaptation. This was shown in our study by the fact that content providers were less international compared to other groups. Thus it can be postulated that firms with standardised products (i.e. hard products) are more favorable towards internationalisation compared with, for example, content providers (i.e. soft services). In addition, there may also be a need to localise software products (e.g. language, packaging, and characters) although many applications designed for professionals do not require adaptation. The internationalisation of 'born global' service firms needs to be researched further, and hopefully, conceptual frameworks, based on an empirical basis, are going to be presented in the near future.

## REFERENCES

Andersen, Otto (1993) On the Internationalization Process of Firms: A Critical Analysis, *Journal of International Business Studies*, Second Quarter, pp. 209–231.

Andersen, Otto (1997) Internationalization and Market Entry Mode: A Review of Theories and Conceptual Frameworks, *Management International Review*, 37/2, pp. 27–42.

Anderson, Erin and Gatignon, Hubert (1986) Models of Foreign Entry: A Transaction Cost Analysis and Propositions, *Journal of International Business Studies*, 1/3, Fall, pp. 1–26.

Armstrong, J. Scott and Overton, Terry S. (1977) Estimating Nonresponse Bias in Mail Surveys, *Journal of Marketing Research*, XIV/August, pp. 396–402.

Bell, Jim (1995) The Internationalization of Small Computer Software Firms – A Further Challenge to 'Stage' Theories, *European Journal of Marketing*, 29/8, pp. 60–75.

Bradley, Frank (1991) *International Marketing Strategy*, Prentice Hall, New York.

Buckley, Peter J. and Casson, Mark (1979) A Theory of International Operations, *European Research in International Business*, pp. 1–8.

Buckley, Peter J. and Casson, Mark C. (1998) Analyzing Foreign Market Entry Strategies: Extending the Internalization Approach, *Journal of International Business Studies*, 29/3, pp. 539–562.

Buckley, Peter J. and Ghauri, Pervez N. (1999) Introduction and Overview. In Buckley, Peter J. and Ghauri, Pervez N. (eds) *The Internationalisation of the Firm – A Reader*, 2nd edition, International Thomson Business Press, London.

Cavusgil, S. Tamer and Zou, Shaoming (1993) Product and Promotion Adaptation in Export Ventures: An Empirical Investigation, *Journal of International Business Studies*, 24/3, pp. 479–507.

Clark, Timothy, Pugh, Derek S. and Mallory, Geoff (1997) The Process of Internationalization in the Operating Firm, *International Business Review*, 6/6, pp. 605–623.

Coviello, Nicole E. and McAuley, Andrew (1999) Internationalization and the Smaller Firm: A Review of Contemporary Empirical Research, *Management International Review*, 39/3, pp. 223–256.

Coviello, Nicole E. and Munro, Hugh J. (1995) Growing the Entrepreneurial Firm: Networking for International Market Development, *European Journal of Marketing*, 29/7, pp. 49–61.

Coviello, Nicole E. and Munro, Hugh J. (1997) Network Relationships and the Internationalization Process of Small Software Firms, *International Business Review*, 6/2, pp. 1–26.

Dunning, John H. (1988) The Eclectic Paradigm of International Production: A Restatement and Some Possible Extensions, *Journal of International Business Studies*, Spring 1988, Vol. 19, pp. 1–31.

Dunning, John H. (1993) The Internationalisation of the Production of Services: Some General and Specific Explanations. In Aharoni Yair (ed.) *Coalitions and Competition: The Globalization of Professional Business Services*, New York, Routledge, pp. 79–101.

Durlacher Research (1999) Application Service Providers, A report by Durlacher Research, July.

Erramilli, M. Krishna (1990) Entry Mode Choice in Service Industries, *International Marketing Review*, 7/5, pp. 50–62.

Erramilli, M. Krishna and D'Souza, Derrick E. (1995) Uncertainty and Foreign Direct Investment: The Role of Moderators, *International Marketing Review*, 12/3, pp. 47–60.

European Information Technology Observatory (EITO) (1998) World-wide ICT Markets by Region, 1998, available on the web at the following address: http://www.fvit-eurobit.de/PAGES/EITO/figures99/index.htm, visited 3.4.2000.

European Information Technology Observatory (EITO) (1999) Europe's ICT Market Outdistances Global Growth – EITO Analysis Sees Increase Rates of Up to 10 per cent in 1999, available on the web at the following address: http://www.fvit-eurobit.de/PAGES/EITO/ABSTRACT/Ab-015.html, visited 3.4.2000.

Hair Hellman, Joseph F., Jr, Anderson, Rolph E., Tatham, Ronald L. and Black, William C. (1998) *Multivariate data analysis*, 5th ed., Englewood Cliffs, NJ, Prentice Hall.

Hill, J.S. and Still, R.R. (1984) Adapting Products to LDC Taste, *Harvard Business Review*, 62, March-April, pp. 92-101.

Hout, Thomas, Porter, Michael E. and Rudden, Eileen (1982) How Global Companies Win Out, *Harvard Business Review*, 60, September-October, pp. 98–105.

Jain, Subhash C. (1989) Standardization of International Marketing Strategy: Some Research Hypotheses, *Journal of Marketing*, 53 (January), pp. 70–79.

Johanson, Jan and Vahlne, Jan-Erik (1977) The Internationalization Process of the Firm: a Model of Knowledge Development and Increasing Foreign Market Commitments, *Journal of International Business Studies*, 8(1), pp. 23–32.

Johanson, Jan and Vahlne, Jan-Erik (1990) The Mechanism of Internationalization, *International Marketing Review*, 7/4, pp. 11–24.

Johanson, Jan and Wiedersheim-Paul, Finn (1975) The Internationalization of the Firm: Four Swedish Cases, *Journal of Management Studies*, October, pp. 305–322.

Kogut, Bruce and Zander, Udo (1993) Knowledge of the Firm and the Evolutionary Theory of the Multinational Corporation, *Journal of International Business Studies*, London; Fourth Quarter, 24/4; pp. 625–646.

Madsen, Tage Koed and Servais, Per (1997) The Internationalization of Born Globals: an Evolutionary Process? *International Business Review*, 6/6, pp. 561–583.

Majkgård, Anders and D. Deo Sharma (1998) Client-Following and Market-Seeking Strategies in the Internationalisation of Service Firms, *Journal of Business-to-Business Marketing*, 4/3, pp. 1–41.

Oviatt and McDougall (1994) Toward a Theory of International New Ventures, *Journal of International Business Studies*, 25/1, pp. 45–64.

Persson, Finn, Rosengren, Jörgen and Wilshire, Michael (1999) Software in Telecoms: The New Battleground, in *McKinsey Telecommunications, The Battle for Value*, McKinsey & Company, UK, pp. 92–103.

Root, Franklin R. (1994) Entry Strategies for International Markets, Lexington Books, New York.

Sharma, D. Deo and Johanson, Jan (1987) Technical Consultancy in Internationalisation, *International Marketing Review*, Winter, pp. 20–29.

TAIK/Mediastudio (1999) Uusmediatoimiala Suomessa 1999, Helsinki.

Terpstra, Vern (1987) *International Marketing*, Dryden Press, Chicago.

Zeithaml, V., Parasuraman, A. and Berry, L.L. (1985) Problems and Strategies in Services Marketing, *Journal of Marketing*, 49, Spring, pp. 34–46.

# Developing Strategies for Growth in HTSFs: Looking Beyond Survival in an Increasingly Competitive Marketplace

WILLIAM KEOGH, VICTORIA STEWART AND JOHN TAYLOR

## INTRODUCTION

This paper illustrates the second year findings from a two-year European Social Fund project that featured, in the first year, the study of 20 innovative new technology based firms (NTBFs) in a number of different sectors, including instrumentation, software and analytical services. Nineteen of these organisations dealt with the oil and gas industry to some extent (Keogh et al., 1999). The second year of the study (ongoing 1999–2000) focused on an additional 40 NTBFS. The dynamic changes that these companies face as they develop products or services for their market niches indicate that value and knowledge, in one form or another, plays a key part in their success (Keogh and Stewart, 2000). Recruiting, selecting and retaining staff is vital for the growth and development of these organisations. One major output objective from this research is an explanation of the relationship between the human resources in this type of organisation and how their knowledge base can be enhanced and harnessed to add value, for example, through personal development such as Investors in People (IiP) whilst, at the same time, recognising their limited resources (see Luckwell and Seaton, 1998).

NTBFs are often involved in the creation and sale of relatively sophisticated products and services in industrial markets. Depending on their requirements, they may need to employ individuals with high levels of academic qualifications in technical areas – who become part of the knowledge base of the organisation. It is recognised that the management teams of the companies comprise the same type of individuals (who may lack experience and training in the strategic management of companies). It may also be the case that owners/managers find it difficult to fully understand the processes that have evolved in their own organisation as it has grown and developed. A greater awareness and understanding of systems and processes in business in recent years are perhaps due to authors such as Senge (1990) and Hammer and Champy (1993). The inter-relationship between the process dynamics and knowledge residing in the organisation requires balance to achieve strategic goals. Mapping organisational processes can aid the owner/manager's understanding of what is going on in the organisation as well as highlighting problem areas (e.g. duplication or wasted effort).

Selection of the sample organisations was not random, and companies were selected on the basis of how innovative they were perceived to be by their peers, by support organisations and by virtue of innovation awards they had achieved. The methodology employed in this study involved semi-structured interview techniques for both phases of each year of the study. Some feedback was given to the participating organisations in year one, and further information will be disseminated to the cohort before the end of the study.

This study was also undertaken to provide insights into the extent to which new technology based SMEs address human resource development as part of the overall strategic management of their operations. To put these observations into context, it should be noted that in most cases there was limited evidence of a strategic management approach in general, and, as such, human resource management was therefore not uniquely deficient. The data collected, however, suggests that project companies have begun to implement a degree of structure to their human resource management as a reflection of overall developments in levels of management sophistication within the company as a whole. The pressure to respond to day-to-day operational demands preclude, or at least make difficult, the development of formalised longer-term plans.

It is evident that the original owner/manager (if this is the case) may not have the desired quality of business or commercial skills necessary to take the company forward. Such deficiencies might include business planning and an understanding of the benefits of the process of attempting to plan strategically. It is important that training plans are included in overall business plans, even if they are not formal, since they can help identify desirable and essential skills when looking for staff and future growth. This paper outlines findings to date, highlights areas of importance, and explores key strategic elements for growth as these organisations compete in the marketplace.

## THE BUSINESS ENVIRONMENT

The Aberdeen region is the principal base for the North Sea oil and gas industry (see Bower and Keogh, 1997), and the UK operations of a significant number of large multinational companies are located within the area. Oil and gas production accounted for 1.7 per cent of the UK's gross value added in 1998 and total income was approximately £17 billion. From this, UK Government revenue is estimated at £2.6 billion in 1998/99 (DTI, 1999). However, it is not the only focus for development in the Aberdeen area as engineering, software, food and tourism are also of prime importance. The key goal for the long-term development of the local economy is to develop an industry base which is sufficiently de-coupled from the local offshore industry to be sustainable in the long term (Grampian Enterprise, 1997), whilst continuing to exploit the opportunities represented by the industry. International activities are of vital importance and, from a sample of 2000 exporters in north east Scotland (Export Partnership, 1999), it was found that 70 per cent of current exporters had been exporting for more than five years, while approximately 40 per cent of exporters stated that at least a third of their turnover was exported.

The presence of the oil and gas industry has, over the last 30 years, given rise to a large number of technology-based companies with a diverse range of specialisms from software to heavy engineering, and it was anticipated that the number of technology-based companies within the region would grow by 10 per cent per annum over a three-year period, with a corresponding increase in export revenues from this sector of the economy (Armstrong and Hughes, 1997). With recent problems in the oil and gas industry, this remains to be substantiated. Technology and innovation provide major opportunities to retain high skills and a high wage base in the local economy and technology businesses are seen as an engine for growth. This means that training and other support mechanisms must be made available to companies. From the initial study, it was found that 19 out of 20 companies sold products and/or services to the oil and gas industry.

In response to these issues, and to the national priorities expressed through Scottish Enterprise, Grampian Enterprise has committed to a technology-led strategy based on the proactive development of technology-based industry as a basis for the long-term sustainability of the regional economy. There are, of course, a large number of other organisations and agencies active, in whole or in part, in relation to wider economic development. This includes Local Enterprise Companies (LECs) and a number of further and higher education institutions and research institutes, each of which has its own focus and priorities.

Not surprisingly, strategic activity is focused on oil and gas related technologies, which will add value to the transfer of skills and knowledge – not just to the United Kingdom Continental Shelf (UKCS), but around the world. The promotion of inward investment within high technology companies in the science and technology and offshore technology parks is actively pursued. Defined subsectors, including electronics/telecommunications, biotechnology/medical technology, environmental technology and high value engineering/instrumentation collectively contribute approximately £730m to the economy. There is a recognised need also to develop skills, particularly in the oil and gas sector (see CILM, 2000) to meet the challenge of internationalisation and diversification to other like industries (Grampian Enterprise, 1997). A major reason for this is that current direct employment in oil and gas in the north east of Scotland is estimated at over 45,000 for both on and off shore. This is forecast to decline by approximately 11,000 workers, including oil related jobs in the north east of Scotland, by the year 2011 (Aberdeen City Council and Aberdeenshire Council, 1997).

To combat many of the above issues, a partnership was formed by bringing together key players such as Grampian Enterprise, the Chamber of Commerce, Aberdeen City Council and Aberdeenshire Council (Grampian Enterprise, 1999). This partnership is known as the North East Scotland Economic Development Partnership (NESEDP) and the main elements of the economic framework include the following:

- the development of the north east as a competitive location, i.e. nationally and internationally;
- continual improvement in the skills base;
- development of a sustainable, competitive business base.

It is within this environment that the NTBFs operate locally, although most of them are thinking internationally.


## RESEARCH METHODOLOGY

The research methodology for the second year of the project was continued from year one (see Keogh et al., 1999). A number of difficulties arose which, broadly speaking, can be categorised as sample selection, sample categorisation and the dynamic changes that organisations faced.

## Sample selection

It was much more difficult in the second year of the study to contact potential innovative, small NTBFs. The original criteria used was that sample organisations were:

- recognised as innovative within the business community;
- possibly involved with a management development programme focused on R&D organisations and offered by the Robert Gordon University;
- located on the Aberdeen Science and Technology Park (this occurred in eight cases in the first year).

To overcome difficulties in sourcing the sample companies, winners of SMART Awards were sought, because they had been recognised by their peers. Location on the Science Parks was discussed with senior staff at Grampian Enterprise (the landlords) as a means of using knowledge of firms' activities – but without breaching confidentiality – and a small number of owner/managers were working with the Robert Gordon University on various activities.

## Sample categorisation

Classifying the companies using the standard industrial classification (SIC) was difficult because most of the organisations selected for the study could be categorised in a number of ways. The principal activity of the sample companies was used to classify them in five groups: software related, engineering, analytical services, instrumentation/electronic and bio-science related. The main problem experienced by the researchers came from the biotechnology related firms where the biotechnology aspect may not be mainstream and may be used as part of a wider process, as found in three organisations.

## Dynamic changes

In year one, dramatic changes occurred in six study companies including one closure and three take-overs by larger firms. It is possible to map the changes in these firms, for example, using a case methodology, but resources for the project were severely limited and a small number of visits had to suffice for each firm. Thus when some firms were visited to obtain updates, their circumstances had radically changed. A case in point is a small biotechnology firm that was a university 'spin-out'. The importance of their technological discoveries in the use of bio-sensors for contaminated land recovery meant that a minister from the Scottish Parliament was present at their official launch and they have also won awards for their innovation.

## Sample selection

The 60 organisations have been sectorally classified as shown in Table 4.1.

Using the EC classification of the SME sector, where the term SME refers to companies employing less than 250 employees, it is possible to further classify the participant companies according to staff numbers, as shown in Table 4.2.

Of those interviewed in year two, 23 were owner managers, 7 were founder directors, and the remaining 10 were senior managers who were not initial company founders. All those interviewed, except one, were male. While 30 of the companies had been established in Aberdeen, the remaining 10 had been founded elsewhere in the UK, with one company originating from the US. Employment numbers for the 40 companies are represented in Figure 4.1, and

**Table 4.1:** *Classification of participant companies by sector*

|  | Total | Year 2 | Year 1 |
|---|---|---|---|
| Software | 12 companies | 8 | 4 |
| Engineering | 14 companies | 7 | 7 |
| Analytical services | 12 companies | 8 | 4 |
| Instrumentation | 13 companies | 9 | 4 |
| Bio-science related | 9 companies | 8 | 1 |

**Table 4.2:** *Classification of participant companies by staff numbers*

| Total organisations | Year 2 | Year 1 |
|---|---|---|
| 14 micro-enterprises (0–9 employees) | 13 | 1 |
| 24 small enterprises (10–49 employees) | 15 | 9 |
| 21 medium enterprises (50–249 employees) | 12 | 9 |
| 1 large enterprise (>=250) |  | 1 |

indicate total staff numbers together with the proportion of staff located in Aberdeen. Figure 4.1 indicates that the sample has a fairly good spread of companies of varying sizes, the majority being micro or small. This reflects the pattern seen in the UK economy as a whole, where 99 per cent of businesses are small. It is worth noting that there appears to be some correlation between the size of company and the relative proportion of employees based in Aberdeen. Because the smallest, notably micro enterprises, have not yet established bases elsewhere, all their employees are in Aberdeen. Once companies grow beyond approximately 20 employees, it would seem that all but one have staff elsewhere. This does not automatically suggest that they have bases outside of Aberdeen, since employees may well be agents or representatives, although in the majority of cases, companies had established bases elsewhere.

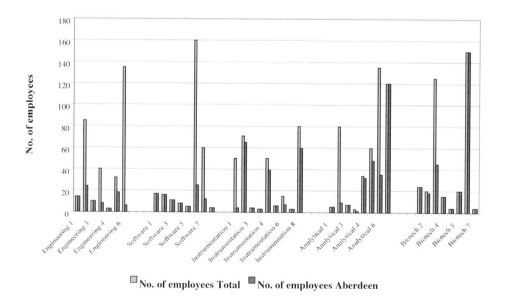

**Figure 4.1:** Employees (year 2 of the study)

## INNOVATION

Pressures faced by the new technology based SMEs in the study reported in this paper come from a number of different sources including the need for financial investment; the need to achieve successful exploitation of core intellectual property; the need for appropriate property and other physical facilities; and the dynamics of local and global economies. It is of critical importance that the staff of the company are appropriately experienced and trained to address these external pressures. It is also important that the staff team is organised and motivated in such a way as to facilitate the development of effective systems of co-operative working, despite what is often a wide spread of experience and commercial (and technical) disciplines. Thus, individuals within the organisation are often helped to realise their own potential in these respects.

Broadly speaking, these firms are in the business of providing innovations and, in some cases, new breakthrough technologies. In order to do this they must have certain inputs and processes in place. Figure 4.2 illustrates a general view of the innovation cycle.

Different approaches to innovation and how value was added emerged from each of the 60 organisations in the study. The role of senior management varied widely, particularly regarding their use of personnel. Their own involvement ranged from making strategic decisions and then having teams work on projects, through to the CEO working on the invention whilst senior managers managed the organisation. What is important, is where and when in the process they involve themselves in order to ensure that value is added. The following example illustrates the way that CEOs (or senior managers) dealt with the invention phase within their product innovation cycles (for an alternative approach see Bower et al., 1998).

### *Example: the process of innovation*

Company A's CEO (also the owner manager) directly employs less than 20 staff, but operates with a number of associates across the UK. Associates are design specialists from a number of engineering disciplines, including electrical, mechanical and acoustic expertise. Engineering consultancy expertise, as well as products,

*Required inputs*

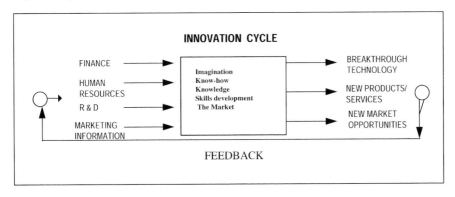

*Desired outputs*

**Figure 4.2:** Innovation cycle

which are developed to meet market demands, is also provided. The main hindering factor has been in recruiting the right people for the company.

The CEO of Company A adds value in a number of ways, but the management of the invention phase is perhaps where he adds most value. He sources the required expertise from experts and buys in their services; project manages the process, divides tasks between the invention team and, at the same time, provides a support network and environment (i.e. workshop, accommodation and facilities). One and a half years on from the initial interviews the CEO has planned expansion with new premises and a forecast that will quadruple turnover. Diversification features strongly in his plans. On the human resource side, their responsibility and involvement motivate his staff in the business. Over and above this, there are financial incentives.

### *Knowledge and learning*

The constant need to update knowledge within the NTBFs was apparent throughout the interviews and this appeared to hold for the customer base of all of the organisations in the sample. The knowledge requirements to achieve success in the marketplace brings together market information, individual knowledge and the drive and determination of the management teams (or owner manager). Updating this knowledge and learning is vitally important for these organisations. Argyris (1996, pp. 84–85) explains that to be successful in the marketplace requires learning by key individuals. He goes on to explain that most people do not know how to learn. In this study, the opportunities open for individuals in some organisations gave them an opportunity to grow intellectually as they were given responsibilities, which would not necessarily have happened if they were part of a larger firm.

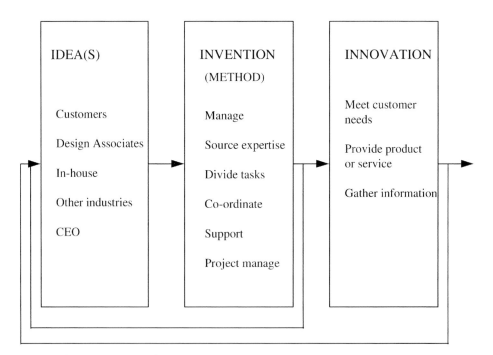

**Figure 4.3:** Innovation in Company A

Education levels were generally high in the sample companies. For example, the biotech companies' employees all had academic qualifications of degree level or above, whilst the engineering companies were lower than the other groups. However, engineering employees did have other qualifications such as Higher National Certificates. Figure 4.4 illustrates employee education at degree level or above.

Developing the skills and education of employees helps them to grow individually by enhancing their tacit knowledge and contributes to the organisation's needs. This is an essential part of organisational learning and adds to the store of in-house knowledge. Garvin (1993, p. 80) defines a 'Learning Organization' as:

> *'an organization skilled at creating, acquiring, and transferring knowledge, and at modifying its behaviour to reflect new knowledge and insights'*

Arie De Geus outlined the problems that many organizations face in adapting and changing to survive (De Geus, 1988) and he made it clear that the way that management thinks must change in order to achieve objectives. This is also the case for the NTBFs where small groups of individuals may work together to plan strategically (either formally or informally). Senge (1990) identified key dimensions that allow the building of organizations that can really learn including: systems thinking, personal mastery, mental models, building shared vision and team learning. It is not clear from the findings of this study to what extent these dimensions have been incorporated into organisational use. Evidence was found, in some companies, of team building and learning (e.g. adapting to change). The vision of owner managers was being communicated to employees in a small number of organisations, while processes were being explored to improve the organisation systemically in at least three cases.

A major issue for many organisations relates to the impact of the changes caused by the advent of enabling technologies, economic pressures which have resulted in the loss of corporate memory from activities such as downsizing, and

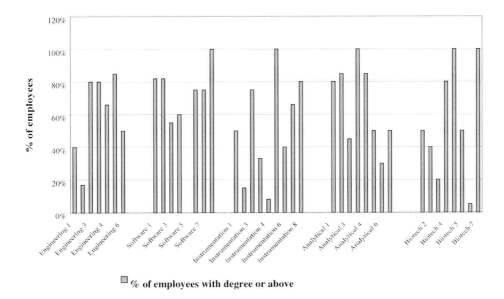

□ **% of employees with degree or above**

**Figure 4.4:** Employee education

changes in international trade which have resulted in a need to obtain new sources of supply). Brooks-Rooney and Foster (1998) explain that organisations need to develop strategies to exploit their intellectual capital and develop best practices to manage their knowledge base. Key issues and challenges for organisations were identified, including 'how to manage knowledge workers' and 'how to identify what knowledge is valuable'. These points are crucial to study firms, as the combination of product or service with information is aimed at enabling end users to act more effectively. Davis and Botkin (1994) have explored issues surrounding economic growth and the types of organisations, which would use their knowledge base to develop 'smart' products. They define knowledge as 'meaning the application and productive use of information'. It was evident that most of the sample organisations are attempting to improve their innovative capacity by making better use of their in-house knowledge, by listening to their customers, and through their willingness to pursue new projects.

## STRATEGIC DECISIONS

From the study, it was apparent that the managers of the NTBFs have to consider a number of key strategic issues that are interrelated, and require not only policies to deal with them, but adaptive processes. Many of their decisions appear to evolve from their emergent strategies. The most important elements for strategic consideration were identified from analysis of the interviews (see Figure 4.5). It is crucial to stress the importance of people and the contribution they make to the development of policies. The transformation of the various inputs is aided by factors such as communication and entrepreneurial activity. Whilst all the factors may be involved in the strategic process, none of these factors necessarily are acted upon independently at any one time, since they are interdependent. So the degree of impact of any one factor, or combination of factors, will depend on the context of the organisation (i.e. its competitive environment, internal resources, level of dynamism, objectives and the overall strategy). Alongside inputs to the NTBFs (Figure 4.5) is the management and control of knowledge. Knowledge and know-how are key assets of innovative companies.

As well as working in organisations, which change due to the innovations they provide, the NTBFs in this study also operate in dynamic, changing environments. There are a number of definitions of innovation but, given the nature of the companies in the study, the most appropriate definition comes from the Organization for Economic Co-operation and Development (1981), which defines technological innovation as:

> 'the transformation of an idea into a new or improved saleable product or operational process in industry or commerce ...'

Understanding the business processes in order to achieve their goals whilst keeping overheads down is also of prime importance for the NTBFs as they tend to be 'lean' organisations. If overheads are too high, then this can seriously impact on the competitiveness of the company as well as cutting profit margins. Support organisations (i.e. at local and national levels) also have a role to play, as well as fiscal policies and the impact of political issues. Feedback, Figure 4.5, leads to changes, corrections and alignment of goals. This feedback exists for such companies in the form of customer contacts, marketing information and the networks they operate within. It can also provide knowledge of their environment. The

*Required inputs*

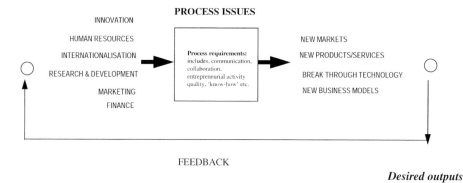

PROCESS ISSUES

INNOVATION

HUMAN RESOURCES                                                                NEW MARKETS

INTERNATIONALISATION                  Process requirements:          NEW PRODUCTS/SERVICES
                                      includes, communication,
                                      collaboration,
RESEARCH & DEVELOPMENT                entrepreneurial activity        BREAK THROUGH TECHNOLOGY
                                      quality, 'know-how' etc.
MARKETING                                                             NEW BUSINESS MODELS

FINANCE

FEEDBACK

*Desired outputs*

**Figure 4.5:** Process issues

processes in each company studied are very different and, although common elements exist, the way they achieve their goals is also very different.

Adding value is not just the province of those companies in the sample who include manufacturing amongst their activities. A number of these organisations managed the design function through suppliers, others brought together sub-assemblies and incorporated them into finished products, while some also offered engineering solutions through problem-solving activities. Added value results from a change in the form, location or availability of a product or service. The increase in market value excludes the cost of externally purchased materials or services. Examination of the process in detail may result in the elimination of non-value adding steps. Porter's explanation of the value chain (1985), that displays total value, and value activities provides a very useful tool for most organisations. Value adding activities are divided into primary and support activities. Most of the activities identified within the NTBFs revolve around explicit knowledge. However, what adds value to the process is the tacit knowledge of key individuals. Consider Figure 4.6, which outlines the 'internationalisation' aspirations of the organisations. The required outputs are new markets and new products/services. In order to achieve these outputs, companies must actively market their innovative offerings in the marketplace.

Before moving on to the marketing stage, it is worth considering what is meant by innovation. It is not enough to say that entrepreneurs are 'innovative' when they have an idea. In order for the organisation to be truly innovative, the product/service must be 'realised' in the marketplace. This requires a whole series of interrelated inputs to the innovation process in order to achieve their desired outputs. When they have something to offer, then they can internationalise their included expertise. As, in the case of a number of the NTBFs of this study, their knowledge and problem solving abilities form part of their product of service portfolios.

*Applying strategy*

This research has explored key aspects of the application of strategic plans, including innovation and the development of successful products, relationships with larger organisations, the process of internationalisation, and the diversification into new markets. The importance of innovation to organisations is illustrated

*Required inputs*

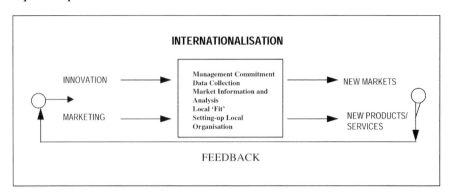

*Desired outputs*

**Figure 4.6:** Internationalisation and the process

in Figure 4.7 (5 rated as very important). Related to this, collaboration was also examined and it was apparent that the NTBFs had had very different experiences with collaborative arrangements, hence the results of approximately 25 per cent in each of the 2–5 ranges.

Related to this, examining marketing strategies revealed interesting findings. Most of the organisations were aiming for low output and high added value: 25 out of the 50 responses indicated this, with 14 focusing on high output and high added value. At the same time, new products, moving into new and mature markets was the predominant strategic choice: with 23 responses, out of 65, looking at new products in new markets, and 17 at relative to new products in mature markets.

## FINDINGS AND DISCUSSION

The two-year research project, which provided the basis for this paper, focused on a relatively small sample of new technology based firms that were recognised as

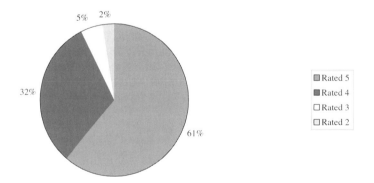

**Figure 4.7:** The importance of innovation to strategic planning

being innovative by their peers and customers. The interrelationship between their business processes, the value which is added to products or services at different stages in their operation, and the importance of increasing their knowledge bases through the development of key staff members, are issues which have been explored in the paper. In order for these small organisations to compete in dynamic markets, they must not only develop the human resource base where tacit knowledge resides, they must also retain and nurture this knowledge base.

The growing importance of maximising knowledge utilisation has been illustrated throughout this paper. Understanding business processes within the organisation can assist the organisations to achieve their goals. However, the concept of adding value within processes can also be used to determine who adds the value and where it should be added.

A number of authors have looked at the successful exploitation of technology in dynamic environments, including Oakey (1995) and Utterback (1996). A crucial issue in achieving success involves enhancing the prospects and skill base within the organisation. This also includes having the capability to identify opportunities as well as managing technological development (see Scott et al., 1996). The knowledge base required to do this stems from many sources and activities, even within small companies, and forms part of the intellectual capital of the organisation. Utterback (1996) explains that '... a strong technological base is as critical to the prosperous survival of a firm as a good understanding of markets and a strong financial position.' Awareness of maintaining their market niche and financial security was evident from answers given throughout the interviews.

The whole area of knowledge within the organisation is complex and, if key people are lost to the company, then knowledge goes with them. Organisational knowledge, the knowledge of individuals and information form the intellectual capital of the organisations. This may not be generally recognised, but may well be achieved intuitively by the organisation. Making use of this combination of information and knowledge has been illustrated by examining the two key areas of innovation and competitiveness within NTBFs. Information and knowledge play a vital role in determining the strategic role of the NTBF, particularly in the areas of research and development. Future products or services will determine the growth (or survival) of these businesses, and it is imperative that they focus their resources in a constructive manner.

The utilisation of a strategic planning process, whether heavily structured or in a more emergent form, is generally seen to be a key determinant of the success of most organisations. Small technology-based firms generally have acutely limited resources to dedicate to staff recruitment and retention, and possibly more than any other type of company, are in a situation where their staff are genuinely their most important asset. Studies of the lack of expertise in the UK are not new and barriers to growth must be identified and steps taken to overcome them.

This study was also undertaken to provide insights into the extent to which new technology based SMEs address human resource development as part of the overall strategic management of their operations. The data collected suggests that the companies have begun to implement a degree of structure to their human resource management as a reflection of an overall development in the level of sophistication of the management of the company as a whole. This might be expected on an intuitive basis, since the pressure to yield to day-to-day operational demands precludes, or at least makes difficult, the development of formalised longer-term plans.

The style of management and blend of skills play an enabling role in the development of strategies within small firms and the examples included in this paper illustrate that there are different ways to meet the end objectives. Value can be added at different parts of the process and individuals with knowledge and skills can also contribute. The knowledge required to do this stems from many sources within even small companies. To illustrate this point, key areas of innovation, competitiveness and human resources were selected to show that they are interrelated and do not stand alone.

It was evident that the original owner/manager may not have the business or commercial skills to take the company forward including the use of business planning and understanding of the benefits of the process of attempting to plan strategically. It is important that training plans are included in overall business plans, even if they are not formal, but can help identify desirable and essential skills when looking for staff and future growth.

Evidence was gathered which demonstrated aspirations towards internationalisation within most of the sample companies, including both exporting and the setting up of overseas organisations. From a European perspective, identification of SME problems and the development of mechanisms to assist with their improvement are vital. From the analysis, it is not always clear how the organisations interviewed address all of the aspects of human resource management that were identified as important. It can be seen that a number of areas that would generally be seen as fundamental to effective human resource management such as job descriptions and individual training needs assessment, may only be partially implemented – possibly because of the small size of most organisations. The overall impression gained is that the issue of human resource development, although being recognised by some as important, is not treated as being of strategic importance. In order to grow, develop new ideas, and reach new markets, the knowledge base of organisations must be nurtured and maintained.

The information requirements of NTBFs tend to be focused on the goals they identified (e.g. on company growth and capture market share). The 'can do' attitude of management, which tends to lead to working informally, can easily be interpreted as unsophisticated. However, where there may be a lack of management skills, contact with customers and a willingness to co-operate in order to solve problems for the customer requires flexibility and the application of the intellectual capital of the NTBF. According to Stewart (1997, p. ix) 'Intellectual capital is the sum of everything everybody in a company knows that gives it a competitive edge'. It was apparent from all of the companies in the sample that they were using intellectual capital intuitively. For example, data was gathered constantly with a view to spotting market opportunities. Key aspects of the use of information and intellectual capital can be illustrated by exploring two main issues for the NTBFs; namely innovation and competitiveness.

The majority of respondent companies do not have sophisticated approaches to identifying current and future staffing needs other than to talk to individuals about current training they feel they might need. Companies rely on identifying needs based on existing staff profiles and loose projections for new business, based on their current financial status. Their ability therefore to react to immediate increases required in staffing levels and to longer-term changes that might be required, is limited. With more time spent on identifying needs at departmental and/or organisation wide level, it should be possible to take a more strategic view of requirements. Companies employed different strategies to stimulate and maintain staff, including bonus schemes, share opportunities and support for leisure activities. By developing a strategy to maintain the competitive position of the organisation, through planning for skills and development needs on a proactive rather than a reactive basis, they will be in a stronger position to cope with such problems (e.g. the unexpected departures of people with key skills).

It was also clear that the significance of Investors in People (IiP) for this type of company would appear to be limited since seven out of 14 organisations were committed to IiP – although two of these had suspended the process. It may be that small companies tend to view schemes such as IiP with a degree of scepticism and, if so, then a different approach is required for this type of SME, which acknowledges their particular circumstances and provides support for the development of relevant systems. The impact of Investors in People on SMEs raises important questions. For example, is it reasonable to expect SMEs, with stretched resources, to embark on a new programme, which will create more internal work? Evidence from this study suggests that the SMEs must develop their people internally in order to achieve the best results.

## ACKNOWLEDGEMENTS

This research has been supported by ESF, Objective 4 – Programme number 984200UK4, project reference 991017SO4. The authors wish to thank participating organisations and the industrialists on the steering committee, Melfort Campbell, Susan Kirkwood and Richard Marsh. Thanks also go to Angela Mulvie, researcher on IiP phase of the study.

## REFERENCES

Aberdeen City Council and Aberdeenshire Council (1997) *Oil and Gas Prospects 1997 Update* Aberdeen.

Argyris, C. (1996) *On Organisational Learning*. Blackwell, Oxford.

Armstrong, I. and Hughes, P. (1997) *Survey of Grampian Manufacturing and Exports in 1995/96*. The Scottish Council Development and Industry, Edinburgh.

Bower, D.J. and Keogh, W. (1997) 'Innovation Management in the Supply Chain and the Limitations of Lean Supply' in Oakey, R. and Mukhtar, S-M. (eds) *New Technology-based Firms in the 1990s, Vol. III*, Paul Chapman, London, pp. 104–113.

Bower, D.J., Shaw, C. and Keogh, W. (1998) 'The process of small firm innovation in the UK oil and gas-related industry'. In Oakey, R. and During, W. (eds) *New Technology-based Firms in the 1990s, Vol. V*, Paul Chapman, London.

Brooks-Rooney, A. and Forster, B. (1998) *Knowledge Management: A Business Imperative* Internal report for Grampian Enterprise.

Centre for International Labour Market Studies, the Robert Gordon University (2000) *Skills Foresight: The Industry Survey, Oil and Gas*. OPITO, Aberdeen.

Davis, S. and Botkin, J. (1994) 'The Coming of Knowledge-Based Business', *Harvard Business Review*, September–October, pp. 165–170.

De Geus, A.P. (1988) 'Planning as Learning'. *Harvard Business Review*, Mar–April, pp. 70–74.

Department of Trade and Industry (1999) *Development of the Oil and Gas Resources of the United Kingdom 1999*. HMSO, London.

Export Partnership (1999) *North-East Scotland, 1998 Export Survey*. European Services North East Scotland, Aberdeen.

Garvin, D.A. (1993) 'Building a Learning Organization'. *Harvard Business Review*, July–Aug., pp. 78–91.

Grampian Enterprise (1997) *Towards the Millennium*. Grampian Enterprise, Aberdeen.

Grampian Enterprise (1999) *Grampian Enterprise Strategy*. Grampian Enterprise, Aberdeen.

Hammer, M. and Champy, J. (1993) *Reengineering the Corporation*. Nicholas Brealey Publishing, London.

Jones-Evans, D. (1996) 'Technical Entrepreneurship, Strategy and Experience'. *International Small Business Journal*, Vol. 14, No. 3, pp. 15–39.

Keogh, W., Evans, G. and Blaydon, C. (1999) 'The Deployment of Strategies for Growth within NTBFs in the Aberdeen Area of Scotland.' In Oakey, R., During, W. and Mukhtar, S-M. (eds), *New Technology-Based Firms in the 1990s, Vol. VI.* Pergamon Press, Oxford.

Keogh, W. and Stewart, V. (2000) 'Innovative New Technology Based Small Firms: Repositioning in a Global Market Place'. Academy of Marketing/AMA 5th Annual Research Symposium on the Marketing-Entrepreneurship Interface, The Robert Gordon University, Jan. 2000.

Luckwell, E. and Seaton, J. (1998) 'An Assessment of the 'Investors in People' Standard for High-Tech SMEs in the UK.' In: Oakey, R.P. and During, W. (eds), *New Technology Based Firms in the 1990s,* Vol. V, Paul Chapman, London.

Oakey, R.P. (1995) *High-technology New Firms: Variable Barriers to Growth.* Paul Chapman, London.

OECD (1981) *The Measurement of Scientific and Technical activities, Frascati Manual 1980.* Organization for Economic Co-operation and Development.

Porter, M.E. (1985) *Competitive Advantage.* The Free Press, New York.

Scott, P., Jones, B., Bramley, A. and Bolton, B. (1996) 'Enhancing Technology and Skills in Small-And Medium-Sized Manufacturing Firms: Problems And Prospects', *International Small Business Journal,* Vol. 14, No. 3 pp. 85–99.

Senge, P.M. (1990) *The Fifth Discipline.* Century Business, London.

Stewart, T.A. (1997) *Intellectual Capital.* Nicholas Brieley Publishing, London.

Utterback, J.M. (1996) *Mastering the Dynamics of Innovation.* Harvard Business School Press, Boston.

# CHAPTER 5

# *Internet Usage in Small Irish Firms*

JAMES GRIFFIN

## INTRODUCTION

Much attention has been paid in recent years to the dynamic nature of the Internet and its growing influence on the business world. The growth of users, both business and home, coupled with the growth of web sites and hosting servers, has opened up what various authors have termed 'a new industrial order' (Hamel and Sampler, 1998) or 'a vast new untapped market' (Forrester, 1999). Use of the Internet by business has entered a 'proliferation stage' (Feher and Towell, 1997).

But to fully appreciate such hyperbolae, and the extraordinary growth in recent years of the Internet through its graphical interface – the world wide web (WWW) – we must examine its historical development. The Internet is not a new concept; it has existed in various forms for quite some time. The origins of the Internet are squarely set in the Cold War era of the 1950s. The earliest known form is the ARPANET (Advanced Research Projects Agency Network), established in 1957 as a direct response to the launching of the SPUTNIK satellite by the then USSR (Zakon, 2000).

Indeed, the first published paper on the technical basis of the Internet occurred as far back as 1961 with MIT's 'Information Flow in Large Communications Networks' by Leonard Kleinrock, which was the first treatment of packet switching theory.

It is the aforementioned graphical interface (i.e. for the WWW) that has created the growth and dynamic change the Internet is currently undergoing. However, it was not until 1991 that the WWW was introduced by CERN, developed by programmer Tim Berners-Lee who invented the HTML language behind the WWW.

It is the WWW that provides the graphical interface and URL (universal resource locator) system of linking 'pages' of information together that provides what we think of as the Internet today. Since its inception, the growth of the WWW can be defined as exponential. From Table 5.1 the growth in the number of host servers (one host may have multiple sites by using different domains or port numbers) has doubled every three months since 1993, and has only recently slowed to a, still impressive, doubling every eight months (Gromov, 1998).

The art of estimating how many people are online throughout the world is, at best, an inexact science (Nua, 2000). The figures in Table 5.2 are based on individual country demographics and survey reports. An Internet user is defined as an adult or child that has used the Internet once in the last three months. When

**Table 5.1:** *WWW growth*

| Date | Sites | Date | Sites | Date | Sites |
|------|-------|------|-------|------|-------|
| 06/93 | 130 | 04/97 | 1,002,512 | 10/98 | 3,358,969 |
| 09/93 | 204 | 05/97 | 1,044,163 | 11/98 | 3,518,158 |
| 10/93 | 228 | 06/97 | 1,117,255 | 12/98 | 3,689,227 |
| 12/93 | 623 | 07/97 | 1,203,096 | 01/99 | 4,062,280 |
| 06/94 | 2,738 | 08/97 | 1,269,800 | 02/99 | 4,301,512 |
| 12/94 | 10,022 | 09/97 | 1,364,714 | 03/99 | 4,389,131 |
| 06/95 | 23,500 | 10/97 | 1,466,906 | 04/99 | 5,040,663 |
| 01/96 | 100,000 | 11/97 | 1,553,998 | 05/99 | 5,414,325 |
| 06/96 | 252,000 | 12/97 | 1,681,868 | 06/99 | 6,177,453 |
| 07/96 | 299,403 | 01/98 | 1,834,710 | 07/99 | 6,598,697 |
| 08/96 | 342,081 | 02/98 | 1,920,933 | 08/99 | 7,078,194 |
| 09/96 | 397,281 | 03/98 | 2,084,473 | 09/99 | 7,370,929 |
| 10/96 | 462,047 | 04/98 | 2,215,195 | 10/99 | 8,115,828 |
| 11/96 | 525,906 | 05/98 | 2,308,502 | 11/99 | 8,844,573 |
| 12/96 | 603,367 | 06/98 | 2,410,067 | 12/99 | 9,560,866 |
| 01/97 | 646,162 | 07/98 | 2,594,622 | | |
| 02/97 | 739,688 | 08/98 | 2,807,588 | | |
| 03/97 | 883,149 | 09/98 | 3,156,324 | | |

*Source: Zakon, 2000*

more than one survey is available on a country's demographics, the mean is taken, or, in the case where one study may be more comprehensive/reliable than another, the results from the former are presented.

If the numbers of host servers (and consequently web sites) can be described as 'increasing exponentially' then a similar term can be applied to the rate of Internet adoption by the general population.

Table 5.2 shows that, in a single year, user rates doubled (or increased more rapidly) in every region of the globe. The figures, therefore, seem to support the claims of authors that the Internet is indeed 'A unique global opportunity' (Dutta and Segev, 1999). It is time therefore, to examine what these authors have to say in more detail.

## BACKGROUND

The previous studies that have formed the empirical and theoretical background to this work are presented in Table 5.3. Necessarily, only the key works are discussed here.

All the studies included in Table 5.3 have provided some element that was finally included in the questionnaire designed for the author's own research.

Leech (1999) provides a definition of e-commerce

> '[e-commerce] ... is when you connect to your customers over the web to buy and sell goods'.

He describes this phenomenon as *'the network economy'* and goes on to identify it as including a basic dichotomy of trade types – firstly, business to business trade, and secondly, business to customer trade. This Internet economy trade type has been termed *'dynamic trade'* and it is claimed that it is moving from its early development stage to a new business trading model which will fundamentally alter products and services, how production schedules are determined, and what pricing models are used (Lief, 1998).

**Table 5.2:** *Increase in the number of Internet users 1999-2000*

| Online users March 1999 Area | Million | March 2000 Area | Million |
|---|---|---|---|
| World total | 158.5 | World total | 304.36 |
| Africa | 1.14 | Africa | 2.58 |
| Asia/Pacific | 26.97 | Asia/Pacific | 68.9 |
| Europe | 36.55 | Europe | 83.35 |
| Middle east | 0.88 | Middle East | 1.90 |
| Canada and USA | 88.33 | Canada and USA | 136.86 |
| South America | 4.63 | South America | 10.74 |

*Source: Various.*
*Methodology: Compiled by: Nua Internet Surveys (1999/2000).*

**Table 5.3:** *Literature synopsis*

| Key issues identified | Author | Sample type |
|---|---|---|
| Types of 'dynamic trade' in a 'network economy': <br>• Business to business <br>• Hard goods and services <br>• Business to customer | Lief (1998) <br>Leech (1999) <br>Putnam et al. (1999) <br><br>MORI (1998) | N/A <br>N/A <br>22 large US corporations <br><br>900 European businesses in six countries |
| Business opportunities in Internet applications | Feher and Towell (1997) <br><br>MIDAS-NET (1998) | 500 executives of large US computer firms <br>Top 500 Irish companies |
| Application of business opportunities to a matrix of 'business value' and 'business impact' | Widdifield and Grover (1995) | N/A |
| Typology of Internet adopters and the factors influencing Internet adoption | Iacovou et al. (1995) <br><br>Drennan and Kennedy (1999) | Seven small Canadian firms <br><br>750 Australian small businesses |
| Influence of industrial sector on Internet adoption | Dutta and Segev (1999) | 120 companies from Fortune Global 500 |
| Problems associated with business use of the Internet | Nath et al. (1998 <br>Cockburn and Wilson (1996) <br>Geiger and Martin (1999) | Various large scale, large firm surveys |

In a study of *'early adopters'* of the WWW, Forrester Research (1999) interviewed 22 large US firms that were already buying significant levels of hard goods on the net. Of these, 59 per cent were found also to be already buying services online. Whilst respondents' expenditure on business services was, on average, only 1 per cent of their services budget, they saw it set to rise to 13 per cent by 2001. The types of business services that are finding a niche on the WWW were commodity services bought on a repetitive basis. Travel and sourcing temporary and contract workers are examples of these. The automation of ordering systems for maintenance, repair and operations goods, Internet based marketing, communications and customer services are all moving into the sphere of being based partly or wholly on the WWW. (These have been termed *automated* or *assisted services;* Lief, 1998.)

Direct selling to the customer via a WWW site is the second type of Internet trade identified by the literature. A MORI study carried out in June 1998 asked 900 European businesses in six countries to quantify usage of the Internet for business to customer trade. It found that 25 per cent of those companies with WWW access generated revenue through it. The main benefits they cited were: (1) The ability to handle a larger volume of orders and inquiries (2) Lower per capita transaction costs leading to internal efficiencies (3) Improved market penetration.

Feher and Towell (1997) conducted a particularly interesting study into large firm Internet usage patterns. Their wide-scale study of 500 executives of large American corporations attempted to look at the different applications of what we think of as the Internet (differentiating between email use, browser use and multimedia use). This study is superior to others that have focused on small firms' Internet use in rather general terms.

To this end, Internet uses have been analysed in terms of the three-by-three matrix structure first developed by Widdifield and Grover (1995), which is specifically designed to examine the business value and impact of existing and potential uses of the Internet. Three major categories of business value are considered in this matrix structure when discussing Internet impact. Each is analysed in terms of accomplishing the three different strategic goals of efficiency, effectiveness and innovation – creating a matrix for evaluation as shown in Table 5.4.

Iacovou et al. (1995) developed a conceptual model for studying the factors influencing Internet adoption rates in the small firm. This model posits that there are three major factors influencing Internet adoption – perceived benefits, organisational readiness and external pressures. The model is based on a considerable foundation of previous empirical work (for example see: Widdifield and Grover, 1995; Rogers, 1983; Benbasat, Bergeron and Dexter, 1993; Pfeiffer, 1992; Swatman and Swatman, 1991; Cragg and King, 1995; Treadgold, 1990; as cited in Iacovou et al., 1995). This model has also been modified and applied successfully to a series of studies into small firm Internet adoption in specific industry sectors by Drennan and Kennedy (1999). A revised version of this model appears later in the *Methodology* section of this paper.

It is also believed that the taking of a non-sectoral approach may identify industry sector as another important factor in Internet adoption rates in small firms (an approach taken by several other researchers in the field – see, for example, Dutta and Segev, 1999 and Cockburn and Wilson, 1996).

An increasing amount of space is given in the literature to the problems being faced by online companies and the fears of those not online – mostly relating to factors such as productivity losses, security, accessibility and privacy issues. This has forced studies to identify any potential correlations between perceived problems and Internet adoption/usage (Nath, 1998; *The Economist*, June 1999; Cockburn and Wilson, 1996). This factor could be viewed as the 'flipside' to the 'perceived benefits' factor and, as such, is akin to the concept of 'external pressures' being

**Table 5.4:** *Internet impact on business value*

| Impact | Compression of Time | Overcoming geographical restrictions | Restructuring relationships |
|---|---|---|---|
| *Efficiency* | Accelerate process | Economies of scale | Bypass intermediaries |
| *Effectiveness* | Reduce float time | Global control | Source scarce knowledge |
| *Innovation* | Service excellence | New markets | Build umbilical cords |

measured as both opportunities and threats, introduced by Drennan and Kennedy to the Iacovou et al., conceptual model in 1999.

Indeed, it is this conceptual model, and the modifications developed by further studies discussed above, that have formed the basis of the questionnaire design used in the research of this paper. Indeed, many of the issues discussed above will resurface in the author's research findings.

## RESEARCH NEED

Dandridge and Levenburg (1999) tell us that studies of business Internet usage in general have focused on the large firm. This is supported by the brief literature review in Table 5.3. The only studies that included small firms in their sample were those of Iacovou and Drennan and Kennedy (Table 5.3). The MIDAS-NET survey in Ireland may have included small firms that appeared in the Top 500 list, but these were at best a small minority of the sample and were not the focus of the research.

Furthermore, Iacovou et al. (1995) correctly suggest that many factors have been identified as influencing Internet adoption and usage rates in business but go on to make the point that 'as these factors have been generally identified through studies of large organisations their applicability to small business is questionable …'. Pfeiffer (1993) tells us that smaller organisations have been shown to have different technology adoption patterns than large firms. Kehoe (1992) has argued that the small or micro firm is as much affected by 'this dynamic entity' (i.e. the Internet) as any large organisation.

All of this evidence makes the point that there appears to be a gap in current literature and academic research as regards Internet adoption and usage rates in the small firm sector.

It is this research need and the identification of suitable supporting empirical research models that led the author to the following research goals:

1. To measure the extent and nature of Internet usage amongst Irish small firms.
2. To analyse the effects and expected effects of Internet usage.
3. To identify the factors influencing these adoption rates

## RESEARCH METHODOLOGY

The subsequent conceptual model for the research is presented in Figure 5.1. It is a reworking of the original conceptual model posited by Iacovou et al., in 1995, and amended by Drennan and Kennedy in 1999, it has been designed to include the potentially influential issues of perceived problems and industrial sector on Internet adoption and use.

The conceptual model in Figure 5.1 gives rise to what can be posited as a basic hypothesis that underlies the research (H0). As follows:

**H0** = Extent of Internet usage is a function of perceived benefits, organisational resources, and external pressures perceived as opportunities or threats.

This hypothesis gives rise to three separate sub-hypotheses that can be tested individually. Namely:

**H1** = Small firms with management that recognises all of the potential benefits of Internet usage will be more likely to be adopters of the Internet and,

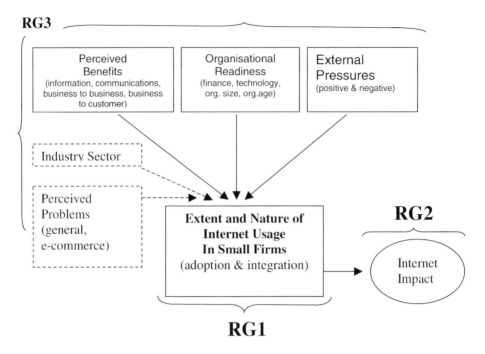

**Figure 5.1:** Conceptual model for Internet research in SMEs

consequently, will enjoy higher benefits than those whose managements have lower levels of recognition of the perceived benefits.

**H2** = Firms with higher organisational readiness will be more likely to be adopters and, consequently, will be more likely to enjoy higher benefits than firms with low levels of readiness.

**H3** = Small firms that encounter pressure, either from their partners, or from the competition, government, suppliers or other sources, will adopt Internet usage more frequently than those that do not encounter any such pressures.

Separate sections of the questionnaire were especially designed to directly test these hypotheses. These 'influencing factors' *(independent variables)* are measured through *grouped Likert-style rating questioning*. Each factor is broken down into a number of sub-factors. Perceived benefits of Internet usage is separated into four main categories (Internet as an information source, as a communications system, in business to business trade, and in business to customer trade), each being further sub-divided. Organisational readiness is divided into six relevant issues, external pressure into seven sub-sections, and perceived problems sub-divided into two categories.

Internet usage (the dependent variable) is comprised of two factors (i.e. e-mail use and Internet browser use), which the respondent is asked to rate separately.

### Pilot testing

Preliminary pilot testing of the proposed cross-sectoral research has been completed by the author. A sample of 20 small and micro-enterprises based in the Tait Business Centre, a business incubator in Limerick City, and 20 other randomly chosen small companies in the Limerick area were selected. It is important to note at this juncture that a small company in Ireland is defined as under 50 employees and having a turnover of under IR£3 million (Task Force on Small Business Report, 1994).

The technical nature of many IT related questionnaires could raise issues for the choice of a suitable method of administration (Proudlock et al., 1999). It is because of this issue that half the companies in the total sample of 40 companies were surveyed by personal interview and the other 20 randomly chosen companies received a postal questionnaire. Comparison of quality and level of response was made to choose the most appropriate canvassing method for the full study to be completed towards the end of 2000.

The 30-question questionnaire was administered to all candidates. Personal interviews were conducted over a five-day period, each lasting approximately 30 minutes. Of the 20 personal interviews conducted, 12 usable interviews were achieved. A response rate of 50 per cent (10 firms) was achieved from the postal surveys. Total response to the pilot study was therefore 22 firms (a response rate of 55 per cent). It is the analysis of these grouped responses that is discussed in the 'Findings' section shortly.

The randomly chosen Limerick-based firms were sourced through the Kompass Directory at www.kompass, i.e. the online version of the Golden Pages at www.goldenpages, i.e. the Irish Business Internet Directory and the Software Directorate of Ireland database. As companies were simply listed alphabetically, a sampling interval of i = 32 provided a representative sample (see also Geiger and Martin, 1999).

As described above, the questionnaire measures the 'Influencing Factors' mostly through Likert-style rating questioning. The questionnaire also aims to identify and rate the differing areas of Internet use and future use in these firms. This is achieved again through rating a provided list of common uses (and reasons for non-use) of the Internet in firms, and common problems resulting from Internet use or non-use. These lists of factors are derived from the large and growing body of literature on business uses of the Internet and previous studies (see Table 5.3).

This pilot study was used to validate conceptual models and research methods. It is also intended to identify the most suitable method of administering the questionnaire whilst providing useful preliminary data in the field of Internet use in the small firm. The findings are presented here in the next section.

## FINDINGS

Table 5.5 has a breakdown of respondent details that give the subsequent results some perspective.

As can be seen, all industrial sectors were canvassed, and a large response was gained from firms in the computer industry, which was to be expected. All the firms in this sample fall into the definition of small firms in Ireland. A high average educational level was also found – in keeping with descriptions of Irish entrepreneurs (Fleming, 1999). The average age of businesses in the sample was 3.5 years.

The importance of the Internet to business has been emphasized consistently in recent literature. The results of this exposure are shown in Table 5.6 where a significantly high average response is given by respondents when asked to rate the

**Table 5.5:** *Respondent details*

| Sector | % of sample | No. of employees | % of sample | Highest education level achieved | % of sample |
|---|---|---|---|---|---|
| Financial | 9 | 1–5 | 46 | Secondary | 14 |
| Manufacturing | 14 | 6–10 | 18 | Diploma | 18 |
| Computing | 36 | 11–15 | 4 | Degree | 45 |
| Transport | 18 | 16–20 | 9 | Masters | 5 |
| Retail | 5 | 26–30 | 9 | PhD | 14 |
| Other | 9 | 46–50 | 14 | Trade/prof. qualification | 4 |
| Tourism | 9 | | | | |

**Table 5.6:** *Perceived IT and Internet importance*

| | Average rated response (/5) |
|---|---|
| How important are Internet and IT developments to your firm? | 4.4 |
| How important do you believe the Internet is in your industry sector? | 4.5 |
| How important do you believe the Internet will be to your industry sector within the next 6–12 months? | 4.7 |

importance of the Internet now, and in the future, on a scale of 1 to 5 (1 being the lowest and 5 being the highest).

Table 5.7 gives us a very important 'snap shot' of current Internet usage rates in small Irish firms. E-mail is a very common Internet based application, and firms indicating that they use it to a great extent in their day-to-day business support this trend. The specific use of Internet browsers also rated highly at 3.8, but this is considerably lower than the rated use of e-mail at 4.5.

The majority of respondents indicated that they had their own web sites (i.e. 68 per cent). Of firms without a web site, 100 per cent intended to set one up within 12 months. A vast majority of firms claimed to have received business value through the Internet already, with 96 per cent expecting to receive value within 12 months – the specifics of the business values gained or expected are examined in Table 5.8.

From Table 5.9 it is obvious that respondents are generally happy with the effectiveness of web sites. The factors that received the highest average ratings were the more 'direct benefits' of advertising, provision of information to customers and the generation of 'off-line' sales, all of which rated over 3 out of 5. There remains a certain reluctance to include e-commerce elements into web sites, which is grounded in the belief that the Internet is not ready for extensive e-commerce use in many respondent industry sectors, the computer sector being the only one where a majority believed that it was. It may be this very point that is holding back small Irish firms from developing better integrated Internet policies.

Tables 5.10–5.13 are derived from respondents' answers to a series of rating questions in the final four sections of the questionnaire. Each factor was sub-divided into a number of separate 'sub-factors' to allow for more depth of answering. In these tables we gain an insight into the importance of various factors that have been suggested as influences on Internet adoption and usage in the small and large firms. The full tables, presented here, show the different factors

**Table 5.7:** *Internet usage in the firm*

|  | Average rated response (/5) |
|---|---|
| To what extent do you use e-mail in your business? | 4.5 |
| To what extent do you use Internet browsers in your business? | 3.8 |

**Table 5.8:** *E-commerce and web site activity*

|  | Yes (%) | No (%) |
|---|---|---|
| Is the Internet ready to use extensively for e-commerce within your industry? | 50 | 50 |
| Does your firm have its own web site? | 68 | 32 |
| Plans to set up web site? | 100 | 0 |
| Plans to incorporate online selling? | 43 | 57 |
| Any business value realised from the Internet in the past 6 months? | 77 | 23 |
| Any business value expected from the Internet in the next 6–12 months? | 96 | 4 |

**Table 5.9:** *Perceived usefulness of web sites*

| Business factor | Average rated response (/5) |
|---|---|
| Direct selling online e-commerce | 2.4 |
| Generating inquiries for offline sales | 3.4 |
| Advertising your firm | 3.5 |
| Providing information to customers | 3.3 |
| Providing information to suppliers/retailers | 2.3 |
| Providing after sales service to customers | 1.8 |

included in each major area of influence as taken from the conceptual model discussed earlier.

Small firms value the Internet mostly as an 'information source' and secondly as a source of 'business to customer trade'. Perceived benefits from the Internet in the areas of 'business to business trade' and as a 'communication tool' were surprisingly lower. Each of the four factors in the 'information source' category scored well above average. Only four other factors in the other three general categories scored significantly highly. Two were involved with business linkages (as a communication tool and in business to business trade), whilst the other two dealt with market entry and customer service (in business to customer trade). These factors could be described as the more traditionally obvious benefits of Internet usage.

In general, small firms responded very positively when questioned about issues of organisational readiness to develop their Internet usage. In all sub-factors, as we can see from Table 5.11, a considerably higher than average response score was achieved. The organisational readiness factor, when averaged out to an importance rating of 3.65, turns out to be the second highest rated factor of all with regard to Internet usage (the highest being the benefits perceived from using the Internet as an information source).

When questioned about the pressures influencing Internet adoption and usage in their firms, respondents rated only two factors significantly higher than average.

**Table 5.10:** *Perceived benefits arising from the Internet*

| As an information source (4 sub-factors were presented here) | Average rated response (/5) | As a communication system (4 sub-factors were presented here) | Average rated response (/5) |
|---|---|---|---|
| | 3.95 | | 2.98 |
| **Business to business trade** (4 sub-factors were presented here) | **Average rated response (/5)** | **Business to customer trade** (4 sub-factors were presented here) | **Average rated response (/5)** |
| | 2.78 | | 3.46 |

**Table 5.11:** *Organisational readiness to further develop Internet usage*

| | ARR | | ARR |
|---|---|---|---|
| Allocate financial resources | 3.9 | Technical expertise within your firm | 3.2 |
| Personal time | 4.0 | Technical expertise outside your firm | 3.5 |
| Allocate employee time and training | 3.4 | Role competitive strategy | 3.9 |

Overall average rating of 3.65

**Table 5.12:** *External pressure to develop Internet usage due to increasing*

| | ARR | | ARR |
|---|---|---|---|
| Internet use by competitors | 2.5 | Internet use by general population | 3.4 |
| No. of support programs | 1.7 | Amount of media coverage | 2.9 |
| Internet use by trading partners | 2.7 | Desire to create competitive advantage | 3.6 |
| Internet use by customers | 2.0 | | |

Overall average rating of 2.69

**Table 5.13:** *Problems associated with the Internet*

| | ARR | | ARR |
|---|---|---|---|
| Loss of productivity | 1.8 | Misuse of company information | 1.8 |
| Service unreliability | 2.9 | Security for information transfer | 2.6 |
| Information overload | 3.3 | Security for online payment | 2.7 |
| Non-user friendliness | 2.5 | Credit card clearance services | 1.8 |
| Unsure of the potential uses | 1.6 | Negative attitude of online selling amongst your current market | 2.4 |
| Government regulations | 1.4 | | |

*Overall average rating of 2.26*

As seen from Table 5.12, these were a 'desire to create a competitive advantage' (3.6) and 'the increasing use of the Internet by the general population' (3.4). These factors would both fit into the category of 'positive pressures' as put forward by Drennan and Kennedy (1999) where they differentiated between positive and negative pressure to adopt and develop Internet usage.

The importance given to problems associated with increasing use of the Internet by the public (Table 5.13) can be directly correlated with the importance that the same respondents gave to the perceived benefits of the Internet for business to customer trade in Table 5.10.

Only the issue of 'information overload' scored an average response of higher than 3 (at 3.3) and, surprisingly, issues with regard to e-commerce such as security and credit card clearance did not score as highly as previous responses regarding a reluctance to embrace e-commerce systems might have suggested (see Tables 5.8 and 5.9). This finding may suggest that such reluctance is more due to the fact that firms simply do not believe that e-commerce is suitable for their practices, rather than fear or lack of understanding regarding technical issues.

With the exponential growth of the web continuing, it is not surprising that the issue of information overload should be of concern to any business using the web for mostly advertising and business to customer trade, as these respondents currently reveal.

## DISCUSSION

The factors that respondents generally gave high average ratings to are those of advertising, provision of information to customers and generation of off-line sales. These higher rated factors all fall into what previous writers (see, for example, Iacovou et al., 1995) have termed the 'direct benefits' of Internet usage. Firms that derive mostly these direct benefits from Internet usage tend to be characterised by a 'non-integrated' approach to Internet adoption.

A more integrated approach would tend to result in higher direct benefits, and the more indirect benefits of organisation efficiency, better customer service and improved business to business relationships – factors that received a low average rating from small firms. The fact that many small Irish firms seem to have developed web sites relatively early in the history of the WWW (i.e. over 40 per cent were 3 years old) would support the theory that early adoption can lead to poorly designed web sites, poorly planned Internet policy, and one that is poorly integrated with other business systems (Cockburn and Wilson, 1996).

The generally poor rating of business to business trade factors is surprising when we consider that currently this is by far the largest commercial section of the WWW (Putnam et al., 1999; People and Technology Strategies Report, Sept. 1995). This author believes that such a finding may well indicate a key difference between large firm and small firm usage of the Internet.

Table 5.14 shows the average rated responses given to business factors that correlate to the cells of the Widdifield/Grove matrix discussed previously. It should be noted here that these responses indicate what firms perceive to be the most important areas of Internet usage, but they do not necessarily represent current methods of usage in such firms. The high ratings given to the previously described indirect benefits such as service excellence, building business relationships, and increased organisational efficiency through reduced float times, show that the small firms canvassed are aware of the need for a better integrated approach to Internet usage discussed above.

With regard to the conceptual model and hypotheses described earlier, the average responses from Tables 5.10 to 5.13 have been graphed and compared to the average level of Internet usage within the firm. The Internet usage rate of 4.15 is derived from the average rate of e-mail use and Internet browser use in the firm

**Table 5.14:** *Value*

| Impact | Compression of time | Overcoming geographical restrictions | Restructuring relationships |
|---|---|---|---|
| *Efficiency* | Accelerate process **2.86** | Economies of scale **2.64** | Bypass intermediaries **3.09** |
| *Effectiveness* | Reduce float time **3.95** | Global control **3.00** | Source scarce knowledge **3.95** |
| *Innovation* | Service excellence **4.09** | New markets **3.86** | Build umbilical cords **3.73** |

(taken from Table 5.7). This is a very high average use and suggests that the Internet is becoming an increasingly important element of small firm business practice in Ireland.

From Figure 5.2 we can immediately see that the average rating of organisational readiness (3.65) and the perceived benefits of the Internet as an information source (3.95) and in business to customer trade (3.46) are the most influential on the Internet usage rate. It is interesting to compare these findings to those of the Iacovou et al., and the Drennan and Kennedy studies discussed earlier which used a similar structure.

These studies identified that perceived benefits and external pressures, viewed as opportunities, were significantly influential on Internet usage rates. The findings from this study agree with the issue of perceived benefits being influential on Internet usage rates but this study has gone further to identify the specific area of benefit that firms identify as being important.

The high importance of organisational readiness in this study was not found in these other studies, conducted in Canada (Iacovou et al., 1995) and Australia

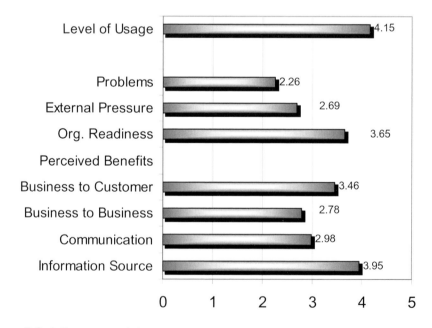

**Figure 5.2:** Influences on Internet usage

(Drennan and Kennedy, 1999). However, the findings of this research suggest that the Irish small firm developed a particularly early acceptance of the importance of the Internet to the future of small business practices.

It is possible that this acceptance of the importance of the Internet to the future development of Irish firms is already changing their organisational structures and strategic planning, thus causing organisational readiness for Internet usage.

## CONCLUSIONS

The Internet and the world wide web have an increasing significance for small and large firms alike. Business practices are changing, and the dynamic environment of the Internet offers organisations new challenges and new benefits. Firms must keep abreast of technological change and move in tandem with it. This is also true of the world of research. There must be a concerted effort to track, measure and identify the uses the Internet offers small business. There is a lag in this area concerning the study of Internet use by the SME sector.

By way of concluding remarks the author would like to note that these results represent a pilot study for a larger planned survey to be undertaken in the summer of 2000. With a sample base of over 300 small firms, it is intended that more detailed regression analysis can be conducted between the independent and dependent variables to confirm the significant relationships that the pilot study has indicated. For the purposes of this paper the sample size was not large enough to conduct such statistical tests.

## REFERENCES

Cockburn, C. and Wilson, T.D. (1996) 'Business use of the WWW'. *International Journal of Information Management.*

Dandridge T. and Levenburg, N. (1999) 'High Tech Potential? An Exploratory Study of very Small Firms' Usage of the Internet'. *International Small Business Journal,* Vol. 18, No. 2, Issue No. 70.

Drennan, J. and Kennedy, J. (1999) 'Internet Use Factors for Small Business'. *ICBS Conference Proceedings.*

Dutta, S. and Segev, A. (1999) 'Business Transformation on the Internet'. *Euoprean Management Journal,* Vol. 17, No. 5, pp. 466–473.

Feher, A. and Towell, E. (1997) 'Business Use of the Internet'. *Journal of Internet Research,* Vol. 7, No. 3, pp. 195–200.

Fleming, P. (1999) 'Education for Enterprise: The Role of a Structured Intervention'. PhD thesis, University of Limerick.

Geiger S. and Martin, S. (1999) 'The Internet as a Relationship Marketing Tool'. *Irish Marketing Review,* Vol. 12, No. 1.

Gromov, G. (1998) 'The Roads and Crossroads of Internet History'. *Internet Valley Online Publishing:* www.internetvalley.com/intval.html 1998

Hamel, Gary and Sampler, Jeff (1998) 'The e-Corporation'. *Fortune Magazine,* Dec. 7, pp. 52–82.

Iacovou, C.L., Benbasat, I. and Dexter, A. (1995) 'Electronic Data Interchange and Small Organisations: Adoptions and Impact of Technology'. *MIS Quarterly,* Dec.

Kehoe (1992)

Leech, J. (1999) 'E-tailing in the Broadband Economy'. *Business and Technology Magazine,* Feb.

Lief, V. (1998) 'Dynamic Trade', Forrester Online Database: *www.forrester.com.* May.

MIDAS-NET (1998) 'Multimedia and Internet Survey'. *BTiS,* University of Limerick

Nath, R., Akmanligil, M., Hjelm, K., Sakaguchi, T. and Schultz, M. (1998) 'Electronic Commerce and the Internet'. *International Journal of Information Management,* pp. 91–101.

Nua (2000) Nua Online Surveys: *www.nua.ie*

Pfeiffer, H.K.C. (1993) *The Diffusion of EDI.* Springer-Verlag, New York, NY.

Proudlock, M., Phelps, B. and Gamble, P. (1999) 'IT Adoption Strategies: Best Practice Guidelines for Professional SMEs'. *Journal of Small Business and Enterprise Development.*

Putnam, M., Dolberg, S., Sharrard, J. and Lanpher, G. (1999) 'The Forrester Report'. *www.forrester.com.* January.

Task Force on Small Business Report (1994) Government Stationary Office, Dublin.

Widdifield, R. and Grover, V. (1995) 'Internet and the Implications of the Information Superhighway for Business'. *Journal of Systems Management,* May/June.

Zakon, R. (2000) Hobbe's Internet Timeline. *http://info.isoc.org/guest/zakon/Internet/History/HIT.html.* April.

CHAPTER 6

# The Barriers to the Deployment of Strategic Planning in High Technology Small Firms – an Empirical Assessment

NICHOLAS O'REGAN, ABBY GHOBADIAN AND JONATHAN LIU

## INTRODUCTION

Clarke (1994, p. 1) contended that 'the last decade brought with it a time of totally unprecedented change'. In particular high technology small firms (HTSFs) now face continual change and an increasing need to adapt to an uncertain future. Some firms that adopted a proactive approach were often the subject of a 'scissors-type' movement as they attempted to meet changing consumer demands, while at the same time, achieving radical organisational and cultural change. To achieve competitive advantage by ensuring that their development is 'steered' rather than based on 'trial and error', it is contended that HTSFs need a greater emphasis on strategic planning. However, the deployment of strategic planning is often complicated by factors such as the external environment, the formality of the strategic planning process, and the barriers to its deployment. A review of the literature suggested that little is known about the influences on strategic planning deployment in HTSFs. Therefore, an understanding of the relationship between the perception of the operating environment, the barriers to the deployment of strategic planning and the formality of strategic plans is of significant importance to HTSFs. This paper is based on an empirical investigation aimed at identifying the impact of the barriers outlined.

## AIMS OF THE RESEARCH

The aims of this paper are to examine:

- the impact of the operating environment on the deployment of strategic planning;
- the barriers to the deployment of strategic planning and to ascertain if they are perceived differently by high or low performing firms;
- the barriers to the deployment of strategic planning experienced by firms with formal (written) strategic plans compared to firms with informal strategic plans;
- the emphasis on strategic planning processes by firms with formal strategic plans compared with firms with informal strategic plans.

The paper begins with a brief literature review on:

- strategic planning;
- the operating environment;
- strategic planning formality;
- the barriers to strategic planning deployment.

It continues by outlining the methodology for the study and presents an analysis of the findings.

## STRATEGIC PLANNING

The literature suggests that a strategic planning approach is needed to maintain competitive advantage and overcome the failure to distinguish between operational effectiveness and strategy (Porter, 1996; Skinner, 1996). A strategic planning approach is also seen as one of the most effective ways for firms, regardless of size or sector, to cope with the changes in their business environment (Hart and Banbury, 1994). However, the literature points out that while most large firms emphasise strategic planning (Ancona and Caldwell, 1987), the position in relation to SMEs is blurred and unclear. McKiernan and Morris (1994) suggest that as few as one in six small firms have a strategic plan. Later studies found that evidence of strategic planning is much higher in SMEs. Larsen et al., (1998) found that 87.5 per cent of high growth companies review their strategies at least yearly. Baker et al. (1993) cited in Larsen et al. (1998), found that 86 per cent of successful US small firms engage in strategic planning at least annually. However, in a study of UK SMEs, Deakins and Freel (1998) commented that SMEs were often 'naive about planning and the development of strategy'. This could be argued to result from a range of contingency factors that act as barriers to the deployment of the strategic plan.

A number of research studies show that small firms employing strategic concepts performed better than those that do not (Bracker et al., 1988). Joyce et al. (1996) found that 'strategic' small firms were more likely to have greater capability to grow and expand, innovate and introduce new products to the market place. Roper (1997) also studied small firms and found that 'strategic' firms were more likely to grow and achieve greater profitability.

## OPERATING ENVIRONMENT

The operating environment is 'the sum total of all the forces that affect a company's actions' (De Geus, 1997). A range of issues affect the operating environment from its dynamism, turbulence, technological change, substitute products, or new firms entering the markets to the changing regulatory environment (Kargar and Parnall, 1996). However, many of these factors lie outside the immediate control of management (Bourgeois, 1996). Studies on the impact of the operating environment of firms on strategic planning show relationships in both size categories, Covin and Slevin (1989); Storey et al. (1987) and Kargar and Parnell (1996) in relation to small firms, and by Mills and Friesen (1992) and Thompson (1996) in relation to larger firms.

## STRATEGIC PLANNING FORMALITY

It could be argued that a formal strategic planning process is a deliberate attempt to include factors and techniques that could be used in a systematic way to achieve specified tasks. In essence, it involves the establishment of a clear goal and the necessary processes to achieve it (Armstrong, 1982). Empirical studies found a mixed picture in relation to the value of a formal strategic planning. Studies carried out by Ramanujam and Venkatraman (1987) and Shrader et al. (1984) in large firms found a significant influence. A significant impact was also found by Bracker et al. (1988) and Lyles et al. (1993) in relation to small firms. However, McKiernan and Morris (1994) found that a formal strategic planning process in SMEs often failed to provide a holistic view of the firm. Another study on the formality of strategic planning in SMEs showed inconclusive results (Parks et al., 1991).

While it is difficult to either accept or reject the contention that strategic planning positively influences the financial performance of the organisation, the majority of studies are in agreement that the strategic planning process exerts a positive influence on performance. It could be argued that the following quotation from Lyles et al., (1993: 42) encapsulates the position:

> 'the elements of goal formulation, developing distinctive competencies, determining authority relationships, deploying resources, and monitoring implementation receive more effective attention when small businesses engage in formal planning.'

As a detailed consideration of formal and informal strategic planning processes was outside the scope of this paper, a written or unwritten strategic plan was used as a surrogate measure of formality. This approach is appropriate for the consideration of strategic planning in smaller firms and is consistent with the work of Bracker et al. (1988), Gilmore (1971) and Robinson and Pearce (1983).

## THE BARRIERS TO STRATEGIC PLANNING DEPLOYMENT

There is no accepted definition of a barrier to implementation or growth (Barber et al., 1989; Cambridge Small Business Research Centre, 1992). Indeed, Piatier (1984, p. 146) suggested that a survey 'can do no more than provide an idea, and possibly an improvised measurement of the perception of the barrier by the person questioned'. Accordingly, this section of the study did not seek to establish a comprehensive range of barriers but, rather, to identify some general barriers derived from the literature that related to the constraint or hindrance of the implementation of strategic planning.

## METHODOLOGY

The sample consisted of 1000 HTSFs throughout the UK, selected on a random sampling basis. Small firms were defined as having fewer than 250 employees. While the factors impacting on strategic planning outlined are extensive, they are by no means exclusive. A series of semi-structured exploratory interviews were conducted with the managing directors of 20 manufacturing SMEs, selected on a random basis from the electronics and engineering sectors, to ascertain their perceptions of the most important issues impacting on the deployment of their firm's strategic plan. The results of the exploratory interviews confirmed that contingency factors such as the barriers to the implementation of strategic planning were some of the main issues facing high technology SMEs. Further interviews were conducted with local and national SME representative bodies as they influence the operations of SMEs (Bennett, 1998). These interviews confirmed the results of the exploratory group interviews.

Data was gathered by means of a postal survey questionnaire. 194 valid responses were received. The questionnaire consisted of questions to infer the emphasis on the attributes of strategic planning, the barriers to its deployment and the operating environment using a five-point 'Likert type' scale, with a response of 1 indicating that an item that received 'no emphasis' and 5 indicating that an item received 'strong emphasis'. The reliability of the dimensions of the environment types was determined by establishing their alpha weighting using Cronbach's Alpha Co-efficient (Cronbach, 1951). Construct validity was assessed using factor analysis. As the eigenvalues are well over 1, and the item loading well over 0.50, with the majority well over 0.70, it was concluded that the scales had good construct validity. Statistical analysis using the Wilcoxon test was carried out on each attribute based on the size of the difference between the two pairs of variables.

## ANALYSIS OF THE OPERATING ENVIRONMENT

The factor analysis of the attributes used to describe the operating environment loaded onto two factors: dynamic and changing, and market threats focuses environment types. Table 6.1 shows that there were a number of significant differences between firms that perceived their operating environment as dynamic and changing compared with firms that perceived their operating environment as market threats focused. While firms in a dynamic environment placed a greater emphasis on all the characteristics of strategic planning than firms perceiving their operating environment as market threats focused, it should be noted that only four attributes were statistically significant at $p<0.005$ (asterisked as *) and a further nine attributes were statistically significant at $p<0.05$ (asterisked as **). The results are outlined in Table 6.1.

A statistical analysis of the mean scores indicated that none of the attributes of the internal capability, products and performance, departmental co-operation and management time characteristics were statistically significant. A possible explanation for this may lie in the perception of these characteristics by both environment types as core characteristics which form a foundation for the use of the remaining characteristics.

The principal differences between the two types of firms were in the following characteristics and their attributes:

(a) The external orientation attributes of *general economic and business conditions ($z = -2.86$ and $p<0.005$), followed by *technological trends* ($z = -2.74$, $p<0.05$) and *competitive position and trends* ($z = -2.27$, $p<0.05$) were statistically significant. This finding was expected, as firms in a perceived dynamic and changing environment tend to place a greater emphasis on looking outwards by scanning the environment and establishing the necessary actions to ensure a 'fit' with the emerging environment.

(b) The resources for strategy attributes of *involvement of ad hoc working groups.* ($z = -0.24$, $p<0.05$), followed by the availability of *relevant and adequate information from available sources* ($z= -2.38$, $p<0.05$), and *the involvement of consultants* ($z = -2.36$, $p<0.05$) were statistically significant. None of these findings were surprising as firms perceiving their environment as *dynamic and changing* often need *ad hoc* groups to consider emerging opportunities/weaknesses. It could

**Table 6.1:** *Emphasis on the characteristics of the strategic planning process by firms perceiving their environment as dynamic and changing or market threats focused*

| Strategic planning characteristics | Dynamic/ changing | Market threats | Z Statistic |
|---|---|---|---|
| *Internal capability* | | | |
| general managerial ability | 3.38 | 3.30 | −0.86 |
| financial strengths/weaknesses | 3.39 | 3.36 | −0.19 |
| human resources strengths/weaknesses | 3.42 | 3.41 | −0.40 |
| *Products and performance* | | | |
| past performance | 3.78 | 3.73 | −0.31 |
| current products strengths/weaknesses | 4.22 | 3.94 | −0.19 |
| *External orientation* | | | |
| general economic/business conditions | 3.94 | 3.47 | −2.86* |
| technological trends | 4.10 | 3.58 | −2.74** |
| competitive position and trends | 4.06 | 3.67 | −2.27** |
| *Departmental co-operation* | | | |
| understanding of all functions by employees | 3.60 | 3.56 | −0.32 |
| cross functional support | 3.81 | 3.70 | −0.71 |
| functional co-ordination | 3.68 | 3.67 | −0.33 |
| efforts to achieve functional agreement | 3.66 | 3.62 | −0.65 |
| *Resources/employees* | | | |
| ad hoc working groups | 2.52 | 2.40 | −0.24** |
| relevant/adequate information | 3.61 | 3.59 | −2.38** |
| involvement of consultants | 2.00 | 1.70 | −2.36** |
| other physical/financial resources | 3.25 | 3.24 | −0.29 |
| *Management time* | | | |
| involvement of line managers | 4.03 | 4.02 | −1.50 |
| managing directors time | 4.38 | 4.36 | −0.21 |
| *Use of analytical techniques* | | | |
| use of analytical techniques | 2.95 | 2.40 | −3.68* |
| ability to use techniques | 2.94 | 2.81 | −3.22* |
| willing to seek outside assistance | 2.78 | 2.56 | −0.91 |
| *Staff creativity* | | | |
| coping with surprises/crises | 3.61 | 3.35 | −1.98** |
| adapting to unanticipated changes | 3.78 | 3.63 | −0.99 |
| identify new opportunities | 4.15 | 3.88 | −1.96** |
| identifying key problem areas | 3.66 | 3.50 | −1.56 |
| generating new ideas | 3.87 | 3.61 | −1.48 |
| generating/evaluating strategy alternatives | 3.71 | 3.27 | −3.09* |
| anticipating barriers to strategy imp. | 3.51 | 3.18 | −1.86 |
| *Strategy a control mechanism* | | | |
| value as a control mechanism | 3.43 | 2.98 | −2.61** |
| a monitoring control technique | 3.27 | 2.91 | −1.92 |
| a mechanism for revising strategy | 3.35 | 2.93 | −3.39* |
| ability to communicate management thinking down the line | 3.62 | 3.47 | −0.85 |
| communicate staff thinking up the line | 3.49 | 3.20 | −1.76 |
| a mechanism for integrating functions | 3.08 | 2.91 | −0.83 |
| a mechanism for managerial motivation | 3.39 | 3.06 | −2.11** |

\*  *p<0.005*
\*\* *p<0.05*

be argued that in a dynamic and changing environment the availability of relevant and adequate information is vital to enable changes to be made in the strategic planning process. Often, firms in a dynamic environment may need to engage consultants to provide the expertise that they lack in the preparation of a strategic plan covering emerging problems or potential opportunities.

(c) The use of structured/analytical approach attributes of *the use of analytical techniques* ($z = -3.68$, $p<0.005$), and *the ability to use techniques* ($z = -3.22$, $p<0.005$) were statistically significant. Both attributes were emphasised to a greater degree by firms perceiving their environment as dynamic. This can be explained by the need to utilise a range of mechanisms to adjust the strategic planning process to meet the changes in the emerging external environment. Interestingly, the remaining attribute of this characteristic, *willingness to seek outside assistance,* did not differ to a degree that was statistically significant. A possible explanation is that most firms have the ability to use a limited number of analytical techniques.

(d) The staff creativity attributes of *ability to cope with surprises, crises, and threats* ($z = -1.98$, $p<0.05$), the *ability to identify new opportunities* ($z = -1.96$, $p<0.05$), and finally, the *capacity to generate and evaluate a number of strategic alternatives* ($z = -3.09$, $p<0.05$) were statistically significant. The emphasis on these attributes by firms perceiving their environment as dynamic can be explained by the requirement to deal with constant and varied change in a dynamic environment.

The control mechanism attributes of *value as a control mechanism* ($z = -2.61$, $p<0.05$), *a mechanism for revising current strategy* ($z = -0.339$, $p<0.005$) *and a mechanism for managerial motivation* ($z = -2.11$, $p<0.05$) were statistically significant. *Control* and *managerial motivation* can be argued to be necessary elements in a *dynamic* environment to enable firms to compete effectively. A mechanism for revising current strategy had the strongest significance ($p<0.005$), which arguably reflected the importance of having an up-to-date strategic plan. The analysis of the perception of operating environment indicated that firms perceiving their environment to be *dynamic and changing* placed a higher emphasis on the attributes of a majority of the strategic planning characteristics than firms that perceived their operating environment as *market threats focused.* However, the differences in only a small number of attributes were statistically significant. In conclusion, these results suggest that the operating environment influences a number of important attributes used to describe strategic planning but it is not a significant variable. It was therefore logical to conclude that the strategic planning process was influenced more significantly by other factors than the operating environment. HTSFs are more likely to experience dynamic/changing markets. This study identified the key distinguishing factors.

## BARRIERS TO THE DEPLOYMENT OF STRATEGIC PLANNING

Firms with a perceived increased market share were classified as high performing firms and firms with a perceived decreased market share were classified as low performing firms. Questions on the achievement of the company's initial goals and objectives and financial results expected were used to confirm the classification. A Wilcoxon test was carried out to ascertain the difference in the extent to which deployment problems were experienced by high and low performing firms. The analysis is shown in Table 6.2.

**Table 6.2:** *Extent to which strategic planning implementation problems were experienced by high and low performing firms*

| Implementation barriers | High performing firms | | Low performing firms | | Z statistic |
|---|---|---|---|---|---|
| | Mean | Frequency | Mean | Frequency | |
| Communication was inadequate | 2.18 | 7 (7%) | 2.34 | 6 (17%) | −1.47 |
| Crises distracted attention from implementation | 2.35 | 18 (17%) | 2.51 | 7 (20%) | −2.26* |
| Implementation took longer than anticipated | 3.31 | 45 (42%) | 3.37 | 17 (49%) | −0.31 |
| Employees capabilities not enough | 2.40 | 19 (18%) | 2.66 | 9 (26%) | −1.12 |
| Overall goals of strategy not well enough understood by staff | 2.11 | 7 (7%) | 2.26 | 3 (9%) | −1.43 |
| Co-ordination of implementation not effective enough | 2.59 | 20 (18%) | 2.69 | 18 (52%) | −1.69 |
| Unanticipated problems arose | 2.81 | 19 (18%) | 2.86 | 8 (23%) | −0.54 |
| External factors impacted in implementation | 2.74 | 25 (23%) | 2.94 | 13 (37%) | −0.71 |

\* $p < 0.05$

The results indicated that all the implementation barriers were experienced to a greater extent by low performing firms than by high performing firms. However, the differences were statistically insignificant with the exception of the barrier *crises distracted attention from implementation,* which was statistically significant ($z = -2.26$ at $p<0.05$).

These findings can be interpreted as indicating that successful firms found it easier to focus on the implementation of the strategy planning process, whereas in low performing firms there was a greater degree of uncertainty and a lower degree of confidence. This was confirmed by the significance of the barriers *crises distracted attention from implementation,* which implied that the operations of low performing firms were disrupted to a far greater extent than high performing firms. Overall, the analysis indicated that similar barriers to strategy implementation existed in high and low performing firms. This finding was not surprising as both categories operate, either directly or indirectly, in the same market environment. However, it indicates that the barriers to implementation are not as significant as perceived by the exploratory group discussions. These findings are consistent with the work of Kargar and Blumenthal (1994), who found that high success firms experienced implementation problems to a broadly similar extent to that of low success firms.

## THE IMPACT OF FORMAL PLANNING ON THE ELIMINATION OF POTENTIAL BARRIERS

The previous section outlined that implementation barriers with the exception of 'crises distracted attention from implementation', did not differ significantly between high performing firms and low performing firms. Arguably this may have resulted from the preparation for such barriers in the strategic planning process. It was, therefore, necessary to ascertain if firms deploying a formal planning process experienced the same barriers to the same extent as firms that used an informal planning process.

Responses were divided into two categories; firms deploying a formal strategic planning process (a written strategic plan was used as a surrogate measure for formality), and those that did not have a written strategic plan. A Wilcoxon test was carried out to ascertain the difference in the extent to which implementation problems were experienced by both categories of firms. The results of the analysis are outlined in Table 6.3.

The results indicated that all eight barriers/problems to the implementation of strategic planning were experienced by both firm types. Only one barrier/problem was statistically significant in that *external factors impacted on implementation* ($z = -2.95$ at $p<0.005$).

Overall, it can be concluded that formal and non-formal planning firms experienced similar implementation problems. These findings are consistent with the findings of Kargar and Blumenthal (1994). An analysis of the findings indicated that the problem of *implementation taking longer than expected* had the highest mean scores in both formal and non-formal planning firms. However, it must be noted that a higher significance rating given to the implementation problems by formal strategic planning firms implied that all the barriers/problems were better prepared for in formal planning firms than in non-formal planning firms. This indicated that formal planning was more likely to enable firms to meet any potential barriers and problems with greater confidence. This finding can be argued to result from the tendency by formal strategic planning firms to be more outward looking or external environment orientated. While it was contended that many of the implementation barriers were already prepared for during the strategic planning process, the results did not provide any information on the degree of emphasis on the strategic planning characteristics by formal or non-formal planning firms. A further analysis was carried out to ascertain if a similar perceived emphasis on the characteristics of strategic planning exists in firms with formal and non-formal strategic planning processes.

**Table 6.3:** *The extent to which strategy implementation problems were experienced by firms with formal and non-formal strategic plans*

| Implementation barriers | Formal planning mean | Non-formal planning mean | Z statistic |
|---|---|---|---|
| Crises distracted attention from implementation | 2.44 | 2.61 | −1.39 |
| Implementation took longer than anticipated | 3.43 | 3.22 | −0.74 |
| Employees capabilities were not enough | 2.54 | 2.43 | −0.09 |
| Communication was inadequate | 2.25 | 2.26 | −0.26 |
| Overall goals of strategy were not well enough understood by staff | 2.19 | 2.10 | −0.88 |
| External factors impacted on implementation | 3.06 | 2.61 | −2.95* |
| Co-ordination of implementation not effective enough | 2.64 | 2.69 | −0.69 |
| Unanticipated problems arose | 2.89 | 2.93 | −0.68 |

*p<0.01*

A Wilcoxon test was carried out on the mean scores to ascertain the difference in the extent to which implementation problems were experienced by high performing firms and low performing firms. Firms with a perceived increased market share were classified as high performing firms and firms with a perceived decreased market share were classified as low performing firms. The responses to an additional question on the degree to which the company achieved its initial goals and objectives, and financial results, was used to confirm the classification of firms as high or low performing. The results are shown in Table 6.4.

The results indicated that all the implementation barriers were experienced to a greater extent by low performing firms than by high performing firms. However, the differences were statistically insignificant, with the exception of the barrier *crises distracted attention from implementation* which was statistically significant $(z = -2.26$ at $p<0.05)$.

These findings can be interpreted as indicating that successful firms found it easier to focus on the implementation of the strategy planning process, whereas in low performing firms there was a greater degree of uncertainty and a lower degree of confidence. This was confirmed by the significance of the barriers in that *crises distracted attention from implementation,* which implied that the operations of low performing firms were disrupted to a far greater extent than high performing firms. Overall, the analysis indicated that similar barriers to strategy implementation existed in high and low performing firms. This finding was not surprising as both categories operate, either directly or indirectly, in the same market environment. However, it indicates that the barriers to implementation are not as significant as perceived by the exploratory group discussions.

## THE IMPACT OF FORMALITY ON STRATEGIC PLANNING

A Wilcoxon test was carried out on the mean scores to ascertain the difference in the extent to which implementation problems were experienced by formal planning and non-formal planning firms as shown in Table 6.5.

**Table 6.4:** *Extent to which strategic planning implementation problems were experienced by high and low performing firms*

| Implementation barriers | High performing Mean | Low performing Mean | Z statistic |
|---|---|---|---|
| Communication was inadequate | 2.18 | 2.34 | −1.47 |
| Crises distracted attention from implementation | 2.35 | 2.51 | −2.26* |
| Implementation took longer than anticipated | 3.31 | 3.37 | −0.31 |
| Employees capabilities not enough | 2.40 | 2.66 | −1.12 |
| Overall goals of strategy not well enough understood by staff | 2.11 | 2.26 | −1.43 |
| Co-ordination of implementation not effective enough | 2.59 | 2.69 | −1.69 |
| Unanticipated problems arose | 2.81 | 2.86 | −0.54 |
| External factors impacted in implementation | 2.74 | 2.94 | −0.71 |

*$p<0.05$

**Table 6.5:** *Emphasis on strategic planning by firms with formal and non-formal strategies*

| Strategic planning characteristics | Formal planning firms (mean) | Non-formal planning firms (mean) | Z score |
|---|---|---|---|
| *Internal capability* | | | |
| general managerial ability | 3.47 | 3.16 | −1.70 |
| financial strengths/weaknesses | 3.44 | 3.33 | −1.03 |
| human resources strengths/weaknesses | 3.52 | 3.31 | −1.44 |
| *Products and performance* | | | |
| past performance | 3.77 | 3.73 | −0.09 |
| current products strengths/weaknesses | 4.14 | 4.03 | −0.08 |
| *External orientation* | | | |
| general economic/business conditions | 3.84 | 3.57 | −1.15 |
| technological trends | 4.02 | 3.64 | −1.68 |
| competitive position and trends | 4.10 | 3.61 | −2.43** |
| *Departmental co-operation* | | | |
| understanding of all functions by employees | 3.70 | 3.42 | −1.02 |
| cross functional support | 3.80 | 3.72 | −0.46 |
| functional co-ordination | 3.69 | 3.68 | −0.67 |
| efforts to achieve functional agreement | 3.65 | 3.64 | −0.40 |
| *Resources/employees* | | | |
| ad hoc working groups | 2.77 | 2.28 | −1.95 |
| relevant/adequate information | 3.76 | 3.41 | −2.53* |
| involvement of consultants | 2.15 | 1.75 | −1.49 |
| other physical/financial resources | 3.43 | 3.04 | −1.90 |
| *Management time* | | | |
| involvement of line managers | 4.12 | 3.84 | −1.64 |
| managing directors time | 4.39 | 4.25 | −1.08 |
| *Use of analytical techniques* | | | |
| use of analytical techniques | 3.00 | 2.09 | −4.36* |
| ability to use techniques | 3.00 | 2.27 | −3.47* |
| willing to seek outside assistance | 2.94 | 2.32 | −3.42* |
| *Staff creativity* | | | |
| coping with surprises/crises | 3.52 | 3.48 | −0.10 |
| adapting to unanticipated changes | 3.79 | 3.66 | −0.92 |
| identify new opportunities | 4.05 | 4.02 | −0.92 |
| identifying key problem areas | 3.70 | 3.44 | −1.76 |
| generating new ideas | 3.88 | 3.67 | −2.04** |
| generating/evaluating strategy alternatives | 3.55 | 3.46 | −0.09 |
| anticipating barriers to implementation | 3.43 | 3.25 | −0.78 |
| *Strategy a control mechanism* | | | |
| value as a control mechanism | 3.37 | 3.01 | −1.76 |
| a monitoring control technique | 3.31 | 2.82 | −2.74** |
| mechanism for revising strategy | 3.45 | 2.89 | −2.99* |
| ability to communicate management thinking down the line | 3.64 | 3.43 | −0.84 |
| communicate staff thinking up the line | 3.42 | 3.27 | −0.38 |
| a mechanism for integrating functions | 3.07 | 2.91 | −0.65 |
| a mechanism for managerial motivation | 3.35 | 3.10 | −0.80 |

\*   *p<0.005*
\*\* *p<0.05*

The analysis indicated that the emphasis on the characteristics of strategic plan-ning by formal planning firms was higher in all the characteristics and their attributes than the degree of emphasis given by informal strategic planning process firms. The differences in emphasis in the majority of attributes were not statistically significant, with the exception of a number of characteristics which are outlined as follows:

(a) The external orientation attribute *competitive position and trends* was statistically significant $(z = -2.43, p<0.005)$. It could be argued that formal strategic plan-ning ensures that the competitive position and trends are stressed to a greater degree than in non-formal planning firms.
(b) The resources for strategy attribute *availability of relevant and adequate informa-tion* $(z = -2.53, p<0.005)$ was statistically significant. The availability of relevant information is central to the strategic planning process. The greater emphasis by formal planning process firms compared to non-formal planning firms was no surprise.
(c) All the attributes of the *use of analytical techniques* characteristic were empha-sised to a higher degree by formal planning firms than non-formal planning firms. The difference of emphases was statistically significant in respect of each attribute. This finding can be explained by the tendency by firms with a written strategic plan to depend more on analytical assessment than on 'instinct' or 'gut feeling'.
(d) The staff creativity attribute *generating new ideas* was statistically significant $(z = -2.04, p<0.05)$. It could be argued that formal planning process firms were more aware of the need staff creativity for greater competitive advantage.
(e) The control mechanism attributes: *strategy as a monitoring mechanism* $(z = -2.74, p<0.05)$, and as a *mechanism for revising strategy* $(z = -2.9, p<0.005)$ were statisti-cally significant. This indicated the greater degree of emphasis given by formal planning firms in the review of activities and in the monitoring processes used.

In conclusion, while all the attributes were given higher emphasis by formal plan-ning firms than in non-formal planning firms, only a limited number of attributes in five characteristics were statistically significant. Accordingly, the contention that there is a significant difference between the emphasis given to the characteristics of strategic planning by formal and non-formal strategic planning firms was rejected.

## CONCLUDING REMARKS

The analysis shows that firms in a dynamic and changing environment emphasised all the characteristics of strategic planing to a higher degree than firms in a market threats focused environment. The results were statistically significant for the all the attributes of the external orientation characteristic and some of the attributes of the other characteristics. This implies that the external environment influences the external orientation of HTSFs and the resources that they devote to strategic planning. It also influences the use of/the ability to use analytical techniques as well as coping with surprises/crises, identifying new opportunities and generating or evaluating strategic alternatives. The remaining attributes of staff creativity and the control mechanism characteristics are consistent with an external orientation approach.

The barriers to the deployment of strategic planning were experienced to a greater extent by low performing firms. The differences were statistically insignificant. However, the results imply that high performing firms are better prepared, possibly as a result of their strategic planning processes. A further analysis indicated that firms with formal strategic planning experienced the barriers to planning deployment to the same extent as firms using a non-formal approach. Finally, the study found that there was no significant difference on the emphasis on strategic planning attributes by formal firms compared to non-formal planning firms.

In conclusion, the results suggested that the operating environment, the barriers to strategic planning deployment and the formality of strategic planning influence a small number of important attributes used to describe different strategic planning, although they were not significant variables. Therefore, it was logical to conclude that strategic planning in HTSFs was influenced more significantly by other variables rather than the operating environment, barriers to strategic planning deployment or the formality of strategic planning. The results suggest that the barriers to deployment are the same for firms irrespective of their strategic planning process. However, the successful results show that firms that engage in formal planning are better equipped and prepared to deploy their chosen strategy.

## REFERENCES

Ancona, D. and Caldwell, D. (1987) 'Management Issues facing New Product Teams in High Technology Companies'. In: Lewin, D., Lipsky, D. and Sokel, D. (eds) *Advances in Industrial and Labour Relations*, Vol. 4. Greenwich CT: JAI Press, pp. 191–221.

Armstrong, J.S. (1982) 'The Value of Formal Planning for Strategic Decisions'. *Strategic Management Journal*, Vol. 3, No. 3, pp. 197–211.

Barber, J., Metcalfe, J.S. and Porteous, M. (1989) *Barriers to Growth in Small Firms*. London: Routledge.

Bennett, R.J. (1998) 'Business Associations and their potential contribution to the competitiveness of SMEs'. *Entrepreneurship and Regional Development*, Vol. 10, pp. 243–260.

Bourgeois, L.J. (1996) *Strategic Management: From Concept to Implementation*. Fort Worth, TX: The Dryden Press.

Bracker, J., Keats, B. and Pearson, J. (1988) 'Planning and Financial Performance Among Small Firms in a Growth Industry'. *Strategic Management Journal*, Vol. 9, No. 6, pp. 591–603.

Cambridge Small Business Research Centre (1992) *The State of British Enterprise*. Department of Applied Economics, University of Cambridge.

Clarke, L. (1994) *The Essence of Change*. Hemel Hempstead: Prentice Hall.

Covin, J.G. and Slevin, D.P. (1989) 'Strategic Management of Small Firms in Hostile and Benign Environments'. *Strategic Management Journal*, Vol. 10, No. 1, pp. 75–87.

Cronbach, I.J. (1951) 'Coefficient Alpha and the Internal Structure of Tests'. *Psychometrika*, Vol. 16, No. 3, pp. 297–334.

Deakins, D. and Freel, M. (1998) 'Entrepreneurial learning and the growth process in SMEs'. *The Learning Organisation*, Vol. 5, No. 3, pp. 144–155.

De Geus, A. (1997) 'The Living Company'. *Harvard Business Review*, Vol. 75, No. 2, March-April, pp. 51–59.

Gilmore, F. (1971) 'Formulating strategy in smaller companies'. *Harvard Business Review*, May-June. Vol. 49, No. 3, pp. 71–81.

Hart, S. and Banbury, C. (1994) 'How Strategy-making Processes can make a Difference'. *Strategic Management Journal*, Vol. 15, No. 4, pp. 251–269.

Joyce, P., Seaman, C. and Woods, A. (1996) In Blackburn, R. and Jennings, P. (eds) *Small Firms: Contributions to Economic Regeneration*. London: The Institute for Small Business Affairs.

Kargar, J. and Blumenthal, R.A. (1994) 'Successful implimentation of strategic decisions in small community banks'. *Journal of Small Business Management*, Vol. 32, No. 2, pp. 10–23.

Kargar, J. and Parnall, J.A. (1996) 'Strategic planning emphasis and planning satisfaction in small firms: an empirical investigation'. *Journal of Business Strategies*, Vol. 13, No. 1 pp. 42–64.

Larsen, P., Tonge, R. and Ito, M. (1998) The Strategic Planning Process in Growing Companies'. *Journal of General Management*, Vol. 24, No. 1, pp. 53–67.

Lyles, M.A., Baird, I.S., Orris, J.B. and Kuratko, F.F. (1993) 'Formalised Planning in Small Business: Increasing Strategic Choices'. *Journal of Small Business Management*, Vol. 31, No. 2, pp. 38–50.

McKiernan, P. and Morris, C. (1994) 'Strategic Planning and Financial Performance in UK SMEs: does formality matter?' *British Journal of Management*, Vol. 5, Special Issue, S31–S41.

Mills, D.Q. and Friesen, B. (1992) 'The Learning Organization'. *European Management Journal*, Vol. 10, No. 2, pp. 146–156.

Parks, B., Olson, P.D. and Bokor, D.W. (1991) 'Don't mistake Business Plans for Planning'. *Journal of Small Business Strategy*, Vol. 2, No. 1, pp. 15–24.

Piatier, A. (1984) *Barriers to Innovation*. London: Frances Pinter.

Porter, M.E. (1996) 'What is Strategy'. *Harvard Business Review*, Vol. 74, No. 6, Nov/Dec, pp. 61–78.

Ramanujam, V. and Venkatraman, N. (1987) 'Planning and Performance: A New look at an old question'. *Business Horizons*, Vol. 30, May-June, pp. 19–25.

Robinson, R.B. and Pearce, J.A. (1983) 'The Impact of Formalised Strategic Planning on Financial Performance in Small Organizations'. *Strategic Management Journal*, Vol. 4, No. 3, pp. 197–207.

Roper, S. (1997) 'Strategic Initiatives and Small Business Performance: An Exploratory Analysis of Irish Companies'. *Entrepreneurship and Regional Development*, Vol. 9, pp. 353–364.

Shrader, C.B., Taylor, L. and Dalton D.R. (1984) 'Strategic Planning and Organizational Performance: A Critical Appraisal'. *Journal of Management*, Vol. 10, No. 2, pp. 149–171.

Skinner W. (1996) 'Three Yards and a Cloud of Dust: Industrial Management at Century End'. *Production and Operations Management Society*, Vol. 5, No. 1, Spring.

Storey, D.J., Keasey, K., Watson, R. and Wynarczyk, P. (1987) *The Performance of Small Firms: Profits, Jobs and Failures*. London: Croom Helm.

Thompson, J.L. (1996) 'Strategic Effectiveness and Success: the Learning Challenge'. *Management Decision*, Vol. 34, No. 7, pp. 14–23.

# CHAPTER 7

## Equity Gaps in Depleted Communities: An Entrepreneurial Response

HARVEY JOHNSTONE

### CONTEXT

Industrial Cape Breton currently has a population of about 120,000. Throughout the twentieth century many of its residents made their living in resource-based industries such as fishing, forestry, coal and steel. However, resourced-based firms in the area have suffered steady employment losses since the 1960s. Officially, unemployment is now reported to be 20 per cent, although when adjusted to national rates of labor force participation, the figure rises to 32 per cent. Furthermore, many of those included in these statistics are chronically unemployed. Since the 1960s, the population of the region has also declined steadily. By the late 1990s Cape Breton's image as the 'industrial heart of the Atlantic region' was based more on past achievements than present realities. In short, Cape Breton is a depleted community.

Over the past 35 years a litany of government schemes aimed at re-developing the economy have been attempted. These schemes have not reduced the high rates of unemployment. At least by that measure, one can say unequivocally, the government schemes have failed. One of the more recent public policy initiatives has been an attempt to promote and encourage new firms operating in the Information Technology (IT) sector. Today, Cape Breton has a number of firms with young, well-educated entrepreneurs who hope to identify and pursue opportunities in the new economy. This approach to development looks to the new prominence of the small firm for theoretical justification.

### THE NEW PROMINENCE OF THE SMALL FIRM AND PUBLIC POLICY

The new prominence afforded the small firm sector (Johnstone, 1998) has provided justification for two policy approaches aimed at boosting faltering local economies. The first directs attention towards existing and potential entrepreneurs in an effort to increase the rate of new firm formation (NFF). This approach has been used in both the United Kingdom and the United States. However, research has found large differences in regional rates of NFF (Keeble, 1993). Furthermore, related research shows that variables contributing to the regional differences in rates of NFF, although identifiable, are very difficult to manipulate (Reynolds, 1994; Mason, 1991). Finally, at least for depleted communities, the association between higher rates of NFF and net employment growth is very weak

(Johnstone, 1998). Together, these results raise questions about the efficacy of such policy initiatives.

The second kind policy initiative springing from the new prominence of the small firm sector aims to stimulate *growth* in SMEs. Fast-growth firms account for the majority of new jobs created in many economies (Storey, 1987). Thus, SME formation and growth is of great importance to those who are concerned with development policies. But designing effective policies to stimulate growth may be difficult because research also indicates the rarity of finding firms with the potential for rapid growth. For instance, Birch's research, for the period between 1980 and 1986, reported more than 90 per cent of gross new jobs in the United States were created by 15 per cent of the firms (Birch, 1987).

In Atlantic Canada, high failure rates of SMEs indicate that small firms in this region have trouble surviving and growing (Gorman and King, 1998). Difficulties in surviving and growing entrepreneurial firms can be accounted for by several factors. The Atlantic Provinces Economic Council (APEC, 1994) indicates that management skills are lacking in the Atlantic Region; in particular, expertise in managing growth and exports are missing from Atlantic Canada. Lack of adequate funding is another reason why many businesses find it difficult to expand (APEC, 1994). How then can SME growth in Atlantic Canada be encouraged?

One possibility, direct financing, is among the more important vehicles for stimulating growth in SMEs. Public policies directed towards establishing economic development funds, such as incentives to banks for small business loans, and other funding schemes have been undertaken. At the same time, governments use these initiatives to address issues of regional disparity by directing funds at specific areas. Within the context of the Cape Breton economy, the Atlantic Canada Opportunities Agency (ACOA) and Enterprise Cape Breton Corporation (ECBC) are examples of government organizations undertaking these types of initiatives. Typically banks and development agencies offer debt financing. This is the traditional type of financing taken on by small businesses. Unfortunately, there are some significant problems associated with debt financing for today's small businesses. Canadian firms tend to be over-leveraged on bank debt and, according to some observers, this over-use seriously limits opportunities to expand (APEC, 1994).

Alternatively, small firms that finance their operations through equity capital enjoy several benefits. Equity investments are longer term, unsecured with high liquidity risk, and the investor(s) usually participates in the management of the company. This is a much better fit with the needs of SMEs. No longer is collateral needed to secure the financing, repayment is flexible and long-term, and some management expertise can usually be gained. In return, the entrepreneur relinquishes some personal control of the company. Those that offer equity financing are known as venture capital investors. The literature identifies two types: formal and informal (Lumme et al., 1998).

1. *Formal venture capital* funds have operated for a number of years in North America and Europe. Using a pool of funds gathered from a number of investors and managed by a separate entity, formal venture capital funds tend to:

   ● avoid risk, by concentrating their investments on expansions and buy-outs;
   ● invest in firms that are in the later stages of their development;
   ● invest primarily in areas near their home base (Mason and Harrison, 1991).

   Because formal venture capital funds tend to operate in these ways they leave equity gaps in the venture-financing scheme. Equity gaps are of several types:

- *Spatial equity gaps* are left because most venture capital funds are concentrated in metropolitan areas leaving out rural and smaller urban areas.
- *Stage equity gaps* exist because venture capital funds concentrate on later stage firms. Thus, start-up and early stage firms are less likely to access this form of funding.
- *Sectoral equity gaps* exist because venture funds tend to invest in industries where they have experience. Especially in emerging sectors, formal venture capital may be difficult to find.

2. *Informal venture capital,* provided by business angels, usually fills in the gaps left by formal venture capital. Business angels tend to invest in early-stage businesses and they invest outside of metropolitan areas. Business angels are usually older, wealthy males with experience in business (Feeney et al., 1998). They invest for the medium to long term and also provide the targeted firm with valuable management expertise (thus they are said to provide 'smart money'). Returns on investment are usually tied to profitability, ensuring the investor's interest in the business and the entrepreneur's ability to pay. (APEC, 1994). Angels tend to protect their investments by getting involved in the firms they invest in. Thus, firms financed through business angels not only gain financial benefits, they also benefit from the business expertise and contacts provided by their angels. The informal venture capital market has thus been identified as a means by which SMEs can be aided in growth (Mason and Harrison, 1994b).

This research focused specifically on the Cape Breton informal venture capital sector (supply side) and the IT sector (demand side). We tested for mismatches between the 'supply of' and 'demand for' local venture capital.

## METHODOLOGY

A pre-tested 'supply side' questionnaire was developed. A list of informal venture capitalists (business angels) was compiled from various sources and interviews were requested. A total of 21 interviews were conducted. A pre-tested 'demand side' questionnaire was developed and distributed to entrepreneurs listed in a directory of locally based IT firms. The sample of IT firms was not meant to be exhaustive. Instead, the responses were filtered to identify those respondents whose firms were focused on growth. A total of 14 useable responses were received. By most research standards the sample sizes are small; however, in small communities this scale can be representative because the populations of investors and firms are not large. In addition, the results were compared to recent regional and national studies to gauge validity.

## DEMAND SIDE RESULTS

Fourteen IT firms were profiled in this survey. Almost all described themselves as being in the 'initial sales' or 'early stages of growth' phases. These firms were asked to outline their investment needs over the coming 3–4 years indicating both immediate needs and investment requirements over the medium term. Table 7.1 summarizes the results of the surveyed IT firms.

The investment needs of these firms amounted to $24,127,000 over 4 years. This is an average of $6,031,750 per year. The median amount needed per firm was $1,175,000 over 4 years. These estimates may be low. When compared to other

**Table 7.1:** *IT sector investment needs*

| | Mean | Year | Median | Year | Totals | Annual needs |
|---|---|---|---|---|---|---|
| Round 1: | $355,500 | 1.04 yrs | $175,000 | 1 | $4,977,000 | |
| Round 2: | $689,286 | 2.50 yrs | $500,000 | 2 | $9,650,000 | |
| Round 3: | $678,571 | 3.92 yrs | $500,000 | 4 | $9,500,000 | |
| Totals | $1,723,357 | | $1,175,000 | | $24,127,000 | $6,031,750 |

sources, local entrepreneurs appear to be underestimating the financing required to grow their firms. For example, OECD figures suggest that high growth firms need on average $750,000 to fund the start-up phase and $1,500,000 for the initial growth stage (OECD, 1998). Thus, it may be more appropriate to say that the annual need is *at least* $6,000,000.

When IT entrepreneurs were asked to indicate the kind of assistance they hoped to receive from informal investors (business angels) the strongest responses were for assistance in the areas of marketing, industry contacts and management (see Figure 7.1). There was little interest shown in having other forms of advice. When asked which functional areas needed the most improvement, the responses were marketing, management and exporting. The majority of the entrepreneurs had extensive formal training, primarily in technical areas. Most had university degrees and many had graduate training. However, the three areas where entrepreneurs had the least formal training were marketing, legal issues, and exporting. Of these, only legal advice seemed to be readily available through external professional services.

## SUPPLY SIDE RESULTS

Table 7.2 shows how much informal venture capital is available to IT businesses in Cape Breton from our business angel respondents. Based on past investment amounts, only $226,000 will be available for Cape Breton IT firms from Cape Breton investors. The $226,000 appearing in Table 7.2 represented about 5.5 per cent of the $4,000,000 available annually. A small number of those interviewed had

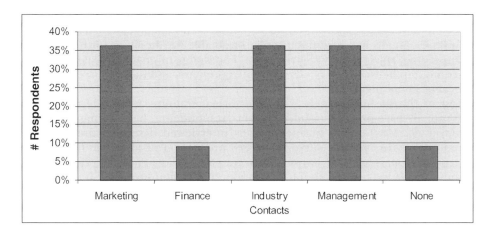

**Figure 7.1:** Expertise sought in an Angel Investor

**Table 7.2:** *Investment dollars available to IT sector*

|          | Supply                        |               | Demand                    |                          |                  |                  |                |
| -------- | ----------------------------- | ------------- | ------------------------- | ------------------------- | ---------------- | ---------------- | -------------- |
|          | Invested<br>(past 5 yrs)      | % of<br>total | Available<br>per year     | Total needs<br>(4 yrs)    | Needs/<br>year   | Unmet<br>needs   | %<br>unmet     |
| Software | $975,000                      | 97            | $220,000                  | $23,527,000               | $5,881,750       | ($5,661,750)     | 96.30          |
| Hardware | $25,000                       | 3             | $6,000                    | $600,000                  | $150,000         | ($144,000)       | 96.00          |
| Totals   | $1,000,000                    |               | $226,000                  | $24,127,000               | $6,031,750       | ($5,805,750)     | 96.30          |

relatively large sums to invest annually (say >$250,000). Elsewhere I refer to these as 'deep pocket investors'. Most of those interviewed had smaller amounts to invest. Of those interviewed 35 per cent said their practice was to invest alone. This figure is considerably higher than figures reported in other studies. While the greater reluctance to syndicate is relevant and probably limits the supply of meaningful investment, most of the 'deep pocket investors' had indicated their practice was to co-invest. It should be noted however, that in some cases, the practice was for 'deep pocket investors' to co-invest with institutional investors rather than with other angels. To the extent that institutional investors are reluctant to invest at the early stages of business development, the practices of these angels may be directed toward more mature opportunities and away from entrepreneurial firms examined here. Nonetheless, relatively large sums could be assembled from this group of investors. However, with little experience in the sector, and reluctance on the part of many local investors to syndicate, the supply of locally based informal venture capital for these particular types of locally based entrepreneurial ventures appeared to be quite limited.

Even limiting total IT demand to the profiled firms, Table 7.2 shows that almost 96 per cent of the expressed needs for investment in IT firms will go unmet. These firms will be forced to look elsewhere for financing, or their anticipated growth will not occur. The IT sector has been one of the few promising areas of development in the Cape Breton economy, but without further investment, its future is threatened. Such a 'dollar mismatch' between supply and demand establishes that action, aimed at increasing informal investment dollars, is urgently needed.

When asked to indicate the areas of the business in which they preferred to be involved, local business angels ranked finance, planning and operations as most important (see Figure 7.2). In contrast, the IT entrepreneurs were looking for advice on marketing, exporting/industry contacts and management. Thus, even if the business angels had investment dollars available for the IT sector it would not be considered 'smart money'. This kind of 'knowledge mismatch' creates a qualitative equity gap between the needs of IT entrepreneurs and the resources provided by local business angels.

Most of the business angels had little formal training, with only two having professional backgrounds, while further respondents had strong technical backgrounds. Most of the business angels interviewed described themselves as entrepreneurs. In national surveys a larger proportion of angels indicated they were professionals such as lawyers or accountants (Feeney et al., 1998). Local business angels were asked about their preferences when investing. In particular, they were asked whether they considered co-investing to be a viable option. Thirty-five per cent indicated that they did not co-invest (see Figure 7.3). This is a significant feature of the local economy. Nationally, the percentage willing to co-invest is much higher. This implies that many local investors would not be inclined to syndicate. Furthermore, only 20 per cent of investors interviewed were

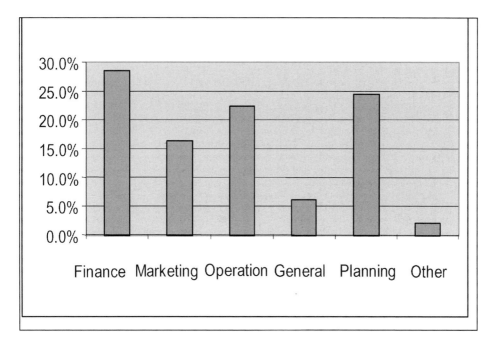

**Figure 7.2:** Expertise provided by Angel Investors

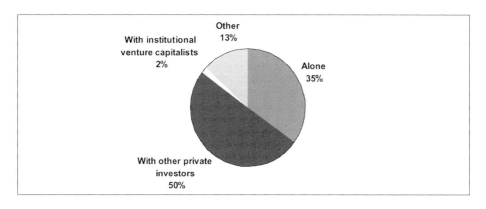

**Figure 7.3:** Investing practices of Angel Investors

comfortable investing alone in computer software deals. Local angels also indicated that they would not be inclined to syndicate with a 'lead' investor who had more experience in a sector than they did. These features suggest that it would be very difficult to attract local investment for projects operating in sectors like IT so long as the sector has been untested by local business angels. The results also suggest that, unless a local entrepreneur can attract a business angel with deep pockets, it may be very difficult to raise large sums through syndication (see Figure 7.4).

Despite the current focus on the IT industry in Cape Breton, to date local business angels have largely avoided this industry. There may be several reasons to explain this apparent lack of interest in the IT sector. Business angels tend to

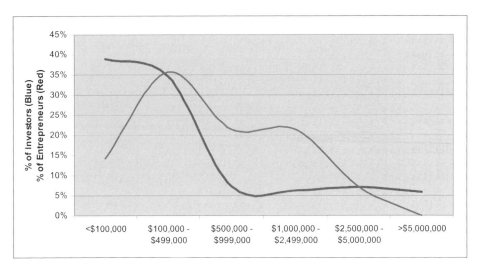

**Figure 7.4:** Equity gap: demand vs supply

invest in industries in which they are comfortable; that is, they tend to invest in industries where they have experience. IT and advanced technology industries are new to Cape Breton and thus we do not have business people who have gained experience and are willing to invest in these industries. The sector may simply be too young here. Local investors are not comfortable investing in this sector. As well, local investment dollars are being attracted to competing opportunities in offshore natural gas. Even the small amounts currently available to IT firms may be redirected toward other investment possibilities. The potential of the Sable and Laurentian gas projects will certainly draw significant amounts of investment from local business angels. The IT industry in Cape Breton will have to compete with these projects for the limited investment dollars available in Cape Breton. Thus, there is a need for an artificial means of interesting investors in this sector.

## THE SITUATION

The IT industry in Cape Breton has enjoyed considerable success in its infant years. It now faces new challenges as it begins to grow. In order to realize the growth potential of many of these firms, financing must be found. Local investors are not currently investing enough in the IT sector to satisfy its needs. Thus, there is a need for immediate action to fill both qualitative and quantitative equity gaps in Cape Breton.

There are a number of strategies that can be used to promote venture capital. The Organization for Economic Co-operation and Development (OECD) reviewed and evaluated several such measures in its 1998 publication 'Technology, Productivity and Job Creation: Best Policy Practices'.

## AN ENTREPRENEURIAL RESPONSE

One of the difficulties associated with proposed remedies (intended to right faltering informal venture capital systems) that are included in reports like the OECD, is that they call for actions by individuals who stand to lose nothing if action is delayed. In the meantime, those who are caught on the demand side of the equity gap, the entrepreneurs, can lose everything. The IT entrepreneurs identified in this study do not have the luxury of time – they need an immediate solution or they will be out of business.

Faced with this reality the IT entrepreneurs have acted. They have created a new company called GENA, which stands for Gap Equity Network Association. GENA was formed to close the equity gaps identified in this research. The solution lies in attracting private investment capital to the region. GENA envisages the creation of a public-private mechanism that will 'kick-start' investment in the IT sector of Cape Breton. GENA believes that creating the first high-growth success stories will lead to the creation of a locally based private investment culture necessary to sustain the IT business sector in Cape Breton. GENA's mission is to attract financing and provide the guidance necessary to enable locally based businesses to succeed at all stages of growth and development, with a primary focus on early-stage companies. In part GENA is modeled on the Small Business Investment Companies (SBICs) operating in the United States.

In 1958, the United States Government recognized that lack of investment capital was impeding the growth of early-stage businesses. In response, it created the Small Business Investment Company (SBIC) program, which matched private investment dollars with public dollars at a rate of up to 300 per cent. The program has been very successful, facilitating billions of dollars of investment, with a list of investments that includes Intel, Apple and Federal Express.

The SBIC program forms part of the inspiration for GENA's proposed Investment Matching Program. Like SBIC, the GENA program proposes the use of public funds to leverage private investment dollars to reduce risk. And like SBIC, the GENA program is privately managed. The program aims to lever the know-how and a sense of ownership of the private investor. In GENA's view it is 'smart money' that helps businesses succeed. Unlike SBIC, entrepreneurs adopting the GENA approach can shop around for an investor who provides the best fit to the business. GENA also differs in terms of the way in which money exchanges between government, GENA and entrepreneur. Finally, because GENA is an initiative of the demand side group, entrepreneurs do not have to wait for investors to set up a SBIC.

The key to a successful investment program is to maintain enough flexibility to attract a variety of investors while maintaining enough tightness to ensure all investments are made in good faith. Some investors like to invest on their own while others prefer to become involved with a group of investors. Some wish to invest in single entities while others prefer the reduced risk of investing in a group of companies. A key attractiveness behind the Investment Matching Program is that it facilitates the flexibility to attract a wide array of private investors.

At this time the voucher system described below is in the proposal phase and there has been no commitment by government to match private investments. Nonetheless, GENA is operating and has contacted several groups of external investors. GENA has also succeeded in attracting more than $1,000,000 of inward investment.

The premise behind this proposed program is to match private investment dollars with government dollars. In order to increase the attractiveness of investment opportunities to potential investors, it is essential that the matching government dollars are pre-approved. By vouchering investment opportunities, the potential investor is granted this assurance. The flexibility of the voucher enables each entrepreneur to find 'smart money' that is specifically tailored to his/her business needs.

## *Details of the voucher system*

1. Entrepreneur approaches GENA's Managing Director to request qualification for an Investment Matching Voucher.
2. The Managing Director reviews the opportunity to make sure it is eligible and 'investment ready'. Where deficiencies are identified recommendations are made to the applicant.
3. The Managing Director completes the preliminary review and sends eligible applications to the due diligence process. A third party such as a nationally recognized accounting firm would conduct the due diligence process. The guidelines and review process will be predetermined and will apply to all applicants. Cost and payment of process will be determined.
4. The due-diligence phase is described as follows:

   ● A review to make sure that the company does indeed qualify for government matching funds, as required by the parameters set out by the government and GENA board. This 'credibility check' includes:

       – A review of the company history such as verifying that it is a Canadian corporation headquartered in Cape Breton, is in good standing with the receiver general, and showing management trustworthiness, etc.
       – A 'reality check' to confirm that the company objectives can conceivably be accomplished. This is not a formal review of the business opportunity, but rather a review of the plausible nature of the business objectives.
       – A matching cap and date to determine the maximum amount of investment that can be matched within a given time period by the company.

   This level of due diligence will be required to be completed within a designated period of time.
5. The completed documentation is sent to the Voucher Committee for approval. Working under specific guidelines, the Voucher Committee members vote to accept or reject the application.
6. The successful applicant is given an Investment Matching Voucher. With this in hand, the entrepreneur can then find any investor to invest knowing their private money will be automatically matched with government dollars at the specified ratio. The investor retains all equity as negotiated with the entrepreneur.
7. Once the entrepreneur finds the investor, the details of the investment are sent to the Voucher Review Subcommittee for final approval and distribution of funds as an interest bearing, conditionally repayable loan. A cheque for the matching funds will be made out, payable to both the company and the investor. The matching funds may be paid out in one or more installments if necessary to match the private investment.
8. Once the investment becomes liquid (via dividends, buyout, etc.), the investor repays the loan, with interest. Any losses are borne between the investor and government at the matching ratio.

It remains to be seen how effective GENA will be in closing the equity gaps identified in this research. Nonetheless the GENA initiative demonstrates, in the clearest terms, the drive these young entrepreneurs have and their commitment to make their firms grow. This research shows that entrepreneurs who choose to operate within depleted economies can take very little for granted. If these IT companies do survive, they will have established elements of infrastructure that will smooth the way for those to follow. While it may be difficult to quantify such a contribution, unquestionably, it would be significant.

# REFERENCES

Atlantic Canada Opportunities Agency (1998) 'The State of Small Business and Entrepreneurship in Atlantic Canada 1998'. Atlantic Canada Opportunities Agency.

Atlantic Provinces Economic Council (1994) 'Equity Capital Investment: A Key to Entrepreneurial Expansion in Atlantic Canada'. Submitted to the Working Committee on Venture Capital appointed by the Conference of Atlantic Premiers.

Birch, David (1987) *Job Creation in America: How our Smallest Companies Put the Most People to Work*. Free Press: New York.

Brouwer, Maria and Hendrix, Bart (1998) 'Two Worlds of Venture Capital: What happened to U.S. and Dutch Early Stage Investment'. *Small Business Economics*, 10, pp. 333–348.

Coveney, Patrick, and Moore, Karl (1998) Business Angels: Securing Start Up Finance. John Wiley and Sons, Toronto.

Farrell, A.E. (1998) 'Informal Venture Capital Investment in Atlantic Canada: A Representative View of "Angels"'. Submitted to Atlantic Canada Opportunities Agency.

Feeney, L., Johnstone, H. and Riding, A. (1998) 'A Profile of Informal Investors in Canada: A Comparison of Canadian and Maritime Investors'. Submitted to The Canadian Council for Small Business and Entrepreneurship Annual Conference, Mount Saint Vincent University, Halifax, Nova Scotia, Fall 1998.

Gladstone, David (1988) *Venture Capital Handbook*. Pretence Hall, New Jersey.

Gorman, Gary and King, Wayne (1998) 'The Dynamics of Firm Growth in Atlantic Canada and Canada (1989–1995)'. Submitted to the 28th Annual Atlantic Schools of Business Conference, Fall 1998.

Groupe Secor Inc. (1998) 'Financing Knowledge-Based Small Business'. Research paper prepared for the Task Force on the Future of the Canadian Financial Services Sector, September 1998.

Harrison, Richard and Mason, Colin (eds) (1996) *Informal Venture Capital: Evaluating the Impact of Business Introduction Services*. Woodhead-Faulkner Limited, Hertfordshire, England.

Harrison, Richard T. and Mason, Colin (1997) 'International Perspectives on the Supply of Informal Venture Capital'. *Journal of Business Venturing*, Vol. 7, pp. 459–475.

Johnstone, H. (1998) 'Small Firms and Regional Development The Impact of New Firm Formation on Britain's Depleted Communities'. In *Proceedings of the Canadian Council for Small Business and Entrepreneurship Conference*, Halifax, Nova Scotia, October 1998.

Johnstone H. and Kirby, D. (1999) 'Regional Development and the Small Firm – Limits on the Prospects for Small Firm Led Growth'. In the *Proceedings of the 44th International Council for Small Business*, Naples Italy, June 1999.

Keeble, D., Walker, S. and Robson, M. (1993) New Firm Formation and Small Business Growth in the United Kingdom: Spatial and Temporal Variations and Determinants. *Employment Department, Research Series No. 15*, Sheffield.

Lumme, A., Mason, C. and Suomi, M. (1998) *'Informal Venture Capital: Investors, Investments and Policy Issues in Finland'*. Kluwer Academic Publishers, The Netherlands.

Manweller, Richard L. (1997) *Funding High-Tech Ventures*. Oasis Press, Oregon.

Mason, Colin (1991) 'Spatial Variations in Enterprise: the geography of New Firm Formation'. In R. Burrows (ed.) *Deciphering the Enterprise Culture: Entrepreneurship, Petty Capitalism and the Restructuring of Britain*. Routledge, London, pp. 74–106.

Mason, Colin and Harrison, Richard (1991) 'Venture Capital, the equity gap and the north-south divide in the UK'. In M. Green (ed.) *Venture Capital: International Comparisons*. Routledge, London, pp. 202–247.

Mason, Colin and Harrison, Richard (1992a) 'A Strategy for Closing the Small Firms' Finance Gap'. In Kevin Caley, Elizabeth Chell, Francis Chittenden and Colin Mason (eds) *Small Enterprise Development*. Paul Chapman, London.

Mason, Colin and Harrison, Richard (1992b) 'The Supply of Equity Finance in the UK: a Strategy for Closing the Equity Gap'. *Entrepreneurship and Regional Development*, Vol. 4, pp. 357–380.

Mason, Colin and Harrison, Richard (1993) 'Strategies for Expanding the Informal Venture Capital Market'. *International Small Business Journal*, 2:4, pp. 23–37.

Mason, Colin and Harrison, Richard (1994a) 'The Role of Informal and Formal Sources of Venture Capital in the Financing of Technology-Based SMEs in the United Kingdom'. In R. Oakey (ed.) *New Technology Based Firms in the 1990s*. Paul Chapman Publishing Ltd, London, pp. 104–124.

Mason, Colin and Harrison, Richard (1994b) 'Informal Venture Capital in the UK'. In A. Hughes and D. Storey (eds), *Finance and the Small Firm*. Routledge, London, pp. 64–111.

Murray, Gordon C. (1998) 'A Policy Response to Regional Disparities in the Supply of Risk Capital to New Technology-based Firms in the European Union: The European Seed Capital Fund Scheme'. *Regional Studies*, 32:5, pp. 405–419.

Odenthal, John (1994) 'Equity Capital Investment: A Key to Entrepreneurial Expansion in Atlantic Canada'. Atlantic Provinces Economic Council, submitted to the Working Committee on Venture Capital appointed by the Conference of Atlantic Premiers.

Organization for Economic Co-operation and Development (1998) 'Technology, Productivity and Job Creation: Best Policy Practices'. OECD.

Reynolds P., Storey, D.J. and Westhead, P. (1994) Cross National Comparisons of the Variation in New Firm Formation Rates. *Regional Studies*, Vol. 28, No. 4, pp. 443–456.

Riding, Allan L. (1998) 'Financing Entrepreneurial Firms: Legal and Regulatory Issues'. Research paper prepared for the Task Force on the Future of the Canadian Financial Services Sector. September 1998.

Storey, D. and Johnson, D. (1987) *Job Generation and Labour Market Change*. MacMillan, London.

Watson, Lisa M., Haines, George H. Jr. and Riding, Allan, L. (1998) 'Decision Making by Canadian Angels: A Qualitative Analytic Approach'. Presented at The Canadian Council for Small Business and Entrepreneurship Annual Conference, Mount Saint Vincent University, Halifax, Nova Scotia.

# CHAPTER 8

# Modelling Returns to R&D: An Analysis of Size Effects

PETER BROUWER AND HENRY NIEUWENHUIJSEN

## INTRODUCTION

Since Schumpeter in his book *Capitalism, Socialism and Democracy* (1942) put forward the hypothesis that large enterprises are the most effective innovators, much research has involved the study of size and R&D. Many authors have discovered through empirical research that the proportion of firms doing R&D increases with size, to the extent that in the highest size classes the proportion is 100 per cent (e.g. Villard, 1958; Nelson et al., 1967; Bound et al., 1984 and Cohen et al., 1987). These empirical results have been interpreted as support for Schumpeter. However, studies also show that the relationship between R&D and size is proportional (Scherer, 1984; Bound et al., 1984 and Cohen et al., 1987). Moreover, some authors have found that the number of innovations per dollar of R&D spent is disproportional to size (e.g. Acs and Audretsch, 1991). The last two theses can be interpreted as a rejection of Schumpeter's hypothesis. Cohen and Klepper (1996) recently put forward the idea that, because of cost spreading, large firms have an advantage when conducting R&D, which conforms to Schumpeter's view. Furthermore, Nooteboom (1994) stated that there is an indication of dynamic complementarity between large and small firms in the innovative process. This means that large and small firms are more effective innovators at different stages in the life cycle of a technology or product. In sum we conclude that earlier studies on the relationship between R&D and size give unambiguous results. The question remains whether large or small firms profit more from their specific R&D activities.

In this study we deal with the direct effects on productivity of the 'in-house' R&D expenditures of firms. In particular the differences in the output elasticities of R&D expenditures between large and small firms are investigated.

## MODELLING PRODUCTIVITY EFFECTS OF R&D

In order to assess the effects of R&D activities on productivity most studies employ a Cobb-Douglas production function.[1] The advantage of estimating a production function is that it is relatively simple, and the data necessary for this estimation are usually available. In its standard form, the production function relates the volume of production to the input factors of labour, capital and material consumption. By including a measure of R&D as an additional explanatory variable in the production function we can obtain an estimate of the output elasticity of R&D.

As a measure of R&D the concept of stock of knowledge capital (Hall and Mairesse, 1995) is used. It is assumed that past R&D expenditures form stocks of knowledge in a way similar to the formation of the stock of physical capital through investments. The knowledge stock increases each year as a result of new R&D expenditures. Furthermore a certain depreciation rate for knowledge capital is assumed. Hall and Mairesse (1995) show that, using the *Perpetual Inventory Method* (PIM), the initial knowledge stock is proportional to initial R&D expenditures. This implies that, in cross sections, R&D expenditures can be used as a measure of R&D in the production function.

The production function can be estimated at different levels of aggregation. For our purpose of estimating the effects of R&D activities on production, it is best to use data at the firm level. Using aggregated data can introduce an aggregation bias due to a skewed distribution of R&D expenditures across firms. In this case, a small number of large firms with high R&D expenditures will dominate the results. When these firms operate at a multinational level, aggregated data are not suitable for measuring the productivity effects of R&D, since R&D activities in one country will affect productivity in another country. In the Netherlands most R&D expenditures are concentrated within five multinational companies (see Minne, 1997).

Clearly, estimating a Cobb-Douglas production function is a simplification of reality. This simplification can lead to biased estimates of the output elasticity of R&D expenditures, caused by the influence of variables not included in the production function. To correct for the omission of variables that are related to the characteristics of the particular sector in which a firm operates we can include sector dummies when estimating the production function.

Besides sector-specific characteristics there may also be firm-specific characteristics that influence estimations of the output elasticity of R&D expenditures. However, including a dummy variable for each firm is not feasible since that would introduce too many coefficients to be estimated. When panel data are available, the firm-specific characteristics can be eliminated by using either growth figures (first differences) or variables related to their mean (within transformation) in the estimation. Unfortunately both methods are rather sensitive to measurement errors. To avoid the influence of measurement errors one can use so-called 'long differences' of variables. This entails using mutations of variables over a longer period of time and requires the observation of firms at two moments several years apart. Especially for smaller firms, of which only samples are surveyed, this is often not feasible.

Another assumption made implicitly when using a production function concerns the exogeneity of input factors. The production function determines the level of output based on the level of the different input factors. However, in practice there can also be a reverse relationship between output and input factors when the level of output may determine the level of input factors employed. This is true especially for the input factors of labour and materials. The interdependence of the levels of output and input factors is usually referred to as the problem of simultaneity.

It will be clear that the advantage of the simple estimation of a production function to assess the productivity effect of R&D comes at the cost of possible biases in the estimates of the output elasticities. Besides the already mentioned complicating factors, R&D not only influences production, but it will most likely also have an effect on the demand for the products of a firm. In fact, increasing the demand by introducing new products is probably one of the main reasons why firms engage in R&D activities.

Van Leeuwen and Nieuwenhuijsen (1999) propose a model comprising a production function and a demand function, both including R&D as an additional explanatory variable. By estimating this model in its reduced form and using long differences and within transformations of the variables, they take into account both the simultaneity issue and the influence of firm-specific characteristics, while incorporating the demand effects of R&D. The sample available in Van Leeuwen and Nieuwenhuijsen (1999) consists of large enterprises.

In our study we distinguish between the productivity effects of 'in-house' R&D for small and medium-sized enterprises (SMEs) and large enterprises (LEs). Because only data for 1994 are available, we begin by estimating the Cobb-Douglas production function, including R&D expenditures in 1994 as additional explanatory variable, for the cross section. Since the estimates for the output elasticities of R&D expenditures obtained in this way may be biased, we also estimate a version of the model by Van Leeuwen and Nieuwenhuijsen. This allows us to determine how the estimated output elasticities are affected by taking into account several of the issues discussed in this section, and consequently, how much confidence we can have in the estimates from the extended Cobb-Douglas production function.

## DATA

Data available from Statistics Netherland on Dutch manufacturing firms at the firm level are analysed for 1994. The database links data from the R&D survey with selected variables from the production statistics. From the R&D survey data are available on the number of R&D and other employees and the amount of 'in-house' R&D expenditures. R&D expenditures are divided into labour costs, costs of materials and investments. The variables from the production statistics include sales, number of employees, capital depreciation costs and material consumption.

With this dataset it is possible to avoid estimation biases caused by the double counting of R&D inputs.[2] In the estimations, labour and material inputs are adjusted to account for the amounts used for R&D. For capital input the adjustment could not be made since no data was available for total investments in fixed capital. However, R&D investments in fixed capital comprise only 10 per cent of total R&D expenditure. Hence, we are able to solve the double-counting problem for 90 per cent of the dataset.

The total number of firms available is 203. Table 8.1 shows the distribution of the number of firms for different size classes, based on the total number of employees in a firm. We define small and medium-sized enterprises (SMEs) as firms consisting of less than 100 employees, while large enterprises (LEs) consist of 100 or more employees. From Table 8.1 we see that there are no data available for firms with less than 10 employees. Thus, our sample of SMEs consists mainly of medium-sized enterprises.

Summary statistics for SMEs and LEs are presented in Table 8.2. The statistics indicate some notable differences between SMEs and LEs, supporting the thesis that the influence of R&D expenditures on productivity differs between these groups of firms. Not surprisingly it is immediately clear that LEs are more capital-intensive than SMEs, as evidenced by the higher average depreciation costs per employee for these firms. It is striking to note that SMEs show a higher average

**Table 8.1:** *Number of firms in dataset by size class*

|      | Number of employees | Number of firms in dataset |
|------|---------------------|----------------------------|
| SMEs | 10–<20              | 3                          |
|      | 20–<50              | 9                          |
|      | 50–<100             | 65                         |
| LEs  | 100–<200            | 61                         |
|      | 200–<500            | 45                         |
|      | 500 and more        | 20                         |

**Table 8.2:** *Summary statistics (averages)*

|                                             | SMEs | LEs   |
|---------------------------------------------|------|-------|
| Number of firms                             | 77   | 126   |
| Number of employees                         | 68   | 606   |
| Sales (× NLG 1,000,000)                      | 21   | 182   |
| In-house R&D-expenditures (× NLG 1000)       | 418  | 12761 |
| Value added per employee (× NLG 1000)        | 103  | 129   |
| Depreciation costs per employee (× NLG 1000) | 11   | 19    |
| R&D intensity (% of sales)                  | 2.36 | 2.02  |

*Source: Statistics Netherlands.*

R&D intensity, as defined by the 'in-house' R&D expenditures as percentage of sales. Furthermore, we see that labour productivity for SMEs is 20 per cent smaller than for LEs.

In our estimations, we use sector dummies to account for differences between sectors that might influence the estimates of the effects of R&D expenditures on productivity. We define four sectors based on the two-digit Standard Industrial Classification (SIC) of Statistics Netherlands. The four sectors are: Food, Beverages and Tobacco (SIC 15 and 16), Chemical Industry and Allied (SIC 23–25), Metal Industry (SIC 27–35) and Other Manufacturing (i.e. textiles, wearing apparel, wood products, paper and paper products, printing and publishing, furniture and manufacture of building materials), (SICs 17–22, 26, 36 and 37).

## RESULTS

We have estimated the productivity effects of R&D expenditures by employing an extended Cobb-Douglas production function, with R&D as an additional explanatory variable besides labour, capital and materials. This production function is given by:

$$Q_i^s = A\ C_i^{\alpha} L_i^{\beta} K_i^{\gamma} M_i^{\delta},\qquad(1)$$

where:

$Q^s, C, L, K, M$: Volume of production, capital, labour, R&D expenditures and volume of material consumption, respectively

$\alpha, \beta, \gamma, \delta$:   Output elasticity of capital, labour, R&D expenditures and material consumption, respectively
A:        Constant term of production function
i:        Index denoting firm.

Equation (1) is estimated in its loglinear form using capital depreciation costs as proxy for capital and including sector dummies to account for sector-specific characteristics. It is estimated for the complete sample and for SMEs and LEs separately. The results are presented in Table 8.3.

From Table 8.3 we see a significant positive productivity effect of R&D expenditures ($\gamma$) for the entire sample of 0.045. This result is comparable to the magnitude of the productivity effects of R&D found by Van Leeuwen and Nieuwenhuijsen (1999) for mainly large Dutch manufacturing firms.

Examining the productivity effects of R&D expenditures for SMEs and LEs separately it appears from Table 8.3 that this effect is larger for the larger firms. The estimated output elasticities of R&D expenditures for SMEs and LEs are 0.035 and 0.048 respectively. To test whether the difference in productivity effects for SMEs and LEs is significant we apply two Chow tests for parameter stability.[3] We first test the hypothesis that the extended Cobb-Douglas production function is the same for SMEs and LEs. Assuming the same production function for all firms amounts to restricting all parameters of the production function to be equal. This hypothesis cannot be rejected at the 5 per cent-significance level as the value of the Chow test statistic is 1.03, whereas the 5 per cent critical value for the $F_{8,187}$ distribution is 1.99. We then test the hypothesis of an equal output elasticity of R&D expenditures for SMEs and LEs, while assuming all other parameters of the production function to be equal. This hypothesis cannot be rejected either at the 5 per cent-significance level, as the value of the Chow test statistic 1.09 is less than 3.89, the 5 per cent critical value for the $F_{1,194}$ distribution. Hence, the Chow test does not reject the hypothesis of equal output elasticities of R&D expenditures for SMEs and LEs.

The insignificance of the differences in estimates between SMEs and LEs may result from the high concentration of medium-sized firms in the sample (see Table 8.1). There are especially few small firms in the dataset.[4]

Furthermore, using an extended Cobb-Douglas production function to assess the productivity effects of R&D expenditures leaves out possible complicating factors, which might lead to biased estimates of these effects.

First, the demand effects of R&D are ignored. It is likely that the introduction of new products will have a positive effect on the demand for products of a given

**Table 8.3:** *Estimates of Cobb-Douglas production functions for 1994\*,\*\**

| Variable | Complete sample | SMEs | LEs |
|---|---|---|---|
| Output elasticity: | | | |
| Material consumption ($\delta$) | 0.645(42.042) | 0.641(22.961) | 0.650(34.622) |
| Labour ($\beta$) | 0.233(10.715) | 0.243(4.662) | 0.248(8.874) |
| Capital ($\alpha$) | 0.102(8.198) | 0.093(3.549) | 0.100(7.184) |
| R&D expenditures ($\gamma$) | 0.045(5.110) | 0.035(1.951) | 0.048(4.841) |
| Number of observations | 203 | 77 | 126 |
| $R^2$ | 0.99 | 0.97 | 0.99 |

\*  *Estimated in loglinear form, including sector dummies.*
\*\* *t-values in parentheses.*

firm. Not including the demand effects might result in biased estimates for the productivity effects.

Second, the production function does not account for possible simultaneity. By using a production function we assume that the production factors of labour, capital, materials and R&D are exogenous variables which determine the volume of production. The reverse may also be true in that the volume of production may influence the levels of the production factors. This simultaneity can influence the estimates of the output elasticities. The problem of simultaneity mainly arises when using time-series data.

Third, although we account for sector-specific characteristics by including sector dummies, there may also be an influence of firm-specific characteristics. When panel data are available, estimating equation (1), using either growth figures or deviations from firm-specific averages of the variables can eliminate these firm-specific influences. However, both methods are sensitive to measurement errors in the data.

The first two of these problems (demand effects and simultaneity) can be dealt with by estimating a more extensive system of equations, proposed by Van Leeuwen and Nieuwenhuijsen (1999). Besides a production function, analogous to equation (1), a demand equation is introduced which includes R&D as an additional explanatory variable

$$Q_i^d = D\, P_i^{\eta} K_i^{\phi}. \tag{2}$$

Where:

$Q^d$, $K$:  Volume of demand and R&D expenditures
$D$:    Constant determining position of demand curve
$P$:    Relative price of final product (compared to competitors)
$\eta$:    Demand elasticity of price of final products
$\phi$:    Effects of R&D capital on position of demand curve
$i$:    Index denoting firm.

The system of equations (1) and (2) can be represented in its loglinear form, with lower case letters representing the natural logarithms of variables:

$$q_i^s = a\ + \alpha c_i + \beta l_i + \gamma k_i + \delta m_i \tag{3}$$
$$q_i^d = d\ + \eta p_i + \phi k_i. \tag{4}$$

Equations (3) and (4) cannot be estimated in a straightforward fashion since it remains unclear which variables are exogenous and endogenous. However, assuming profit maximisation, short-term constant physical capital and production were being equal to demand, three equations can be derived that can be estimated directly. Appendix I provides a detailed explanation of the derivation. In the derived model, turnover, employment, and material consumption depend on R&D capital, tangible capital, material prices, and wages (indices are left out):

$$q = \pi_q + \frac{\alpha}{1-\varepsilon(\beta+\delta)}c + \frac{\gamma - \dfrac{\phi}{\eta}(\beta+\delta)}{1-\varepsilon(\beta+\delta)}k - \frac{\beta}{1-\varepsilon(\beta+\delta)}w_l - \frac{\delta}{1-\varepsilon(\beta+\delta)}w_m. \tag{5}$$

$$\pi_l + \frac{\varepsilon\alpha}{1-\varepsilon(\beta+\delta)}c + \left(\frac{\varepsilon\gamma-\varepsilon\dfrac{\phi}{\eta}(\beta+\delta)}{1-\varepsilon(\beta+\delta)}-\frac{\phi}{\eta}\right)k$$

$$-(1+\frac{\varepsilon\beta}{1-\varepsilon(\beta+\delta)})w_l - \frac{\varepsilon\delta}{1-\varepsilon(\beta+\delta)}w_m \tag{6}$$

$$m = \pi_m + \frac{\varepsilon\alpha}{1-\varepsilon(\beta+\delta)}c + \left(\frac{\varepsilon\gamma-\varepsilon\dfrac{\phi}{\eta}(\beta+\delta)}{1-\varepsilon(\beta+\delta)}-\frac{\phi}{\eta}\right)k$$

$$-\frac{\varepsilon\beta}{1-\varepsilon(\beta+\delta)}w_l - (1+\frac{\varepsilon\delta}{1-\varepsilon(\beta+\delta)})w_m \tag{7}$$

$w_l$ and $w_m$ respectively denote wages and price of materials (intermediate goods). $\pi_q$, $\pi_l$ and $\pi_m$ are constants in equations (5) through (7). $\varepsilon$ equals $1+1/\eta$.

In short, the equations can be written as:

$$q_{it} = \pi_q + \pi_{ql}w_l + \pi_{qm}w_m + \pi_{qc}c_{it} + \pi_{qk}k_{it} \tag{5a}$$
$$l_{it} = \pi_l + \pi_{ll}w_l + \pi_{lm}w_m + \pi_{lc}c_{it} + \pi_{lk}k_{it} \tag{6a}$$
$$m_{it} = \pi_m + \pi_{ml}w_l + \pi_{mm}w_m + \pi_{mc}c_{it} + \pi_{mk}k_{it}. \tag{7a}$$

All coefficients in equations (5a)–(7a) can be expressed in terms of the structural parameters in equations (3) and (4). By estimating the system of equations (5)–(7) we take into account both the demand effects of R&D expenditures and the issue of simultaneity. To deal with firm-specific characteristics as well, we can include wages at the firm level. This will probably cause biases in the estimates of the output elasticity of labour ($\beta$), as it will incorporate the influences of the firm-specific characteristics. This is of no great concern, however, since we are not particularly interested in the estimates of $\beta$.

Table 8.4 shows the estimates of the structural parameters of equations (1) and (2) for both SMEs and LEs. These estimates are obtained by estimating the system of equations (5)–(7), including wages at the firm level and sector dummies, using a *seemingly unrelated regression* (SUR) procedure.

From the results for SMEs in Table 8.4 we conclude that the extensive system of equations cannot be estimated meaningfully for these firms. The only parameter significant at the 5 per cent-significance level is $\eta$, the price elasticity of demand. Together with the value of $\eta$ (−9.174) this indicates that SMEs may be operating under conditions close to perfect competition.[5] Since we find no significant demand effects of R&D expenditures for SMEs, it seems at least partially justified to assess the productivity effects of R&D expenditures for SMEs by estimating an extended Cobb-Douglas production function.

For LEs the estimation of equations (5)–(7) yields significant estimates for most structural parameters. The unfeasible (and insignificant) estimate of $\beta$ (−0.016) is probably due to the inclusion of wages at the firm level, as a result of which it incorporates the influences of firm-specific characteristics. LEs do exhibit a

**Table 8.4:** *SUR estimates of structural parameters for 1994\*, \*\**

| Variable | SMEs | Les |
|---|---|---|
| Output elasticity: | | |
| Material consumption ($\delta$) | 0.896 | 0.876 |
| | (1.584) | (12.999) |
| Labour ($\beta$) | −1.807 | −0.016 |
| | (−0.457) | (−0.245) |
| Capital ($\alpha$) | 0.620 | 0.109 |
| | (0.475) | (4.639) |
| R&D expenditures ($\gamma$) | 0.112 | 0.045 |
| | (0.488) | (3.176) |
| Price elasticity of demand ($\eta$) | −9.174 | −6.665 |
| | (−2.257) | (−5.988) |
| R&D elasticity of demand ($\phi$) | −0.030 | 0.160 |
| | (−0.174) | (2.101) |

\*   *Estimated with wages at the firm level and including sector dummies.*
\*\* *t-values in parentheses.*

significant influence of R&D expenditures on demand (0.160), even though the price elasticity of demand is also substantial (−6.665). However, of most interest to us is the estimate of the output elasticity of R&D expenditures ($\gamma$). The estimate of $\gamma$ obtained from estimating the extensive system of equations for LEs (0.045) is very close to the estimate found by estimating the extended Cobb-Douglas production function (0.048). Furthermore the results for LEs are comparable with the results found by Van Leeuwen and Nieuwenhuijsen (1999). They used a panel of large Dutch manufacturing firms comprising information for the years 1985, 1989 and 1993. Their 'within' estimates are presented together with our results for LEs in Table 8.5. The table shows that the estimates of the impact of R&D on

**Table 8.5:** *Estimates of structural parameters LEs; cross section 1994 and within estimates 1985–1993\**

| Variable | Cross section\*\* 1994 | Within estimates\*\*\* 1985–1993 |
|---|---|---|
| Output elasticity: | | |
| Material consumption ($\delta$) | 0.876 | 0.775 |
| | (13.0) | (13.5) |
| Labour ($\beta$) | −0.016 | 0.081 |
| | (−0.25) | (0.8) |
| Capital ($\alpha$) | 0.109 | 0.066 |
| | (4.6) | (6.9) |
| R&D expenditures ($\gamma$) | 0.045 | 0.047 |
| | (3.2) | (2.1) |
| Price elasticity of demand ($\eta$) | −6.665 | −1.717 |
| | (−6.0) | (−8.1) |
| R&D elasticity of demand ($\phi$) | 0.160 | 0.192 |
| | (2.1) | (4.3) |

*Source: Van Leeuwen and Nieuwenhuijsen, 1999*
\*       *t-values in parentheses.*
\*\*     *Estimated with wages at the firm level and including sector dummies.*
\*\*\*   *Estimated with firm-specific effects (within transformation: deviation of mean score of variable), sectoral wages and dynamic sector dummies.*

demand and productivity are almost equal. The output elasticity of labour is different. The firm-specific effects cause this, which biases the output elasticity in the cross-sectional estimates. Because in Van Leeuwen and Nieuwenhuijsen a panel is available, they can make a correction for firm-specific effects by using 'within' estimates.

In sum, the estimations of the extended Cobb-Douglas production functions provide evidence for a larger output elasticity of R&D expenditures for large firms. However, the difference in parameter estimates for SMEs and LEs is not statistically significant at the 5 per cent-significance level. The estimates may be biased due to the omission of demand effects of R&D expenditures, simultaneity, and the influence of firm-specific characteristics. When estimating a more elaborate system of equations to account for these issues, we find no significant estimates for SMEs due to the high price elasticity of demand. This indicates that the demand effects of R&D are of limited importance to SMEs. For LEs, we find significant demand effects of R&D, but the estimated output elasticity of R&D is very close to the estimate found using the extended Cobb-Douglas production function. Furthermore the results for LEs are comparable with the results found by Van Leeuwen and Nieuwenhuijsen (1999) who investigated mainly large firms. The findings indicate that the extended Cobb-Douglas production function is an adequate model for estimating the output elasticity of R&D expenditures. The estimates of the output elasticities of R&D expenditures obtained in this way do not reveal a significant difference between SMEs and LEs. However, this may be due to the high concentration of medium-sized firms in our sample.

## SUMMARY

It is generally accepted that R&D contributes to economic growth. R&D activities lead to improvements in production processes and introduction of new products. R&D activities influence the performance of the R&D performing firm, but via 'spill-overs' the performances of other firms (within or outside the sector) are also influenced.

This chapter considered direct effects of R&D at the firm level. The main objective of the study was to measure the productivity effects of R&D. In particular the differences in the output elasticities of R&D expenditures between large and small firms were investigated.

To measure the output elasticity of R&D a Cobb-Douglas production function was estimated. We used data from 203 Dutch manufacturing firms for 1994, available from Statistics Netherlands. We found positive and significant productivity effects of R&D for both large and small firms. Small firms were defined as firms with less than 100 employees, while large firms had 100 or more employees. The estimated output elasticities were 0.035 for small firms and 0.048 for large firms. Testing the significance of the difference between small and large firms reveals that the difference is not significant.

Some tests on robustness of the results were performed. A model incorporating both productivity effects and demand effects of R&D was also estimated. The model corrects for simultaneity and missing variables. A disadvantage of the model is that it can be used only if there is a demand effect of R&D. Hence, in situations close to perfect competition, the model is not suitable. In this study the model was estimated for both small and large firms. The model gave no interpretable results for small firms. It appears that, for the population of small firms, the market situation is close to perfect competition. For the large firms plausible results were found. The estimate of the output elasticity for large firms was 0.045 and the estimate of the demand effect was 0.160. These results are close to the results found by Van Leeuwen and Nieuwenhuijsen (1999), where they used data from especially large firms. In sum, we conclude that the Cobb-Douglas estimates of the output elasticity of R&D expenditures for small and large firms are robust.

## NOTES

1. Instead of the Cobb-Douglas production function one could also estimate more complicated functional forms. Two possible candidates would be the CES and Translog functions. As, for instance, Griliches and Mairesse (1984, p. 342) note this will not matter for the estimation of the productivity effect of R&D expenditures.
2. See Schankerman (1981). See also Bartelsman et al. (1996) and Hall and Mairesse (1995) for a comparison of empirical results with and without adjusting for double-counting.
3. See e.g. Stewart (1999, pp. 101–102) for a description of the test statistic.
4. Defining three different groups of firms based on size, we find similar results.
5. In theory $\eta$ equals $-\infty$ under perfect competition.

## REFERENCES

Acs, Z.J. and D.B. Audretsch (1991) R&D, firm size and innovative activity. In Acs, Z.J. and D.B. Audretsch (eds) *Innovation and Technological Change: An International Comparison.* New York: Harvester Wheatsheaf.

Bartelsman, E.G., van Leeuwen, G., Nieuwenhuijsen, H.R. and Zeetenberg, C. (1996) 'R&D productivity growth; evidence from firm-level data in The Netherlands". Netherlands Official Statistics, CBS, Vol. 11, Autumn, pp. 52–69.

Bound, J., Cummins, C., Griliches, Z., Hall, B.H. and Jaffe, A. (1984) Who does R&D and who patents? In Z. Griliches (ed.) *R&D, Patents, and Productivity.* The University of Chicago Press for the National Bureau of Economic Research.

Cohen, W.M. and Klepper, S. (1996) A reprise of size and R&D. *The Economic Journal*, Vol. 106, pp. 925–951.

Cohen, W.M., Levin, R. and Mowery, D. (1987) Firm size and R&D-intensity: a re-examination. *Journal of Industrial Economics*, Vol. 35, pp. 543–565.

Griliches, Z., and Mairesse, J. (1984) Productivity and R&D at the Firm Level. In Z. Griliches (ed.) *R&D, Patents, and Productivity.* The University of Chicago Press for the National Bureau of Economic Research.

Hall, B.H., and Mairesse, J. (1995) Exploring the relationship between R&D and productivity in French manufacturing firms. *Journal of Econometrics*, Vol. 65, pp. 263–293.

Leeuwen, G. van and Nieuwenhuijsen, H.R. (1999) Distinguishing between productivity and demand effects of R&D. Research paper no. 9905, Statistics Netherlands.

Minne, B. (1997) *International battle of giants. The role of investment in research and fixed assets.* Onderzoeksreeks Directie Marktwerking, Ministry of Economic Affairs (The Hague).

Nelson, R.R., Peck, M.J. and Kalachek, E.D. (1967) *Technology, Economic Growth and Public Policy.* Washington D.C.: Brookings Institution.

Nooteboom, B. (1994) Innovation and Diffusion in Small Firms: Theory and Evidence. *Small Business Economics*, Vol. 6, pp. 327–347.

Scherer, F.M. (1984) *Innovation and Growth: Schumpeterian Perspectives*, Cambridge, Mass.: MIT Press.

Schankerman, M. (1981) The effect of double counting and expensing on the measured returns to R&D. *Review of Economics and Statistics*, Vol. 63, pp. 454–458.

Schumpeter, J.A. (1942) *Capitalism, Socialism and Democracy.* Harper and Row (New York).

Stewart, J. (1991) *Econometrics.* Philip Allan (Hertfordshire).

Villard, H. (1958) Competition oligopoly and research. *Journal of Political Economy*, Vol. 66, pp. 483–497.

# APPENDIX I:  DERIVATION OF PRODUCTION FUNCTION AND DEMAND EQUATION

In the underlying appendix, we present the relation between the parameters in the structure model and the reduced model. The structure model consists of a production function and a demand equation. The reduced model consists of three equations. The model has been presented earlier by Van Leeuwen and Nieuwen-huijsen (1999).

We start with the following equations for the variables in volumes:

$$Q_{it}^s = A_i e^{\mu t} C_{it}^\alpha L_{it}^\beta K_{it}^\gamma M_{it}^\delta \tag{1}$$

$$Q_{it}^d = D_i P_{it}^\eta K_{it}^\phi. \tag{2}$$

Where:

$Q^s$, $Q^d$, $C$, $L$, $K$, $M$: Volume of production, demand, capital, labour, R&D capital and intermediate (material) consumption

$\alpha$, $\beta$, $\gamma$, $\delta$: Output elasticity of capital, labour, R&D capital and material consumption

$\mu$: Disembodied technological development

$A$: Constant term of production function

$D$: Constant determining position of demand curve

$P$: Relative price of final product (compared to competitors)

$\eta$: Demand elasticity of price of final products

$\phi$: Effect of R&D capital on position of demand curve

$i,t$: Indices denoting industry and year.

In logarithms we obtain:

$$q_{it}^s = a_i + \mu t + \alpha c_{it} + \beta l_{it} + \gamma k_{it} + \delta m_{it} \tag{3}$$

$$q_{it}^d = d_i + \eta p_{it} + \phi k_{it}. \tag{4}$$

Notice, that in the case of cross sections, R&D-expenditures are used in state of R&D capital. The parameters in equations (3) and (4) cannot be estimated directly since it is not clear which variables are exogenous and endogenous. Based on the hypotheses of profit maximization and short-term constant physical and R&D capital, a system of three equations can be derived that can be directly estimated. Derivation is presented below (indices i and t will henceforth be omitted).

We maximize the so-called Lagrangian function and assume that $q^s = q^d = q$:

$$LG(\alpha, \beta, \gamma, \delta, \mu, \eta, \phi, \lambda) = PQ - W_c C - W_l L - W_m M - W_k K - \lambda(Q - F(X)),$$

where:

$W_f$  equal to the price of production factor ($f = C, L, M$ en $K$)

$F(X)$ production function such as (1), thus $X = (C, L, M, K)$. $\tag{5}$

Furthermore, lower case symbols refer to the logarithmic transformation of variables.

First-order conditions give:

$$\partial LG/\partial \lambda = 0 \Rightarrow Q = F(X). \tag{6}$$

$$\partial LG/\partial Q = 0 \Rightarrow (\partial P/\partial Q)Q + P - \lambda = 0 \Rightarrow P(1 + 1/\eta) = \lambda. \tag{7}$$

$$\partial LG/\partial L = 0 \Rightarrow w_l = \lambda \beta Q/L,$$
$$\text{with } (7) \Rightarrow l = ln(1 + 1/\eta) + ln(\beta) + p + q - w_l. \tag{8}$$

$$\partial LG/\partial M = 0 \Rightarrow w_m = \lambda \delta Q/M,$$
$$\text{with } (7) \Rightarrow m = ln(1 + 1/\eta) + ln(\delta) + p + q - w_m. \tag{9}$$

We rewrite the demand curve:

$$p = q/\eta - (\phi/\eta)k - d/\eta, \tag{10}$$

and define:

$$\varepsilon = (1 + 1/\eta). \tag{11}$$

Including equations (10) and (11) in equation (8) gives:

$$l = ln(\varepsilon) + ln(\beta) - d/\eta - (\phi/\eta)k + \varepsilon q - w_l \text{ for } l. \tag{12}$$

For $m$ we include equations (10) and (11) in equation (9):

$$m = ln(\varepsilon) + ln(\delta) - d/\eta - (\phi/\eta)k + \varepsilon q - w_m. \tag{13}$$

With respect to q, including equations (12) and (13) in equation (3) gives:

$$q = \pi_q + \frac{\alpha}{1 - \varepsilon(\beta + \delta)}c + \frac{\gamma - \dfrac{\phi}{\eta}(\beta + \delta)}{1 - \varepsilon(\beta + \delta)}k - \frac{\beta}{1 - \varepsilon(\beta + \delta)}w_l - \frac{\delta}{1 - \varepsilon(\beta + \delta)}w_m. \tag{14}$$

Including equation (14) in equations (12) and (13) gives:

$$l = \pi_l + \frac{\varepsilon \alpha}{1 - \varepsilon(\beta + \delta)}c + \left( \frac{\varepsilon \gamma - \varepsilon \dfrac{\phi}{\eta}(\beta + \delta)}{1 - \varepsilon(\beta + \delta)} - \frac{\phi}{\eta} \right)k$$

$$- (1 + \frac{\varepsilon \beta}{1 - \varepsilon(\beta + \delta)})w_l - \frac{\varepsilon \delta}{1 - \varepsilon(\beta + \delta)}w_m \tag{15}$$

and

$$m = \pi_m + \frac{\varepsilon\alpha}{1 - \varepsilon(\beta + \delta)} c + \left( \frac{\varepsilon\gamma - \varepsilon\frac{\phi}{\eta}(\beta + \delta)}{1 - \varepsilon(\beta + \delta)} - \frac{\phi}{\eta} \right) k$$

$$- \frac{\varepsilon\beta}{1 - \varepsilon(\beta + \delta)} w_l - \left( 1 + \frac{\varepsilon\delta}{1 - \varepsilon(\beta + \delta)} \right) w_m \tag{16}$$

The constants $\pi_q$, $\pi_l$ and $\pi_m$ in equations (14) through (16) are important; they depend on sector and year. In the case of panel estimates, the constant can even be included in a firm-specific way.

In the case of perfect competition and zero impact of R&D on enterprise sales-opportunities, the equations are less complicated ($\eta = -\infty$, $\varepsilon = 1$ and $\phi = 0$). Our data set allows for a complete estimation of the correct system as presented in section 4:

$$q_{it} = \pi_q + \pi_{ql} w_l + \pi_{qm} w_m + \pi_{qc} c_{it} + \pi_{qk} k_{it} \tag{17}$$

$$l_{it} = \pi_l + \pi_{ll} w_l + \pi_{lm} w_m + \pi_{lc} c_{it} + \pi_{lk} k_{it} \tag{18}$$

$$m_{it} = \pi_m + \pi_{ml} w_l + \pi_{mm} w_m + \pi_{mc} c_{it} + \pi_{mk} k_{it}. \tag{19}$$

The coefficients $\pi_{ql}$, $\pi_{qm}$, $\pi_{qc}$, $\pi_{qk}$, $\pi_{ll}$, $\pi_{lm}$, $\pi_{lc}$, $\pi_{lk}$, $\pi_{mb}$, $\pi_{mm}$, $\pi_{mc}$ and $\pi_{mk}$ are functions of the structure parameters. Equations (17) through (19) are rewritings of equations (14) through (16).

Equations (15) and (16) prove that, among others, the following relations hold for the coefficients in equations (17) through (19):

$$\pi_{lc} = \pi_{mc} \tag{20}$$

$$\pi_{lk} = \pi_{mk}. \tag{21}$$

Equation (21) implies that a rise in R&D capital has identical effects on labour and material intermediate consumption. On the basis of equation (20) this also holds for physical capital.

CHAPTER 9

# Managing Training in SMEs for Holistic High Performance

ZULF KHAN AND MARK COOPER

## IMPORTANCE OF SMALL TO MEDIUM ENTERPRISES (SMEs)

In recent years the number of small and medium sized enterprises (SMEs) in Britain has been growing rapidly. Ninety-nine per cent of firms now employ fewer than 250 people, and 60 per cent of the workforce work in SMEs. These firms represent a major growth area of the British economy, and are the seedbed of much innovation. At the same time, competition is driving many British firms towards higher quality markets and into service and knowledge based industries, which require higher levels of skill and knowledge from their workers.

It has been argued that Britain's economic survival depends upon this shift, which calls for a general upgrading of the skills and knowledge of the whole work-force (DfEE, 1999). Rothwell and Zegveld (1982) report that SMEs have unique advantages over large firms including their technological capabilities and their ability to serve niche markets: through close contact with customers they keep abreast of fast changing market demands, and are able to react quickly and efficiently to both market and technological changes.

## NEGLECT OF TRAINING

Until recently British Employers felt no need to explain or justify their long-standing neglect of employee training. For decades training has been considered as a minor activity; having little or nothing to do with the organisation's perform-ance; and representing a heavy drain on operational capital (Hallier and Butts, 1999). The training of small business and its performance is currently high on the policy agenda for the UK government. The Department for Education and Employment (DfEE) has commissioned much research activity including a paper titled 'Training provision and development of SMEs' (Storey and Westhead, 1997), which places great emphasis on the reasons why SMEs provide less job related training compared to large firms, and suggests several explanations:

1. *The 'ignorance' explanation* – This implies that small firms are less likely to provide job-related formal training for their employees because business owners/managers are unaware of the full benefits of training. In some cases small firm owners have feelings of antipathy towards educational institutions that provide training. Surveys (Storey and Westhead, 1997) have shown that individuals who do not hold any formal educational qualification establish

approximately one third of new firms. Such small firm owners are often opposed to what they view as formalised learning, which they associate with school.

2. The '*market forces explanation*' states that:

- Owners of small firms are overwhelmingly concerned with short-term survival issues, whereas most training benefits are long-term.
- There is a high probability that trainees in small firms will be poached by other (large) employers.
- Absence of internal labour markets in small firms.
- Promotion for managers (certainly to the top position within the business) is less likely in small firms where this post is likely to be occupied by the owner.

Another reason why SMEs may be reluctant to provide training is the difficulty in assessing the benefits of training. As Hendry (1991) points out:

*'In practice, in most companies, the absence of effective systems to support evaluation and the rarity of cost-benefit analysis make the demonstration of such benefits (training) diffi-cult. It is generally easier to identify the costs of not training than to say what particular benefits on-going training produces.'*

In many cases the benefits of training do not result in immediate pay-back, and the larger time horizon is seen as a negative factor by many SMEs.

A recent survey by Joyce et al. (1995) showed that four-fifths of establishments with less than five employees did not have any employees with individual training plans. However, establishments with more than 25 employees reported that some employees had individual training plans. Similarly a survey of 48 small firms in the Hampshire region of England found that only five firms (10 per cent) had a struc-tured induction and on-going training programme in operation and eight firms (17 per cent) had no training at all. Furthermore, none of the firms employed outside consultants to advise on training and training needs (Hankinson, 1994). Shields (1998) found that small employers funded significantly less training than their larger counterparts throughout the decade (1984–1994). Hendry et al. (1991) report that there is a general reluctance to spend money on training. A number of SMEs, even those with turnovers approaching £2 million, believe that little money is available to put into formal training and development. Sargeant (1996) states that the preoccupation of entrepreneurs with the day-to-day concerns of running their business is another reason why SMEs are reluctant to provide training. SME managers are more preoccupied with keeping the business afloat. This clearly demonstrates that emphasis on training initiatives is required in order to improve the business performance of SMEs.

Companies need to be proactive rather than reactive in terms of training to reap the full benefits, and anticipate technical and cultural changes. Training should be in line with the company's overall strategy and not used as a 'stand alone' measure to bring about the success of a company. The majority of SMEs do not identify training needs from the business plan before providing training, and few evaluate training effectiveness. This suggests that training provided on an ad 'hoc basis' is a continuing feature of this sector (Kerr and McDougall, 1999). As Tate (1997) points out 'Training is an important lever to bring about change if anchored sensibly to a sound business agenda, but it is just one lever among many and a weak one if pulled on its own'. The training is most effective when organisa-tions learn to be cautious in how they use individuals' capability, marrying talent with healthy cultures, systems and processes, and serving well-conceived business goals (Tate, 1997). It is noted that the most successful SMEs provide much more training than on average (DTI Publications, 1996).


## ORIGINAL EQUIPMENT MANUFACTURERS (OEMs)

SMEs are at the centre of interest in the quality debate for several reasons. One is that larger organisations will not be able to improve the quality of their products, services and processes, unless their suppliers or the second tier suppliers also grow to a high level of quality maturity (Wiele and Brown, 1998).

SMEs are increasingly facing pressures to continually improve their quality, service, and delivery (QSD) from domestic markets, global competition, and original equipment manufacturers (OEMs), putting pressure on their supply chain – which in the majority of cases are other SMEs. While it is evident that OEMs view the supply chain as a direct extension of their organisation, for companies to grow successfully within an extended enterprise their employees must be developed in order that they can deliver superior performance when benchmarked against competing value chains. Large businesses such as IBM, Rank Xerox, and British Airways are in the 'premier league' when it comes to such activities. However, their achievements and progress to date could be hampered if they do not extend the improvement boundary beyond their organisations. This is especially so for those organisations who obtain their raw materials, components, sub-assemblies, semi-finished products, and services, from suppliers, many of which are small businesses (SMEs; Yusof and Aspinwall, 2000).

Dankbaar (1996) reports how Japanese car manufacturers developed organisational innovations and management techniques, which enabled them to lead the global industry in productivity, quality, and flexibility. Today, it is widely recognised that these organisational innovations were responsible for the great competitive successes of Japanese industry during the past decades. The report also highlights how European car suppliers and their supply chains began to implement Japanese methods such as JIT, Kaizen, TPM, TQM, etc. Accordingly, to realise these structural changes, it was necessary to invest in training in new skills, training in new attitudes, in new forms of co-operation, and in a new entrepreneurial culture. Continuous training was a precondition and a consequence for continuous improvement.

In the leaner, results-orientated organisations of today, training must be a deliberate organisational strategy and not a reaction to problems or political decisions based on managerial whim (Anderson, 1994). Training plays a vital role in making change happen. Skills that once lasted for generations are now redundant. New skills have to be identified and trained (Wills, 1994). Hence employees need to be multi-skilled in order to achieve maximum flexibility and help develop the interest of the individual.

To take full advantage of the quality management systems and technologies available today it is important that companies understand that it is not enough just to educate the workforce (i.e. NVQs etc.) but it is also important to train their workforce through involvement. The tremendous power associated with learning through involvement has been recognised and accepted for most of the past century. Even still, when it comes to employee training, especially when financial resources are limited, many companies favour a more cost-sensitive, but far less cost effective, approach. They turn to education instead of training (Hughey and Mussnug, 1997). Before people commit themselves to belief and action they need to know how the organisation will treat them. Most people have no desire to become the Chief Executive Officer and are quite happy with their position in the firm. However, they may have concerns about training; job rotation; job stability; challenging, interesting and varied work; the broadening of their responsibilities; and a clear view of what is expected of them and their relationship with other people (Gilbert, 1998). The most important word in employee development is training (Gilbert, 1998). Training can instil interest and commitment from employees towards the company, hence making cultural change easier to bring about.

## CONTINUOUS IMPROVEMENT AND TQM TRAINING

It is critical that companies consider both technical (hard skills) and soft-skills training. Management often recognise that training in technical skills delivers real benefits, but will blanch at the thought that training in non-technical areas can also be of great value (Bedingham, 1997).

Soft-skills training such as listening, leadership and teamwork can provide companies with world class status because these skills are at the core of continuous improvement, and hence total quality management (TQM). Total quality management is an example of a business strategy that cannot succeed without a huge investment in training (Wills, 1994). Probably the biggest benefit for training, arising from introducing TQM, is that it will provide a focus for all activities. *Ad hoc* unsystematic training is replaced by integrated, ongoing training (Brown, 1994). Patel and Randell (1994) believe TQM to be an approach and a vehicle to get people talking together and to get training done, and to be a catalyst for commitment.

Reeve (1994) notes that early failures with TQM arose because simply providing everyone in the organisation with a small amount of awareness training will not change attitudes and behaviour overnight. This can be taken akin to many other training initiatives where only 'introductory' training is carried out, without any further follow ups.

For an organisation to achieve flexibility, responsiveness and the ability to adapt quickly to changes within its environment, the implementation of a sound strategy for continuous improvement is essential (Kaye and Anderson, 1999). Training for continuous improvement is specific where it provides insight into the workings of specific processes. It is generic where it provides workers with tools for the analysis of problems, instils different attitudes towards the organisation, and helps people to deal with, and even support, continuous change (Dankbaar, 1996). While change should be a continuous process, it should not be a reaction to a crisis. All parts of the organisation must be prepared to accept that change is continuous. If change is continuous, improvement should also be continuous. This is achieved by doing everything better while eliminating waste. The Japanese call this Kaizen (Huda, 1992). For a successful continuous improvement programme training is a prerequisite. Training will equip people with the tools and skills to take part in the improvement process (Patel and Randell, 1994). Quality training programmes are a must for organisations if they are to reach their goal for continuous improvement (Motwani et al., 1994). The beginning and the end of continuous improvement is training. The beginning of the end is lack of training (Huda, 1992).

The findings related to SME training needs show that greater importance needs to be applied by SME managers. Wilkes and Dale (1998) highlight that the overall trend arising from their research was that SMEs require (1) training and introduction to the benefits of continuous improvement and, (2) a guide, specifically prepared, which maps out a step-by-step progression towards TQM including assessment methods and models.

It is evident that SMEs need to undertake more training to assist their companies through often-troubled waters and ever increasing competition and change. But in the same instance it is important to direct training towards a company's mission and also for training to be in line with the company's strategy. Also because of the changes in new and updated technologies, it is imperative for companies to provide training in a proactive and structured manner rather than in a reactive *ad hoc* manner. It is also apparent that SMEs are under pressure from OEMs to increase their QSD while at the same time retaining favourable prices. Thus a culture of continuous improvement can help an organisation to not only attain reasonable QSD but to continually improve the whole enterprise. As stated in the literature, quality and change cannot be successfully implemented without training. Training is a worthwhile tool and may help to facilitate change and make SMEs more competitive.

The literature search has highlighted that further research needs to be carried out (empirical and qualitative) to further the knowledge in this area of important work.

## REFERENCES

Anderson, G. (1994) 'A proactive model for training needs analysis'. *Journal of European Industrial Training*, Vol. 18, 3.

Bedingham, K. (1997) 'Proving the Effectiveness of Training'. *Industrial and Commercial Training Journal*, Vol. 29, 3.

Bowen, W.P. (1997) 'Family Internet'. *Training for Quality*, Vol. 5, 2.

Brown, A. (1994) 'TQM Implications for Training'. *Training for Quality*, Vol. 2, 3.

Dankbaar, B. (1996) 'Training issues for the European Motor Industry'. *Journal of European Industrial Training*, Vol. 20, 8.

DfEE (1999) 'Graduate Skills and Small Business'. DfEE briefing paper.

DTI Publications (1996) 'Competitiveness: Creating the Enterprise Centre of Europe 1996a'. HMSO, London.

Gilbert, J. (1998) 'A job for life' into 'A life of jobs'. *Empowerment in Organisations*, Vol. 6, 6.

Hallier, J. and Butts, S. (1999) 'Employers discovery of training: Self-development, Employability and Rhetoric of partnership'. *Employee Relations Journal*, Vol. 21, 1.

Hankinson, A. (1994) 'Small Firms Training: The reluctance prevails'. *Industrial and Commercial Training*, Vol. 26, 9.

Hendry, C. (1991) Corporate Strategy and Training. *Training and Competitiveness*, p. 106, Kogan Page Ltd. London.

Hendry, C., Jones, A., Arthur, M. and Pettigrew, C. (1991) 'Human Resource Development in Small to Medium Enterprises'. *Department of Employment research paper*, no. 88, p. 66.

Huda, F. (1992) *Kaizen: The Understanding and Application of Continuous Improvement*, p. 34, Technical Communications Publishing. Herts.

Hughey, W.A. and Mussnug, J.K. (1997) 'Designing Effective Employee Training Programmes'. *Training for Quality*, Vol. 5, 2.

Joyce, P., McNulty and Woods, A. (1995) 'Workforce Training: are small firms different?' *Journal of European Industrial Training*, Vol. 19, 5.

Kaye, M. and Anderson, R. (1999) 'Continuous Improvement: The ten essential criteria'. *International Journal of Quality and Reliability Management*, Vol. 16, 5.

Kerr, A. and McDougall, M. (1999) 'The Small Business of Developing People'. *International Small Business Journal*, Vol. 17, 2.

Motwani, G.J., Frahm, M.L. and Kathawala, Y. (1994) 'Quality Training: The Key to Quality Improvement'. *Training for Quality*, Vol. 2, 2.

Patel, A. and Randell, G. (1994) 'Total Quality Management – The Solution to more Training in Britain?' *Training For Quality*, Vol. 2, 1.

Reeve, C.R. (1994) 'Investing in Training'. *World Class Design Manufacture*, Vol. 1, 1.

Rothwell, R. and Zegveld, W. (1982) *Innovation and the small and medium sized firm*, 45. Frances Pinter (Publishing Ltd), London.

Sargeant, A. (1996) 'Training for growth: how can education providers assist in the development of small businesses'. *Industrial and Commercial Training*, Vol. 28, 2.

Shields, M. (1998) 'Changes in the determinants of employer-funded training for full-time employees in Britain, 1984–94'. *Oxford Bulletin of Economics & Statistics*, Vol. 60, 2.

Storey, J.D. and Westhead, P. (1997) 'Training Provision and the Development of SMEs'. *DfEE report* 26.

Tate, W. (1997) 'Training the Stuff of Legends'. *Industrial and Commercial Training*, Vol. 29, 2.

Wiele, T. and Brown, A. (1998) 'Venturing down the TQM path for SMEs'. *International Small Business Journal*, Vol. 16, 2.

Wilkes, N. and Dale, B.G. (1998) 'Attitudes to self assessment and quality awards: A case study in small and medium sized companies'. *Total Quality Management*, Vol. 9, 8.

Wills, M. (1994) 'Managing the Training Process: Putting the Basics into Practice'. *Journal of European Industrial Training*, Vol. 18, 6.

Yusof, M.S. and Aspinwall, E. (2000) 'A conceptual framework for TQM implementation for SMEs'. *The TQM Magazine*, Vol. 12, 1.

CHAPTER 10

# Barriers in Co-operation between Small and Large Technology-Based Firms: A Swedish Case Study

MAGNUS KLOFSTEN AND CARINA SCHÄRBERG

## INTRODUCTION

Collaboration between firms of all sizes is becoming increasingly important in an era that is complex, global, and technologically uncertain. During the economic restructuring of the 1970s and 1980s it became clear that few big firms can go it alone (Harrison, 1994). Thus many large firms are seeking partnerships with smaller firms, with complementary assets, as a way to expand. Both small and large firms may have a number of reasons for forming an alliance. Faulkner (1995) speaks in terms of external stimulus, i.e. regionalisation or globalisation, fast technological change, shortening of product life cycles and high economic uncertainty. In addition new transportation and communication systems have provided firms with the enhanced means for collaboration (Castells, 1996).

A strong motivation for collaboration can be found in resource dependency theory, which maintains that firms depend on other firms within that environment to acquire the needed resources. Thus, through collaboration a firm can gain access to the 'complementary' resources needed for survival (Yuchtman and Seashore, 1967; Aldrich and Zimmer, 1986; Teece, 1986a, 1986b). These complementary assets include expertise in the areas of R&D, production, marketing, and distribution, among other assets and resources required for developing a new product. Faulkner (1995), in his investigation of ten case studies, found that complementary assets were identified by nine alliances to be the most important criteria in partner selection. The need for complementary resources has been underscored by a number of other studies that have identified access to resources, skills, competences and marketing as reasons for collaboration. Occasionally firms may need added resources to protect a product they have designed but have failed to fully develop. Added resources mean a larger size that produces scale economies and credibility (Faulkner, 1995; Mønsted, 1998; Parkhe, 1991). Faulkner's (1995) case studies also highlighted that the reputation of a partner, together with access to new and strong brand names, are important aspects of motivation for entering into alliances. Added resources can help firms successfully transfer organisationally embedded knowledge from one area to another, referred to as the 'transfer of organisational learning' (Kogut, 1988). Slowinski et al., (1996) found, in their longitudinal study of 50 alliances between small and large technology-based firms, that large firms often lack technology when they have identified a market opportunity, and that this is the reason for collaborating with world-class small firms. Likewise, Rothwell (1991) have stated that the respective drawbacks of large and small firm's innovation can be overcome by joining forces.

Researchers have adopted the use of various terms described in the literature, which refer to a range of inter-firm agreements, such as 'global strategic partnerships' (Perlmutter and Heenan, 1986), 'joint ventures' (Hamel et al, 1989; Harrigan, 1985) and 'strategic alliances' (Lorange and Roos, 1992; Mønsted, 1998). Moreover, participation in strategic alliances has been identified as an important strategy option for small technology-based firms (Porter and Fuller, 1986; Forrest, 1990). An increasing research interest in the area can be noted by recent works (Esposito et al., 1993; Mayer et al., 1997; and Weaver 1998).

## NEGOTIATING DIFFERENCES

There are many differences between large and small firms' motives for sharing resources. Rothwell (1991) identified a number of respective advantages of small and large firms for co-operation. Whereas small firms were mainly concerned with behavioural issues, such as management, dynamism, organisation and flexibility, large firms were more interested in the benefits of material resources. Firms may also have different strategic positions. One way of looking at strategic alliances is by focusing on the strategic positions of each partner in terms of two dimensions. One dimension concerns the strategic importance of the particular business (core business or peripheral) and how it fits within the overall portfolio of that partner, and the second dimension considers the firm's relative position in the business; whether it is a leader or follower (Lorange and Roos, 1992). Lorange and Roos (1992) argue that regardless of the underlying motives the main concern for each party is related to how much to put in, and how much to retrieve from the strategic alliance.

Differences between partners can also be classified by defining different kinds of collaborative mechanisms. In strategic alliances, one can determine the degree of vertical integration or market transactions used to negotiate differences or resource sharing (Lorange and Roos, 1992). Lorange and Roos (1992) define four types of strategic alliances: (1) an 'ad hoc pool' type of alliance in which a minimum of resources are often used on a temporary basis by complementing each other, where the output is returned to the firms in their totality; (2) the 'consortium' type of alliance which takes place when the parties are willing to put in more resources, but still the value created is returned to the partners, i.e. R&D consortium; (3) the 'project-based venture', which involves a minimum of strategic resources through a common organisation and where resources are not distributed except as dividends, and (4) the 'full-blown joint venture', where all necessary resources are available and remain in the alliance itself, and a new free-standing organisation is created for long-term purposes.

## POTENTIAL BARRIERS TO COLLABORATION

There are several potential barriers to collaboration that can lead the collaborative process to break down. First, firms may have different and conflicting interests in collaboration that may create barriers to collaboration because each party may not get what they want out of the co-operative process. Large firms may find that smaller firms lack many of the skills promised. Small firms may find large firms distracted by commitments to dominant markets (Feldman, 1998a). Moreover, an abundance of resources and a legacy of industry leadership, whether real or perceived, makes it particularly difficult for a large firm to admit to itself that it has something to learn from a smaller partner (Hamel, 1991). Faulkner (1995) states that an alliance between a very small and large partner is unlikely to be successful in the long term as the large firm might acquire the smaller one.

Secondly, while firms may come to share complementary resources, they may have different views as to what these resources are and their potential value. This can create problems in negotiating arrangements between firms. One problem is that it may be difficult for collaborating parties to assess technologies because of secrecy concerns for proprietary release of resources. Underlying this problem is that one collaborator may become suspicious of the other. The problem of trust has been outlined in many studies. Doz (1988) reported that hidden agendas were commonplace in technological partnerships. His observation of smaller firms' fear that co-operation with a larger partner was the first step towards acquisition are well founded.

Thirdly, cultural differences and communication problems between partners may create problems in collaboration between the firms. One party may have very specialised know-how that can not be readily transferred to the other for further development. In some cases companies may have technical specialists who can learn from mechanical engineers. Communication can also be blocked between partners because of intermediaries who act as buffers, such as consultants who inadvertently prevent one party from learning from the other (Feldman, 1998a, 1998b). Faulkner, (1995) argues that while there is evidence to suggest that failed strategic alliances cite incompatible cultures as a key reason for alliance failure, only four out of ten cases identified culture as an important selection criteria for partners.

## OVERCOMING THE BARRIERS TO COLLABORATION

There are many ways in which potential barriers to collaboration can be overcome. Firstly, the differing interests between collaborating parties can be overcome if the needs of the two partners are balanced, similar in strength, although different in nature. Nevertheless, resource imbalances need not create differential interests in collaboration. Killing (1983) found that alliances built on one partner are more dominant when the other removes much of the ambiguity of the relationship as clarity of authority improves. Partners do not seem to resent this as long as benefits from the alliance exceed the costs, i.e. a win-win situation.

Some research suggests that firms whose strategies complement one another can also overcome the potential barrier of differential interests (Faulkner, 1995). Faulkner argued that partner relationships are more important as a predictor of successful alliances than any other economic, organisational or structural factors. In other words, the potential barrier of differential interests can be overcome by selecting the appropriate partner. According to Hlavacek et al. (1977) three research criteria can be used when selecting an appropriate partner. The first is to select a partner with complimentary strengths and resources. Secondly, the partner should be an expanded and entrenched marketing organisation with a highly favourable image to the end-user market you want to serve. The third criteria is to select a partner of an appropriate size, but still having the aggressive nature of a small company.

As suggested earlier, different firm sizes may have differential interests in collaboration, as alliances are not always set up between firms of similar size. However, Killing (1983) suggested that major size mismatches may cause problems, but they may also lead to higher profits if the larger partner has leadership. Seven of the alliances were formed between companies of similar size and strength. Of those alliances two were judged to be the most dynamic, namely Rover/Honda and ICL/Fujitsu, in which one was the stronger partner, i.e. Honda and Fujitsu. Only the ICL/Fujitsu alliance was found to be clearly unbalanced in terms of partner size and strength.

Turning to the second potential barrier to collaboration, the different views of potential assets, concerns for secrecy and suspicion that block collaboration can also be overcome by long-term exchanges between collaborators. In addition, trust building exercises among collaborators can reduce suspicions about valued assets. The work of Mowery and Harrison suggests that strategic alliances can reduce the severity of revelation of valuable information regarding a technological asset, because 'the prospective partners will typically experiment with the collaboration before any money changes hands' (Harrison, 1994, p. 136–137). Sanctions can also be implemented for firms that violate breeches of trust; 'the sanctions must be great enough to prevent a break in the first place or social ties can provide a basis for breaches to be repaired' (Sabel, 1993 as cited in Cooke, 1998, p. 17).

A third potential barrier to collaboration suggests that cultural differences that block collaboration can be overcome through cultural complementarity. In the long term partners must understand the cultural differences between each other, have a will to compromise, have mutual trust for each other and share a strong commitment to project goals. The 'fit' between each partner, in turn, may be strongly influenced by the degree of 'significant' differences in size between the companies (Faulkner, 1995). Slowinski et al. (1996) supports Faulkner in that partner selection methods should maximize compatibility and complementarily. Tailor-made contracts negotiated specifically for the alliance should provide milestones that establish clear objectives even though they are likely to be modified or possibly abandoned. Developing conflict resolution techniques that can help mangers resolve problems while they are small and still solvable, is also important.

## AIM AND SCOPE

The above review suggests that there is a significant need to address research on collaboration between large and small technology-based firms. Previous researchers have tended to focus on alliances between equally strong multinational companies (Doz, 1988; Parkhe, 1991). Furthermore, the motives for entering alliances (Kogut, 1988), their various forms (Killing, 1988), criteria for partner selection (Faulkner, 1995), the formation process (Lorange and Roos, 1992), differences between companies, development processes (Doz, 1996), contract forms and evaluation are all exhaustively described in the management and strategic research literature. The purpose of this study is to describe and analyse different barriers to co-operation in strategic alliances between small and large technology-based firms. These barriers are divided into three types: (1) differential interests, resources and size; (2) differential assets, secrecy and trust, and (3) cultural differences and communication problems.

In the following sections of this paper our methodological approach is briefly described. The main part is dedicated to describing SoftLab's relationship with Ericsson. We begin with an overview of the company and the overall development of the relationship. Thereafter we focus on the co-operation process described by means of the barriers and their appearances at different times.

## METHOD

During the spring of 1999 ten interviews were conducted with selected persons within SoftLab and Ericsson. The respondents were founders and owners of SoftLab, as well as key employees in both firms with knowledge of the relationship between the companies. The interviews were semi-structured and lasted on average for about 1–1.5 hours. In spite of the structure of the interview guide the respondent could shape the order in which the questions were handled. Data collected included annual reports of SoftLab for 1982–1997 as well as other internal documents such as transparencies, reports and board-meeting protocols. For the latter we have had access between 1989–1997. In the protocols, we searched for statements in relation to Ericsson and other clients as well as motives and changes that have appeared in the relationship. We have had less access to documents produced at Ericsson.

   Because the last two years have been turbulent for SoftLab we chose to handle that period towards the end of the interview. In some cases informants conveyed, at the scheduling of the meeting, that they did not want to discuss or comment on what happened with SoftLab. (They put a natural end-point but this also made me aware of the need for some kind of epilogue. We would like to assert, with the vocabulary of Scott (1990), that we had 'restricted access'.)

## THE CASE OF SOFTLAB

SoftLab was founded in 1982 by two researchers at Linköping University. The original idea was to do consulting in computer technology, as earlier they had conducted assignments at Ericsson through a university–industry co-operative agreement. Their objective was to develop effective and appropriate programs, build long-term relationships with clients by focusing on client benefits as well as function as a learning organisation. The clients of SoftLab are described as world leaders in telecommunications, electronics, industrial robots, and users of advanced information systems in their production of goods and services.

### The initiating stage (1982–1986)

Parallel to the creation of the embryonic SoftLab, a relationship with Ericsson was initiated and built up slowly. This relationship was founded on trust between the two partners. SoftLab is a minor consulting company, and one among many for Ericsson to choose from. The turnover increased from almost half a million SEK and reached close to SEK3 million, during the five-year period, and the number of employees increased from two to nine.

### The re-creating stage (1987–1990)

Earlier networking within the group provided the foundation for SoftLab to re-create its relationship with Ericsson. This allowed SoftLab to build up its relationship with Ericsson. Despite the down-swings which resulted from specific projects being terminated, the relationship survived because of the SoftLab ability to carry through other projects. This created continuity between the project management teams. At the end of the period, the number of employees increased to 19 and the turnover to SEK11 million.

### The development stage (1991–1996)

During this period the reciprocal dependence was at its peak. The relationship became more formalised as SoftLab took responsibility for product support. By then one person within SoftLab was responsible for supporting the relationship, which meant that personnel changes thereafter affected the relationship. At a later stage the co-operation was affected by the tendency to choose competence development projects within SoftLab. This led to competitiveness between the different Ericsson-companies because of scarce resources within SoftLab. This created a competitive side to the relationship, which was further undermined by unclear goals within SoftLab, which implied that control was increasing within Ericsson. The number of employees increased to 66 while the turnover at the end of the period came close to SEK50 million.

### What happened then?

At the end of 1996, exit possibilities and return on investment were discussed among the owners. There were on-going discussions with Rational Software Corporation, and an American software engineering company, quoted on the NASDAQ, on an acquisition. Other alternatives discussed were to bring the company towards a quotation on the stock exchange and to let Ericsson acquire SoftLab. The latter was refused and the owners decided that further negotiations would take place with Rational. The acquisition of SoftLab by Rational was made in early 1997, but a year later it became obvious that the relationship with Rational was not functioning as planned. The two companies exhibited differences in their values. Conflict between the two companies came to a head, and by the beginning of 1998 the relationship ended. Rational decided to sell the SoftLab unit to Ericsson and a new company – Ericsson Soft-Lab – was formed. SoftLab continued to grow and the company reached a turnover of SEK92 million with about 85 employees.

## CO-OPERATION AND ITS EVOLUTION

Table 10.1 gives an outline of how the co-operation evolved and illustrates the barriers to co-operation at different periods, and how they have been manifested. The co-operation process is described by means of three stages. In terms of the three stages we would like to indicate the major changes that have occurred in the alliance over the years. However, we will not discuss whether the co-operation took place sequentially as previous researchers have done (Faulkner, 1995 and Ring and Van de Ven, 1994).

### To initiate a co-operation (1982–1986)

During the period 1982–86, SoftLab was working towards building its reputation through a number of co-operative agreements. Co-operation did not precede a formal selection process of a number of possible suppliers (which is usually the case when selecting partners), but was more a consequence of personal contacts. The importance of a rumour a partner might create is underlined by Faulkner (1995) who asserts that a partner's reputation depends to a large degree on what motivates a partner to start co-operating.

**Table 10.1:** *Barriers in the co-operation between SoftLab and Ericsson*

| Barrier | Initiating (1982–86) | Re-creating (1987–90) | Developing (1991–96) |
|---|---|---|---|
| Conflicting/ differential interests, resources and size | Common interest | Mutual dependence | Unequal dependence Competitive situation |
| Differential assessment of assets, secrecy and trust | SoftLab – awareness of differences Ericsson – unnoticed project termination | Mutually prioritised position | Good confidence Attitude differences |
| Cultural differences and communication problems | Adopt – apply | Event management of information and stochastic, linked to each other | SoftLab internally splitted goal-picture Ericsson unclear management |

Dependence is undoubtedly linked to SoftLab's turnover. Likewise, Ericsson's dependence is related to their competence and skill. Killing (1983) shows that co-operation with a dominant partner decreases the vagueness in the relationship as authority becomes clearer, a win-win situation exists, and both parties are pleased. While Ericsson took the role of initiator in a project called 'Mimer', they decided to leave the project, and thus their role in the project became difficult to define. For SoftLab this project was a matter of survival. The Ericsson project was put down hastily and resources were transferred to the 'Mimer' project. Thus SoftLab survived the hollow in the utility rate.

### Conflicting/differential interests, resources and size

SoftLab was a minor part of Ericson's purchasing of consulting services as it only had two founders and a couple of employees. Even if SoftLab worked within one department at Ericsson, they were still considerably smaller. They had common interests, which took the form of Ericsson striving for competence development and access to knowledge via the usage of SoftLab as consultants. Furthermore, SoftLab strived to increase their commercial side by learning about market pricing as well as assuming the role of competence consultants. Their business consisted of other things, such as courses and education within specific niches for different Ericsson units. The competence consulting role was deliberated in their attempt to bring the projects in-house without accounting for consulting hours as a goal in itself.

### Differential assessment of assets, secrecy and trust

The existing resource differences between SoftLab and Ericsson became evident when projects were being terminated. This was something that seems to have passed by relatively unnoticed within Ericsson, even if it was not economically feasible for SoftLab. Project terminations were a natural part of an on-going business for Ericsson, and high-risk projects tended to be given to consulting firms. SoftLab disregarded the economic situation concerning earlier clients. Furthermore, Ericsson was unaware of the consequences this brought about for SoftLab.

## Cultural differences and communication problems

Cultural differences between Ericsson and SoftLab were not a diverging factor in the co-operation. Naturally, there were some differences concerning for example Ericsson and SoftLab's views on dynamics, decision making process and flexibility, but no more than what they regarded as being common to SMEs and large companies. SoftLab was managing this by adopting parts of what they regarded as 'positive' parts of the Ericsson culture, such as the order in document handling. The parties' understanding of each others' differences, and the will to compromise affected cultural differences and communication problems. Given the strong cultural similarities between Ericsson and SoftLab, both companies expressed a will to compromise and develop the relationship.

## To re-create a co-operation (1987–1990)

During the period 1987–1990, the co-operation was characterised by a re-creative effort, which meant that contacts were resumed with earlier clients, and initiated with other companies to enhance SoftLab's stability. However, towards the end of this stage turbulence re-emerged as major projects were being terminated.

## Conflicting/differential interests, resources and size

There was no evidence or signs of diverging interest in terms of technology and technology content, which was emphasised systematically by Ericsson's management. However, SoftLab's qualities were being ignored in the long-term. Furthermore Ericsson began to lack confidence in SoftLab's capabilities. A mutual dependence existed between Ericsson and SoftLab in terms of competences and resources. The dependence took several forms, for example in some cases SoftLab agreed to delay its invoicing to Ericsson, which was not customary for an ordinary supplier. This also indicates that SoftLab's role developed from being a consulting firm, to having a personal relationship with purchasers and managers within Ericsson.

## Differential assessment of assets, secrecy and trust

The alliance got off to a good start, but after several years, both firms felt a need to adjust its terms. In essence, both sought to reduce risk and gain exposure in new industries and technologies through the use of strategic alliances. SoftLab decided, for example to reduce its dependence on other alliances, and concentrate its efforts on projects with Ericsson. On one occasion SoftLab attained remuneration from a project termination.

## Cultural differences and communication problems

Communication was to some extent informal and did not cause many problems. Communication was organised through close co-operation on projects, which managed the information flow between the two companies. Moreover, there was no formal regularity concerning meetings and information exchange at the management level, and interaction took place on a need-to-know basis. SoftLab having access to the Ericsson internal networks also made communication easier to some extent. The adoption of the Ericsson culture by SoftLab became apparent.

## Developing co-operation (1991–1996)

During the period 1991–1996 the relationship between the companies became strongly affected by a pronounced expansion by SoftLab. This growth strategy led to diversification and the opening up of new offices in both Uppsala and Stockholm. SoftLab aimed to reduce their dependence on Ericsson, by acquiring another customer base in which Ericsson would have little knowledge concerning their activities. Moreover, 40–70 per cent of the turnover was derived from assignments for the Ericsson group. The relationship was most affected by the general agreement on support and maintenance, which was signed as a formal long-term agreement between 1991/92. While SoftLab agreed to offer second-line support, and attained responsibility for product support and maintenance, strategic responsibility remained with Ericsson. The exchange of information between Ericsson and SoftLab was closely monitored at the beginning of the relationship. However, as the relationship developed, some managers became more willing to share information. Thus, in some cases, managers facilitated the development of trust through personal contacts and a shared informal understanding. As SoftLab's business began to grow, contacts were transferred from top-management to business area management. This happened at the same time as management positions within Ericsson became unclear towards the mid-90s.

SoftLab's motives for entering the support and maintenance relationship included increased stability, and securing a foundation for expanding their activities. Furthermore, there was the intent to secure a source of income, and lower the market changes. Ericsson was their major client, and represented more than 50 per cent of the total market for technical consulting services. During this period a number of discrepancies arose as to whether the relationship was of central interest to both parties. For example, SoftLab was responsible for upgrading parts of the AXE Support System, even though this system was not part of Ericsson's core business. The findings support Mønsted (1998), who argued that co-operation is of central interest to both parties in order for them to be willing to invest in the relationship.

### Conflicting/differential interests, resources and size

At the beginning of the 1990s SoftLab's high technology business projects were considered by Ericsson to be the reason behind the competition between them. They felt threatened by SoftLab's consultants who had the authority to execute technically demanding projects, while the search for background information was conducted within Ericsson. The problem was compounded by the fact that SoftLab supplied external consultants with information in order for them to carry through the assignments, which caused personnel problems at Ericsson.

SoftLab grew to a comparable size of the internal development department at Ericsson. As confidence grew between the two parties, they began to realise their respective competences. For example, during the early 1990s Ericsson began building competences in compilers and languages.

The conflicting interests of the two companies emerged towards the end of the alliance agreement. SoftLab prioritised profit and competence development, which resulted in 'the traditional client' feeling of being left out 'in the cold', even though they had co-operated for a long period of time. They considered themselves as not being able to compete with the more technically demanding and exciting projects from Ericsson's new clients.

Moreover, a number of Ericsson's units had a divergent pricing policy, which affected the relationship even though SoftLab chose Ericsson's most profitable projects. Apart from conflicting interests, their differences can be explained in terms of two aspects: (1) partly they can be explained in terms of differences between new clients, in which there were also differences in technology heights of the projects and, (2) partly these diverging interests can be explained in terms of differences between low marginal services in the support and maintenance agreement and high marginal services in new technology development. At the same time these differences were perceived by Ericsson in a way that led to increased interchangeability between a number of consultants at SoftLab. This affected the former privileged position that had been built up over the years in some units at Ericsson. Moreover, Ericsson observed differences in the management of some business areas in SoftLab. This implied that Ericsson perceived its relationship with SoftLab ambiguously. This led to some distrust and thus undermined the previous confidence they had developed and shared.

### Differential assessment of assets, secrecy and trust

Ericsson's trust in SoftLab was based on personal relationships at the management level between the two companies. However, changes within the management structure at Ericsson had a negative impact on the relationship. The level of trust was reduced, and a higher level of control was initiated. This control process culminated in a quality assessment in the autumn of 1996. Ericsson also noted the unwillingness of SoftLab to undertake certain assignments. SoftLab complained about the lack of resources, which were controlled more or less by Ericsson, who were of the opinion that they had to compete for assignments. In many cases differences in attitudes between the companies concerned the will to carry on with projects and client satisfaction. These differences did not emerge during the earlier phases of the relationship.

### Cultural differences and communication problems

The alliance became troubled because managers were unable to communicate clearly and thus did not clearly understand each other's intent – their goals and purposes. SoftLab prioritised short-term profit and projects at the technological edge. Additionally, internal communication difficulties within SoftLab hampered its relationship with Ericsson. Communication also became difficult because for some time the Processes and Tools Unit had no Managing Director, thus leaving SoftLab without a counterpart. With the management being unclear about Ericsson, SoftLab began to anticipate what Ericsson expected from the relationship. Presumably there may have been differences of opinion between those advocating outsourcing and those saying that support and maintenance are too strategically sensitive to be outsourced to a minor company such as the Linköping "spin off". This ambiguity made the relationship insecure. During discussions with Rational, SoftLab discovered that Ericsson were anxious about being too dependent, and about a hostile take-over.

## CONCLUSIONS

The purpose of the case study was to describe and analyse different barriers to co-operation between small and large technology-based firms. The focus is on SoftLab, a spin-off firm from Linköping University, and its co-operation with Ericsson. A snapshot concerning SoftLab's evolution will be described before presenting the main findings of the study. SoftLab was founded in 1982, and focused on consulting in the areas of language design and compiler construction. The business idea was built on creating long-term, strategic partnerships with their clients to improve their competitiveness by implementing, developing and administering customer made support systems and methods. The firm initially had a slow growth and it was not until 1990 that SoftLab attained a turnover of SEK10 million and 19 employees. The 1990s were characterised by a focus on growth, which was reflected in a tripling of both the number of employees and turnover.

The main findings of this study are:

- The transition between different forms of co-operation are sliding, which is also reflected in the literature of the research area in general (Lorange and Roos, 1992; Faulkner, 1995; Mønsted, 1998), where the terminology differs between the authors and also what characterises different forms of co-operation.
- Each of the three barriers (conflicting/differential interests, resources and size; differential assessment of assets, secrecy and trust; cultural differences and communication problems) has conveyed both a positive and a negative influence on the relationship at different stages.

The development of the co-operation can be described in three stages: an initiation stage characterised by personal contacts followed by a re-creative stage. In the last stage, where the aim was developing co-operation, the relationship is deepened and formalised.

During 1982–86, SoftLab began as a micro company with six employees and a turnover of SEK2.4 million. Its relationship with Ericsson was marked by stability and growth. The relationship with Ericsson was built up slowly, on trust and problem-solving on a need-to-know basis. Problems resulting from projects being terminated were handled by SoftLab, by the transfer of personnel resources to new projects.

The crisis in 1985–86 implied a need for risk spreading, searching for new clients and developing new niche markets. SoftLab strived to enhance stability. Its relationship with Ericsson was marked by a will to re-create the earlier co-operation. Continuity was something that both companies strived for, as individuals, as well as projects, became more and more inter-twined. SoftLab had continuous support from Ericsson at several entities and organisational levels, which influenced decisions on using their services. Thus, as the networks within the group increased, the two companies became physically linked. In 1989 the relationship again suffered as a major project was terminated.

During the 1990s SoftLab was marked by growth and there were continuous attempts to distinguish between those projects emanating from Ericsson and those which were not. This implied several re-organisations. A growth strategy was taken in order to reduce their dependence on Ericsson. Growth in the telecom business meant more assignments for SoftLab, who chose to concentrate on those projects which were most economically rewarding and fulfilling. The relationship was initially underlined by annual agreements. However, mutual dependency between the two led to a more long-term, formalised co-operative agreement in a second-line product support contract. SoftLab became a more co-operative partner. Information was now exchanged on a more formalised basis.

An unforeseen internal split was created by SoftLab because of competition for scarce resources between the two companies. This led to an internal struggle for resources between different Ericsson units. Increasing mistrust developed between the parties and Ericsson ascertained to increase control over SoftLab. As the relationship produced the basis for the exit possibilities, SoftLab was sold to an American company.

The relationship was also examined in terms of its characteristics and three kinds of barriers. The barriers included:

- conflicting/differential interests, resources and size;

- differential assessment of assets, secrecy and trust;
- cultural differences and communication problems.

In this study, interest, resource and size barrier were developed through both parties having a common interest in each other via mutual dependence.

Assets, secrecy, and trust were evaluated in terms of unequal assets. During the last phase, while both companies trusted each other, some differences of opinion began to emerge. The alliance suffered from mistrust and poor communication. Opportunities for further evolution of the alliance were not obvious. Ericsson being in the stronger negotiating position sold SoftLab to an American company.

## REFERENCES

Aldrich, H.E. and Zimmer, C. (1986) Entrepreneurship through social network. In Smilor, R. and Sexton, D. (eds) *The Art and Science of Entrepreneurship*, pp. 2–23. Cambridge, Ballinger.

Castells, M. (1996) *The Rise of Network Society*. Oxford, Blackwell Publishers.

Cooke, P. (1998) Introduction: origins of the concept. In Braczyk, H.-J., Cooke, P. and Heidenreich, M. (eds) *Regional Innovation Systems*, pp. 2–25. London, UCL Press.

Doz, Y.L. (1988) Technology partnerships between larger and smaller firms: some critical issues. In Contractor, F.J. and Lorange, P. (eds) *Cooperative Strategies in International Business*, pp. 3–30. Lexington, MA: Lexington Books.

Doz, Y.L. (1996) The evolution of cooperation in strategic alliances: initial conditions or learning processes? *Strategic Management Journal*, Vol. 17, pp. 55–83.

Esposito, L.S. and Raffa, M. (1993) The complexity in the relationships between large and small firms some empirical evidence. In *Frontiers of Entrepreneurship Research*, Babson College, Mass.

Faulkner, D. (1995) *International Strategic Alliances: Co-operating to Compete*. McGraw-Hill, UK.

Feldman, J.M. (1998a) Defence diversification and civilian spin-offs at Saab: lessons from the 1970s and 1980s. Working Paper, Department of Technology and Social Change, Linköping University, Linköping, Sweden.

Feldman, J.M. (1998b) The conversion of defence engineers' skills: explaining success and failure through customer-based learning, teaming and managerial integration. In Susman, G.I. and O'Keefe, S. (eds) *The Defence Industry in the Post-Cold War Era: Corporate Strategy and Public Policy Perspectives*. Oxford, Elsevier Science.

Feldman, J.M. and Klofsten, M. (1998) Interaction, growth and decline: the rise and fall of a Swedish medium-sized firm. Working Paper, Department of Technology and Social Change, Linköping University, Linköping, Sweden.

Forrest, J.E. (1990) Strategic Alliances and the small technology-based firm. *Journal of Small Business Management*, July, pp. 37–45.

Hamel, G. (1991) Competition for competence and interpartner learning within international strategic alliances. *Strategic Management Journal*, Vol. 12, pp. 83–112.

Hamel, G., Doz, Y.L. and Prahalad, C.K. (1989) 'Collaborate with your competitors and win'. *Harvard Business Review*, Vol. 67, No. 1, pp. 133–139.

Harrigan, K.R. (1985) *Strategies for Joint Venture Success*. Lexington, MA, Lexington Books.

Harrisson, B. (1994) *Lean and Mean*. New York, Basic Books.

Hlavacek, J.D., Davey B.H. and Bioudo, J.J. (1997) 'Tie small business technology to marketing power. *Harvard Business Review*, Vol. 55, No. 1, pp. 106–116.

Kaufmann, F. (1995) Internationalisation via co-operation – strategies of SMEs. *International Small Business Journal*, Vol. 13, No. 2, pp. 27–33.

Killing, J.P. (1983) *Strategies for Joint Venture Success*. New York, Praeger.

Killing, J.P. (1988) Understanding alliances: the role of task and organisational complexity. In Contractor, F. and Lorange, P. (eds) *Cooperative Strategies in International Business*, pp. 55–68, Lexington, MA, Lexington Books.

Kogut, B. (1988) Joint ventures: theoretical and empirical perspectives. *Strategic Management Journal*, Vol. 9, pp. 319–332.

Lorange, P. and Roos, J. (1992) *Strategic Alliances – Formation, Implementation, and Evolution.* Cambridge, Mass, Blackwell Publishers.

Mayer, G.D., Alvares, S.A. and Blasick, J. (1997) Benefits of technology-based strategic alliances: an entrepreneurial perspective. In *Frontiers of Entrepreneurship Research.* Babson College, Mass.

Mønsted, M. (1998) Networking for legitimacy – overcoming uncertainties in small high-tech firms. Paper presented at the Conference on Small Business Research, Växjö.

Parkhe, A. (1991) Interfirm diversity, organizational learning, and longevity in global strategic alliances. *Journal of International Business Studies,* Vol. 4, pp. 579–601.

Perlmutter, H.V. and Heenan, D.A. (1986) Cooperate to compete globally. *Harvard Business Review,* Vol. 64, No. 2, pp. 136–152.

Porter, M.E. and Fuller, M.B. (1986) Coalitions and global strategy. In Porter, M.E. (ed.) *Competition in global industries,* pp. 315–344, Boston, Mass., Harvard Business School Press.

Ring, P.S. and Van de Ven, A.H. (1994) Developmental processes of cooperative interorganizational relationships. *Academy of Management Review,* Vol. 19, No. 1, pp. 90–118.

Rothwell, R. (1991) External networking and innovation in small and medium-sized manufacturing firms in Europe. *Technovation,* Vol. 11, No. 2, pp. 93–112.

Sabel, C. (1993) Constitutional ordering in historical context. In Scarpf, F. (ed.) *Games in Hierarchies and Networks,* pp. 65–123, Frankfurt, Campus.

Scott, J. (1990) *A Matter of Record.* Polity Press, Cambridge, UK.

Slowinski, G., Seelig, G. and Hull, F. (1996) Managing technology-based strategic alliances between large and small firms. *Advanced Management Journal,* pp. 42–47.

Teece, D.J. (1986a) Towards an economic theory of the multiproduct firm. In Putterman, L. (ed.) *The economic nature of the firm: a reader,* pp. 250–265. Cambridge, Cambridge University Press.

Teece, D.J. (1986b) Profiting from technological innovation: implications for integration, collaboration, licensing and public policy. *Research Policy,* Vol. 15, No. 6, pp. 285–305.

Weaver, K. (1998) An examination of inter-firm co-operation in technologically intensive firms: a synergistic choice for small to medium sized enterprises. Paper presented at the Babson Conference, Twente, The Netherlands.

Westney, D.E. (1988) Domestic and foreign learning curves in managing international cooperative strategies. In Contractor, F. and Lorange, P. (eds) *Cooperative Strategies in International Business,* pp. 339–346. Lexington MA, Lexington Books.

Yuchtman, E. and Seashore, S.E. (1967) A system resource approach to organizational effectiveness. *American Sociological Review,* Vol. 32, pp. 891–903.

# CHAPTER 11

# *Local Skills and Knowledge as Critical Contributions to the Growth of Industry Clusters in Biotechnology*

CHRIS HENDRY AND JAMES BROWN

## INTRODUCTION

The role of regional clusters as an engine for economic growth has been widely studied by both academics and government agencies (Saxenian, 1994; Swann et al., 1998; Sainsbury, 1999). Central and regional government in the UK have adopted the principles of cluster development in a positive manner, with Scottish Enterprise and the Welsh Development Agency pioneers in developing appropriate methodologies (Peters and Hood, 2000).

In an analysis of the biomedical and information technology sectors in California, Finegold (1999) considered geographic clusters as 'high-skill ecosystems' (HSEs), with a focus on continual evolution and self-sustaining growth. Drawing on parallels with evolutionary theory, he argued that one of the key factors in achieving this is 'nourishment', which he interprets as the availability of an accessible pool of labour at all levels of skills and experience. Porter and Sölvell (1998) also subscribe to this view. The growth and performance of firms is then the result of an environment that encourages localised information flows and the creation of specialised pools of knowledge and skill.

Our findings on the opto-electronics industry in the UK, however, cast doubt on the effectiveness of clusters, and the extent to which concentrations of opto-electronics firms have moved beyond simple 'co-location' to become dynamic entities (Hendry and Brown, 1999). Of the three supply-side positive externalities mentioned by Krugman (1991), only the provision of specialised intermediate goods and services (i.e. technical and business services) plays an evident role in facilitating the development of new small firms.

It is possible, however, that these factors are industry specific. The biotechnology industry has a different structure and character to opto-electronics. Biotechnology firms are more tightly grouped round major university centres (Hendry, 1999) and market sectors are more closely aligned with different aspects of the technology (Swann and Prevezer, 1996). Cluster effects may therefore be more pronounced, and certainly more capable of being supported by outside agencies.

This paper builds on our earlier work (Hendry and Brown, 1999; Hendry et al., 1999) and reports on an empirical project that applies the survey instrument used in the opto-electronics case to a selection of UK dedicated biotechnology companies. A particular aspect of the research is to test the Finegold hypothesis in relation to the extent to which individual firms perceive the benefits of being situated in a localised area of high technology activity.

## THE FINEGOLD MODEL

In a general-purpose framework for analysing national comparative advantage, Porter (1990) identified four sets of inter-related factors (firm strategy, structure, and rivalry; factor conditions; demand conditions; and related and supporting industries) as key determinants. However, this model may be inappropriate for an emerging technology-based industry, such as biotechnology, where there is greater emphasis on research and development, and commercialising new scientific knowledge. Finegold (1999) has developed a more dynamic model for high-technology industries in highly concentrated geographic areas. Finegold proposes that localised concentrations of companies, which he calls high-skill ecosystems (HSEs), can be self-sustaining and capable of organic growth, provided that certain characteristics are in place. The four elements of the Finegold model are:

### Catalyst

The essential starting point is a catalyst (or set of catalysts) to trigger the development of new high-skill enterprises. In Finegold's view, this is not an isolated incident that happens entirely by chance, but is the result of several factors coming together with a 'strong element of historical contingency'.

### Nourishment

From an ecosystem perspective, being able to generate and sustain technological competence within a region is dependent on a continuing supply of 'nutrients'. This comes down to two basic things – human and financial capital. Human capital is envisaged at both the high-science level, with its requirement for advanced academic qualifications, and at the engineering level, which is more concerned with the process of transferring technology from the research laboratory through manufacturing to the market place. The financial aspect is clearly important but, as this paper is focused on skills, it is reviewed in more detail elsewhere (Hendry and Brown, 2000).

### Supportive environment

A supportive environment is the set of local factors that encourage the growth of new high-technology industries. These are broadly comparable to the local factors described by Porter (1990), and include for example such general features as a good transport and telecommunications infrastructure. Additionally, Finegold argues that this should be extended to include externalities that are specifically aimed at supporting the 'knowledge workers' that are important for high technology companies. These might include attractive social and recreational 'lifestyle' conditions, as well as a relaxed business and regulatory environment that is more tolerant of risk and more supportive of entrepreneurial, pioneering behaviour.

### Interdependence

The three elements considered above can organise companies into clusters with a range of external economies of agglomeration, and may be applicable to any group of companies in the same industry, located in the same geographic area. Finally, Finegold maintains that to achieve HSE status the region needs a high degree of co-operation among the participating companies and agencies.

This last factor may well be industry-specific. In biotechnology, inter-organisational networking is recognised as being crucial (Senker and Sharp, 1997). This is because, in the early stages of the industry, knowledge and resources are broadly distributed across a variety of institutions – universities, private research institutes, new biotechnology companies, and old pharmaceutical companies. Neither the range of core technologies, nor the required skills (basic research, applied research, clinical testing procedures, manufacturing, marketing, and knowledge of regulatory processes) are likely to be found under one roof (Powell et al., 1996). The result is that a multiplicity of organisational arrangements has evolved for co-operation in biotechnology, which therefore makes it a good test case for the model.

## RESEARCH DESIGN

Our purpose is to examine the behaviour of geographically localised clusters of business enterprises operating in the biotechnology sector. We followed the approach suggested by Storper and Harrison (1991) and focused on the local 'production unit' as the unit of analysis. This 'production unit' is defined as a research and development or production unit in biotechnology, operating from a single site in a defined locality, and is either an independent company or part of a larger commercial organisation. For convenience, these are all referred to as 'firms' or 'companies'. In this paper, we also use the terms 'cluster' and HSE interchangeably.

Identifying the relevant population of firms for survey purposes is difficult because many different types of company claim they are in biotechnology. Industry guides and directories list many companies (and other institutions) whose real activities are something different from, but have application to biotechnology. In a wider study of clusters these companies are important because they provide the supporting network of firms that Finegold considers to be essential for interdependency. In this more limited perspective, we focus on dedicated biotechnology firms, in order to get their views on skills requirements and the capability of this supportive environment to meet their needs.

As the focus is on the biotechnology industry in the UK, the BioIndustry Association (BIA) directory for December 1999 was taken as the starting point. This lists some 260 members. After checking each entry, 82 were selected for inclusion in the survey as being sizeable biotechnology companies engaged in the research and development of new products. The excluded companies were either in services (legal, financial, consultancy), education (typically university departments or individuals) or were 'sole traders' or subsidiaries of foreign companies with no research presence in the UK. They were excluded on the grounds that they were unlikely to be able to complete the sections on employment levels and skill requirements as required by the study.

The second consideration was the inclusion of pharmaceutical companies from the Association of British Pharmaceutical Industry list of members, which numbers about 80 (although some of these appear in the BIA list). After discussion with industry experts, 12 were selected and included in an attempt to focus on that part of the pharmaceutical industry that is actively concerned with research and development in biotechnology. Essentially this comes down to those companies with

R&D facilities that do work on biotechnology, and the survey was addressed to the research director on these sites.

A number of companies were also selected from the regional biotechnology associations in Kent and the eastern region. Again, both of these membership lists included many companies that were considered peripheral to the study (as well as some already on the BIA list). Accordingly some 8 out of 55 were selected from Kent and 30 out of 290 from the eastern region.

Finally, *Genetic Engineering News* (1999) was consulted. This is an American publication that lists companies in biotechnology and related industries. One hundred and ninety four companies are listed for the UK. However, an examination of the list reveals that many are subsidiaries of American equipment or reagent suppliers with limited biotechnology research and development capabilities. In addition there are overlaps with the previous lists and accordingly some 28 companies were selected for the survey.

These sources provided a total of 160 companies. Further inspection suggested that some of these were concerned more with infra-structural activities, such as incubator centres and other forms of facilities management, while an initial mailing revealed some unknown companies. For example one multi-national responded with comments, but did not complete the survey. This resulted in a total sample of 142 firms.

The survey was conducted during February 2000, and an initial mailing was followed up with a reminder to firms that had not responded. A total of 45 (31.7 per cent) useable responses were received. The regional distribution of the respondent sample compares well with the target population and this shows a high degree of geographical representation with the possible exception of Wales, which provided no responses at all. The survey responses were analysed using SPSS. Descriptive statistics were used to analyse cluster characteristics of formation and development, followed by an analysis of variation across the regions.


## CLUSTER CHARACTERISTICS

The first objective was to determine the nature and extent of biotechnology clustering in the UK. Companies were grouped according to the DTI regional definitions and boundaries. A straightforward count of the number of firms in each geographic region revealed two clusters in England, each cluster centred around Cambridgeshire and the Thames Valley respectively. The second cluster was concentrated to a lesser extent in South Wales and Central Scotland. Taking this pattern into account and using the knowledge gained about the development of the industry from previous studies, firms were classified into three groups of roughly equal size.

*The Eastern Group* covers the DTI Eastern Region. East Anglia was identified in the 1960s as a centre for the development of high-technology industry, along the lines of Silicon Valley, and benefited from the opening of the first university Science Park in England. The area has a number of research centres, which were early entrants into biotechnology, including the Medical Research Council. This group can be regarded as a concentrated group, as much of the industry centres on Cambridge as the focal point.

*The Southeast Group* covers the DTI Southeast Region. This extends from Oxfordshire to Kent. This is a widely spread region without a clear central point, but it includes a number of university, industrial and hospital medical research centres, each of which has given rise to the formation of new biotechnology companies.

*The RestUK Group* comprises those companies not in the two groups above. As a first step, we regard this as the non-cluster group, as the geographic concentration of companies is considerably less than in the other two. Sainsbury (1999) similarly identified Cambridge and Oxford as the two most developed UK clusters in biotechnology. No doubt, some local concentrations are in place, such as the important cluster in Scotland around Glasgow and Edinburgh, but in the main the RestUK group is quite distributed. In the absence of obvious significant clustering, these firms can be regarded as an approximate control group.

Further details on the three groups can be found in the report to the Science, Technology and Mathematics Council, which sponsored this work (Hendry and Brown, 2000).

## INTERPRETING THE DATA WITHIN THE FINEGOLD MODEL

### Catalyst

In a description of the circumstances surrounding the start of the Californian high skill eco-system in biotechnology, Finegold states that one of two groundbreaking discoveries was made in Cambridge, but not commercialised because of the lack of patents. The importance of being close to a research centre for the creation of HSEs is clear, but the implication that Cambridge suffered as a consequence of not having patenting processes in place is perhaps without exception as there are a number of reasons why companies start up in particular regions.

The results from the survey regarding the reasons for choice of location and start-up reveal that the three most frequently occurring responses, from a set of choices, were (1) near key research centre (51 per cent), (2) availability of a scientific work-force (42 per cent), and (3) low-cost premises (33 per cent). The first two reflect the importance of a university or other research centres. Extending the analysis across the three clusters does not reveal any significant variation – although it is unusual that in the Southeast (a high-cost locality) a disproportionate number of firms main-tain that low-cost premises were an attraction. This suggests that they may benefit from special arrangements, which were not apparent in this study.

The fact that distributions across the regions, relating to the proximity to a research centre and a scientific workforce, do not differ significantly between the clustered regions (Eastern and Southeast) and the non-clustered RestUK, suggests that proximity to a university is a necessary, but not in itself a sufficient reason, for a cluster to start. Additional factors may have been involved. The survey does not indicate comprehensively what these might be, but the second tier of explanations may provide a clue. These show that low cost premises (33 per cent), technical workforce (20 per cent), lifestyle preferences (20 per cent), good transport (20 per cent) and proximity to a science park (22 per cent) may also play a part. Thus it is likely that a number of factors play a part.

### Nourishment

In order to analyse the issues relating to human capital, we broke down employ-ment into four job categories – research and development, laboratory, manufacturing and administration. Only 17 (out of 45) companies expressed needs for manufacturing skills. Therefore, conclusions must be viewed with caution. Administration is a broad category that includes sales, marketing and management. Research and development is the largest category, with 41 per cent of staff. When combined with the 28 per cent in laboratory, giving a total of 69 per cent scientific and technical staff, it indicates the high-skill research content of the biotechnology industry at this early stage of development.

In the skills analysis section, the survey requested respondents to indicate those skills considered to be (a) 'important' and (b) 'lacking', in each of the four job categories. Three general comments can be made about the responses. First, inter-personal skills and attributes scored high across all job categories. Second, the top (or equal top) need in each job category was 'flexibility'. As respondents were mainly senior management, this is perhaps not surprising, but it does contrast with the requirement for technical skills expressed in the reasons for choice of loca-tion. Third, the response rate to the 'skills lacking' question was about half (a maximum of 40 per cent) compared to that for 'skills important' (typically 70–80 per cent). It is a matter of opinion whether this should be a cause for satisfaction about the state of skill provision, or a matter of concern.

Specific findings concerning skills and training are:

1. For research and development staff, there is a clear requirement for formal qualifications, which firms rely on the university sector to provide. R&D staff are perceived to be lacking in project management, communications, and entrepreneurial skills.
2. For laboratory staff, the requirement is for skills that facilitate co-operation within the workplace – namely, flexibility, willingness to learn, and communica-tions. Communications, teamworking, and initiative taking ('entrepreneurial' skills) are perceived to be lacking.
3. The figures for manufacturing are probably too small to comment seriously, other than to suggest there is a skills deficiency in IT.
4. For administration, the top skill requirements are flexibility and teamwork, but advanced information technology also comes out as a key problem. As this is the commercial part of the organisation, we assume this is not a reference to sophisticated use of information technology for research purposes, but rather for business use (possibly a reference to e-commerce).

To summarise this section, the overall impression is that, apart from the necessary requirement for research and development staff with high academic qualifica-tions, the skills issues are more to do with effective work organisation and productivity. The significance, for all job categories, of in-company training and training on the job (Table 11.1), which build on basic education in university, college, and further professional training, reinforces this picture.

### Supportive environment

Respondents were asked to indicate (on a scale of 1–3) the value of different kinds of institution in supporting skills development. The clear leader was 'biotech-nology association' with 1.9 (34 companies), and 'professional institution' second with 1.6 (25 companies). Other associations also scored high at 1.6 (19 compa-nies). These are national rather than local institutions, with an industry-specific and professional development role. For local institutions, the scores are typically lower, at around 1.4 for Chamber of Commerce, Regional Development Agencies and regional industry forum.

Another approach was to ask questions about factors inhibiting development. The answers reveal the lack of a 'local economic strategy for biotechnology' (scoring 1.6 for 37 companies, increasing to 1.7 for 24 companies in five years time) as important, suggesting a picture of a weak local development infrastructure. On the other hand, 'public attitudes to biotechnology' were also

**Table 11.1:** *Different sources of training and skills development that are regarded as 'valuable' by respondents for each of four job categories (Research and development R&D, Laboratory LAB, Manufacturing MAN and Administration ADM). The number given is the number of companies (expressed as a percentage of the total responding at all for that category of job) indicating it to be of value*

| | R&D | | LAB | | MAN | | ADM | |
|---|---|---|---|---|---|---|---|---|
| Number of companies reporting at least one source of training value (N) | 40 | | 36 | | 17 | | 44 | |
| Per cent of N indicating specific training source | % | Rank | % | Rank | % | Rank | % | Rank |
| University | 92.5 | 1 | 58.3 | | 35.3 | | 52.3 | |
| FE college | 12.5 | | 61.1 | 3 | 64.7 | 3 | 40.9 | |
| School | 10.0 | | 19.4 | | 41.2 | | 25.0 | |
| Sector training organisation | 10.0 | | 16.7 | | 17.6 | | 18.2 | |
| Other training organisation | 5.0 | | 8.0 | | 0.0 | | 11.4 | |
| TEC | 0.0 | | 19.4 | | 5.8 | | 11.4 | |
| Professional seminars and courses | 60.0 | 3 | 28.6 | | 29.4 | | 54.6 | 3 |
| Industry seminars | 50.0 | | 33.3 | | 41.2 | | 36.4 | |
| Private training company | 22.5 | | 13.9 | | 23.5 | | 30.2 | |
| In-company training | 55.0 | | 63.9 | 2 | 94.1 | 1 | 88.6 | 1 |
| Training 'on the job' | 82.5 | 2 | 83.3 | 1 | 88.2 | 2 | 79.6 | 2 |
| Personal networks | 45.0 | | 19.4 | | 35.3 | | 43.2 | |

regarded as a problem (at level 1.6 now, rising to 1.9 in five years time), indicating serious concern about the national climate for biotechnology.

However, evidence from industry experts and from the membership lists of the BIA, ERBI and, to a lesser extent, Kent-Bio, suggests there is a flourishing network of venture capitalists, legal experts, public relations, and recruitment consultants. Many of these are concentrated in the London area, and are therefore accessible to both Eastern and Southeast regions. Evidence for a local supportive environment is therefore somewhat mixed. Company perceptions (as 'consumers') are often at variance with those of organisations that exist to promote (and sell) infrastructure support.

### Interdependence

Finegold distinguishes between three different types of interdependence: (1) horizontal (partnering with organisations that have complementary experts), (2) vertical (collaborations along the value chain), and (3) personal networks. In this section we examine the prevalence and importance of these types of linkages, with the added feature of distinguishing between local (within a 50 mile radius), national (within the UK), and international connections.

We do this by first looking at commercial partnerships (both vertical and horizontal), then non-commercial partnerships (typically this will be horizontal arrangements with research organisations), and finally personal networks.

### (1) Commercial networks

*Primary Commercial Network.* The extent to which a biotechnology firm collaborates with other companies can be considered from two different aspects. The first one is density (the number of companies in the sample having at least one form of collaboration, expressed as a percentage of the total in the sample), and the second intensity (the average number of different types of collaboration per actively collaborating company). The survey asked for details of collaborations with other biotechnology companies, pharmaceutical companies, and 'other' commercial enterprises. In each case, a number of alternative kinds of collaboration were suggested and respondents were asked to indicate all those they used. Additional information was requested to indicate whether the collaboration involved a company in the locality, the UK, or internationally.

The number of companies with at least one form of collaboration is shown in the second column in Table 11.2. Numerically and proportionally, collaborations with other biotechnology companies scored highest (at 84 per cent), but collaborations with pharmaceutical companies scored slightly lower (62 per cent).

Table 11.2 also illustrates the intensity of collaborative activity. Column 3 shows the average number of different types of collaboration across the three geographic regions. It is clear that the general pattern is one of increasing intensity as the location of the collaborative partner moves to the international arena. This appears to be consistent across the different types of partner and the pattern is maintained across the three clusters. (The figures for collaborations with 'other' companies are too low to indicate anything about the pattern of behaviour across the clusters).

Within this general picture, however, the intensity of collaborations with biotechnology companies at the local level is twice as high as for pharmaceutical companies. This pattern is consistent across all three clusters, particularly for the eastern region. At the national level, this relative emphasis on links with biotechnology rather than pharmaceutical companies is repeated, although less marked. Southeast companies have a low level of collaboration with pharmaceutical companies nationally. Overall, this suggests that horizontal partnering between (small) biotechnology companies is more common than vertical supply chain relationships with (large) pharmaceutical companies at local and national levels. This effect is particularly marked in the eastern region at the local level, and probably reflects the tighter clustering around Cambridge.

The idea of collaborating along the value chain is well established in many industrial sectors. However, the degree of collaboration with horizontally equivalent companies is unusual (at least in the UK). This may reflect the early stage of product development and the need to draw on complementary resources where product development is complex. More detailed analysis shows that collaborations in research and product development score consistently higher than those for process development and marketing, which bears this out. Meanwhile, collaborations with pharmaceutical companies are far more pronounced at the international level, where marketing considerations, patent registration, and resourcing international research expertise become important.

*Secondary Commercial Network.* In addition to the primary commercial network, there is also a secondary network of supporting services that may be especially important for new companies that have not yet developed specialised resources in-house. Thus, a secondary aspect of a firm's commercial network is the extent to which it uses service-based companies for general business purposes (legal, accounting and training), and for technical support (product design, fabrication facilities, and product testing).

Respondents were therefore asked whether or not they used business and technical services at local, national and international levels. Not surprisingly, the extent of such links decreases towards the international end of the scale. The fact that almost 20 per cent of all firms make use of technical services outside the UK

**Table 11.2:** *Distribution of the average number of collaborative links between biotechnology companies and different types of partner. This is summarised initially in terms of the number of links at local, national and international levels, and then, for those areas where there is significant activity, a break-down is provided across the three clusters*

| Collaboration type | Number of companies with some form of collaboration | The average number of types of collaboration | Variation of average figure across the three regions | | |
|---|---|---|---|---|---|
| | | | Southeast | Eastern | RestUK |
| Biotechnology companies | 38 | | | | |
| Local | | 0.5000 | 0.2727 | 0.8571 | 0.3077 |
| National | | 1.5526 | 0.9091 | 1.7857 | 1.8462 |
| International | | 1.9211 | 1.8182 | 1.9286 | 2.0000 |
| 'Pharma' companies | 28 | | | | |
| Local | | 0.1786 | 0.1250 | 0.3636 | 0.0000 |
| National | | 1.1071 | 0.2500 | 1.5455 | 1.3333 |
| International | | 2.1786 | 2.1250 | 2.4545 | 1.8889 |
| Other companies | 15 | | | | |
| Local | | 0.1333 | | | |
| National | | 1.5333 | | | |
| International | | 2.0000 | | | |
| Universities | 45 | | | | |
| Local | | 2.1136 | 1.6154 | 2.2500 | 2.4000 |
| National | | 3.2727 | 3.3077 | 3.4375 | 3.0667 |
| International | | 1.2045 | 1.3077 | 1.3750 | 0.9333 |
| Government research | 29 | | | | |
| Local | | 0.7931 | | | |
| National | | 1.8276 | | | |
| International | | .3448 | | | |
| Private research | 15 | | | | |
| Local | | 0.4667 | | | |
| National | | 1.6667 | | | |
| International | | 0.5333 | | | |

suggests a strong international dimension, reinforcing the picture of strong global relationships in the supply chain.

For technical services, the use of nationally based facilities is highest at 69 per cent, with international second at 42 per cent, and local at 29 per cent. For business services, on the other hand, local scores 69 per cent, national 60 per cent, and international 11 per cent. The two key functions, therefore, are local business services and national technical services. While this may simply reflect the availability of services, we might have expected the local effect to be more pronounced in those regions (Eastern and Southeast) where clusters are more extensively developed. However, this is not the case, as the averages are much the same across the three regions.

Specific attention to the role of service companies may throw more light on this. Certainly the extensive supply of business services relating to biotechnology in the highly economically and technologically active regions of East Anglia, London and the Thames Valley, suggests that the provision of services is a significant factor in the development of the UK biotechnology industry.

## (2) Institutional networks

Similarly we asked about the extent of collaborative activity with universities, government research centres, and private research centres, covering a range of activities through recruitment, use of facilities and equipment, product ideas, advice and consultancy, commissioning of research, and student placement.

The university infrastructure clearly stands out as the most important institutional link, with all firms having at least one form of university collaboration, and an average intensity of 2.1 at local level, 3.3 at national level, and 1.2 at international level (Table 11.2). Although contact with government and private research enterprises is lower, there is a consistent pattern, with the national research infrastructure scoring higher than the local or international arenas. This presumably reflects a greater concentration of resources into a few national centres, which are also more accessible than international institutions. Local universities score higher on the intensity scale for the RestUK, suggesting pockets of intensive collaborative activity across the country focused on local centres of expertise.

## (3) Personal networks

A key aspect of the generic HSE model, as a source of innovation and economic growth, is the use of knowledge resources from the locality that are external to the company and based on personal networks. In this section, we look at the non-transactional links that relate more directly to knowledge transfer, as the process of acquiring information of any sort which, when placed in the context of a specific firm, can be translated into practical outcomes.

The survey offers two approaches to this. Firstly, we asked for comments on the value of a number of different networks for 'skills development'. The clear leaders in this are the industry and professional associations, with scores in the range 1.6 to 1.9 (on a scale from 1–3). These are very much national institutions, although Eastern and Southeast regions score slightly higher than the RestUK, which may reflect the fact that these associations are typically located in London.

Next in importance are the regional institutions, such as development agencies, forums, and Chambers of Commerce, which scored around the 1.4 mark. Companies in the RestUK rated these more highly than those in the Southeast and Eastern regions. Although the differences are not numerically significant, it is interesting to see that the pattern is reversed. A possible explanation is that in the two regions near London, the abundance of supporting institutions may result in some devaluation of local bodies, whereas in the RestUK these assume greater importance, whether or not they are intrinsically stronger.

The second approach is to look at personal networks. In the industrial cluster model, as exemplified by Silicon Valley, Saxenian (1994) stresses the creative value of the movement of technical engineers from one company to another within the locality. This was difficult to assess in this type of survey. Although we did not specifically test for the existence of personal networks, we made some inferences from answers to questions on sources of training and problems in the locality. The responses indicated only moderate support for the value of personal networks in skills development, with less than 45 per cent of companies regarding them as valuable. This contrasts with the 80 per cent who valued on-the-job training. Taken together, these two indicators do not suggest that there is a well-developed set of personal networks operating locally for skills development purposes, outside those internal to the company. Networks for high-level skills (and knowledge transfer) are national, operating through professional and industry associations.

## CONCLUSIONS

Cooke and Morgan (1993) point out that clusters are hard to imitate and transfer to other regions. They may be very effective in certain well-documented localities, but the strong dependence upon an indigenous social and cultural tradition and an effective entrepreneurial contribution makes the cluster model a difficult one to transplant into other areas. This dependence on strong local roots contrasts with the picture from our research into opto-electronics and biotechnology clusters, which shows firms having a global (and national) rather than local perspective towards market opportunities and technological advances.

The ability of firms to link into global networks promotes competitiveness and innovation by providing access to leading edge technologies (Kanter, 1995). This is enhanced by the use of sophisticated information and communications networks. On the basis of such global information and communication trends, together with new forms of global governance, institutions and strategic alliances, location proximity may be unnecessary.

As Bartholomew (1997) points out, the issue is not whether local or global networks are more likely to produce world-class companies and successful clusters, but how to put the two together. This is a key theme in the papers edited by Howells and Michie (1997), who postulate the need for a clear analytical link between the study of globalization of technology and the study of national systems of innovation. These two strands of literature on the dynamics of technical change have so far been more or less unconnected, and should be considered complementary.

The real issue, then, is how does the Finegold hypothesis contribute to this desired synthesis?

In this concluding section, we review the four Finegold factors from this viewpoint.

### *Catalyst*

In the case of biotechnology, it seems clear that a necessary precondition for the development of a cluster is the presence of a research centre (Swann et al. 1996). This is fairly self-evident and well documented in UK biotechnology by Sainsbury (1999). The survey confirms the clustering effect around Cambridge and Oxford, and suggests that the existence of clusters in UK biotechnology depends on a university with world-class reputation and research. This is less so in opto-electronics (Hendry and Brown, 1999), where, although clusters are in much the same parts of the UK, the influence of the original industrial base as a catalyst for the growth of clusters is perhaps more significant. In both cases, though, the importance of life-style factors and the inertial effect of people staying in the area where they developed their expertise are also important.

### *Nourishment*

Clearly, in the case of a science-based industry, such as biotechnology, the strong supply of highly qualified scientists is pre-eminent. The survey bears this out, with scientific staff in the great majority. However, qualifications should be noted. First, the percentage number of firms using national universities as a recruitment source is 62 per cent, compared to 40 per cent for local, and 9 per cent for international ones. The Southeast and Eastern clusters show slightly less dependency on local (compared to national) university links than the 'non-cluster'. This suggests that the availability of a local highly educated scientific work force is not a significant factor in the development of biotechnology clusters, but it is important in the national context.

The second qualification for the high-science requirement is that the highest scores for skill needs across all job categories are in the areas of personal skills and attributes. This suggests a focus on effective work organisation and productivity. The example of Celltech is instructive in this respect (McNamara and Baden-Fuller 1999). Its recovery from near bankruptcy was the result of the application of established managerial techniques, including the formation of new interdiscipli-nary team structures and the infusion of new organizational processes. Thus, the availability of a scientific workforce scores high in the initial location choice, and is a precondition for early company formation. However, personal skill factors come to the fore when companies need to start developing best practices in work organization.

### Supportive environment

Finegold identifies the need for a good transport and communications infrastruc-ture as essential ingredients of a supportive environment. More importantly, he stresses features that might attract knowledge workers, such as attractive living and working conditions, and a relaxed regulatory environment that encourages exper-iment and risk. This is a key area for policy makers and one that will take on increased importance in the UK as the Regional Development Agencies get underway. Our survey shows, however, that the institutions that score highest as sources of support (and training) for the development of skills are national industry and professional associations, rather than local bodies.

Clearly, there is a significant amount of work to be done by the new Regional Development Agencies to overcome the 'lack of a local strategy for biotechnology', and to stimulate the extensive networks of local service companies, which appar-ently exist. The strategy of the two established development agencies in Wales and Scotland, and the networks they support in opto-electronics – the Welsh Opto-electronics Forum, and Scottish Opto-electronics Association – may be instructive. Notably, both have encouraged an international approach that aims at promoting their indigenous industries onto a wider stage.

### Interdependence

Inter-organisational networks are important, but the real question is whether concentrations of these networks within localised clusters are especially beneficial for knowledge transfer and skills development. The evidence states that collabora-tions are very important, with 84 per cent of companies indicating at least one collaboration with a biotechnology company (horizontal linkage), and 64 per cent indicating at least one collaboration with a pharmaceutical company (vertical linkage). But when the total number of types of collaboration are summed for each geographic region, there is a clear picture of increasing activity as the loca-tion of the collaborating company moves from local to national to international space. If increased activity (and therefore increased resource commitment) can be taken as an indicator of expected returns, this would suggest that the case for local commercial collaborations conferring special benefits are far from proven. While the most developed cluster, around Cambridge, did score much higher than the other two clusters on local collaborations, this was still less than national and international collaboration.

On the other hand, for the secondary network, the pattern is one of stronger local (and national) linkages for business services, and national (and international) linkages for technical services. This suggests that the beneficial effect of local inter-company links may depend more on service companies that support business development, rather than support for the core technological competences of the firm. Similar results were found for opto-electronics (Hendry and Brown, 1999).

Biotechnology is an industry at a very early stage of development. Few companies have products on the market, and none in the UK are yet making a profit from their biotechnology operations (Arthur Andersen, 1997; Hendry, 1999). It is an industry, in the UK, that has a remarkably rich 'supportive environment', that central government has recognised and encouraged. Clusters have made strong progress, but are nevertheless still mostly embryonic. Typically, for a young industry, local business services are important. But already biotechnology firms are strongly linked with national networks for technical services and international networks with other biotechnology and pharmaceutical companies. This confirms the need to connect the theory and analysis of high-technology clusters with globalisation, and the role of extra-regional networks in innovation.

## ACKNOWLEDGEMENTS

We are grateful to the Science, Technology and Mathematics Council, who sponsored this work, and to Bill McNichol and Pauline Moylan for their support.

## REFERENCES

Arthur Andersen (1997) *UK Biotech '97 – Making the Right Moves*. London.

Bartholomew, S. (1997) 'National systems of biotechnology innovation: Complex interdependence in the global system'. *Journal of International Business Studies*, 28, 2: 241–266.

Cooke, P. and Morgan, K. (1993) 'The Network Paradigm – New Departures in Corporate and Regional Development'. *Environment And Planning D: Society and Space*, 11, 5: 543–564.

Finegold, D. (1999) 'Creating Self-sustaining, High-skill Ecosystems'. *Oxford Review of Economic Policy*, 15, 1: 60–81.

Genetic Engineering News (1999) *Directory of Biotechnology Companies*. Larchmont NY: Mary Ann Liebert.

Hendry, C. (1999) *New Technology Industries*. Sheffield: Department for Education and Employment.

Hendry, C. and Brown, J. (2000) *Creating High-skill Ecosystems in the UK Biotechnology Industry*. London: Science Technology and Mathematics Council.

Hendry, C. and Brown, J. (1999) 'Clustering and Performance in the UK Opto-electronics Industry'. Seventh High Technology Small Firms Conference, Manchester Business School.

Hendry, C., Brown, J., DeFillippi, R.J. and Hassink, R. (1999) 'Industry clusters as commercial, knowledge and institutional networks: opto-electronics in six regions in the UK, USA and Germany'. In A. Grandori (ed.) *Interfirm Networks: Organisation and industrial competitiveness*. London and New York: Routledge, pp. 151–184.

Howells, J. and Michie, J. (eds) (1997). *Technology, Innovation and Competitiveness*. Cheltenham: Edward Elgar.

Kanter, R.M. (1995). *World Class: Thriving Locally in the Global Economy*. New York: Simon and Schuster.

Krugman, P. (1991). *Geography and Trade*. Cambridge, MA: MIT Press.

McNamara, P. and Baden-Fuller, C. (1999) 'Lessons from the Celltech Case: Balancing Knowledge Exploration and Exploitation in Organizational Renewal'. *British Journal of Management*, 10.

Peters, E. and Hood, N. (2000) 'Implementing the Cluster Approach: Some Lessons from the Scottish Experience'. *International Studies of Management and Organization*, (forthcoming).

Porter, M.E. (1990) *The Competitive Advantage of Nations*. London: Macmillan.

Porter, M.E. and Sölvell, Ö. (1998) 'The Role of Geography in the Process of Innovation and the Sustainable Competitive Advantage of Firms'. In A.D. Chandler, P. Hagstrom and O. Solvell (eds) *The Dynamic Firm; The Role of Technology, Strategy, Organization, and Regions*. Oxford: Oxford University Press.

Powell, W., Koput, K. and Smith-Doerr, L. (1996) 'Interorganisational Collaboration and the Locus of Innovation: Networks of Learning in Biotechnology'. *Administrative Science Quarterly*, 41: 116–145.

Sainsbury, D. (1999). *Biotechnology Clusters: Report of Team Led by Lord Sainsbury, Minister for Science*. London: Department of Trade and Industry.

Saxenian, A. (1994). *Regional Advantage: Culture and Competition in Silicon Valley and Route 128*. Cambridge, Massachusetts: Harvard University Press.

Senker, J. and Sharp, M. (1997) 'Organizational Learning in Co-operative Alliances: Some Case Studies in Biotechnology'. *Technology Analysis and Strategic Management*, 9, 1: 35–51.

Storper, M. and Harrison, B. (1991) 'Flexibility, Hierarchy and Regional Development: The Changing Structure of Industrial Production Systems and their Forms of Governance in the 1990s'. *Research Policy*, 20: 407–422.

Swann, G.M.P., Prevezer, M. and Stout, D. (1998) *The Dynamics of Industrial Clustering*. Oxford: Oxford University Press.

Swann, P. and Prevezer, M. (1996) 'A Comparison of the Dynamics of Industrial Clustering in Computing and Biotechnology'. *Research Policy*, 25, 7: 1139–1157.

CHAPTER 12

# Entrepreneurial Networking in the Dutch Manufacturing Sector: The Role of Key Decision Leaders in SME-Based Alliances

WIM DURING AND AARD J. GROEN

## INTRODUCTION

Increasingly companies recognize the potential advantage of inter-firm alliances in creating value. Regarding the motivation for firms to co-operate, recent writings (e.g. Håkansson, 1987; Iacobucci, 1996; Granovetter, 1992; Burt, 1992) suggest that the reason why firms consider a cooperative strategy is the potential to create synergetic value by combining resources to develop, produce and market goods and services. More specifically Powell et al. (1996) argue that the rapid pace of technological development, and its associated high costs, underlie the motives of firms when cooperating with regard to technological development. Previous alliance oriented research has mostly focused on strategies of, and effect of alliances on, the large firm. Nooteboom (1994) contends that, through using alliances, small and medium sized firms can gain synergetic benefits by, on the one hand exploiting their flexibility due to their smallness, and on the other hand gaining economies of scale and scope attributable to large firms (see also Groen and Nooteboom, 1998). Some evidence of the specific position of the SME is presented in Monsted (1998) where it is argued that the process of forming strategic alliances is more opportunistic for the SME, and less a part of a formal corporate strategy.

Our focus in this chapter is on the role of the entrepreneur in alliance behavior. This is a first elaboration of the recently developed concept of 'entrepreneurial networking'. During and Klein Woolthuis (1997) define entrepreneurial networking as 'a means by which SMEs develop new activities or ventures in cooperation with other firms, with a strong personal involvement of the entrepreneurs in the cooperation process.' This is part of our interest in the entrepreneurial process of creating, developing and exploiting new (technology-based) market opportunities. This process is a core activity for small technology-based firms. As for small firms in general, the particular and dominant role the entrepreneur plays in the firm, and thus also in cooperation between firms, is an important point. The specific situation and background of the small and medium sized companies and their entrepreneurs will influence the way they operate in these processes (During and Oakey, 1998).

Specifically, this research is thus focused on, as described by Dickson and Weaver (1997): '(the use by SMEs of) structured agreements which establish exchange relationships between co-operating firms, but do not involve a "free standing wholly owned subsidiary".' This study deals with alliance behavior of Dutch manufacturing small and medium sized enterprises.

The objectives of our study are two-fold. First, we will explore the extent of previous alliance experience and current alliance use. To explore this we will gather information on a rich variety of co-operative relationships. This heterogeneous set of alliances will be analyzed to see whether types of alliances can be discerned. Second, we will show the significance of variations in the opinions of entrepreneurs regarding the organizational determinants of the alliance processes as an explanation of firm-level alliance use. In the next part of the chapter, we will develop propositions from theory on this topic.

## DETERMINANTS OF ALLIANCE INVOLVEMENT

From previous research it is evident that alliance involvement is dependent on individual, organizational and environmental factors. In this section we discuss individual, and especially, organization based determinants that prompt individual decision leaders to become involved in alliances.

## INDIVIDUAL DETERMINANTS

In the context of a small business, the dominant role that the entrepreneur plays in cooperation between firms is a key issue. Lumpkin and Dess (1996: 138) contend that 'an individual entrepreneur is regarded as a firm' and that the 'small business firm is simply an extension of the individual who is in charge.' Given the importance of the individual leader, Covin and Slevin (1991:10) view entrepreneurial attitude as an overall strategic orientation that has a significant impact on how organizational leaders interpret and respond to organizational and environmental stimuli. Lumpkin and Dess (1996) argue that a decision leader's entrepreneurial orientation, in interaction with organizational and environmental factors, will significantly influence the performance of a firm. Recent findings by Dickson and Weaver (1997) suggest that entrepreneurial orientation, in interaction with the individualism/collectivism orientations of the decision leader, is positively related to alliance use in the light of perceived opportunities for growth and profit. Apparently, decision leaders with a high entrepreneurial orientation have a higher potential for pursuing opportunities and leveraging alliance advantage. Co-operation between firms is thus partially dependent on the individual psychological orientations of the decision leader and the way that these affect his or her perception of opportunities and constraints in the environment. For the Dutch sample we also found a positive correlation between the decision leaders entrepreneurial orientation and alliance experience and current alliance use (Weaver et al., 1999).

## ORGANIZATION-BASED DETERMINANTS

Various firm-based aspects can also define incentives for individual decision leaders, in order to turn their orientation into actions. The first aspect is related to the strategic necessity of entering alliances. Das and Teng (1997) show that being a strong player in one's own market makes it easier for a firm to develop successful alliances. One might expect that small firms seldom have such a strong position, where the strength is, for example, associated with size and based on competitive position in terms of market share. However, evidence suggests that small, but highly competent, firms can be successfully involved in long-term alliances with big companies (e.g. Håkansson, 1987). Such small firms tap into the resources of the larger firm (e.g. marketing resources), which are of strategic importance to them when entering alliances. As mentioned above, rapid technological development might be another strategic reason for small firms to enter into alliances (Nooteboom, 1994; Powell et al., 1996). According to some authors (Luimes and Spitholt, 1994; Douma, 1997; Das and Teng, 1997), the 'organizational fit' between alliance partners is an important determinant of alliance success. Hamel et al. (1989) stress the importance of shared goals as an important strategic imperative and how these may result in a broad set of specialized skills to build a core competence and serve clients needs. Williamson (1985, 1991), however, argues that firms also enter into alliances with different, and sometimes conflicting goals, when compared to their partners. Moreover, according to Williamson the risk of opportunistic behavior cannot be excluded in situations where partners have dissimilar goals.

Also an organization-based aspect associated with positive alliance outcomes is the 'cultural fit' between organizations (Douma, 1997). Groen and Nooteboom (1998) refer to 'cultural fit' as cultural capital, defined as the base of knowledge and experience available in a specific firm that is built over time with following positive experiences (Håkansson, 1987). From a small technology based firm perspective, During and Oakey (1998) suggest that the technology-base and the specific technological expertise of a firm will play an important role in a firm's ability to successfully engage in alliances. Luimes and Spitholt (1994) stress the strategic importance of the 'human fit' between participants in facilitating the alliance. When people do not like each other at all, one might expect that cooperation over long periods of time is difficult. The more operational organizational aspects in terms of a clear division of tasks, and flexibility within the organization, is also important.

A further organizational aspect that might influence the likelihood of firms entering into alliances is previous experience with alliances and other networking expertise (Groen, 1994; Groen and Nooteboom, 1998). Closely related to this is, as mentioned above, is the personal experience of the entrepreneur with regard to alliances (During, 1998). Therefore, we expect that the opinions of key decision leaders with respect to the organizational aspects of alliances are related to their experience with, and current use of, alliances.

We propose the following general propositions:

- The use of an alliance is associated with the opinion of the key decision leader on the importance of its strategic relevance.
- Alliance experience is associated with the opinions of the key decision leaders about organization-based aspects of the alliances (e.g. cultural fit, human fit, organizational form).
- Current alliance use is associated with the opinions of key decision leaders regarding organization-based aspects of alliances (e.g. cultural fit, human fit, organizational form).
- Decision leaders currently using alliances will differ from non-users regarding their opinions about organizational success factors.

## RESEARCH DESIGN AND OPERATIONALIZATION

### Research design

To explore the alliance behavior of small and medium sized manufacturing enterprises we have used a questionnaire developed by the Strategic Alliance Research Group (SARG) (Weaver et al., 1999). This questionnaire was translated into Dutch and back into English to ensure equivalent meanings (cf. Brislin, 1980). Some additional questions were drawn up but we will not cover these topics in this article.

From a sample of 435 independent firms with 5 to 200 employees, 131 firms responded to the questionnaire (Weaver et al., 1999). A limitation of this approach is the use of a single type of data, from responses taken in a single point in time. Thus it is difficult to grasp dynamic developments with this type of research method.

However, it offers a good possibility to identify the experience, opinions and perceptions of key decision leaders. Triangulation, to compare several types of data, and also more longitudinal data would offer greater insights into the processes of alliance behavior. Regarding the latter point, some retrospective questions based on the experience of the respondent, offer a partial solution.

### Operational measures

- *Alliance experience:* Alliance experience was determined by asking respondents the number of times their company had used one or more of 13 different forms of alliances specified in the last five years.
- *Current alliance use:* Current alliance use was measured by asking respondents if they were currently involved in alliances.
- *Entrepreneurial orientation.* Entrepreneurial orientation uses criteria drawn from Covin and Slevin (1989, 1991). An eight-item, five-point scale (alpha = 0.81) assesses the tendencies of the owner/manager towards risk taking, innovation, and proactiveness towards competitors. Due to the small sample, we differentiated between key decision leaders with high and low entrepreneurial orientation on the basis of mean scores on the criteria used to define the entrepreneurial orientation construct.
- *Opinions about organizational aspects of alliances.* In the survey, a number of items are included which measure the perception of managers regarding strategic aspects such as the reasons for entering alliances, perceptions on possibilities of how to grow, and the potential for entrepreneurial networking. Furthermore, questions are asked about organizational factors, including the autonomy of partners, shared visions, the use of information systems, explicit goals, tasks, and responsibility divisions, all of which help to explain the success or failure of alliances.

## RESULTS

In this section, we initially present a general description of the sample and discuss previous alliance experience. Second, we will explore the influence of some individual, organizational, and environmental variables as determinants of current alliance use.

### General description

In Table 12.1 some characteristics of the sample are presented. A look at the table shows that the target key decision leaders reached were male, export orientated, proficient in at least one foreign language, and on average, employed approximately

**Table 12.1:** *Sample characteristics (n = 131)*

| Individual related characteristics | |
| --- | --- |
| Titles: director or assistant director | 79.4% |
| Average age | 44.9 years |
| Male | 90.8% |
| Foreign language proficiency | 82.9% |
| Equity interest | 68% |
| Firm related characteristics | |
| Size (average number of employees) | 42.9 |
| Exporters | 63.1% |
| Top three export markets | Germany, Belgium, United Kingdom |

43 people. Almost 80 per cent of respondents reported prior alliance experience, but only slightly over one-third reported that they were currently involved in alliances. The average number of alliances they are currently involved in was 6.54, the majority with domestic partners. We observed that the export activities of firms (63 per cent) are predominantly in the direct neighboring countries of the Netherlands. This is not surprising, when we consider the significance of the Netherlands as a major distribution center in Europe.

## Alliance experience

More specifically we asked decision leaders if they were involved in alliances such as sub-contracting based alliances, equity-based alliances, joint ventures, or functional (R&D, marketing, production or distribution) oriented alliances (see Table 12.2). We did not expect firms to be active in all types of alliances, but expected a mix of alliance types to exist. To explore this expectation, we performed an exploratory factor analysis. Based on an identified four-dimensional structure, we designed scales of types of alliances. Types of alliance could be correlated because firms active in one type of alliance also might be active in another. This meant that the dimensional structure did not need to be orthogonal. We used the Oblimin rotation method, which allows for correlated factors, while for scale construction we followed steps proposed by Maradi (1981). Moreover, we explored factor based scales as well as using a factor score generated by SPSS through the regression method. For the factor-based scale construction method, items with loadings above a conservative cut-off point (i.e. > 0.40) were taken up in the scale. This is a straightforward method of scaling, but it has the disadvantage that available weighting information is disregarded. However, the factor-scores method uses this information in weighting the scores on items on the basis of the loadings of the items on a factor. Using a regression technique, factor-scores per respondent are made. From a correlation analysis it showed that the comparable scales from the two methods correlated more than 0.90. We checked the Cronbach's alpha for each of the scales constructed. Because of the exploratory nature of the analysis, and the relatively small sample size, in the remainder of the article we use the more easy to interpret factor-based scales.

An examination of the results of the factor analysis enables us to reduce the data into four underlying dimensions. The first dimension is built up from the two items on technology alliances (i.e. score > 0.4 in the pattern matrix). We see in the structure matrix (the matrix with correlations between items and factors) that no other item comes close to the factor (highest is distribution agreements 0.47), which indicates that technology alliances are separable from the other types of alliances. The Cronbach's Alpha of 0.85 indicates a reliable scale. Based on this scale

**Table 12.2a:** *Factor analysis*

| (n = 131)          Items* | Technology-based alliances | Equity-based alliances | Operation-based alliances | Export based alliances |
|---|---|---|---|---|
| Joint venture with small companies | 0.218 | 0.276 | −0.001 | 0.138 |
| Joint ventures with large companies | −0.001 | 0.004 | −0.01 | **0.544** |
| Short-term outside contracting | −0.008 | 0.002 | **0.821** | −0.151 |
| Long-term outside contracting | −0.005 | −0.002 | **0.658** | 0.189 |
| Licensing | −0.009 | 0.332 | 0.108 | −0.002 |
| Long-term marketing agreements | 0.200 | −0.003 | 0.152 | 0.317 |
| Long-term distribution agreements | 0.279 | −0.006 | 0.226 | 0.352 |
| Long-term production agreements | 0.143 | 0.002 | **0.426** | −0.006 |
| Equity investments from small to medium sized companies | 0.002 | **0.949** | −0.122 | −0.007 |
| Equity investment from other companies | −0.14 | **0.606** | 0.132 | 0.29 |
| Export management or trading companies | −0.002 | 0.112 | −0.000 | **0.775** |
| Technology alliances for research and development (process) | **0.550** | 0.268 | 0.006 | 0.214 |
| Technology alliances for research and development (product) | **1.020** | 0.005 | −0.005 | −0.002 |
| Purchaser-supplier alliance | 0.180 | 0.198 | 0.148 | 0.100 |
| Eigen values | 4.48 | 1.63 | 1.20 | 1.07 |
| Per cent of variance explained | 31.9 | 11.7 | 8.6 | 7.7 |
| Alpha | 0.85 | 0.75 | 0.65 | 0.60 |
|  | (2 items) | (2 items) | (3 items) | (2 items) |
| Percentage of firms active in types of alliances | 30% | 50% | 70% | 50% |

*Extraction method: Maximum likelihood. Rotation Method: Oblimin with Kaiser Normalization Rotation converged in 7 iterations*

we established the number of firms with experience of such alliances. This showed that 30 per cent of the firms had experience of technological alliances.

The second dimension is built up from the equity investment items. From the structure matrix we see that the item on technology alliance for process innovation correlates moderately high at 0.59. This indicates that equity investments are relatively often undertaken to achieve process innovation goals. The Cronbach's Alpha is 0.75, which also indicates a strong scale. Half of the firms had prior experience with this kind of alliance.

The third dimension relates to operation based activities such as outside contracting and production alliances. The Cronbach's Alpha of 0.65 indicates a moderate reliable scale. These types of alliances were mentioned by 70 per cent of the firms.

'Export management' and joint-ventures with large companies load heavily on the fourth dimension. This dimension might relate to export oriented alliances with large companies. The Cronbach's Alpha is 0.60, which is the lowest point acceptable in exploratory analysis.

**Table 12.2b:** *Factor analysis alliance type: structure matrix*

| | | Factors | | | |
|---|---|---|---|---|---|
| (n = 131) | Items* | Technology-based alliances | Equity-based alliances | Operation-based alliances | Export based alliances |
| Joint venture with small companies | | 0.37 | 0.42 | 0.17 | 0.33 |
| Joint ventures with large companies | | 0.16 | 0.24 | 0.03 | 0.53 |
| Short-term outside contracting | | 0.20 | 0.14 | 0.76 | 0.03 |
| Long-term outside contracting | | 0.27 | 0.19 | 0.68 | 0.32 |
| Licensing | | 0.27 | 0.39 | 0.22 | 0.19 |
| Long-term marketing agreements | | 0.36 | 0.21 | 0.30 | 0.41 |
| Long-term distribution agreements | | 0.47 | 0.24 | 0.41 | 0.48 |
| Long-term production agreements | | 0.30 | 0.14 | 0.47 | 0.09 |
| Equity investments from small to medium sized companies | | 0.31 | 0.89 | 0.08 | 0.30 |
| Equity investment from other companies | | 0.26 | 0.71 | 0.29 | 0.53 |
| Export management or trading companies | | 0.30 | 0.43 | 0.20 | 0.81 |
| Technology alliances for research and development (process) | | 0.76 | 0.59 | 0.40 | 0.54 |
| Technology alliances for research and development (product) | | 0.97 | 0.41 | 0.35 | 0.31 |
| Purchaser-supplier alliance | | 0.35 | 0.35 | 0.30 | 0.28 |
| Eigen values | | 4.48 | 1.63 | 1.20 | 1.07 |
| Per cent of variance explained | | 31.9 | 11.7 | 8.6 | 7.7 |
| Alpha | | 0.75 | 0.74 | 0.66 | 0.72 |
| Percentage of firms active in types of alliances | | 30% | 50% | 70% | 50% |

*Extraction method: Maximum likelihood. Rotation Method: Oblimin with Kaiser Normalization*
*Rotation converged in 7 iterations*

**Table 12.2c:** *Factor analysis alliance types: factor correlation matrix*

| Factor | 1 | 2 | 3 | 4 |
|---|---|---|---|---|
| 1 | 1.000 | 0.395 | 0.399 | 0.362 |
| 2 | 0.395 | 1.000 | 0.234 | 0.426 |
| 3 | 0.399 | 0.234 | 1.000 | 0.238 |
| 4 | 0.362 | 0.426 | 0.238 | 1.000 |

*Extraction Method: Maximum Likelihood. Rotation Method: Oblimin with Kaiser Normalization.*

## DETERMINANTS OF ALLIANCE EXPERIENCE AND CURRENT ALLIANCE USE

In this section we will consider if key decision leaders who are making current use of alliances differ from non-users in their opinions about organization-based strategic goals, and operational organizational success factors.

### The opinions of entrepreneurs on strategic organizational aspects of alliances

In the survey key decision leaders were asked to give opinions on the importance of strategic aspects of alliances. In Table 12.3, results of a factor analysis of these alliance opinions items are presented. To come to this result we again followed Maradi's steps of exploratory factor analysis. We obtained a vector of factor loadings using maximum likelihood and varimax rotations. Items in this first matrix that did not load to one of the factors were deleted. Furthermore we checked if we could interpret the outcome and developed here also factor-based scales. We report four dimensions, although based on the eigen-vector criterion, five factors would be acceptable. Looking at the screen plot of eigen-vectors, and the interpretability of the scales, we decided to constrain the description to these four factors.

The first factor refers to the perceived necessity for companies to form alliances. The second factor is about teaming with big companies, while the third refers to the entrepreneurial networking of the key decision leader, resulting from a belief in creating opportunities for growth through personal relationships. A fourth 1-item factor is increased attractiveness of the firm for attracting external funds.

Two items: namely, 'creating strategic alliances is an alternative to being acquired' and 'for business interested in growth, alliances offer excellent opportunities' did not load on any of the factors. One way to proceed would be to re-estimate the factors without these items. We do not attempt this here because of the risks of capitalizing on chance in this relatively small sample, but when this strategy was pursued, the first two factors 'necessity to form alliances' and 'teaming with big companies' stay significant, which is an indication of stability regarding these factors.

We calculated Cronbach's alpha for each scale using the bold figures. The results indicate that the first two factors hold together in a one-dimensional scale. The Cronbach's alpha from the third factor, which we interpreted as entrepreneurial networking, is low.

Based on the scales built upon this four-factor solution we subsequently consider how these factors correlate with alliance experience (Table 12.4).

From Table 12.4 we infer that there is a significant positive correlation between key decision leader opinion about the necessity to form an alliance and experience with alliances. Second, there is a positive correlation between entrepreneurial networking and previous experience with alliances.

We also checked if the group of decision leaders currently involved in alliances significantly differed from those not currently involved with respect to the four strategic aspects factors mentioned above using an ANOVA. The results indicate that the key decision leaders using alliances differ significantly from those that are currently not involved in alliances with respect to their opinions about necessity for alliances and entrepreneurial networking. The results show no differences between current alliance users and non-users with respect to teaming with large companies and increased attractiveness. However, for reasons of space limitation we do not present the table. On the basis of this analysis the proposition that decision leaders, currently using alliances, will differ from non-users regarding their opinions about organization-based strategic aspects of alliances is supported for two of the four factors.

### Entrepreneurs opinions on operational organizational alliance success factors

We asked the key decision leaders to indicate what operational organizational factors in their opinion are important to the success of the alliance. In Table 12.5

**Table 12.3:** *Results of factor analysis of opinions about strategic organizational aspects of alliances*

| Items* | 1 Necessity to form alliances | 2 Teaming with big companies | 3 Entrepreneurial networking | 4 Increased attractiveness |
|---|---|---|---|---|
| **1.** With respect to alliance quality … | | | | |
| a) The most important factor in the continuation of a strategic alliance is the chemistry between key individuals | 0.106 | 0.002 | **0.407** | .003 |
| b) It is essential for small companies to have supporters inside big companies to have successful alliances | 0.109 | 0.16 | **0.50** | –0.06 |
| c) In spite of having a monopoly on the business of smaller companies who are alliance partners, large companies rarely behave like arrogant bureaucracies | –0.03 | **0.52** | 0.19 | 0.14 |
| d) The stability of contact persons within alliance partnership companies are a key element in preventing problems. | 0.21 | 0.03 | **0.41** | 0.23 |
| **2.** With respect to necessity for alliances | | | | |
| a) In the future, both large and small companies increasingly will be required to enter into strategic alliances to achieve success. | **0.64** | –0.006 | 0.359 | 0.27 |
| b) Small companies must recognize that they are not self-sufficient. | **0.75** | 0.12 | –0.001 | 0.06 |
| c) It is not enough to be 'small' and entrepreneurial in the future | **0.59** | 0.06 | 0.06 | 0.04 |
| d) Large and small companies will have to increasingly 'network', i.e., enter into strategic alliances, to achieve success | **0.73** | –0.06 | 0.32 | –0.06 |
| e) Small businesses have the ability to identify potential alliance partners and to strike deals that can be mutually profitable. | –0.003 | 0.02 | 0.53 | –0.08 |
| **3.** With respect to growth through alliances… | | | | |
| a) Small companies do not simply enter alliances as lifelines. | **0.42** | 0.103 | 0.33 | 0.002 |
| b) Creating strategic alliances is an alternative to being acquired. | 0.03 | –0.05 | –0.04 | 0.142 |
| c) A strategic alliance can, in the future, increase the attractiveness of a business that decides to go public, seek venture capital, or be acquired. | 0.08 | 0.11 | 0.06 | **0.95** |
| d) For businesses interested in growth, strategic alliances offer excellent opportunities. | 0.282 | 0.186 | 0.36 | 0.30 |

**Table 12.3:** *Continued*

| Items* | 1 Necessity to form alliances | 2 Teaming with big companies | 3 Entrepreneurial networking | 4 Increased attractiveness |
|---|---|---|---|---|
| 4. With respect to teaming with big companies… | | | | |
| a) Big companies have become increasingly receptive to joint projects with smaller, entrepreneurial companies. | 0.04 | **0.61** | 0.06 | 0.05 |
| b) Big companies have learned how to form alliances with small companies without diminishing the small companies' creativity and entrepreneurial strengths. | 0.04 | **0.86** | −0.05 | −0.09 |
| c) Big companies are capable of utilizing the entrepreneurial capabilities of small companies without diminishing the autonomy of the smaller companies | 0.03 | **0.81** | .18 | −0.02 |
| Eigen values | 3.7 | 2.4 | 1.4 | 1.3 |
| Percentage of variance explained | 24 | 15 | 9 | 8 |
| Alpha | 0.80 | 0.79 | 0.56 | Single item |

*Extraction method: Maximum likelihood.*
*Rotation Method: Varimax with Kaiser Normalization*
*Rotation converged in 7 iterations*
*\* All items employed a 5-point Likert-type response scale.*

**Table 12.4:** *Correlations between strategic aspects and alliance experience*

|  | Necessity | Entrepreneurial networking | Teaming with big companies | Increased attractiveness |
|---|---|---|---|---|
| Alliance experience | 0.282* | 0.323* | −0.028 | −0.073 |
| Sig. (2 tailed) | 0.001 | 0.000 | 0.752 | 0.409 |
| N | 129 | 128 | 128 | 129 |

\* *Pearson correlations significant at the 0.01 level (2-tailed)*

we present the results of a factor analysis of alliance success items. Results of the factor analysis show that a common vision for the alliance, key communicators identified, clear and similar goals, similar decision styles, management support and rapid reaction potential score relatively high.

The first factor in Table 12.5 refers to a clear alliance organization indicating the importance of a common vision of the alliance, clear and similar objectives and goals, the identification of key communicators and top management support. The second factor refers to the importance attributed to a flexible alliance organization. Items that hold together are flexible funding and evaluation systems, adaptive legal agreements between alliance companies, top management support and safeguards against any unfriendly takeover by any one company in the alliance. The third factor refers to the availability of systems that would enable firms to act rapidly. Items refer to real-time information systems and flexible funding and evaluation systems. The fourth factor refers to cultural similarity and includes items such as similar decision styles and cooperative corporate cultures. The items on flexible funding and evaluation systems, and support of the CEO, loaded both on two factors. We decided to keep them in this exploratory analysis as we see no interpretation problems for these items in both scales, although for future scaling, rephrasing of the items might be useful. The systems factor is still not very strong and could possibly be improved by using different wording. Building four Likert scales based on the items with a higher loading then 0.4 (bold type face in Table 12.5) we see that the Cronbach's alphas of these scales indicate high to reasonable internal consistency. To test proposition 2c, in which we proposed that the opinions of entrepreneurs on organizational aspects of alliances might differ in relation to their experience, we looked at the bivariate correlations between the four factors and alliance experience. This showed that only clear organization correlated significantly (0.34) with the degree of alliance experience of the firms. We also checked if the group of decision leaders currently involved in alliances significantly differed from those not currently involved with respect to their opinion on the four success factors mentioned in Table 12.5, using an ANOVA. The results indicate that the key decision leaders using alliances differ significantly from those that are currently not involved in alliances with respect to their opinions about the importance of a clear and flexible alliance organization as an important determinant of alliance success. The results show no differences between current alliance users and non-users with respect to the other two success factors, namely information systems and cultural similarity. For reasons of space limitation we will not present the table. On the basis of this analysis the proposition that decision leaders currently using alliances will differ from non-users regarding their opinions about organizational success factors is supported for two of the four factors.

**Table 12.5:**  *Results of factor analysis of operational organizational alliance success items*

| (n = 131)  Items* | Factors | | | |
|---|---|---|---|---|
| | 1 Clear alliance organization | 2 Flexible alliance organization | 3 Systems | 4 Cultural similarity |
| 1. In your opinion how important are the following factors for the success of the alliance? | | | | |
| a)  Separation/autonomy of alliance participants | 0.18 | 0.07 | 0.02 | −0.22 |
| b)  Common vision for the alliance | **0.74** | −0.05 | 0.15 | −0.09 |
| c)  Free-market environment | 0.32 | 0.28 | 0.28 | −0.48 |
| d)  Real-time information systems | 0.05 | 0.07 | **0.84** | 0.12 |
| e)  Flexible funding and evaluation systems | 0.21 | **0.42** | **0.47** | −0.03 |
| f)  Key communicators identified | **0.56** | 0.18 | 0.34 | −0.01 |
| g)  Clear and similar objectives and goals | **0.86** | 0.22 | 0.01 | 0.11 |
| h)  Adaptive legal agreements between alliance companies | 0.13 | **0.57** | 0.03 | 0.20 |
| i)  Similar decision styles | 0.05 | 0.33 | 0.15 | **0.66** |
| j)  Cooperative corporate culture | 0.30 | 0.31 | 0.22 | **0.53** |
| k)  Support of the chief executive officers of each company | **0.60** | **0.45** | −0.08 | 0.09 |
| l)  Safeguards against an unfriendly takeover by any one company in the alliance | 0.02 | **0.64** | 0.06 | 0.13 |
| m)  Alliance structures will allow rapid response to problems | 0.20 | **0.55** | 0.24 | −0.07 |
| Eigen values | 3.93 | 1.78 | 1.31 | 1.14 |
| Percentage of variance explained | 30.2 | 13.7 | 10.1 | 8.8 |
| Alpha | 0.78 | 0.69 | 0.55 | 0.65 |

*Extraction method: Generalized least squares; Rotation Method: Varimax with Kaiser Normalization; Rotation converged in 7 iterations; All items employed a 5-point Likert-type response scale.*

# DISCUSSION AND CONCLUSION

Here we will discuss the results following the two research goals and propositions made earlier in this paper.

## Strategic organizational determinants of alliance use

Results of a factor analysis suggest that there are four groups of underlying strategic reasons for the decision leaders to be involved in alliances. First, decision leaders viewed necessity as an important aspect. The respondent companies form alliances because they are deemed necessary (i.e. companies are compelled to form alliances in order to succeed – given general developments in the (global) economy). A second strategic aspect perceived to be important by the respondents is more opportunity related and refer to the advantage gained by teaming with large companies in order to, for example, acquire resources. The results suggest that key decision leaders have a positive attitude towards teaming with large companies. A third factor perceived to be important is the potential for entrepreneurial networking. In the opinion of the key decision leaders surveyed, the entrepreneurial capabilities of each separate company, in combination with strong and stable personal ties, have the potential to create excellent opportunities for business growth, and this in turn is ensured by the personal involvement of the key decision leaders. Results of an ANOVA analysis indicated that key decision leaders using alliances differ significantly from non-users with respect to their opinions about the necessity for alliances and entrepreneurial networking. Users seem to find it more necessary to cooperate then non-alliance-users. This indicates that low alliance users might have the possibility to co-operate, but do not see why they should do so. The results indicate no differences between current alliance users and non-users with respect to teaming with large companies and increased attractiveness.

## Operational organizational determinants of alliance use

On the basis of a factor analysis we found four factors which, in the opinion of the key decision leaders, are important determinants of alliance success, namely: clear organization, flexible organization, availability of systems and cultural similarity. Correlational analysis and results of an ANOVA procedure supported the proposition that decision leaders currently using alliances will differ from non-users regarding their opinions about organizational success factors. More specifically this is supported for clear and flexible alliance organization. It is interesting to note that all four factors are essentially in the realm of management control. This finding is in line with theoretical assumptions that agree that the success of alliances is more dependent on the management of the cooperation process than on conforming to a set of initial conditions (Ring and Van de Ven, 1994; Doz, 1996). The factors provide an insight into key decision makers' perceptions with respect to critical success factors within the alliance process. A clearly managed organization, for instance, refers to clear and similar objectives and goals, with a clear vision of what the alliance stands for. Direct support from other key decision leaders is essential in this respect. In addition, key communicators have to be identified within each of the partner organizations. Apparently key decision leaders view a clearly managed organization as a guarantee that people involved in alliance activities can operate in an entrepreneurial way. Furthermore, in case of trouble no time is lost in searching for people who are in a position to act. The essence of a flexible organization is adaptability to changing circumstances and security from an unsolicited change in ownership between alliance partners. Adaptability is necessary, given the unpredictability of the environment of the alliance, but also within the individual partner companies. Operational flexibility is realized through flexible funding, evaluation mechanisms, and information systems. Information systems enable close monitoring of alliance activities, and in combination with flexible funding and evaluation systems, can support managers and help them to realize alliance objectives. As with clearly managed organizations, decision leaders are apparently of the opinion that their personal support is an important condition for realizing operational flexibility. We found no difference in the reported importance of this factor between alliance users and non-users. Furthermore, key decision leaders view cultural similarity as an important success factor. Similarity helps to prevent misunderstandings about meaning and intent, and this is especially important in a volatile and changing business environment.

Results of this study suggest that an increased understanding of key decision leader orientations and opinions could help explain firm-level involvement in alliances. During and Kerkhof (cited in During and Oakey, 1998), who discuss research into the management style of successful European small business managers in eight different countries, noted that Dutch manufacturing companies seem to be particularly oriented towards a project oriented management structure. We need to consider a combination of the degree of subcontracting activity, a favorable attitude towards large companies, and a strong preference for project-based structures when we attempt to explain the low incidence of entrepreneurial networking. A compelling extension of this research would be to understand and explain how individual level orientations and opinions are related to firm level performance. This will call for a research design in which data are drawn from several different partners in the alliance. Another suggestion for future research is to explore if responses to various strategies and success factors within alliances would differ, depending on alliance type, industrial setting, and country. Such an inquiry may also shed more light in understanding why different types of alliances are used in specific countries. Finally, future research should make explicit the reasons for non-involvement in alliances in order to improve the effectiveness of policy initiatives initiated by government and industry associations aimed at stimulating alliance formation.

## ACKNOWLEDGEMENT

The authors acknowledge the contribution of Vivek Nagpaul to the SARG 1 project of which this paper is a part. We published with him elsewhere (Weaver et al., 1999; Nagpaul et al., 1998) on the topic of the use of ICT in managing alliances.

## REFERENCES

Aldrich, H. and Zimmer, C. (1986) 'Entrepreneurship Through Social Networks'. In: Sexton, D. and Smilor, R.W. (eds) *The Art and Science of Entrepreneurship*, Massachusetts: Ballinger Publishing, pp. 3–23.

Brislin, R.W. (1980) 'Translation and Content Analysis of Oral and Written Materials'. In: H.C. Triandis and J.W. Berry (eds) *Handbook of Cross-cultural Psychology*, 2, pp. 389–444. Boston: Allyn and Bacon.

Burt, R.S. (1992) *Structural Holes: The Social Structure of Competition*, Cambridge: Harvard University Press.

Covin, J.G. and Slevin, D.P. (1989) 'Strategic Management of Small Firms in Hostile and Benign Environments', *Strategic Management Journal*, 10, pp. 75–87.

Covin, J.G. and Slevin, D.P. (1991) 'A Conceptual Model of Entrepreneurship as Firm Behavior', *Entrepreneurship Theory and Practice*, 16 (1), pp. 7–25.

Das, T.K. and Teng, B.-S. (1997) 'Sustaining Strategic Alliances: Options and Guidelines', *Journal of General Management*, Vol. 22, No. 4.

Dickson, P.H. and Weaver, K.M. (1997) 'Environmental determinants and individual level moderators of Alliance use'. *Academy of Management Journal*, 40, pp. 404–425.

Douma, M.U. (1997) 'Strategic Alliances: Fit or Failure', Ph.D. thesis, University of Twente, Enschede, The Netherlands, Elinkwijk: Utrecht.

Doz, Y.L. (1996) 'The evolution of co-operation in strategic alliances: initial conditions or learning processes?' *Strategic Management Journal*, Vol. 17, pp. 55–83.

During, W.E., Kerkhof, M., Klein Woolthuis, R.J.A. and de Smit, J.M.J. (1997) In Hans Landstrom, H. Frank. and J.M. Veciana (eds), *Entrepreneurship and Small Business Research in Europe*, Avebury: Aldershot.

During, W.E. and Klein Woolthuis, R.J.A. (1997) 'The Character of Entrepreneurial Networking', Rent V conference paper, Mannheim, Germany.

During, W.E. and Oakey, R. (1998) 'High Technology Small Firms: Entrepreneurial Activity and the Co-operation Process'. In Willem, E., During, W.E. and Oakey, R. (eds) *New Technology-Based Firms in the 1990s, Volume IV*, London: Paul Chapman Publishing.

Dyer, Jeffrey and Singh, Harbir (1998) 'The Relational View: Cooperative Strategy and Sources of Inter-organizational Competitive Advantage'. In: *Academy of Management Review*, Vol. 23, No. 4, pp. 660–680.

Granovetter, M.S. (1973) 'The Strength of Weak Ties', *American Journal of Sociology*, 78 (6), pp. 1360–1381.

Granovetter, M.S. (1992) 'Problems of explanations in economic sociology'. In N. Nohria and R. Eccles (eds) *Handbook of Economic Sociology*, Princeton University Press: Boston, NJ, pp. 453–475.

Groen, A.J. (1994) 'Milieu en MKB: Kennis en Kennissen, milieuinnovatie in de grafische industrie: modelmatig verklaard' (Environment and SME; Environmental innovation in printing industry quantitatively explained). Groningen, Ph.D.Thesis in economics, management and organization, Wolters-Noordhof, Groningen.

Groen, A.J. and Nooteboom, B. (1998) 'Environmental Innovation: Knowledge and Networks'. Paper presented at Egos colloquium, Maastricht, The Netherlands.

Håkansson, H. (ed.) (1987) *Industrial Technological Development: A Network Approach*, London: Croom Helm.

Håkansson, H. (1989) *Corporate technological behavior: co-operation and networks*, London: Routledge.

Håkansson, H., and Johanson, J. (1993) 'Industrial functions of business relations'. In Grabher, G. (ed.) *The Embedded Firm*. London: Routledge, pp. 15–31.

Håkansson, H. and Sharma, H.D. (1996) 'Strategic Alliances in a Network Perspective'. In: Iacobucci, D. (ed.) *Networks in Marketing*. New Delhi, Sage Publications, pp. 108–124.

Håkansson, H. and Snehota, I. (1995) 'Networks in Technological development'. In Håkansson, H. and Snehota, I. (eds) *Developing relationships in business networks*. Routledge, London.

Hamel, G., Doz, Y. and Prahalad, C. (1989) 'Collaborate with your Competitors and Win', *Harvard Business Review*, January-February, pp. 133–139.

Iacobucci, D. (ed.) (1996) *Networks in Marketing*, New Delhi: Sage Publications.

John, G. (1984) 'An Empirical Investigation of some antecedents of opportunism in a marketing channel', *Journal of Marketing*, 21 (2), pp. 278–289.

Larson, A. (1992) 'Network Dyads in Entrepreneurial Settings: A Study of the Governance of Exchange Relationships', *Administrative Science Quarterly*, 37, pp. 76–104.

Luimes, W. and Spitholt, M. (1994) 'Ontvlecting van Concurrentie Onderdelen: Een onderzoek naar de invloed van cultural (mis)fit human (mis)fit en synergie/ antagonie', Ph.D. thesis, University of Twente, Coopers and Lybrand: Hengelo.

Lumpkin, G.T. and Dess, G.G. (1996) 'Clarifying the Entrepreneurial Orientation Construct and Linking it to Performance', *Academy of Management Review*, 21, pp. 135–172.

Macmillan, J.C. (1983) The Politics of New Venture Management. In: *Harvard Business Review*, November-December.

Maradi, A. (1981) Factor analysis as an aid in the formation and refinement of empirically useful concepts. In: Jackson, D.J. and Borgatta, E.F. (eds) *Factor Analysis and Measurement in Sociological Research*, London: Sage.

Miles, R.E. and Snow, C.C. (1978) *Organizational Strategy, Structure, and Process*, New York: McGraw-Hill.

Miller, D. (1983) 'The Correlates of Entrepreneurship in three types of firms', *Management Science*, 29, pp. 770–791.

Monsted, M. (1996) 'Strategic alliances as an analytical perspective for innovative SMEs'. In *Proceedings 4th Annual High Technology Small Firms Conference*, 5th, 6th, September 1996, Enschede, the Netherlands.

Monsted, M. (1998) 'Strategic alliances as an analytical perspective for innovative SMEs'. In: During W. and Oakey R.P. (eds) *New Technology-based firms in the 1990s*, Vol. IV, Paul Chapman, London.

Nagpaul, V., During, W.E., Groen, A.J. and Weaver, M. (1998) 'Use of information and communication technology in small to medium sized enterprise-based alliances in the Netherlands manufacturing sector: a key decision leader perspective', *Presented at The R&D Management Conference, Technology Strategy and Strategic Alliances*, 11 pp. Avila, Spain, 30-9/2-10-1998.

Nooteboom, B.H. (1994) 'Innovation and Diffusion in Small Firms: Theory and Evidence', *Small Business Economics*, 6, pp. 327–347.

Nooteboom, B., Berger, H. and Noorderhaven, N. (1997) Effects of Trust and Governance on Relational Risk, *Academy of Management Journal*, 40(2), pp. 308–338.

Powell, W.W., Koput, K.W. and Smith-Doerr, L. (1996) 'Interorganizational Collaboration and the Locus of Innovation: Networks of Learning in Biotechnology', *Administrative Science Quarterly*, 41(1), pp. 116–145.

Ring, P. and Van de Ven, A. (1992) 'Structuring co-operative relationships between organizations', *Strategic Management Journal*, Vol. 13, pp. 483–498.

Ring, P. and Van de Ven, A. (1994) 'Developmental Processes of Cooperative Inter-organizational Relationships', *Academy of Management Review*, Vol. 19, No. 1, pp. 90–118.

Verspagen, B., Kleinknecht, A.H. and Hollanders, en H. (1998) De innovatie achterstand van Nederlandse bedrijven (The innovation lag of Dutch companies), Rotterdam, RIBES.

Weaver, M., During, W., Groen, A., Nagpaul, V. and Dickson, P. (1999) 'Entrepreneurial Orientation as a Predictor of Perceived Environmental Uncertainty and of Alliance Involvement: the Case of Small to Medium Sized Manufacturing Enterprises in the Netherlands'. In: Ray Oakey, Wim Duirng and Syeda-Masooda Mukhtar, (eds) *New Technology Based-Firms in the 1990s, vol. VI*, Pergamon.

Williamson, O.E. (1985) *The Economic Institutions of Capitalism: Firms, Markets, Relational Contracting*, New York: Free Press.

Williamson, O.E. (1991) 'Comparative Economic Organization: The Analysis of Discrete Structural Alternatives', *Administrative Science Quarterly*, 36, 269–296.

CHAPTER 13

# New Product Development (NPD) Alliances between Research Institutes and SMEs: The Development, Technology Transfer and Spin-Off of Advanced Material Burners

PETRA C. DE WEERD-NEDERHOF AND AARD J. GROEN

## INTRODUCTION

Changes in market demands imposed upon organizations are important driving forces for change within organizations. Changing the functionality of products in the value creation processes for clients, or delivering value in other parts of the value chain raise questions for the management of organizations; namely can we do this ourselves? Can we purchase elements necessary for upgrading our value creation process, or should we collaborate? In many circumstances firms choose to focus on developing their core competences and collaborate or use the market mechanism to outsource those parts that do not fit within their core competence profile (Hamel and Prahalad, 1994). However, when looking into processes, such as technology development related to product development, this choice might occur at several stages in the development process. In the first phases of the NPD process, developers have to consider if they are sufficiently knowledgeable on all facets of the technology. Other actors might develop parts of the development process more efficiently. This is specifically relevant in cases where research institutes take the initiative for collaboration in NPD, since they cannot manufacture and sell the new products themselves, and often also lack experience with (manufacturing) process development. This means that, for the commercialization of NPD activities, research institutes have to rely on external parties to transfer knowledge about their prospective new product (which is often a prototype). These external parties then have to create a production and marketing process.

This approach of generating knowledge in a research setting and commercializing it in a production and marketing setting is problematic because of the need to develop complex dependencies between the research process and organization experienced in the production and marketing of new products. For example market demands might determine important choices to be made in the research phase of new product development processes. On the other hand, of course, outcomes of the research process may determine what is possible in the production and marketing phase of the product. The involvement of many different actors collaborating in order to carry out these processes often adds to the complexity. Generally, heterogeneous networks of specialized research groups and integrators also play a growing role in NPD processes (Rip and Groen, 2000). The strategic technology partnerships necessary for such collaboration can be carried out in a wide variety of organizational modes, ranging from (strategic) alliances to new ventures (Tidd et al., 1997). Hagedoorn (1996) argues that *'these different modes of co-operation have a distinctive impact on the character of technology sharing, the organizational context and the possible economic consequences for participating companies'*. One mechanism used in this context is to create 'spin off' companies in collaboration with network partners, which increasingly are often (new) small- to medium sized enterprises (SMEs). In terms of the different types of collaboration distinguished by Tidd et al. (1997), the complete 'spin off' is a new venture which '*is essentially a divestment option, where the corporation wants to pass over total responsibility for an activity, both commercially and administratively'*. In carrying out NPD in heterogeneous networks, the management of research institutes and collaborating partner/SMEs are faced with various problems concerning the establishment and management of their alliances. Managing NPD in cases of complete 'spin off' does not only require the management and support of the actual technology and product development processes, but also processes of technology transfer, and even the organizational design of the newly formed company. The success of these processes may be affected by decisions taken as early as during the signing of the license agreement in a specific case. These problems boil down to questions of determining **with whom** to form an alliance, which is strongly influenced by the reasons **why** and **how** to align.

## OBJECTIVES OF THE PAPER

The objective of this paper is to explore NPD alliances between research institutes and SMEs. Combining a process-based contingency model with a social systems model develops a framework for description and analysis of NPD alliances. In applying the framework to the case of the development of an advanced material burner, we focus on a relationship in which the research institute seeks collaboration in order to generate a 'spin off' company for the production and commercialization of a specific piece of developed technology. The paper starts with a theoretical section that ends with the presentation of the analytical framework. The next section presents the case study, which consists of a retrospective part (i.e. the development of the advanced material burner, started more than ten years ago), as well as an analysis of current NPD alliances. Our focus is on the discussion of the suitability of the above framework for the description and analysis of these processes and alliances, and on the retrospective part of the case study.

## BUILDING A FRAMEWORK FOR ANALYSIS

From the introduction above it is clear that, in the analysis of heterogeneous networks of organizations carrying out NPD activities, more multi-dimensional analysis is necessary to better understand the complex nature of the collaborative development processes. Our basic point of departure in dealing with this is an approach in which we focus on *processes of interaction* between *actors* in a network developing new technologies. The framework for description and analysis of NPD alliances is first of all based on a process-based contingency model designed for description and analysis of the new product development process (de Weerd-Nederhof, 1998). Although this model is developed and tested with the organization as the focal analysis level, it has the advantage that it allows the NPD process and function to be examined across organizational barriers, which is crucial for NPD undertaken by research institutes. Since it is also a contingency model, it facilitates the taking into account of contingencies, both internal and external to the organization. The second cornerstone for the development of the framework is a more generic social system model developed from the work of Parsons (1951, 1977). This model adds a set of dimensions to the framework by erecting an analytical space in which social complexity can be reduced systematically in a multi-level and multi-dimensional analysis of relations within networks (Groen, 1994, 2000). Below we will discuss both models in more depth, after which we present the key-elements of the framework.

## The process-based contingency model tailored to NPD

The process-based contingency model treats organizations as purposeful systems of people and resources which, using multiple technologies, together achieve certain 'activities' or 'processes' in order to transform inputs into outputs (Boer and Krabbendam, 1991). The main assumption underlying the model explicitly refers to the link between effectiveness and configuration. An organization is assumed to be effective if the constituent elements of the organization are compatible with each other and with their environment. The model thus explicitly acknowledges that organizations do not operate in a vacuum: they depend on their context for inputs, outputs and (human) resources. The specific (contextual) elements relevant to a particular organizational subsystem can be identified through an examination of the input-output relationships of the constituent processes. When identifying and describing NPD contexts one is immediately confronted with the fact that NPD is:

> 'typically a collective achievement, not an individual activity. No single individual (function) can master the diverse knowledge which is required in today's demanding environment in order to effectively and efficiently conceptualize, design, produce, and market new products (...). All product development projects are characterized by high levels of reciprocal interdependence between parties that participate in, are interested in, or are affected by product design decisions'. (Emmanuelides, 1993)

NPD systems in which research institutes are included almost by definition cross organizational borders. The first step in describing the **(who)** elements of the NPD process-based model is the identification of a partner, which can be different for each company and for each particular NPD project.

The process of partner search is crucial since it determines the specific form of the alliance (i.e. formal or informal) and whether letters of intent or detailed research contracts or license agreements, etc. will underwrite it. To start with the latter point, Bidault and Cummings (1994) mention the tension between what they call the dynamics of technological innovation (requiring adjustable and flexible management processes) and the logic of partnering (emphasizing clarity and explicitness). According to them, *the nature of the innovation* project, as well as the *characteristics of the partnership* (including the *context* in which it is operating and the reasons **why** it is being formed), should be taken into account when designing the specific form of the alliance. Alongside the fact that research institutes need to find (external) partners who will carry out the producer business functions 'in-house' (such as manufacturing and product marketing/sales), the process of partner search may be guided by the need for quality inputs to the NPD process, which according to Hart and Baker (1994), require the accommodation of third parties ensuring, for example, user-relevance and supplier-support. Alignment should, however, not only occur for reasons of uncovering opportunities and identifying market demands, it is just as important for NPD systems to be aware of *constraints* imposed upon new product development. These might involve legislation on product safety, product liability, environmental laws, or already existing patents.

Biemans (1992) suggests five characteristics of interactions: type of interaction (vertical/horizontal; competitive/complementary); purpose of interaction (task performance or task simulation); intensity of interaction; duration of interaction and formalization of interaction. Following the recommendation of Hart and Baker to view alignment and alliances in terms of interactions in networks, in a process-based contingency model, these characteristics are used to describe the alignment (**how**) involving the partners and functions in terms of an outside NPD process. The operationalization of the process-based contingency model tailored to NPD (de Weerd-Nederhof, 1998) further contains separate mapping tools for the description of goals (strategic, adaptive and operational), processes (primary, management and support), people (NPD workers and managers), tools and techniques (techniques, IT, equipment), and organizational arrangements. Organizational arrangements are described at individual (i.e. jobs, roles), group (i.e. teams, procedures) and organizational (i.e. structure, culture) levels. Analysis of the above described NPD system is facilitated by assessing performance fit as well as configurational fit, both in terms of the already performance dimensions of operational effectiveness and strategic flexibility. *Performance fit* is the degree to which the strategic, adaptive and operational goals set for the product concept performance fit with market demands and firm competencies and the NPD process performance requirements of speed, productivity and flexibility, set in the context of how actual performance is achieved regarding both performance dimensions. *Configurational fit* is determined by identifying the features of the NPD configuration, which either contribute to the matches or cause the gaps in the performance fit. Note that the concept of fit is *dynamic*, meaning that it should be possible to deal with (continuous) changes in operational effectiveness and strategic flexibility issues. In fact, it is stressed that NPD management is an act of balancing short- and long-term issues as well as finding a balance in satisfying internal and external stakeholders. In line with this, shortcomings in one configurational element can dynamically balance strengths in another. For example it was found that badly designed horizontal linkages, hindering in-depth contacts between members of cross-functional teams representing the same business function, may – especially in small organizations – be balanced by an innovative climate and strong leadership (de Weerd-Nederhof, 1998).

## Social system model

In common with the process-based contingency model, the social system model treats actors as purposeful systems of people interacting with each other. In Parsons' definition of a social system, an actor is seen in a dynamic context in which interaction between actors is a central mechanism of the development of the system:

> 'Reduced to the simplest possible terms, then, a social system consists in a plurality of individual actors interacting with each other in a situation which has at least a physical or environmental aspect, actors who are motivated in terms of a tendency to the

optimization of gratification *and whose relation to their situations, including each other, is defined and mediated in terms of* culturally structured and shared symbols.' (Parsons, 1964, pp. 5–6, emphasis added)

In this definition four mechanisms are built: the interaction mechanism; the motivation or goal setting mechanism; the optimization of gratification or economizing mechanism, and a pattern maintenance mechanism. During interaction, actors use resources in such a way as to expect good results regarding goal attainment. Actors search for economically efficient ways to reach goals, and use culturally structured and shared symbols learnt through experience or in educational systems. Actors behave sub-optimally due to bounded rationality, and although a social system might look stable when seen from a high level of analysis, during specific interaction processes they need not be in balance. The interesting point in the original Parsons' theory is the explicit concern for the multi-dimensionality of social system interactions, and the enthusiasm for multi-level analysis. In social system theory, actors act in four dimensions, which are hypothesized as multi-level enabling and constraining mechanisms. For each of the mechanisms actors have an amount of 'capital' available. During interaction, actors use this capital more or less successfully, which leads to recursive relations between capital use in one situation, and later possibilities.

1. Actors interact with other actors choosing network positions and relating in a complex way, but are dependent on other actors' actions towards them. This leads to social capital.
2. Actors set goals and try to attain them, but are also constrained by the goals of other actors (i.e. political/strategic capital).
3. Actors maintain patterns of behavior and value patterns, but are influenced by the patterns of others (i.e. cultural capital).
4. Actors adapt their processes to work as efficiently as possible, but also have to use or compete for production systems of others (i.e. economic capital).

Although it is clear that the social system model starts from interaction between actors, structural and institutional influences are also evident. Structural influences can be analyzed by network analysis providing a picture of positions of actors in a field of technological development. In this sense the social system model can be linked with the three levels of organizational arrangements in the process-based contingency model, and it enhances its analytic strengths by viewing the network structure as more explicit, and as an endogenous part of the analysis. In Figure 13.1, relational analysis of relations between two actors is depicted. Adding to a structural analysis of relations in a network, the content analysis can be built up by the three other mechanisms. Figure 13.2 lists the main characteristics of all four mechanisms, which will be discussed in relationship to each other in more detail below.

*Pattern maintenance mechanisms* relate to, for example, technological regimes (Rip et al., 1995), which guide actors in choosing specific solutions to specific technological problems. In the domain of innovation adoption research, Gatignon and Robertson (1985) point out that actors with different propensities towards innovation decide and learn in different ways than 'non-innovators'. When analyzing collaborative relations in new product development processes this leads to questions about differences between the actors involved, and their propensity to innovate. Furthermore, not all knowledge creation processes are explicit for the actor. Michael Polany's (1966) concept of 'tacit knowledge' – the fact that

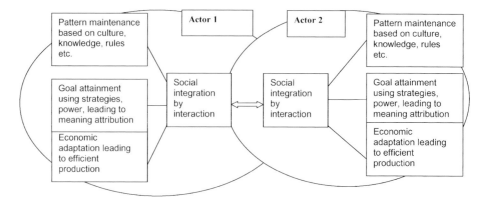

**Figure 13.1:** Two-actor model of network of actors in social system perspective

*1 Goal attainment mechanisms (strategy related):*
Using power/authority.
Jockeying for position in the network, searching for power bases to influence partners and other actors.
Alliances with actors who have congruent goals, leading to economies of scale, skill, or scope.

*2 Pattern maintenance mechanisms (culture related):*
Building up knowledge by interacting.
Making rules explicit (contract, convenants, trustworthy relations).
Building on culture: congruent value systems defining role-relation patterns.

*3 Adaptation mechanisms (economic efficiency related):*
Make buy or make decisions related to efficiency.
Change production system in relation to a chain of activities.

*4 Social integration mechanisms (network related):*
Networking using holes in network structure.
Cohesive interaction with other actors.
Equivalent interaction as 'role models'.

**Figure 13.2:** Mechanisms to influence and to be influenced by

individuals appear to know more than they can explain – offers insights into why firms with the same kind of information about an innovation (cp.) do not necessarily behave in the same way (Kogut and Zander, 1992; Nooteboom, 1992; Nonaka and Takeuchi, 1995). The scheme of interpretation of information is a function of cognitive skills built up in earlier interactions with other actors in other contexts. Von Hippel (1988) defined know-how as the 'accumulated practical skill or expertise that allows one to do something smoothly and efficiently'. Know-how becomes a part of the value system of the social system defining more or less acceptable/possible (changes in) behavior. Although 'blue-print' information about an innovation seems to be generally applicable, it might not fit with the know-how of the firm. In that case the cognitive distance between know-how of the firm and the cognitive skills necessary to adopt an innovation is large. In other words compatibility in relation to current practice in the social system of the innovation is relatively low.

The important aspect here is that one has to assess the knowledge available in the social system to explain or predict whether an innovation is compatible to this context. Or in other words is the social system able to learn the adaptations necessary to adopt an innovation? A useful concept here is *'cultural capital'* from

Bourdieu, (1973, 1980) who indicates closeness to the central values of a social system based on the level of education an actor received, and by reproduction of these values through experience. It stands for the cognitive strength of an actor in a social system, but is generated in a process of reproduction and accumulation of knowledge in interaction with other actors. More specifically for firms, Cohen and Levinthal (1990) developed the concept of 'absorptive capacity' to indicate the ability of a firm to adapt to newly available knowledge. Differences of absorptive capacity between collaborative partners may lead to serious distortions of knowledge transfer from one to another.

In the *economic domain*, differences in *efficiency* explain differences in the success of actors exploiting new technology. Analyzing the compatibility of economic processes of actors collaborating on new product development shows important demands on the product development process.

From the analysis above it is clear that the social system dimensions are not independent. Central to the analysis of dependencies is the interaction process between actors and the consequent structure of networks that follows, which returns us to the *integrative network* dimension. One might see this as an analysis of fit between cultural, strategic, and economic patterns and processes between the two partners, although it is not assumed that there should be a fit on all dimensions in order to be able to cooperate. Problems with one type of fit might be solved by a good fit in another dimension. For example, one partner having too little knowledge and experience to be able to judge the quality of the work of the other, might be solved by using a third actor, trusted by both actors in a partnership, to solve disputes. In Twente the use of 'flight leaders' coaching cooperating high-tech small firms in networks between the university and other larger firms is an example of balancing a relational misfit. Here, in acknowledging the dynamics of the multi-dimensional fit, and stressing the possibility of problems, as well as the need for balancing, the analytical approach of the social system model again links with the one advocated in the process-based contingency model, where also the dimensions are not independent: strategic flexibility in fact is a prerequisite of future operational effectiveness.

### Framework for description and analysis of NPD alliances

Combining the process-based contingency model tailored to NPD with the social system model as described above, we arrive at a framework for description and analysis which centers around the primary processes of technology and product development and technology transfer. This means that the *description* first of all focuses on the input, output, activities and phases of these two processes, as well as, of course, on the management and support processes linked to them. The description of people and organizational arrangements carrying out these processes (configurational elements of the process-based contingency model) is achieved following the social system model involving people as individual actors. The structural and cultural organizational arrangements are represented by the interaction mechanisms at the individual, firm and environmental levels, and constitute the multi-level network of actors in the social system perspective.

*Analysis* starts with an assessment of the operational effectiveness and strategic flexibility of the NPD system as a whole (incorporating technology and product development and technology transfer), and then 'zooms in' on the process phases of the constituent processes by analyzing in more detail the fit of the four different interaction mechanisms. Figure 13.3 presents the elaborated mapping tool, which is the starting point for this part of the analysis.

*Mapping of goal attainment processes:*
- Which goals have actors set (content)
- Mapping of power, influence or authority base of actors involved (strategic capital)
- Mapping of dynamics of goal attainment (games)

*Mapping adaptation mechanisms:*
- Describe nature of economic production processes of actors involved
- Describe possibilities of going it alone or possibilities of buying (make or buy)
- Analyze economies of scale, skills, or scope by alliance compared to working apart

*Mapping of pattern maintenance mechanisms:*
- What knowledge is used in partnership, differences and communalities?
- What management style is used by partners involved?
- Role of rules and contracts versus trust in business practice of NPD network partners
- What organizational arrangements are in use?
- Formal versus informal practices
- Attitude towards innovative elements in the NPD process
- Which techniques are being used by partners?

*Mapping the network of involved or influential actors:*
- What position in network of knowledge, power, economy are actors in (structural holes, brokerage position, prominence)?
- What type of cohesive interaction takes place between whom (frequency, duration, intensity: weak versus strong ties)?
- Find equivalent interaction patterns as role model

**Figure 13.3:** Elaborated mapping tool combining process-based contingency model (tailored to NPD) and social system model for description of NPD alliances

## THE CASE OF ADVANCED MATERIAL BURNERS

### *Methodology*

The empirical data gathering was carried out as a qualitative case study in two phases. Firstly, a retrospective case study describing and analyzing the development of advanced material burners mainly from the viewpoint of HeatCo in terms of the primary, management and support processes, as well as the people involved (from HeatCo and BurnerInc) NPD tools used, and organizational arrangements in place, included the mechanisms for internal and external alignment (described in detail in de Weerd-Nederhof, 1998). In total nine people were interviewed and documentation was studied. This included an article written by the former general manager of HeatCo on the improvement of market orientedness of the research institute, project information on the advanced material burner development projects, brochures, and the business plan of BurnerInc.

The second phase of the case study concerned the evaluation and analysis of the development of the advanced material burner as well as the current situation regarding the 'spin off' company and its interactions with the research institute, from the viewpoint of BurnerInc and the (national) subsidizing agency (StoER = Stimulation of Energy Research) which heavily funded the development and technology transfer activities (described in detail in Vos, 2000). In total eight people were interviewed from BurnerInc, HeatCo and the subsidizing agency StoER. In two workshop-type meetings the descriptive and analytic findings were discussed with representatives from BurnerInc, StoER and HeatCo.

### *Basic information on HeatCo*

HeatCo is an energy research institute (founded in 1955), employing 900 people distributed between seven different business units. Each autonomous business unit covers a specific energy product-market combination. The development of the advanced material burners took place in the business unit concerned with fossil fuels. HeatCo's overall mission is energy innovation: the development of technologies for a safe, clean and efficient supply of energy. It is a specific company policy not to manufacture any product developed 'in-house', since industrial companies licensing the technology from HeatCo must do this. Note that up to the beginning of the 1980s HeatCo was almost 100 per cent government funded. Subsequently the annual subsidy was drastically decreased and HeatCo had to start earning income through co-operation with industrial parties. In the near future, further changes in government funding will take place, obliging HeatCo to establish many more formal alliances with industries, covering most of their activities.

### Developing the advanced material burner: background information

Based on an initiative from an energy producer, and financially supported by StoER, the starting point of this project was to develop an advanced material burner. The main application of this burner was in central heating systems, but use in industrial ovens was also envisaged. The main advantages of the advanced material burner would have to be low NOx emission, low noise, lower cost, and continuous modulation. The burner would be a substitute for existing burners. The programme was begun at the end of the 1980s with an envisaged duration of about six years. However, it was more or less completed from the viewpoint of HeatCo after 10 years.

The project was started as a combined initiative of HeatCo and an energy producer. Halfway through the programme a license agreement was made with a burner manufacturer, but after some time this company decided not to proceed. It took quite some time to find a new manufacturer, and this was BurnerInc, a small company established as a 'spin off' company specifically for the purpose of producing and marketing the advanced material burner. By this time, the performance of other types of burners had considerably improved and part of the competitive advantage was lost. BurnerInc had no experience in the market sector and no market share. The potential market was huge, but it was also a slow moving, conventional technology aimed market with strong price competition and high durability or demand. The advanced material burner was cheaper than metal burners (and also scored better in terms of durability), but more expensive than another type of advanced material burner, which, however, made more noise. Furthermore the advanced material burner was a new, unfamiliar product, and was more fragile than the metal burners, which was a problem with regard to its installation and/or replacement in central heating systems. Technical performance was superior in terms of low noise, its ability to burn different gas mixes and withstand higher temperatures. It was the latter product characteristic that was finally crucial in obtaining customer orders for both central heating as well as industrial oven applications. Note that in choosing its product specification BurnerInc was largely dependent on technological choices made by HeatCo.

### Describing and analyzing NPD alliances.

Figure 13.4 summarizes the description of the technology and product development processes in the case of the advanced material burner, indicating that the most important phases, milestones and bottlenecks as well as the actors involved in the NPD alliances. Three trajectories are distinguished in the description: Technology development at HeatCo, Transfer to (and founding of) BurnerInc, and Roll out (and consolidation) by BurnerInc. After the assessment of the operational effectiveness and strategic flexibility below (mainly from the viewpoint of HeatCo), we will for the purpose of further analysis, elaborate upon the issues listed in Figure 13.4, concerning the interaction mechanisms.

### Operational effectiveness and strategic flexibility

The development of the advanced material burner illustrates the fit of the alignment mechanisms relative to the *operational effectiveness* of HeatCo. Specifically the systematic (external) 'target group' approach (see Figure 13.5) is potentially a positive contribution to fit with (other) market demands (such as price and manufacturability), but this strongly depends on the type of target groups that can be and are involved in practice. First of all this has to do with the dilemma of whether to involve customers and end-users early in the process, at the risk of them losing interest through initial failures. Also, to obtain funding from StoER for just a feasibility study, it is not necessary to involve a customer or end-user since this can be done in co-operation with a branch organization. Thus there is less pressure for the early involvement of potential producers like BurnerInc.

The researchers at HeatCo are very much focused on building competencies and flexibility into the NPD process which positively contributes to *strategic flexibility* in terms of future product concept effectiveness. However, most interviewees felt that more attention should be paid to contributing to future NPD process effectiveness, which is also part of *strategic flexibility*, in the way that HeatCo aligns with its target groups. The focus is very much on individual projects within the overall programmes. Improvements within these projects are not always directly linked to improvements in the overall NPD process. In order to become an even more attractive partner in NPD, which is necessary to generate future income, it is crucial to improve the ability to undertake and adequately complete overall NPD processes, which is referred to by StoER as an overall trajectory approach. This requires HeatCo when forming its alliances and determining alignment mechanisms, to pay attention to overall time to market as well as price and manufacturability of the product, technology transfer and continuous anticipation of market demands and constraints (in the primary NPD processes). This 'overall trajectory' approach also has implications for StoER, which may act as the already mentioned 'flight leader', together with BurnerInc.

### Interaction mechanisms

*Goal attainment*
The strategic goals of two of the three main actors involved can be directly related back to their mission. StoER is a government funded organization whose mission it is to stimulate (and financially support) the durable development of society in the areas of energy and environment research. An important area of concern is energy conversion. HeatCo's overall mission is energy innovation involving the development of technologies for a safe, clean and efficient supply of energy. Its main goals, in terms of which the different scientific products of HeatCo can be characterized, are threefold:

● to contribute to mid and long term energy policy (knowledge development);
● to serve as a 'knowledge base': expanding knowledge on energy technology (knowledge development);

| Technology & product (& process) development (phases) | Technology Development at HeatCo | Transfer to BurnerInc | | | Roll Out by BurnerInc |
|---|---|---|---|---|---|
| | Technology development & conceptual product design | Product planning phase | Product/process design | commercial preparations phase | market introduction |

Main actors, their goals & main activities:

| Actor | Technology Development at HeatCo | Transfer to BurnerInc | | | Roll Out by BurnerInc |
|---|---|---|---|---|---|
| StoER | Subsidize development and alignment of target groups | Subsidize HeatCo projects | | TURNAROUND: subsidize BurnerInc projects | financial support to programmes within larger framework |
| HeatCo | Development, design and testing | Research market potential / Redesign prototypes | | techn. support / applied development (EE) | technological support |
| BurnerInc | | Research market potential | Process design | prototypes | producer of Adv. Mat. installations / customer-specific solutions / membrane filtration |

Other actors involved:

|  | |
|---|---|
| Energy producer | Advise and some measurements |
| Central heating systems manufacturer | Advise & input / Provide CH system |
| Branch organization | Advise & input |
| First burner manufacturer | Field & durability tests |

**Milestones**

- initiative from energy producer
- definition of starting points
- technical feasibility established
- proof of Principle
- contact 1st burner manufacturer
- life tests in CH systems
- proof of concept / 1st report man.process
- contact BurnerInc / 1st prototype burner
- commercial market feasibility study
- field tests CH systems
- process development
- Advanced material breaks down!
- production line for advanced material
- various prototypes

Roll Out by BurnerInc:
- first delivery
- shift to more installation building
- paper drying
- Industrial burner
- product improvements
- area heating- new product development
- last project within StoER framework

**Figure 13.4:** Description of the development and technology transfer of the advanced material burners

| Time → | Technology development at HeatCo | | Transfer to BurnerInc | | Roll out by BurnerInc |
|---|---|---|---|---|---|
| **Technology transfer (phases)** | Prospecting | Develop/t est | Prospecting | Develop/test | Adoption |
| *Actors & main goals/activities* | | | | | |
| StoER | | | | | Partial financial support |
| HeatCo | Licence option | Build in burners in CH systems | Adv. Mat. lab. | Adv. Mat. lab & Burner lab | |
| BurnerInc | | | Practical knowledge Adv. Mat. market demands | Manufacturing knowledge Adv. Mat. | Product & process improvement | Research assignments from BurnerInc to HeatCo and advice from BurnerInc concerning new applications Advanced Material burner |
| *Other actors involved:* First burner manufacturer | Licence option | Tests | | | |
| *Milestones* | agreement with manufacturer | manufacturer drops out | practical knowledge Advanced Material | • transfer from Fossil fuels BU to Energy Engineering (EE) • trainee for process development • transfer of research notes | |
| | | | request for secondment of specialist from Fossil Fuels BU to BurnerInc | • secondment specialist • appointment of account manager within EE BU | • project 'support on request' • support concerning: raw materials analysis; laboratories; secondments and 'on the job' training |

**Figure 13.4:** *Continued*

| | HeatCo | Governmental agencies like StoER | Industry, e.g. BurnerInc |
|---|---|---|---|
| Definition of starting points | XXX* | | |
| Feasibility | XX | XX | X |
| Basic geometry | X | XXX | X |
| Field/life/durability tests | X | XXX | XX |
| Prototype development | | XX | XXX |
| Market introduction | | X | XXX |

* The number of Xs indicates the degree of involvement.

**Figure 13.5:** Financial involvement of target groups per phase at HeatCo (adopted from one of the interviewees)

- to contribute to concrete (short-term) practical applications (product development).

In addition, HeatCo believes it performs an important societal function, which is to ensure that small and medium-sized enterprises benefit from their scientific products. However, their specific choice of projects to be undertaken is very much influenced by the operational target of obtaining adequate funding for their man-hours since, as has been indicated above, HeatCo is increasingly more dependent on subsidizing agencies and industries for an increasing part of its income. For the development of the advanced material burner, HeatCo particularly needed BurnerInc to attain the above third goal. However, when the relationship was established this goal was already largely attained from HeatCo's viewpoint whereas, for BurnerInc, this was only the start. BurnerInc was specifically founded as a 'spin off' company to manufacture and market the advanced material burners. In the start up period the company's goals reflected that objective. Gradually as they began to grow, their goals shifted more to be aimed at continuity, enlarging the product portfolio and becoming more independent from HeatCo.

Because of their important role as financiers, StoER might have exercised much more power throughout the above described trajectories, but they did not, most probably because they had such high regard for HeatCo and HeatCo's judgments on the feasibility of the projects. Thus, HeatCo initially, and for quite a long time, was the actor with the highest authority, exercising the actual power in the partnership, mostly due to their technological knowledge base. Halfway through the second trajectory (Transfer to (and founding of) BurnerInc) a strategic change was initiated by StoER (i.e. transit from influence and authority to control), when they rejected a project proposal submitted by HeatCo, and decided to grant only project proposals submitted by BurnerInc concerning the further development and roll out of the burners from that point onwards (see Figure 13.4). Thus, there was a transition from StoER exercising only some influence and authority to their taking the control granted by their funding means. After that, BurnerInc also became more and more a mature partner in the network. In terms of Mitchell et al. (1997), from the viewpoint of BurnerInc, at the start up phase they depended on HeatCo as a stakeholder that has power over the firm, a relationship that changed to a mutual power-dependence relationship (although still not with equal partners) where the basis for the legitimacy of the relationship is formed by contracts, such as the 'Support on Request' project facilitated and financed by

StoER. This is again changing towards a situation where HeatCo (and in future also StoER) as a stakeholder has interests in BurnerInc but legitimacy is not specifically implied anymore (Savage et al., 1991: 61). 'Mitchell et al. (1997: 862) have argued that a partner may have an interest in the actions of an organization and ... have the ability to influence it.'

*Pattern maintenance*

As may be clear from the above, in the case of the development of advanced material burners, HeatCo possessed all technological knowledge needed for product and process development. From Figure 13.4 it can be seen that BurnerInc actually entered the technology and product development process quite late. Some problems with very expensive raw material, not suitable for batch production, might have been prevented by their earlier involvement. The most important knowledge 'assets' possessed by BurnerInc were the basis for their entrepreneurial spirit: namely some marketing and manufacturing knowledge but not at all in the field of the advanced material burners. What knowledge StoER possessed concerning facilitating this type of partnerships, was not actively brought into the network until late in the second trajectory (see Figure 13.4). The founders of HeatCo originated from industry and were independent entrepreneurs in metal manufacturing. They had very little (cultural) commonalities with the scientists and academics working at HeatCo. Needless to say, the differences in management style, and even in jargon used, were very big. BurnerInc's managing director had undertaken enthusiastic talks with HeatCo's president, who very much inspired him to take part in the adventure, winning his trust and convincing him that both companies would be in it together all through to the end. Even though the only formal contract was the license agreement, BurnerInc was convinced that they would get full support from HeatCo all the way. Surely, related to attaining the goal of contributing to short term practical applications, HeatCo meant to do just that, but both partners did not realize that considerable expertise was lacking in terms of how to transfer technological knowledge to BurnerInc and how to pursue an overall NPD trajectory.

The only formal technology transfer mechanism used initially was the handing over of the scientific reports mentioned in the license agreement. Later on during the transfer, there was much more actual co-operation in projects between HeatCo and BurnerInc, which is one of the 'best practices' recommended by Souder et al. (1990). Figure 13.4 shows that BurnerInc tried several times to get someone from the Fossil Fuels Business Unit seconded (another 'best practice' recommended by Souder), but HeatCo were very reluctant to do that. BurnerInc now considers the appointment of an account manager as well as the 'Support on Request' project as big improvements. In the start up phase BurnerInc was located at HeatCo's premises, which of course facilitated informal contacts. After their move to another industrial area, some staff from HeatCo started working at BurnerInc. An important point to mention here, from BurnerInc's viewpoint, was that they were not only concerned with taking part in the partnership and the technology development and transfer processes, but because they were founded as a 'spin off' company, they had to set up and institutionalize a complete new, fast growing organization from scratch, adding to the complexity of organizational development processes. Speaking in terms of the mapping tool (Figure 13.3 left lower quadrant), organizational arrangements, practices and techniques were not in place but had to be developed alongside the other processes.

*Adaptation*

Due to the specific company policy not to manufacture any in-house developed product, HeatCo is not concerned with make or buy decisions. Thus, they cannot pursue an overall NPD trajectory on their own, either from a financial viewpoint (see Figure 13.5), or in terms of manufacturing and marketing. However, there are differences in the degree of involvement. Initially, HeatCo had contacts with a burner manufacturer who already had market access and some manufacturing experience. When this co-operation did not work out, and HeatCo decided to support the 'spin off' of BurnerInc, they entered into a process where their involvement would be much larger than usually anticipated. Specifically the late involvement of BurnerInc caused inefficiencies in the manufacturing process such as the already mentioned example of very expensive raw materials. Also difficulties in transferring the laboratory processes into batch production caused considerable inefficiency and reworking.

When working on expanding their product portfolio, during the roll out phase of the advanced material burners, BurnerInc was also faced with make-or-buy decisions regarding their R&D and NPD function. Almost automatically they turned to HeatCo for this, although now slowly but surely (and after evaluating the development of the advanced material burners) they recognized that, for certain phases in the development process, other partners might have to be involved. Otherwise, it might be necessary to further develop their own NPD function in house. This notion, and the carrying out of it, ensured that BurnerInc were also an economically more independent actor.

*Network of involved or influential actors*

The structure of the network or partnership is briefly depicted in Figure 13.6. BurnerInc (Actor 2) fills in a structural hole for HeatCo (Actor 1) towards the market, by fulfilling the marketing and manufacturing function. StoER has (or should have) a brokerage position, first of all by facilitating the partnership through financial means; but later on in the process also facilitating the technology transfer process by actively intervening at the already mentioned turnaround point (again, see Figure 13.5). As the foregoing sections have already indicated, the strength of ties, as well as the frequency and duration of interaction between HeatCo (for most of the time the prominent actor!) and BurnerInc, varied per phase. It is now, with the maturing of BurnerInc and the finishing of the roll out of the (first generation) advanced material burners, heading towards a balance with loosened, but not uncoupled, ties. Interaction between StoER and BurnerInc is now also becoming more efficient, especially, of course, after the turnaround.

At HeatCo, the target group approach (see again Figure 13.4) has been strengthened and improved for future projects concerning firm formation. For example the issue of closer and earlier involvement of manufacturers is now explicitly stressed. Largely based on the experiences with Burner Inc and HeatCo,

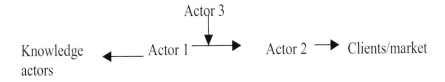

**Figure 13.6:** Network structure

172 NEW TECHNOLOGY-BASED FIRMS IN THE NEW MILLENNIUM

StoER in its current programmes acts much more as a facilitating 'flight leader' and they actively apply a formalized overall trajectory approach for technology development. This trajectory approach, insofar as it was based on this case, captures interaction patterns, which may serve as a role model. The case study described here, as it applies to BurnerInc, served as an evaluation of the overall trajectory and has also delivered useful insights.

### Summary of managerial implications for technology and product development and technology transfer

Very briefly summarized, the managerial implications that can be derived from this empirical data boil down to:

- the importance of and the availability of knowledge concerning the carrying out and management of an *overall trajectory approach* to the carrying out of the NPD processes;
- planning (well in advance) and formalizing (even including in licensing agreements) technology transfer processes and mechanisms such as the secondment of development engineers;
- actively carrying out important facilitating roles such as the 'flight leader' role by actors within StoER.

## CONCLUSIONS AND FURTHER RESEARCH

The objective of this paper was to explore NPD alliances between research institutes and SMEs. To this end we have developed and presented above a framework for the description and analysis of NPD alliances: a combination of a process-based contingency model with a social systems model. In applying the framework to the case of the development of an advanced material burner, we have focused on a relationship in which the research institute seeks collaboration to generate a 'spin off' company for the production and commercialization of a specific piece of developed technology. Our conclusions, apart from the managerial implications briefly summarized above, mainly concern the suitability of our framework for the description and analysis of this type of processes and alliances, and on the retrospective part of the case study. First of all we want to stress that this is a first attempt at operationalizing the framework, and we applied the analysis part to case material mainly gathered solely by using the process-based contingency model. Therefore, the analysis of the interaction mechanisms following the dimensions from the social systems model is somewhat limited, and not as well structured as might be possible. Furthermore, specifically the multi-level approach, which would allow us to discuss individual, group-level and organizational actors, has not been applied systematically in the analysis. Further operationalization of the mapping tool(s) enabling a more detailed analysis is the first pathway for further research we have to explore.

However, when comparing and combining the analysis of operational effectiveness and strategic flexibility with the analysis of the interactions mechanisms, the results are very promising in that much more insight is gained on the nature and strengths and weaknesses of the heterogeneous networks in which research institutes and SMEs are involved when pursuing new product development. This encourages us to pursue further the framework, and apply it to more cases in order to get a grasp of the diversity of networks in NPD, also concerning other actors (see de Weerd-Nederhof, 2000). The content and the usefulness of the case study as an evaluation for BurnerInc, HeatCo and StoER points at the added particular value for high technology small firms which is another line of further research we will pursue (During and Groen, 2000).

## ACKNOWLEDGEMENTS

Harry Vos gathered a large part of the empirical data during his graduation assignment at BurnerInc. This data was complemented by an earlier case study of HeatCo published in de Weerd-Nederhof (1998). The authors wish to specifically thank the general manager and the managing director of BurnerInc for their co-operation. Parts of this paper are based on earlier publications by the first author in co-operation with Olaf Fisscher (de Weerd-Nederhof and Fisscher, 1998) and Rob Bartholomew (Bartholomew and de Weerd-Nederhof, 1997).

## REFERENCES

Bartholomew, R.A. and de Weerd-Nederhof, P.C. (1997) Appraisal, Selection and Organization of New Product Development Projects. Case Studies of two European Energy Sector Companies. *4th EIASM Product Development Conference*, Stockholm, Sweden, May 26–27.

Bidault, F. and Cummings, Th. (1994) Innovating through alliances: expectations and limitations, *R&D Management*, **24**, 1, pp. 33–45.

Biemans, W. (1992) *Managing Innovations within Networks,* Routledge, London, UK.

Boer, H. and J.J. Krabbendam, (1991) Organising for market-oriented manufacture, *POMS Conference*, New York City, USA, November 11–13.

Bourdieu, P. (1973) Cultural reproduction and social reproduction. In: R. Brown (ed.), *Knowledge, education and cultural change*. London: Tavistock.

Cohen, W.M. and Levinthal, D.A. (1990) Absorptive capacity: A new perspective on learning and innovation. *Administrative Science Quarterly*, 35, pp. 128–152.

Deuten, J.J., Rip, A. and Jelsma, J. (1997) Societal embedding and product creation management. *Technology Analysis & Strategic Management*, 9, 2.

During, W. and Groen, A.J. (2000) *Knowledge Intensive Entrepreneurship in Networks*. Research program University of Twente Entrepreneurship Centre (forthcoming).

Emmanuelides, P.A. (1993) Towards an integrative framework of performance in product development projects. *Journal of Engineering and Technology Management,* 10, pp. 363–392.

Gatignon, H. and Robertson, T.S. (1985) A Propositional Inventory for New Diffusion Research. *Journal of Consumer Research,* Vol. 11.

Granovetter, M. (1985) Economic action and Social Structure: The Problem of Embeddedness. *American Journal of Sociology*, Vol. 91, No. 3 (November), pp. 481–51.

Granovetter, M. (1992) Problems of Explanation in Economic Sociology. In Nohria, N. and R.G. Eccles (eds) *Networks and Organizations*. HBS: Boston.

Groen, A.J. (1994) Milieu en MKB: Kennis en Kennissen, milieuinnovatie in de grafische industrie: modelmatig verklaard, Groningen Thesis in economics, management and organization, Wolters-Noordhof, Groningen.

Groen, A.J. (2000) Marketing en Prestaties van de onderneming; net werken of netwerken? *Tijdschrift voor Bedrijfskunde,* Vol. 72, No. 2, pp. 72–80.

Hagedoorn, J. (1996) Trends and patterns in strategic technology partnering since the early seventies. *Review of Industrial Organization*, **11**, 601–616.

Håkansson, H. and Johanson, J. (1993) *Industrial functions of business relations*. In Grabher, G. (ed.) *The Embedded Firm*. London: Routledge, pp. 15–31.

Hamel, G. and Prahalad, C. (1994) *Competing for the Future*. HBS, Boston.

Hart, S.J. and Baker, M.J. (1994) The multiple convergent processing model of new product development. *International Marketing Review*, **11**, 1, pp. 77–92.

Klein Woolthuis, R.J.A. (1999) Sleeping with the enemy. Ph.D. thesis University of Twente, Enschede.

Kogut, Bruce and Zander, Udo (1992) Knowledge of the Firm, Combinative Capabilities, and the Replication of Technology. *Organization Science*, Vol. 3, No. 3, August.

Mitchell, R.K., Agle, B.R. and Wood, D.J. (1997) Toward a theory of stakeholder identification and salience: defining the principle of who and what really counts. *Academy of Management Review*, Vol. 22, No. 4, pp. 853–886.

Nonaka, I. and Takeuchi, H. (1995) *The Knowledge Creating Company*. Oxford.

Nooteboom, B. (1992) Towards a dynamic theory of transactions. *Journal of Evolutionary Economics*, 2, pp. 281–299.

Parsons, T. (1951) (1964) *The Social System*. New York: The Free Press.

Parsons, T. (1977) *Social systems and the evolution of action theory*. New York: The Free Press.

Polany, M. (1966) *The Tacit Dimension*. London: Routledge.

Ring, P., Smith and Van de Ven, A.H. (1994) Developmental processes of cooperative interorganisational relationships. *Academy of Management Review*, 19(1), pp. 90–118.

Rip, Arie, Misa, Thomas J. and Schot, Johan W. (eds) (1995) *Managing Technology in Society. The Approach of Constructive Technology Assessment*. Pinter Publishers, London.

Rip, A. and Groen, A.J. (2000) Many Visible Hands. In Rod Coombs, Ken Green, Vivien Walsh, and Albert Richards (eds) *Demands, Markets, Users and Innovation*, Edward Elgar.

Savage, G.T., Nix, T.H., Whitehead, C.J. and Blair, J.D. (1991) Strategies for assessing and managing organizational stakeholders. *Academy of Management Executive*, 5, pp. 61–75.

Souder, W.E., Nashar, A.S. and Padmanabhan, V. (1990) A guide to the best technology transfer practices. *Technology Transfer*, Winter-Spring.

Tidd, J., Bessant, J. and Pavitt, K. (1997) *Managing Innovation. Integrating Technological, Market and Organizational Change*. John Wiley and Sons, Chicester, UK.

von Hippel E. (1998) '*Sources of Innovation*'. Oxford Press, New York.

Vos, H. (2000) Kennisoverdracht kennis instituut richting MKB. Casestudy HeatCo/BurnerInc. Masters Thesis University of Twente, Enschede, The Netherlands.

Weerd-Nederhof, P.C. de (1998) New Product Development Systems. Operational Effectiveness and Strategic Flexibility. Ph.D. Thesis, University of Twente, Enschede, The Netherlands.

Weerd-Nederhof, P.C. de (2000) 'Organizational Architectures for Improved performance of New Product Development Systems. Proposal for a research programme submitted to ASPASIA, a programme from the Dutch Scientific Council NWO, University of Twente, Enschede, The Netherlands.

Weerd-Nederhof, P.C. de and Fisscher, O.A.M. (1998) Strategic Alliances for New Product Development: How Research Institutes Align With Their Target Groups. *1998 R&D Management Conference*, Avila, Spain.

Williamson, O.E. (1975) *Markets and Hierarchies: Analysis and Antitrust Implications*. New York: The Free Press.

Williamson, O.E. (1985) *The Economic Institutions of Capitalism: Firm Markets Relational Contracting*. New York: The Free Press.

# CHAPTER 14

# Academic Spin-Off Ventures: A Resource Opportunity Approach

CÉLINE DRUILHE AND ELIZABETH GARNSEY

## INTRODUCTION

Academic 'spin-off' companies have been of growing policy and research interest since the early 1990s. In their readiness to promote academic entrepreneurship, European governments have supported numerous initiatives aiming to create favourable conditions under which scientists could develop research-based new products. Organisations and schemes have multiplied throughout Europe to teach and nurture entrepreneurship in universities and public research laboratories. As a recent example of this trend, in 1999 both the UK and French governments have sought to foster high-tech enterprise and links between university and industry by launching national competitions between universities to finance the creation of incubators or entrepreneurship centres. Despite this public interest, the process whereby academic institutions actually 'spin out' businesses is not well understood. 'Spin-off' enterprise has been analysed at both aggregate and micro-levels, respectively through statistical analysis and detailed descriptions based on case studies. The main focus of these studies is not on the emergence of the company. Yet the initial stages, prior to venture formation, are a decisive period during which academic-type knowledge is transformed into a business idea.

In this paper we attempt to address this gap, and to provide a conceptual basis for the analysis of the early process of firm formation, using the academic 'spin-out' as an exemplar. The paper proposes to deal with the following question: how do academic scientists recognise an opportunity and create resources from the science base to serve as a basis for a new company? Academic 'spin-off' companies are defined as firms whose products or services stem from technology-based ideas or scientific/technical know-how generated in a university setting by a member of faculty, staff or the student body founding or co-founding a firm.[1] The incubation of an academic spin-off is a long, uncertain, and complicated innovative process. There are many difficulties in spinning a business out of a university, which stem from differences between the academic and business worlds. Academia and industry not only belong to different spheres of social activity and organisation but also produce distinctly different types of knowledge, and are governed by differing research ethics. Partly as a consequence of these differences, the technology, or technical idea, generated in an academic environment, and on which the start-up is based, is often far from being a commercial product. The creation of a science-based enterprise involves all the risks of innovation. The management of innovation has been studied extensively. Most of the factors identified as affecting either success or failure can be found in the special case of academic enterprise. Hence, the proximity to customer needs, the scale of activity, the maturity of technology and markets, the availability of finance, the ownership and strength of intellectual property, and the motivations of the entrepreneur, all play a role in any new venture. Thus understanding the emergence of an academic 'spin-off', not only presents an interest in its own right, but also provides a better insight into the dynamics of innovation and enterprise.

The conceptual framework we develop in this paper focuses on the preparatory phases of a project, prior to the creation of the academic 'spin-off' company, when the potential for a new business is identified. It is rooted in the resource-based theory of the growth of the firm (Penrose, 1959; Garnsey, 1998), which we extend into the stages prior to 'start-up'. The scientist who decides to start a company based on knowledge generated in a 'lab' needs to accomplish entrepreneurial tasks, such as recognising a business opportunity, accessing and securing resources, and matching these creatively. We argue that this is a collective endeavour in which interactions between the potential scientist-entrepreneur and a variety of other individuals and organisations involved in the innovation process play a decisive role. The framework is further developed through a comparison of two case studies based on data collected at the University of Cambridge, in the United Kingdom. Our intent in these empirical examples is to focus on building theory. We do not use the case studies to test formal hypotheses but as a basis for theoretical insights. The cases present an analysis of how the initial business idea evolves and is built through alliances and interactions, thereby allowing the business project progressively to become a reality.

## THE LITERATURE ON ACADEMIC SPIN-OFF COMPANIES: THE INITIAL PHASE AS A NEGLECTED ISSUE

Academic 'spin-off' companies are often described as representing a mediating space between two settings. In some cases they mediate between the world of basic research, from which they originate, and a network of firms that are their clients (Mustar, 1997). In other cases they are said to mediate between academia and industry, thus creating an institutional space that allows scientists to preserve their professional identity while getting involved in business (Stankiewicz, 1994). Academic companies are far from forming a homogenous category. On a spectrum of mediation types between academia and industry, they range from independent businesses to 'shell companies'. In these, the funding of existing academic research programmes is a sufficient incentive to produce the starting-up of a business for academics who have no intention of leaving university, nor of actively pursuing commercial exploitation (Rappert, 1997; Blair and Hitchens, 1998).

The perspectives offered in the literature for the analysis of academic 'spin-off' companies are varied, focusing either on one or several universities (Smilor et al., 1990; Rappert and Webster, 1998; Blair and Hitchens, 1998) or more rarely on national data (Mustar, 1994). Outside the US (Smilor et al., 1990; Brett et al., 1991; Roberts and Malone, 1996), the phenomenon has been analysed in several European countries including the United Kingdom and Ireland (Downes and Eadie, 1998; Rappert and Webster, 1998; Blair and Hitchens, 1998), France (Mustar, 1994, 1997), Sweden (Stankiewicz, 1994) and Italy (Chiesa and Piccaluga, 1998). Mostly empirical, these studies describe significant features of academic 'spin-off' companies. We highlight here some of their conclusions that give an insight into the nature and main features of these companies.

Beyond descriptive typologies, a range of factors featuring academic 'spin-outs' have been assessed, including the reasons for start-up, the role of the university in company formation and development, and major difficulties facing 'spin-out' companies. Positive incentives, such as the recognition of a market opportunity or the drive to try something new, seem to be more important than negative ones, namely the need for additional money and the lack of motivation within the university career structure, in influencing the launching of 'spin-off' companies (Smilor et al., 1990; Chiesa and Piccaluga, 1998). Comparing the perceptions of Scottish and American scientists towards academic 'spin-off' companies, Downes and Eadie (1998) argue that the British research environment, and the agenda and priorities which it imposes, does little to encourage academic researchers toward active involvement in the commercial application of their work. Partly as a result of this, academics considering the possibility of setting up a business tend to regard the process as fraught with difficulty.

The role of the university in supporting 'spin-off' companies varies from one university to the other, but a proactive position appears to be beneficial. Several factors influencing the creation of 'spin-off' companies can be identified, including the technological and R&D strength of the university, the existence of an entrepreneurial culture within the university and its immediate environment, and the presence of rich and diversified technological and economic resources in the local surrounding milieu. Weaknesses in the last two factors can be compensated for, to some extent, by public policy measures. The extent of university involvement in 'spin-outs' covers a wide spectrum from relative disinterest to 'hands-on' control (Etzkowitz, 1998; Blair and Hitchens, 1998). The motivations and expectations of academic entrepreneurs frequently differ from those of their institutions (Blair and Hitchens, 1998).

The managerial competencies of the academic entrepreneur are a controversial issue. It has been argued that academics do not make good entrepreneurs and that the effective exploitation of their technology requires a transfer of the ownership and managerial control to professional managers at an early stage (Stankiewicz, 1994). Others observe that a lack of business experience is felt as a weakness by scientists-entrepreneurs (Smilor et al., 1990). Reporting that academic researchers rarely make good managers, Blair and Hitchens (1998) emphasise the importance of key individuals filling the roles of product champion, 'missionary', and entrepreneur, although these three roles are seldom satisfactorily performed by one person.

However, there are studies which show that academics are able to operate adequately in the business world, given the small size of their companies (Chiesa and Piccaluga, 1998). Early studies of MIT 'spin-outs' showed the capacity of academics to make a successful transition from university to the business world, albeit not without initial difficulty (Roberts, 1991).

Links with the parent institution are shown to be important to the success of the academic 'spin-off' company. Although most academic 'spin-offs' distance themselves from their parent university, in terms of financial and managerial control and research links after the founder has moved out of the university, informal research-based university links are cited as important to the development of many academic 'spin-offs' (Rappert, 1997). Rappert and Webster (1998) underline that academic 'spin-off' entrepreneurs consider that universities contribute to innovation by providing an underpinning of scientific and engineering theory and by assisting firms in finding knowledge and materials not readily available. More generally Mustar (1994, 1997) stresses that the success of 'spin-off' companies especially depends upon their capacity to establish linkages with a broad range of actors, including research labs, local authorities, clients, financial institutions, and other companies. He attributes the lower rate of failure of French academic 'spin-off' companies over traditional SMEs to a networking and linkage capacity very early on in the life of the company.

The literature has generated useful insights into the features of this particular type of entrepreneurship represented by academic enterprise. This work emphasises that academic 'spin-off' companies form a heterogeneous category, functioning as connecting links between the university and industry, as part of a network in which various actors, including academic institutions, customers, and venture capitalists all take part.

However, the preparatory phases leading to the creation of academic 'spin-offs' are a neglected issue in the literature. Even when case studies analyse the early phases of the growth of academic 'spin-outs', they consider them mostly after the launch, and do not study the initial stages during which the existence of the company remains a nebulous project. Moreover within a literature dominated by empirical approaches, no adequate conceptual framework has been developed to reflect the extent to which initial stages are critical for identifying the commercial potential of inventions developed in a university environment.

## CONCEPTUALISING THE INITIAL PHASES OF ACADEMIC ENTERPRISE: OPPORTUNITY RECOGNITION AND RESOURCE CREATION

Starting an academic 'spin-off' company encompasses both entrepreneurship and innovation, as the academic entrepreneur takes an invention produced in an academic environment to the market. Entrepreneurship is often presented as uncertain and risky. This uncertainty is amplified in the case of academic 'spin-off' companies because the capacity of scientists to become entrepreneurs is in question, and these companies are based on university-based knowledge often produced to satisfy academic criteria rather than economic concerns.

To analyse these atypical aspects of entrepreneurship, we build here on the resource-based theory of the firm (Penrose, 1959; Wernerfelt, 1984; Barney, 1986; Grant 1991). The dominant application of the theory has focused on explaining the source of competitive advantage and diversification strategy within large established firms:

> 'The resource-based view has tended to focus its attention on the golden age of the firm when the sustained competitive advantage is supported by valuable resources within the firm, while paying little attention to what happens before and after that period (...). The resource-based view has little to say about entrepreneurs, those whose inventory of resources is remarkably thin. On closer examination, one may argue that these firms lack the large scores of pedestrian resources we associate with established firms (but also overlooked in their analysis), but have in fact, a jewel in the form of an idea, or a vision of how things might be done. This line of enquiry, however, has not been developed, and it is difficult to suggest how far it could be taken (Montgomery, 1995: 262).

We argue that a resource-based approach can illuminate early-stage companies (Garnsey, 1998) and can be extended to the stages prior to 'start-up'. The focus on opportunities and resources provides fruitful theoretical insights into the processes of venture creation.

There are many definitions of enterprise but here we wish to emphasise the following elements: the detection of an opportunity, the mobilisation of resources, the coupling of resources and opportunities, and the creation of value. There is a fifth element to enterprise: when mobilisation of resources is required before the rewards from value creation can be reaped, and resources are committed before revenues are secured, this involves uncertainty and risk. We define enterprise as new activity that connects resources and opportunities to create value. The phases preparatory to the creation of the company are centred on the detection of an opportunity, and on the search for, and access to, various resources, which, when combined, provide the new venture with a suitable base for realising a commercial opportunity. In this section, we review the key concepts of opportunity and resource to bring conceptual clarifications to the emergence of academic enterprise.

## Economic opportunities

Entrepreneurs are motivated by the existence of economic opportunities. Economic opportunities represent the prospect of benefits from a preferred state.[2] Entrepreneurs are alert to misuse of resources; they identify needed resources, secure them as inputs and organise a conversion process that results in outputs more valuable than the costs of production.

The concept of dynamic coordination, or synchronisation, of supply and demand, of the mix of resources, of opportunities and resources, is central to entrepreneurial activity. Entrepreneurs operate as connecting agents and agents of change.

Opportunities arise when new information becomes available, in the light of which the existing allocation of resources appears inefficient (Casson, 1982)[3] or new resources can be created. This new information represents the solution to the problems of producers, distributors or consumers. New ways to solve production or distribution problems can reduce costs; when production costs are reduced, value creation increases and more value can be retained by the producer at a given purchase price. Ultimately, the rewards that can be obtained by meeting needs or solving user problems depend on delivering value and this is a key source of opportunity.

Competition and bargaining position will affect who gains from these opportunities.

Technologies are a key source of new value and new opportunity. Technologies can be defined as new problem-solving devices. New products, new production methods and new forms of organisation offer the prospect of rewards. Technology transfer from one sphere to another, including the science base, can create value through the application of knowledge in new areas of activity.

Opportunities are activated by recognition. The process of opportunity recognition is far from trivial, as opportunities do not appear in a readily-available form. Their recognition is subjective and often depends on access to special knowledge. An entrepreneur will discover opportunities that relate to his or her prior knowledge; experience opens out the perception of opportunity (Shane and Venkataraman, 2000). Entrepreneurs recognise different opportunities in the same technology, and discover opportunities related to the information that they already possess. Academics seldom develop prior knowledge within the university that is useful to the detection of commercial opportunities. As stressed in the literature review, they usually lack the awareness and the understanding of the commercial world that can make it possible to identify gaps and problems in the market that the new technology can solve. We argue that scientists will success-fully recognise an opportunity when they draw on the pool of resources from their wider environment, and are able to create and make good use of a network of contacts in the market place. For instance, academics can pull together valuable information by drawing on various sources including existing users, industrial sponsors of research, academic colleagues in another discipline, or industrial liaison experts in the university. Through this kind of linkage activity, scientists progressively acquire specialist knowledge useful to the recognition of the oppor-tunity. Simultaneously, they build the technological resource that will be used as a basis for the new company.

### The concept of resources

It is worth pursuing further the concept of resources, so often used and so seldom defined, to clarify the ways in which academics employ academic-type knowledge to detect an opportunity and create value. Within the resource-based view, the term resource was originally used to refer to 'anything which could be thought of as a strength or weakness of a given firm' (Wernerfelt, 1984: 172). More recently, however, the expression has tended to refer only to positive assets and attributes explaining the source of competitive advantage:

> '... firm resources include all assets, capabilities, organizational processes, firm attributes, information, knowledge etc. controlled by a firm that enable the firm to conceive of and implement strategies that improve its efficiency and effectiveness' (Barney, 1991: 101).

There are difficulties with such an all-encompassing concept of resources, espe-cially as regards the conceptualisation of the emergence of new ventures. First it is often difficult to identify which of the resources, or combination of resources, in a firm can be said to be valuable. The identification process is often made *ex-post*, once a firm has been successful. Secondly, such a broad concept can result in circular reasoning of the kind criticised by Porter (1991). 'At its worst, the resource-based view is circular. Successful firms are successful because they have unique resources. They should nurture these resources to be successful'. This circular bias is of little help to understand a firm's creation and what resources entrepreneurs mobilise to start the venture independently of its future success. Porter counters:

> 'Resources are not valuable in and of themselves, but because they allow firms to perform activities that create advantages in particular markets. Resources are only meaningful in the context of performing certain activities to achieve certain competitive advantages. The competitive value of resources can be enhanced or eliminated by changes in technology, competitor behaviour or buyer needs which an inward focus on resources will overlook ... An explicit link between resources and activities, along with the clear distinction between internal and external resources (such as relationships and reputation) ... is necessary to carefully define a resource in the first place' (Porter, 1991: 108–109).

These criticisms can be overcome through the use of the idea of the firm as an activity system, and the need for continual iteration between resources and commercial opportunities, each of which is required to complement the other. Going back to the foundations of the resource-based view, Penrose (1959) had an implicit notion of the enterprise as an input-output system, in which resources are converted through 'productive activity' into output, the sale of which provides the firm with further resources needed to continue and expand activities. Resources are all those means required to enable the factors of production to be converted into what Penrose calls the 'productive services' that make output possible.[4] For Penrose, the transformation of resources into productive services is firm specific and occurs in the context of the experience, knowledge and ideas of members of the firm:

> 'Strictly speaking it is never resources themselves that are the inputs in the production process but only the services that the resources can render. The services yielded by resources are a function of the way in which they are used – exactly the same resource when used for different purposes or in different ways and in combination with different types or amounts of other resources provides a different services or set of services …' (Penrose, 1959: 25)

Broadly speaking, the concept of resources covers a variety of means required for action. In ecology, it is defined as a source to be drawn upon. Because the concept implies both means and ends, factors constitute resources when they can be used to achieve a sought-after objective. Further, the value of resources will change over time, and what was once an advantage may one day become an encumbrance, even though the resource itself has not changed. The value of resources is continually in question in a dynamic economic environment. The structure of opportunities is continually shifting. Thus entrepreneurs continually have to weigh up opportunities in the light of available resources, and to assess resources in relation to the opportunities they can facilitate. For this reason, the nature of the industrial environment must be the object of analysis no less than the activities within the firm.

Knowledge produced in a university environment, whether scientific or technological, constitutes an unexploited reserve of potential resources that entrepreneurs can transform and combine with other resources to realise a commercial opportunity. Resources are more likely to sustain value-creation when they are unusual, valuable, hard-to-replicate and not easily substitutable (Barney, 1991). Thus leading edge technological knowledge can be a potent resource if it can be oriented towards commercial applications. The potential resource can only lead to the realisation of a commercial opportunity if it is developed for market applications in combination with other types of resources, such as finance and manpower. Therefore, key tasks of the initial stages of the entrepreneurial process are centred around the recognition of a commercial opportunity in the light of the environment, and the creation of economic resources on the basis of access to, and mobilisation of, complementary resources.

In the next section, two case studies are compared to illustrate how academics detect a business opportunity, search for resources, and refine the opportunity in the light of a changing environment and of the mobilisation of resources. It is particularly interesting to analyse the accomplishment, or absence of accomplishment, of these tasks by academics. They are usually little involved in the business world, therefore the success of their entrepreneurial process relies heavily on an ability to interact with various business actors from which they can draw the resources required, as the two case studies below emphasise.

## TWO CASE STUDIES: RECOGNITION OF OPPORTUNITIES AND CREATION OF RESOURCES BY ACADEMICS FROM THE UNIVERSITY OF CAMBRIDGE, UK

The two case studies are based on participant observation field work in Cambridge University between 1998 and 1999. The academics studied were in the process of starting a company and received the support of a network of local business actors supporting high-tech enterprise in the region, namely the Anglia Enterprise

Network (AEN).[5] Both authors were academic members of this network. One author assisted a senior consultant over a 7 to 12-month period during which the potential academic entrepreneurs progressively built their venture project. Six meetings in one case and five in the other were held during that process with each team of entrepreneurs. Additional information includes e-mails and drafts of business plans produced by the entrepreneurs. Individuals and companies' names have been changed to preserve anonymity.

Since the aim was to understand the process by which academics start a company, it was important to look at enterprise creation 'in the making' in order to follow the evolution of the project and to not be dependent on the recall of the principals in the initial phases, as is usually the case with retrospective interviews. Moreover the observation of current business projects in real time, before it is clear whether the projects will be successful, is relevant to the process of academic 'spin-off' companies beyond ventures that succeed.

### Dr Jones, Mark, and Cambridge Capture Ltd

This first case is in the area of motion capture.[6] As part of her research, Dr Jones, a university lecturer in the Computer Laboratory, was involved in human motion analysis. She supervised a student project on the application of new computer vision techniques to capture motion. The use of capture systems comprised of cameras and sensors was required to carry out the research. However, Dr Jones could not afford the expensive commercial capture systems. This led to the development of their own PC-based system, at a lower cost than the ones sold in the market. In their spare time, Dr Jones and her student, Mark, were both runners and thus interested in motion analysis. This extended their motivation beyond purely academic research and drove them towards market applications. This side-knowledge facilitated their acquisition of a special technological knowledge oriented towards users and the market for motion capture.

Over the course of the one-year project, several events led Dr Jones and Mark to progressively recognise the potential for a commercial opportunity. At professional conferences on the subject, she obtained feedback from end-users in the medical field about their problems with existing software analysis packages and about the high-price of capture systems. While providing useful market information, this was also an incentive for turning the research prototype into a commercial product:

> 'I have had significant feedback from doctors, physiotherapists, podiatrists etc. who were very keen on having a straightforward, useful and affordable analysis package. Many researchers in the field are very frustrated at the inadequate provision of software, and are often forced to write their own analysis programs; this is difficult as most doctors are not mathematicians of signal processors.'[7]

Dr Jones's comparison of her system's technical performance with existing products seemed to corroborate these external opinions about the poor quality of the motion analysis packages. Personal contacts with doctors and local sport organisations enabled Dr Jones to test their system and to form links with potential customers:

> 'I also have the Sports Development Council and the University of Cambridge Tennis Association interested in its development as a sports analysis tool; this latter would be a service function and a research activity.'[8]

The way Dr Jones and Mark developed their technology over the course of the research project extended their special knowledge on motion capture. They were able to create and extend a valuable network of users and professionals in the field and also find potential customers, at least for a sophisticated analysis package. This allowed them to recognise a commercial opportunity.

However, human motion systems had existed for some time, and the market was dominated by a few large companies, mainly in the animation and medical fields. They were therefore cautious and planned a two-stage development, with a soft start based on the development of the analysis package and the later production of a hardware system conditional on the success of the analysis software. The opportunity consisted of the production of:

> '*a user-friendly, well-documented, general purpose system unlike existing systems which have very little in the way of meaningful analysis, and often have incorrect evaluation of certain quantities. The second phase of the project would be to develop our already existing motion-capture hardware. We believe that we can produce a system which would be as robust and accurate as existing capture systems at a fraction of the cost (we estimate a factor of between 5 and 10 less than other systems). The market would thus be opened up to individual practitioners; physiotherapists, podiatrists, sport coaches etc., who are currently priced out of the market.*'[9]

The opportunity that had been identified was based upon the potential of the technology. Realising the opportunity meant the conversion of the research result into a valuable economic resource, and the accessing of complementary resources. In particular, the next steps were to develop a commercial software package and to build a demonstrable hardware prototype. The route to market chosen was defined in order to limit the resources, and in particular finance, necessary to the commercialisation of the technology. Dr Jones and Mark were both keen on producing the software themselves through a new company, although Dr Jones wished to remain in academia. They planned that the development of a software package would take six months. In order to achieve this milestone, they relied on the availability of university facilities, including space and equipment. However, this low-cost route required a high level of personal commitment, as both of them had to carry out competing business and academic duties simultaneously.

Over the following months, Dr Jones and Mark decided to produce the hardware and the software simultaneously. They developed a system working with two cameras being used to investigate and analyse various types of human motion (running, swimming, violin playing), drawing on inputs from expert biomechanists, coaches, and clinicians. In order to build demonstrable prototypes, additional financial resources were required. The AEN consultant with whom they had discussed their project suggested a presentation at the AEN Forum.[10] They decided to raise sufficient funding to build two prototypes and carry out further market research. Even when not raising money, presenting was a useful way to focus the minds of the two scientists, and to move the project forward as it required a sharper business proposal. Thus, Dr Jones and Mark started to look in more detail into the markets for motion capture. The sports and medical markets still seemed the easiest to access, since they offered the opportunity to supply potential users currently discouraged by the high price of motion capture systems.

A weakness of their proposal was with regard to the intellectual property position. Although Dr Jones and Mark owned the intellectual property of their system,[11] substantial research results had already been published. In addition they had not been able to establish whether their own hardware algorithms were patentable. Their technology could be subject to imitation and reverse engineering. Several investors present at the AEN Forum argued that the absence of strong intellectual property protection in a competitive market was limiting interest in the technology. However, two serious offers were made including one from a golfer who was keen on applying the system to golf swing analysis. Therefore Dr Jones and Mark decided to revise their opportunity in order to adapt it to the nature of their technological resources. To benefit from the expertise and knowledge of the investor, they focused on the development of specific applications of the technology in niche areas such as the golf market. The acquisition of expertise in particular niches would allow them to provide, not only a motion capture system, but also a service and consulting activity. This was thought to offer the prospect of generating a more sustainable competitive advantage.

The route to market that was selected involved the forming of a development company that would generate early revenues from the production and selling of motion capture hardware systems to people who could not afford them at present prices. Those revenues would allow the company to carry out further R&D on specific applications in market niches such as golf swing analysis.

Over 12 months, the technological resource originating from academic research had been identified as offering a market opportunity. Moving beyond the early search period, Dr Jones and Mark selected their business project and began to mobilise initial resources. Preliminary financial and management resources (AEN consultant, expertise of the investor) were mobilised to develop the project further. This is a case where technology had reached an advanced stage, although further development was needed to build a commercial prototype. The proximity to users and to the market facilitated the identification of a focused opportunity. However due to the existence of competition, and the lack of strong intellectual property protection, the technological resources on which the new company would be based were neither rare nor hard to replicate. The potential for value-creation seemed to be limited. The opportunity had been refined to take account of the nature and characteristics of the market for this technology.

### Dr Perry and Cambridge Optica Ltd

Dr Perry's case differs from that of Dr Jones and Mark in many respects. Dr Perry formed Cambridge Optica Ltd as a development company based on his research of optical devices while he was a senior researcher in a science department of Cambridge University. Having 'spun out' of the department's research group, Cambridge Optica received strong support from the research group leader, Dr Steele, an entrepreneurial academic well networked in the local Cambridge business scene.

The undertaking resulted from Dr Perry's project and career plans. When he was hired by the department after completing a PhD in physics, he had several research ideas including research on innovative optical devices. Thus, over the course of a three-year project, he carried out research in optical science, a potentially commercial field. At the age of 30, no longer attracted by an academic career, Dr Perry moved into industry where he worked in product development for four years as a project engineer for a laser manufacturer and obtained a management qualification at the Open University. However, as a result of a change in corporate strategy caused by the recession, he had to leave this post. He contacted Dr Steele, who offered him the opportunity to carry out further research in the same optical scientific field as previously performed. At this point, disenchanted with his role as an employee within industry, he developed the idea of starting a venture as a way of taking control. Meanwhile Dr Steele had spun a company out of his lab and acted both as a role model and a support for Dr Perry:

> 'Dr Steele employed me because he knew I could do something of interest to him and because he is loyal. Loyalty is a key thing. Without loyalty, there would have been no business now because you need mutual support, it is scary to start a business, you need help.'[12]

Research was then carried out with a commercial interest in mind. Whereas in the case of Dr Jones and Mark, the recognition of a market opportunity was the main motivation for starting a company, for Dr Perry, entrepreneurship was a key part of a personal and an institutional strategy where the recognition of an opportunity acted as the main factor enabling the realisation of long-term personal plans.

Over the years Dr Steele and Dr Perry created a team, consisting of scientists with multidisciplinary scientific skills. They also wrote a patent application covering the principles underlying the optical devices and based on the results that had been achieved four years before, but kept confidential. This patent was later granted in the UK and in the US. Research was carried out for several years before obtaining significant results leading to commercial applications as described by the inventor:

> 'We got stuck with the technology. We could not progress. Four to five years were spent on research without the breakthrough that was necessary to make the technology widely available. I stayed on because I had a good job; academics have a comfortable way of life. There is a harsh difference between academia and business. It is painful for an academic to go into business.'[13]

A breakthrough was finally achieved in the method to make these optical devices. As possibilities for applications opened, Dr Perry and Dr Steele operationalised the idea of starting a company.

A business manager newly hired by the department and the AEN consultant also came to advise, each acting as catalysts in the business venture. Dr Perry agreed to present his business project at the AEN Forum because the Forum was an appropriate way to find out what investors expected and to test the attractiveness of his project. However, he had only two months to prepare the presentation, and the process of defining the markets and carrying out market research was problematic as these optical devices can have many applications. Two main market segments were broadly defined: the medical and the non-medical markets. His presentation was well attended, confirming the growing interest in this new technology and offering much useful feedback to Dr Perry on his business project. Although some of the investors attending the AEN Forum were ready to invest, Dr Perry did not accept any investment at this early stage because he was not confident enough in his proposal and needed to better define the market opportunity. When a breakthrough finally opened up commercial applications, the group's scientific advance was transformed into a potentially valuable commercial resource through the constitution of a patent portfolio. However, the recognition of a market opportunity was complicated by the novelty of this technology because the identification of users was a difficult task. Among the many potential applications for this new and generic technology, it was necessary to target only the ones that would create maximum value for the new company.

During the following year Dr Perry had to combine his academic commitments and research with developing a commercial strategy. Lack of time was an important issue. Dr Perry and the business manager of the department started to do some market research with the help of engineering and MBA students and developed several business scenarios. Owing to Dr Steele's contacts in the local business community, the scenarios were reviewed by venture capitalists who argued it was necessary to choose more specific applications for the technology. Dr Perry chose a low-cost route centred on using free resources in his environment to define the opportunity. However this case exemplifies Dr Perry's lack of commercial awareness, since he did not know how to use and synthesise the disparate and limited information he received from various sources.

After several months, Dr Perry thought the technology was not progressing at a fast enough rate. Thus, he slowed down the process of raising equity and focused on the research side with his team. They tried to consolidate the technology and to reduce the technical risks for the markets they were considering. Three months later, the positive comments of potential commercial partners and research team members convinced them that the technology base was strong enough. At that time the invention was protected by a portfolio of two patents and two others were underway. The strategy was more focused: as a development company, Cambridge Optica would license the technology to manufacturing partners in the medical market. Non-medical applications were completely abandoned. Medical applications were found to be the most promising and the consumer market would be targeted in priority. On the financial side, Cambridge Optica was working with an accountancy firm to help them find investors. A sum of £700,000 was sought over a three-year period. Dr Perry started to work for the business full-time eight months later. A clear opportunity was identified as well as a route to market, but they required the further development of the resources, especially the filing of new patents that would allow the company to license the technology in specific market segments.

## ANALYSIS OF THE VENTURES

In their entrepreneurial undertaking, both groups of entrepreneurs had to address similar problems: what is the opportunity? Can the proposed opportunity create value for the new company? Do we have the resources required to realise that opportunity and, if not, how do we acquire them? Can knowledge generated by research provide the basis for a new venture?

### *Opportunity recognition and special knowledge*

In the two cases presented above, the scientists lacked a thorough understanding of the commercial world, and did not possess a developed prior knowledge of the markets related to their technology. Therefore the two main difficulties the scientists encountered were related (1) to the identification of the problems that their technology could solve, and (2) to the possibility of generating rewards by solving these problems.

Opportunity recognition was activated by a distinctive way of doing science which allowed the academics to link their technology to the problems of agents in the market place. This study confirms the findings of Armstrong et al. (1999) concerning scientists-entrepreneurs working in liquid crystal technologies. Although the latter related to corporate scientists who were managing directors of high-tech firms, the two case studies analysed in this paper reflect that the scientists performed a similar type of application-oriented science. Dr Perry carried out long-term, speculative research but the ultimate potentiality for commercialisation was perceived early on, as a scientific breakthrough made 'technology push' possible. Dr Jones and Mark carried out user-oriented research which resulted in a prototype

(Von Hippel, 1988). Its commercialisation was progressively perceived as the logical next step to be taken. Both cases are examples of opportunity-driven science.

To counterbalance their lack of prior knowledge about markets, the scientists built special knowledge by drawing upon resources in their environment. Dr Jones and Mark used their medical and sports contacts, as well as the advice from the AEN consultant (and later feedback from potential investors), to acquire special knowledge about the motion capture market. As Dr Jones and Mark were both potential users of the technology and contacts with users had been formed very early on in the course of the research project, the identification of users' problems was facilitated.

In his process of targeting opportunities, Dr Perry utilised students, advisers, venture capitalists, and an accountancy firm, to carry out preliminary market research and give feedback on his business plan. The technology being generic, the early search opened many potential applications that could solve the problems of a range of users. Both cases are the results of collective entrepreneurship rather than the activity of a solo entrepreneur.

### *Opportunity and the creation of a valuable resource*

As mentioned above, another difficulty faced by the entrepreneur was the recognition of applications with commercial prospects. Opportunity recognition and the search for resources differed between the two examples according to the nature and market maturity of the technology concerned. Various problems regarding the identification of the sources of value-creation and the building of resources arise depending on the maturity of the technologies.

In Dr Perry's case, this is an emerging and generic technology, which presents the advantage of being easy to protect, although the market is difficult to identify. Potential applications are numerous but users might not see the uses for the new device. Competitors may be providing substitute solutions to the same problem based on different technologies. Among all the potential applications, those offering realistic possibilities for value-creation by the new enterprise must be identified and pursued. This selection process, carried out alongside scientific and technical development, took a year. Eventually the medical market was detected as offering the best opportunities for rewards. An emerging technology also requires a longer development, which implies a longer delay before profitability and extraction of value. Intellectual property protection was critical in transforming the technology into a valuable and rare resource. Therefore the extended period spent searching for opportunities was not wasted, since it was needed to consolidate the technological resource. A solid IP portfolio was created and further research carried out to reduce technical risks for particular market applications. Fund raising was the key subsequent stage which tested whether the opportunities selected would convince investors.

In the case of Dr Jones and Mark, the technology is more mature and some of these problems have been solved. Technology development is less uncertain and users' needs are clearer since it is much easier to target a market. By virtue of these advantages, the technology presents downsides as it is already in use and hard to protect. Competition exists and the technological resource is not as scarce and hard to replicate as in the above case. Therefore, the possibilities for realising returns are uncertain. Dr Jones and Mark had to refine their target opportunity if they were to access the financial resources needed. They identified niche markets where the competition was not as high and in which their own technical expertise applied to consulting as well as product development.

### Collective entrepreneurship and iteration between opportunities and resources

A successful academic 'spin-off' does not require that the founding academics transform themselves into Schumpeterian heroes, but rather that they create links with others who will enable them to build specialist knowledge, and shape the business project. They need help with identifying a business opportunity and finding the productive resources needed and setting up the venture. In both cases, the use of university facilities and equipment extended the resource base of the new company by allowing the research groups to carry out development, despite very limited financial resources. External expertise including the consultant, the business angel, the department's business manager, venture capitalists and students, was used to support the scientists in their initial entrepreneurial endeavours. The criticism that academics do not make good entrepreneurs outlined in the literature can be tempered by recognition that academics do not need to fulfil the full range of entrepreneurial functions in order to move their technology out of academe. They need to be able to detect and use key resources in their environment. Starting an academic 'spin-off' enterprise is a matter of teamwork and collective entrepreneurship.

Furthermore, it is tempting to consider the technology as the critical resource of an academic 'spin-off' company, on which competitive advantage can be based. However, other resources were needed, including university equipment and facilities and facilitation by knowledgeable individuals and groups who could provide business expertise. These resources were indispensable if transformation of public domain knowledge into an economic resource was to take place. These more mundane resources need recognition, because when taken together, they represent indispensable services to the entrepreneurial process.

The preparatory phase of new enterprise requires an iteration between opportunities and resources in order to create value. A large amount of time and effort was concentrated on recognising and defining the commercial opportunity that might be opened up by the development of a technological resource. Perceptions of the opportunity were modified as the project developed and moved forward and as new resources and competences were brought in. These cases stress that the opportunity recognition process is iterative. The exploitation of the commercial opportunity defines the objective of the new future venture, which in turn influences the type and extent of the resources needed.


## CONCLUSION

Opportunity recognition, the development of technological resources, and the search for complementary resources are identified as the key aspects of an interactive and collective entrepreneurial process by which academic-type knowledge is used as the basis for a new company. The benefit of applying the theory to case evidence is that it offers a systematic basis of comparison between the cases. In taking the evidence back to the theory, the need to consider technology and market maturity becomes clear. These are among the factors that influence the nature of the opportunity, the possibilities for value-creation and the constitution of the resource base for the new company. The analysis of complementary empirical evidence is required in order to pursue this line of enquiry and take the theory further.[14]

## NOTES

1. Other definitions include companies started by faculty members, members of staff, students and/or based on a technology or technology-based idea developed within the university (Smilor et al., 1990)
2. There are other definitions of economic opportunity such as Kirzner's: 'opportunities … consist in the availability of resources today at prices lower than the present value of the prices at which outputs can be sold in the future' (Kirzner, 1979: 113). However, this definition based on a discounted cash-flow approach is static in outlook and does not take into account the versatile character of opportunities in an uncertain economic environment.
3. However, new resources can be created by entrepreneurs, and not simply reallocated as Casson implies. Entrepreneurship stemming from the science base is partly a matter of converting a non-economic resource into an economic resource.
4. Definitions of resources necessarily have an element of tautology because they are identified in relation to objectives that require those means. Some tautology is necessary if the concepts in a theory are to interconnect, but there is a need to be alert to the circular reasoning to which this may give rise (cf Porter's 1991 critique of resource approaches).
5. Started by St John's Innovation Centre in early 1998, the Anglia Enterprise Network, AEN was composed of several local business organisations interested in entrepreneurship support and ended in August 1999. AEN aimed to support academics to realise a business idea, which typically involved the following activities: helping the academics to protect their idea, build a market strategy, write a business plan, raise money, and find managers when necessary.
6. Motion capture means recording information about the movement of a human subject in 3D space.
7. First draft of a business plan.
8. First draft of a business plan.
9. First draft of a business plan.
10. The AEN Forum is an opportunity for entrepreneurs to present their business plan to potential investors, such as venture capitalists and business angels. The ten-minute presentation is followed by break-out sessions where each entrepreneur gives more detailed explanations of the project to the interested investors.
11. The intellectual property system applied at the University of Cambridge allows scientists to retain the intellectual property of their inventions if they are self-funded or funded by the university.
12. Interview with Dr Perry.
13. Interview with Dr Perry.
14. This is the main objective of the PhD research agenda of one of the authors.

## REFERENCES

Armstrong, P., Tomes, A., Erol, R. and Dunmur, D. (1999) Entrepreneurship in science: case studies from liquid crystal application. Paper presented at *The Second International Conference: Entrepreneurship – Building for the Future*, Rennes, Saint-Malo, France, September 30th–October 2nd.

Barney, J.B. (1986) Strategic factor markets. *Management Science*, 32, pp. 1231–1241.

Barney, J.B. (1991) Firm resources and sustained competitive advantage. *Journal of Management*, 17(1), pp. 99–120.

Blair, D. and Hitchens, D. (1998) *Campus companies in the UK and Ireland*. Aldershot: Ashgate.

Brett, A., Gibson, D.V. and Smilor, R.W. (eds) (1991) *University Spin-off companies, Economic Development, Faculty Entrepreneurs and Technology Transfer*. Maryland: Rowman & Littlefield Publishers.

Casson, M. (1982) *The Entrepreneur, an Economic Theory*. Aldershot: Gregg Revivals.

Chiesa and Piccaluga (1998) Transforming rather then transferring scientific and technological knowledge – The contribution of academic 'spin-out' companies: the Italian way. In Oakey, R. and During, W. (eds) *New Technology-Based Firms in the 1990s, Volume V*, London: Paul Chapman.

Downes and Eadie (1998) The creation and support of academic spin-out companies. In Oakey, R. and During, W. (eds) *New Technology-Based Firms in the 1990s, Volume V*, London: Paul Chapman.

Etzkowitz, H. (1998) The norms of entrepreneurial science: cognitive effects of the new university-industry linkages. *Research Policy*, 27, pp. 823–833.

Garnsey, E. (1998) A theory of the early growth of the firm. *Industrial and Corporate Change*, 3, pp. 523–556.

Grant, R.M. (1991) The resource-based theory of competitive advantage: implications for strategy formulation. *California Management Review*, 33, Spring, pp. 119–135.

Kirzner, I.M. (1979) *Perceptions, Opportunity, and Profit*. Chicago: The University of Chicago Press.

Montgomery, C.A. (1995) Of diamonds and rust: a new look at resources. In Montgomery, C.A. (ed.) *Resource-Based and Evolutionary Theories of the Firm, Towards a Synthesis*. Boston: Kluwer Academic Publishers.

Montgomery, C.A. (ed.) (1995) *Resource-Based and Evolutionary Theories of the Firm, Towards a Synthesis*. Boston: Kluwer Academic Publishers.

Mustar, P. (1994) *Science et Innovation – Annuaire Raisonné de la Création d'Entreprises par les Chercheurs*. Paris: Economica.

Mustar, P. (1997) How French academics create hi-tech companies: the conditions for success or failure. *Science and Public Policy*, 24 (1), pp. 37–43.

Oakey, R. and During, W. (eds) (1998) *New Technology-Based Firms in the 1990s, Volume V*, London: Paul Chapman.

Penrose, E.T. (1959) *The Theory of the Growth of the Firm*. Oxford: Oxford University Press.

Porter, M.E. (1991) Towards a dynamic theory of strategy. *Strategic Management Journal*, 12, Winter, pp. 95–117.

Rappert, B. (1997) University spin-offs in the commercialisation of research. *Industry and Higher Education*, 11(5), pp. 270–277.

Rappert, B. and Webster A. (1998) Links between university and their spin-offs, Variation by type and by sector. *Industry and Higher Education*, December.

Roberts, E.B. (1991) *Entrepreneurs in High Technology; Lessons from MIT and Beyond*. New-York: Oxford University Press.

Roberts, E.B. and Malone, D.E. (1996) Policies and structures for spinning off new companies from research and development organizations. *R&D Management*, 26(1), pp. 17–48.

Shane, S. and Venkataraman, S. (2000) The promises of entrepreneurship as a field of research. *The Academy of Management Review*, 25, 1, pp. 217–226.

Smilor, R.W., Gibson, D.V. and Dietrich, G.B. (1990) University spin-out companies: technology start-ups from UT-Austin. *Journal of Business Venturing*, 5, pp. 63–76.

Stankiewicz, R. (1994) Spin-off companies from universities. *Science and Public Policy*, 21(2), pp. 99–107.

Von Hippel, E. (1988) *The Sources of Innovation*. Oxford: Oxford University Press.

Wernerfelt, B. (1984) A resource-based view of the firm. *Strategic Management Journal*, 14, Spring, pp. 4–12.

CHAPTER 15

# Commercialisation and Regional Economic Development: Universities and their Role in the Emergence of New Technologies

SARAH Y. COOPER

## INTRODUCTION

In attempting to identify ways of enhancing levels of innovation and economic activity occurring at the local, regional and national level, attention is being focused upon the roles which different institutions may play in contributing to the development of regional economies. The development of some regional agglomerations has been linked to the presence of specialist research laboratories and educational establishments which have provided a focus for public and private sector investment which has in turn helped stimulate the emergence of firms exploiting newly emerging technologies. The *Commercialisation Enquiry* of 1996 recognised that commercialising scientific and technical research made an important and varied contribution to the Scottish economy but acknowledged that the contribution could be much greater (Scottish Enterprise/Royal Society of Edinburgh (SE/RSE), 1996). Universities were identified as well placed to play a leading role in the commercialisation process as sites of much leading-edge research and the source of many innovative opportunities. Failure to exploit ideas emanating from within their walls, however, is an important loss to both the institutions and wider economy. Commercialisation does not just happen but can be facilitated by the development of the right cultural environment and creation of the right supporting infrastructure.

   This paper explores some of the multifaceted roles which universities play in the emergence and growth of technologies and regional economies, from acting as sources of ideas and of graduates with the skills required by new dynamic firms, to providing access to specialist expertise in the form of academics working at the forefront of their field. The paper also considers some of the factors that have lead universities to look carefully at the potential benefits of commercialisation as a strategy, in particular pressures on funding which mean that greater attention is being paid to identifying alternative income streams. Having considered broader issues related to the role of universities in the emergence of technology-based firms, the paper considers the approach that Heriot-Watt University has been following since early 1997 with regard to encouraging innovation and commercialisation within and beyond its walls. It is perceived that advantages accrue to the wider economy from increased commercialisation activities; thus, the wider benefits for regional economic development are considered in the conclusion to this paper.

## THE UNIVERSITY AND ITS ENVIRONMENT

### Research and education: bipartite roles

Universities have two main aims, education and research (The British Council, 1978). The two should be viewed as mutually supporting, even if some forms of external teaching and research assessment run the risk of concentrating attention on one at the expense of another. A university whose staff engages in leading-edge research is well placed to offer its students an education where they are exposed to the very latest developments in their field. A university with strong links into the commercial world ensures that its students emerge with a sound theoretical understanding of their discipline and a critical appreciation of the applied/practical issues of major importance in the commercial environment in which many will one day work.

The focus of much research in universities, in common with most governmental and voluntary sector research organisations, is at the 'basic' end of the spectrum. Few commercial organisations, by contrast, expend many of their resources on speculative, blue-sky research. In universities the broad balance is perhaps 70 per cent basic research, 20 per cent development and 10 per cent applied work, while it is quite different for most commercial organisations. Universities act as communities of specialists in a wide range of fields, working at the leading edge of research within their chosen specialisation. Thus, some staff within universities are involved in the types of research which results in significant technological breakthrough central to advancement of understanding related to the technological core of some areas of enquiry. As such they have the opportunity to develop know-how of considerable commercial value. Options include the licensing of technology to others to enable them to exploit the technology in return for the payment of an initial fee and a royalty payment, providing an initial payment and subsequent income streams. This is ideal when there is no one who wishes to create a spin-out firm to exploit the technology. Many universities now have in place infrastructure and policy to co-ordinate and control knowledge management strategy, and develop appropriate collaborative relationships.

### Rationales for collaboration

Since the British Council hosted its British-German Seminar on Academic Research and Industry in February 1977, most universities in Britain have become increasingly aware of the need to exploit know-how developed within their walls. One facet of the strategy involves the development of collaborative relationships with external, and particularly industrial, partners. External organisations have similarly become increasingly aware of what the academic community has to offer by way of, for example, technology and expertise:

> 'The prime function of industry is to generate wealth and provide employment. Consequently the majority of research undertaken in industry is short term and strategic (intermediate time scale) research, and it also tends to be innovative in terms of products. Universities on the other hand, are much more involved in the fundamental research and the training of personnel ... There is a need to create a really effective interaction between university and industrial sectors. Unlike Germany where there is much more interaction between university and industry this type of collaboration is not very frequent in Britain. The attitudes within British universities are beginning the change, especially within those with a strong technological background, from being scientifically

*oriented towards having a greater emphasis on the market.'* (The British Council, 1978)

In the UK as a whole, and in Scotland in particular, there has been sustained interest in the benefits of partnership between the educational and business/ industrial communities. The emphasis has been firmly focused on how collaboration could be to the advantage of all parties involved and to the benefit of the wider economy. Two sets of reports have focused specifically on the issue in the UK (Advisory Council for Applied Research and Development (ACARD), 1983; Howells et al., 1998) and Scottish contexts (Scottish Council Development and Industry (SCDI) 1983; SE/RSE 1996). The SCDI (1983) report recognised the distinct culture within universities and the idea that universities were often seen as remote, but acknowledged that the situation was changing, with progress in opening up the research arena for commercialisation and exploitation. The report also suggested that the situation was not uniquely British, but one pertaining in a number of countries. However, more recently it has been suggested that there is still some way to go if universities and commercial organisations are to exploit fully the opportunities that are open to them.

Howells et al. (1998) consider that academic-industry linkages result from four principal mechanisms/sources. These are informal contacts and spin-outs from departments within universities, research performed for industry on a collaborative/contract basis, property-lead initiatives such as science parks, and finally through the exploitation of university research by means of the management of intellectual property rights (IPR). They identify a number of institutional reasons for commercialising research: (a) to generate additional income, (b) to participate in local economic development, (c) to gain prestige for the institution, (d) to fulfil obligations to sponsors, (e) to motivate and reward staff. In addition, they identify individual motivations, which include financial benefits, recognition and the achievement of entrepreneurial status and the wish to make a contribution to society. Universities are ranked annually on the basis of their income from different sources including commerce, research councils and sponsorship. Competition is too strong to be highly ranked in terms of commercial income to demonstrate just how 'in-touch' the universities are.

The development of more commercially aware universities is a positive and logical step from the perspective of intellectual exploitation and there is an appreciation that spanning the academia-industry divide serves multiple interests. These changes are being stimulated by a number of contrasting pressures; as in the commercial world competition is increasingly the name of the game; universities are competing for students and financial resources. Institutions are focused on providing programmes to attract students and equip them with the knowledge and skills required by the commercial world. Financially, universities are being squeezed, as the funding councils are unable to meet all their funding needs/ expectations. Like any business experiencing an insufficient flow of funds, universities have been looking to develop existing and new areas of revenue generation. They are increasingly focusing on ways of maximising returns on their assets, just like a business building upon its core competences. Many of today's businesses recognise that their greatest assets are not their physical resources but their intellectual and systems capabilities; 'professional intellect creates most of the value in the new economy' (Quinn et al., 1996). In universities the focus has consequently fallen on ways to exploit the intellectual capital within their walls. They are turning their attention to technology, which has been developed to ensure that that which has commercial value sees the light of day. Much of the research, which generates technology, is publicly funded; failure to capitalise on this knowledge is both a significant waste and a missed opportunity.

### The university and regional economies

Arguably, those seeking the most positive role models for successful academic-industry interaction look to the United States (US). It is difficult to heed reference to the high technology agglomeration along Route 128 in Boston, Massachusetts, and not think of the Massachusetts Institute of Technology (MIT). Not only has MIT been responsible for the provision of numerous ideas upon which firms in the area have based and developed but also many academics within the university have on-going involvement with firms in the locality and beyond (BankBoston, 1997). On the west coast of the US, Stanford and Berkeley are, similarly, associated with the development of Silicon Valley, with some of the brightest and best making the transition from university, either as students or researchers, into business. Two of the best known, Hewlett and Packard, swapped the research lab for a modest garage where they laid the foundations of their business empire. Meanwhile many universities have been linked with the development of agglomerations of technology-based firms. Storper, (1995) has argued that 'there is a much smaller number of Silicon Valleys and Route 128s'. Today many US academics span the divide between academia and the commercial world; arguably, the most exciting opportunities exist for those in the fields of science, engineering and technology. Some 'academics' do not cross the divide but have associations with the commercial world, holding company positions as well as doing the 'day job'. Academics with close industrial associations are much more common in the US, but an increasing number of UK staff are developing characteristics similar to their trans-Atlantic counterparts.

Universities have a multifaceted role to play within their local economy; they are significant employers of academic, technical, administrative and support staff, and through their undergraduate and postgraduate activities attract a sizeable number of students to their locality for varying length periods, generating beneficial economic multiplier effects. A number of those attracted to work or study at a university tend to remain in the locality once they leave, either to work for other organisations or to establish their own business (Keeble, 1987; Cooper, 1996; Lind-holm Dahlstrand, 1999). Universities are producers of employable, well-qualified individuals and as such, locations in which they are situated are able to attract firms seeking skilled labour. Universities act as a source of technological ideas and of potential entrepreneurs, both emanating from the student and staff community. Accordingly they can act as magnets for local firms seeking close proximity to specific expertise. In some instances technological know-how is made available to existing commercial organisations for exploitation by means of, for example, a licence. In other situations the technology forms the basis of a new venture which may be incubated within the institution before spinning-out. Institutions play varyingly proactive roles in both encouraging the recognition of technology with commercial potential and the support and incubation of business ventures.

## COMMERCIALISATION AND ACADEMIC-INDUSTRY LINKAGES

The four types of academic-industry linkage defined by Howell et al. (1998) discussed provide a framework for discussing the role which universities may play in stimulating economic activity and commercialising their technology.

## External R&D activities

It is widely recognised that the innovation process is a collective activity (Lawton Smith, 1997). While many firms are entering into strategic technology-based alliances, it seems rational that universities and firms will identify incentives for co-operation. Internal R&D may be insufficient to meet a company's needs, and the rapid rate of technology development has encouraged firms to externalise aspects of their R&D acquisition activities in an attempt to fast-track product and process development activities (Lawton Smith, 1990). Some firms turn to specialists within universities to act as R&D suppliers or collaborators. Government research establishments have been linked to the development of clusters of industries working with them (Buswell and Lewis, 1970; Morphet, 1987) and universities have been linked to the development of high-technology businesses. However, Oakey (1985) questions the actual degree of collaboration that occurs between universities and local firms. Given their differing research foci, it is potentially powerful when these two types of organisation collaborate, as the combined force of experts from contrasting ends of the R&D spectrum maximise the output potential of projects. Both parties have the opportunity to learn through the experience and exploit any resultant synergies. One initiative where universities and outside organisations can form fruitful relationships is through the Teaching Company Scheme, operated by the Teaching Company Directorate. Knowledge within universities is transferred to external organisations. Associates employed by the university, but working for the participating industrial/commercial organisation, introduce new ideas into the firm, thereby enhancing its capabilities and hopefully developing its innovative and competitive potential.

While technical links may be maintained over long distances, they are most readily maintained within a local area. Sweeny (1987) considers that, since links or networks are based upon 'person-to-person' contacts, proximity is relatively important, and hence the desire 'to be located within the half-hour contact potential'. He also acknowledges that once having met the telephone provides an alternative, punctuated by the occasional personal meeting. Cooper (1999) identified no spatial bias in favour of proximity to university research partners amongst small software and electronics firms. Enthusiasm for the university science park is predicated on the belief that interaction will occur between firms and academics in the university. There is debate between those who believe that universities and science parks play a role in stimulating industrial development (Monck et al., 1988) and those who question the precise nature of the relationship between universities, science parks and the growth of agglomerations of technology-based firms (Oakey, 1985). While the level of interaction may vary, research-intensive organisations are perceived to be an important part of the innovation infrastructure in improving the network to support and encourage new enterprise development and growth. Modern communication technology enables universities to support the research of organisations not only within their locality, but world wide. Firms and other organisations requiring specialist help tend to seek out the institution that offers the knowledge expertise they need to access, wherever they may be located. Proximity does facilitate meetings, but distance tends not to be insurmountable if the link is what is required (Cooper, 1996).

Currently there is an awareness gap between universities and the commercial world. Firms that could benefit from the assistance of experts available within universities are not accessing the required help. Universities generate technology in-house but are also well placed to help facilitate the emergence of technology and development of business opportunities within other organisations. In 1983 SCDI commented:

*'Most contacts today between universities or colleges and industry arise out of personal knowledge, and mainly concern large companies who are familiar with the universities' system and people, and can readily gain access to the right place. The difficulties lie with the small and medium-sized or young companies who do not always realise their problems, and do not know how to obtain help. They are the section of the economy which has most to gain from better interplay, and are a prime vehicle for innovation.'*

Today the same situation exists, although perhaps it is less marked. Arguably, while an increasing proportion of the graduate workforce are aware that help may be available to them from universities, in their work for others or in their own business venture, graduates are probably unaware of the breadth of assistance that is available within institutions.

## The academic spin-out

As well as producing technological know-how, which can be commercialised, universities also act as a source of entrepreneurs or business founders. Cooper (1973) characterises organisations by their birth rates, in terms of their propensity to 'produce' spin-off entrepreneurs. He suggests that low birth-rate organisations employ large numbers of employees, are organised by function, recruit average technical people, are relatively well managed and are located in areas of little entrepreneurship. By contrast, high birth-rate organisations have small numbers of employees, are product-decentralised, recruit very capable ambitious people, are afflicted by periodic crisis and are located in areas of high entrepreneurship, where role models fulfil the role of encouraging further entrepreneurial activity. Research amongst new technology-based firms suggests that public sector institutions, such as universities and government research establishments, are a minority source of business founders, the majority coming from commercial firms, both large, medium and small (Oakey, 1995; Cooper, 1996; Lindholm Dahlstrand, 1999). Lindholm Dahlstrand (1999) highlights the fact that a relatively large number of new firms are indirect university spin-outs as their founders worked for other organisations within the locality following graduation or resignation, before setting up in business. To reduce risk and build upon existing networks most founders establish firms in the field of technology in which they have worked previously (Oakey, 1995; Cooper, 1996), although the degree of sectoral similarity may vary depending on the size and age of the sector (Cooper, 1998). For example, most electronics spin-outs are generated from other electronics firms, whereas in the software or biotechnology sector few new start-ups originate from within the sector. A sizeable proportion come from organisations that share aspects of the underlying science/technology but are less closely allied (Cooper, 2000).

Cooper's (1973) typology reflects how the type of organisation for which the founder worked influences the breadth of knowledge he develops. Whether founders come from private firms or public sector institutions, such as universities and government research establishments, most provide an environment which allows entrepreneurs to establish firms built upon their research and technical experience. What varies is the degree of exposure to commercial issues. Most technical entrepreneurs have experience primarily in technical areas, since many have held research and technical positions, which provide limited management training. Research has shown that most technical entrepreneurs, whether from an academic or commercial background, lack experience in marketing and finance (Shanklin and Ryans, 1988; Oakey et al., 1993). Cooper (1997) further revealed sectoral variations in expertise. Founders in the electronics sector mainly worked in relatively strict, technical and functional roles, while software founders held predominantly technical/sales positions, developing a combination of technical skills and commercial awareness. When academic entrepreneurs establish a business they are strong on the technical side but tend to lack a commercial base, including knowledge of and contacts with potential suppliers, customers and other technical specialists, to grow a business beyond the start-up stage. Many 'academic' entrepreneurs have strengths in project management, and through co-ordinating research teams have developed relevant people-management skills (Jones-Evans, 1996) to counteract their commercial weakness. Many also team up with others offering complementary skills (Cooper, 1998).

A study was undertaken in the electronics and software industry in the UK to explore the extent of academic spin-outs in industry (Cooper, 1996). The sample size was based on 94 firms. A further two founders were employed in public-sector research establishments. Four of the six academic spin-outs were located in Scotland and four of the total were in the software sector. Spinning-out was not the sole preserve of youngsters; three founders were in their twenties, two in their forties and one was 55 years of age. Three of the spin-outs were started by a multiple of founders, one by three people and two by four individuals started three of the spin-outs. Two of the sole founders benefited from a combination of commercial and academic experience, while the third had only technical experience. In a group of multiple founders the team members contributed complementary expertise. In four of the six cases the academic was the managing director or proprietor (Cooper, 1996).

Four of the university spin-outs were initiated on the basis of the academic's previous expertise. Three firms generated revenue from contract research and factoring, and provided resources to invest in product development. The formation of a management team is important to the development of a successful company. Also the extent of involvement of an academic with external organisations influences the networks developed. An academic with a strong network is likely to come into contact with potential entrepreneurial colleagues outside his workplace. The workplace also provides an environment in which to identify possible business partners (Cooper, 1996). In the cases of multiple founders, some, if not all had worked together previously. This enabled members to evaluate their partners and consider how they might 'get on' in a business setting. Five out of the six firms had been established within 30 miles of the founder's former workplace. Only one founder had been brought up in the same locality in which he established his firm. The majority of founders had moved away from home to take a degree and on completion of their studies had not moved back. In spite of leaving the university four of the six founders maintained informal research links with their institution, and three of the six firms were located in a science park. At start-up all six firms had been micro businesses with fewer than ten employees. During the intervening years, three of the firms had grown from micro-business into employers of sizeable numbers of staff; two employed 20–49 staff and the third employed over 100. Such firms made an important, contribution to their local economy in terms of employment and customer and supplier linkages, which tended to be locally oriented (Cooper, 1998).

### Property-led initiatives

A large number of UK universities have developed science or research parks since Heriot-Watt University established the Research Park at Riccarton, Edinburgh, in 1971, the first in Europe. According to the United Kingdom Science Park Association (UKSPA), a science park is:

*'a business support and technology transfer initiative that: encourages and supports the start up and incubation of innovation led, high growth, knowledge based businesses; provides an environment where larger and international businesses can develop specific and close interactions with a particular centre of knowledge creation for their mutual benefit; and has formal and operational links with centres of knowledge creation such as universities, higher education institutes and research organisations.'* (UKSPA 2000)

In 1997 UKSPA had over 1400 tenant firms providing 27,300 jobs on its 53 Full and Associate Member parks (UKSPA, 1998). What constitutes a science park and the degree of collaboration that exists between tenants and university departments, varies from one to another. Extensive research has been conducted, examining the development and growth of science park-based firms (Westhead and Storey, 1994). A science park located right on the doorstep of a university does not imply that the tenant firms will seek to tap into the expertise within the university. Where such access is sought proximity will facilitate interaction. Increasing numbers of universities are establishing incubator units to provide space for spin-outs aimed at university start-ups. The supported environment provides a sound base on which to develop the embryonic enterprise, until it is ready for larger premises. For example the UK Business Incubation (UKBI) was established to help support a wide range of organisations and partnerships with the development of incubation initiatives. A range of bodies including the Department of Trade and Industry (DTI), Prudential Corporation and the Midland Bank sponsors UKBI. It is intended to fulfil a number of roles which include assisting and supporting new and existing business incubation projects, providing information on best practice, encouraging partnerships including those with universities and ensuring integration of incubation projects with the local business support infrastructure (UKBI, 1999).

### Exploiting IPR

The protection and exploitation of intellectual property (IP) is a complex legal area. A number of universities are realising the value of their IP and many are focusing upon ways of maximising returns from it. Technology transfer offices are becoming common within universities, and are responsible for a range of activities and initiatives. They are assuming responsibility for identifying and alerting staff to the commercial potential of IP and communicating to the business community the services and expertise available. In 1977, prior to the development of the current Research Assessment Exercise (RAE) process, with its focus on volume/quality of publications, it was acknowledged that promotion of university staff was more dependent upon the volume of papers than their 'qualitative merit'. The British Council (1978) stated that 'scientists publish increasing numbers of papers, frequently overlooking the needs of industry'. There is still a strong link/correlation between publications and promotion, but emphasis is growing on other measures of research output. The criteria for any post-2001 RAE are likely to be different, possibly with increased emphasis on industrial involvement. Concentration on publishing can mean that IP may take second place. While staff involved in ground-breaking research develop commercially valuable ideas, resulting know-how may be left on the shelf, its full value unrecognised. This constitutes a major waste of funding and a missed opportunity to recoup expenditure and generate income. When a viable opportunity is identified, a decision has to be taken as to how it can best be exploited. The tendency for academics to disseminate their research findings through the medium of publication can jeopardise the opportunity to protect know-how; academics are being 'educated' about the importance of protection prior to disclosure. Technology ownership also has to be resolved, in terms of whether the know-how was developed wholly or partially in the course of the person's employment, the source of funding, and whether inter-organisational collaboration was involved (SHEFC, 1997; Howells et al., 1998). Access to legal advice is essential for institutions seeking to exploit know-how (SHEFC, 1997, Howells et al., 1998), hence the importance of Technology Licensing Offices.

## UNIVERSITIES AND COMMERCIALISATION: THE SCOTTISH CONTEXT

There are 20 Scottish higher education (HE) institutions including 14 universities; while over 36,000 people are directly employed in these institutions, an estimated 38,000 additional jobs exist elsewhere in the Scottish economy as a result of HE activities (McNicoll, 1995). Meanwhile, 380,000 people in Scotland are involved directly in Scottish HE, either as staff or students (COSHEP, 1998). Nearly 50 per cent of young people in Scotland undertake a programme of full-time study (32 per cent in Britain as a whole) and Scotland records one of the highest European proportions of graduates per head (Scottish Enterprise, 1999). The reputation of Scottish HE is widely recognised; Scotland is a net importer of over 27,000 students from the rest of the UK and approximately 20,000 from over 100 countries (HESA, 1998a). Scotland's HE institutions make an important financial contribution to the economy, with a total annual income in excess of £1.27bn. Funding for HE comes in the form of core public funding for teaching and research, which accounts for approximately 60 per cent of the sector's income; the remaining 40 per cent is generated from a range of public and private sector sources (McNicoll, 1995). Although Scotland has only 9 per cent of the UK's population, its institutions attract in excess of their share of income from funding sources (Table 15.1).

A common measure of research strength is the propensity of the institution's academics to undertake research and publish. Scotland's academics generate 1 per cent of all research publications world-wide/head of population, third highest in the world (SE/RSE, 1996). Scotland is strong in a number of areas, including computer science, opto-electronics; and biotechnology; 18 per cent of PhDs gained by candidates in fields related to biotechnology are awarded in Scotland (Scottish Enterprise, 1999). Research conducted in Scottish HE establishments has been responsible for innovative breakthroughs, which have led to major developments in several leading science and technology areas. For example, the computer game Lemmings, the vaccine for Hepatitis B and the use of nuclear magnetic resonance (NMR) for imaging are all 'products' of HE-based research.

**Table 15.1:** *Scottish higher education: funding performance 1996/7*

| Factor | Scottish share |
| --- | --- |
| Total UK funding council resources for research | 12% |
| Research councils' resources for research | 13% |
| Government research departments' resources for research | 13% |
| EU research resources spent in the UK | 12% |

*Source: COSHEP (1998)*

## Commercialisation and Heriot-Watt University

Universities are developing their own approaches to maximising their contribution to the economy through technology commercialisation and the encouragement of inter-organisational linkages. Heriot-Watt University, for example, has a proactive approach, some aspects of which are considered here. Under the umbrella of Technology and Research Services (TRS), it is involved in a range of initiatives.

The university has approximately 14,000 students, 40 per cent of which are campus-based, the remainder studying through distance learning. Of the 5756 campus-based students, 2742 are in Engineering, 1646 are taking degrees in Management and Languages, and 1368 are in Mathematics and Sciences (Heriot-Watt University, 1999). The university is a major employer with 1790 staff (March 2000) at its Edinburgh, Borders and Orkney Campuses. With strengths in a range of fields including opto-electronics, petroleum engineering and brewing & distilling, the university is well-placed to benefit from links with the commercial world. The university earns a sizeable proportion of its research income from commercial sources (see Table 15.2), and compares favourably with the UK average per employee (see Table 15.3). Many departments and research groups have strong research and technical links with external organisations. Many of these are dependent upon the staff and the nature of their particular networks and connections.

Technology and Research Services (TRS) co-ordinates the university's range of activities in the areas of commercialisation, consultancy and the Research Park. Under its umbrella is the Institute of Technology Management (ITM), established in 1992 to help improve the university/industry interface. Its emphasis is on the transfer of skills and technology from the university into industry through hands-on involvement, with a focus on SMEs. This takes various forms, including business projects, project management and co-ordination through Teaching Company Schemes, and consultancy or technology development and exploitation through commercialisation. It uses its academic, industrial, professional and enterprise networks to enable it to lever-in a wide range of resources, including finance, to support initiatives.

TRS has a five-stage development process through which ideas with commercial potential pass, being evaluated and filtered. Stage One is Initial Evaluation; at this

**Table 15.2:** *Heriot-Watt University income 1998/1999*

| Source | Amount | % share |
|---|---|---|
| Funding council grants | £27.0m | 37 |
| Other operating income | £18.7m | 26 |
| Academic fees and support grants | £13.0m | 18 |
| Research grants and contacts | £12.2m | 17 |
| **Of that:** | | |
| *Research councils* | *£4.7m* | *40* |
| *UK industry, commerce, public corps* | *£3.3m* | *27* |
| *EU government bodies* | *£1.5m* | *12* |
| *UK public bodies* | *£1.0m* | *8* |
| *Other overseas* | *£0.9m* | *7* |
| *Other* | *£0.7m* | *6* |
| Endowment income and interest receivable | £1.8m | 2 |
| **Total** | **£72.7m** | **100** |

*Source: Heriot-Watt University (1999)*

**Table 15.3:** *Industrial and research council funding (£000/FT academic staff member)*

|  | 1995/1996 | | 1996/1997 | | 1997/1998 | |
|---|---|---|---|---|---|---|
|  | **RC** | **IR** | **RC** | **IR** | **RC** | **IR** |
| Heriot-Watt | 12.03 | 11.42 | 14.49 | 9.16 | 13.99 | 9.46 |
| Scotland | 6.96 | 2.26 | 7.2 | 2.62 | 7.32 | 2.72 |
| England | 7.15 | 2.24 | 7.2 | 2.55 | 7.32 | 2.79 |
| UK | 6.83 | 2.18 | 6.9 | 2.47 | 7.03 | 2.73 |

*RC = Research Council Funding per FT member of academic staff in thousands*
*IR = Industrial Research Funding per FT member of academic staff in thousands*
*Source: HESA (1997; 1998b; 1999)*

point ideas are considered to determine whether the idea is attractive and whether or not there is IP which needs to be protected before the idea proceeds any further. Many ideas are rejected at this stage. Surviving ideas proceed to Stage Two – Commercialisation Route Decision – where options for the most appropriate exploitation route are considered. Options include company formation or licensing. Ideas considered for spin-out then pass to Virtual Company and Feasibility (Stage Three), where feasibility is assessed, market analysis carried out and a business plan developed. There are four potential outcomes: no route for commercialisation, licensing to a third party, spin-off a company or joint venture formation. Stage Four is Company Formation, where the firm becomes a separate legal entity from the university, usually the university is one of the shareholders. Stage Five is Further Development where the firm develops and grows, receiving minimal assistance from the university (ITM, 1997).

Since the start of 1997 academics have brought forward over 90 ideas. In 1997, for example, 37 projects were opened from a wide range of departments: Mechanical Engineering (9), Building Engineering (9), Computing and Electrical (7), Civil and Offshore (6), Physics (2), and one each from Chemistry, Centre for Sport and Exercise, Mathematics and Languages. In that year seven new patents were lodged on behalf of the University, and six teams were co-ordinated into virtual companies (ITM, 1998). As at March 2000, the process has facilitated the formation of eight spin-out companies. These have spun-out from the following departments: Mechanical Engineering (1), Physics (1), Learning Technology Centre (2), Languages (1), Textiles (1), Petroleum Engineering (1) and Biological Sciences/Chemical Engineering (1). All are currently micro businesses (0–9 employees), but in total have 31 people working for them. In all cases the university has taken an equity share which varies from firm to firm. Four of the eight firms have been SMART award winners, providing valuable business funding. In addition to a steady stream of patent filings, the university is keen to increase license income. In March 2000 the university had six current licenses, the majority in software; small firms, five of which were in Scotland, held all six licenses.

Heriot-Watt University first explored the possibility of establishing its own Research Park in the 1960s. It was in 1971 that the Research Park became operational with its first tenant moving in during April of that year. At that time it covered an area of 30 acres; following significant expansion the Park now occupies 85 developed acres. Heriot-Watt University currently has 48 campus companies, the smallest of which occupies a unit of approximately 1000 sq. ft, the largest occupies a site of over 13 acres. The campus companies have a combined turnover of approximately £75 million a year in R&D technology-based business, and employ approximately 2000 employees. Of the 48 companies, 11 are Heriot-Watt University spin-outs, and two are spin-outs from other institutions in the Edinburgh area. Approximately 25 per cent of tenants are overseas owned.

Table 15.4 presents a comparison of the domain of Research Park companies and university research. All firms are required to have links to academic departments within the university, and are assisted in brokering 'marriages' with departments. The immediate proximity of the Research Park to university facilitates these links. Approximately 30 per cent of tenants are single-site companies; firms requiring larger scale manufacturing perform this elsewhere. While manufacturing is not permitted, pre-production and bespoke manufacturing, along with small-scale production are allowed. The Research Park is sited within the greenbelt and no direct sales to the public are permitted. Development of incubator units on the Research Park is under consideration to provide accommodation for small start-up businesses. Incubator units are currently under construction at the university's Scottish Borders Campus in Galashiels.

It can be seen how the university is pursuing a number of strands of activity to exploit its own technology and support the activities of other external organisations. Its contribution is multidimensional; it provides graduates for the jobs market, research and consultancy services for external organisations, as well as making technology available. It has in place a mechanism to support the spin-out academic and a Research Park to provide premises for the emergent business. Through these and other activities the university aims to meet the needs of industry and benefit the economy.


CONCLUSIONS

The preceding discussion suggests that there are many ways in which universities may play a role within the economy. Universities provide significant direct and indirect employment. They generate graduates to help meet the demand of today's dynamic businesses for highly skilled staff, and support the innovation activities of a wide variety of organisations, through the development of technology, including the provision of support services and licensed technology. Universities are sometime seen as ivory towers and there is growing evidence that any cultural barrier is not insurmountable. Universities with external links are likely to fulfil a technology transfer role, improving the efficiency and innovativeness of partners with which they work. Some academics develop strong relationships with external actors, but links are dependent upon people and as they are mobile, the nature and strength of links will ebb and flow. As technology evolves and the needs of industry alter the nature and intensity of links will similarly change. The system is dynamic and it is not possible to lock institutions together. Synergy has to be seen to be there for each to want to come to the table.

Table 15.4: *Domain of Research Park companies and university research*

| Activity | Research Park companies | University research |
|---|---|---|
| Marine technology | 20% | 27% |
| Biotechnology | 20% | 11% |
| Information technology | 17% | 31% |
| Business management | 10% | 8% |
| Others | 33% | 23% |

Research and licensing links can raise the profile of the university and enhance its reputation as a generator of useful technology, and hopefully improve the competitiveness of the firms, which acquire technology. Arguably there is a lack of knowledge of what help is available within institutions to help organisations within the local community. The development of events such as Open Doors Days may help to increase awareness of what institutions have to offer, helping both the institution and external organisations concerned.

Universities are an important source of entrepreneurs, spinning-out either directly or indirectly. The barriers to start-up vary between sectors (Cooper, 1996), but there is scope for academics to pursue highly successful entrepreneurial careers in the commercial world. Staff are increasingly encouraged to identify licensing opportunities for in-house developed technology. More academics are also working closely with commercial firms, thereby gaining greater insights into the commercial world. In the long term a minority may be tempted into heading-up a spin-out team or into taking part-time directorships with spin-out companies. Given their relative lack of commercial expertise, the appropriate long-term role of academic entrepreneurs might be questioned, but teams comprising those with complementary skills provide a partial answer.

Universities that generate successful academic entrepreneurs are more likely to see higher levels of spin-out than those where there are few positive role models. It is a question of how you kick-start the virtuous circle. A recent initiative from the UK government may help the process of culture change amongst both staff and students within universities. In 1999 the Office of Science and Technology (OST) launched a major initiative, Science Enterprise Challenge (SEC), aimed at increasing the ability of the UK university community to generate the entrepreneurs of tomorrow. The principal aims of the initiative are to foster the commercialisation of research and new ideas, stimulate scientific entrepreneurialism and result in institutions incorporating the teaching of enterprise into the science and engineering curricula, thereby raising awareness of opportunities and facilitating commercialisation. A total of £25 million has been awarded, for a five-year period, to support the creation of eight centres of excellence. Currently a sizeable number of graduates from science and engineering do not pursue careers in related sectors; time will tell whether SEC will reverse the flow.

While levels of direct university spin-outs are not high, anecdotal evidence suggests that universities act as a magnet, attracting students and researchers who go on to work for other firms in their locality before becoming 'indirect' spin-out entrepreneurs from the commercial sector. Thus, universities, where not acting as direct generators of new firm starts, are able to act as incubators of the entrepreneurial and innovative spirit which develops wings some way down the line. Universities also act as magnets to firms who seek their graduates and/or the development of links to specific centres of expertise. Communications technology is making the maintenance of remote links simpler, but firms desiring physical proximity are still candidates to be attracted.

The ability of institutions to contribute to economic development will vary depending upon their mix of specialisation. Benefits will not accrue simply within the local environment, universities have the potential to spread their effects much more widely. It is likely that each institution will develop its own approach dependent upon its context, but it is apparent that the opportunity is there for universities to have an impact in the areas of human, technological and economic development.

## REFERENCES

Advisory Council for Applied Research and Development (ACARD) (1983) *Improving Research Links between Higher Education and Industry*, joint report of the ACARD in collaboration with the Advisory Board for the Research Councils, London, HMSO.

BankBoston (1997) *MIT: The Impact of Innovation*, Boston, BankBoston Economics Department.

Buswell, R.J. and Lewis, E.W. (1970) 'The geographical distribution of industrial research activity in the United Kingdom', *Regional Studies*, **4**, 3, pp. 297–306.

Cooper, A.C. (1973) 'Technical Entrepreneurship: what do we know?' *R&D Management*, Vol. 3, No. 2, pp. 59–64.

Cooper, S.Y. (1996) 'Small high technology firms: a theoretical and empirical study of location issues', unpublished PhD thesis, Edinburgh, Heriot-Watt University, Department of Business Organisation.

Cooper, S.Y. (1997) 'You take the high road and I'll take the low road: contrasting routes to entrepreneurship in high technology small firms', paper presented to IntEnt97, the 7th International Entrepreneurship Conference, Monterey, California, 25–27 June.

Cooper, S.Y. (1998) 'Entrepreneurship and the location of high technology small firms; implications for regional development', pp. 247–267. In R.P. Oakey and W. During (eds), *New Technology Based Firms in the 1990s*, London, Paul Chapman.

Cooper, S.Y. (1999) 'Sectoral difference in the location and operation of high technology small firms: some issues for economic development', pp. 171–184. In R.P. Oakey, W. During and S-M Mukhtar (eds), *New Technology Based Firms in the 1990s*, London, Pergamon.

COSHEP (1998) Scottish Higher Education Key Facts, COSHEP website, www.coshep.ac.uk/factcard.html.

Heriot-Watt Unversity (1999) *Annual Report 1999*, Edinburgh, Heriot-Watt University.

HESA (1997) *Resources of Higher Education Institutions 1995/96*, Cheltenham, HESA.

HESA (1998a) *Students in Higher Education 1996/97*, Cheltenham, Higher Education Statistics Agency.

HESA (1998b) *Resources of Higher Education Institutions 1996/97*, Cheltenham, HESA.

HESA (1999) *Resources of Higher Education Institutions 1997/98*, Cheltenham, HESA.

Howells, J., Nedeva, M. and Georghiou, L. (1998) *Academic-Industry Links in the UK*, Manchester, PREST.

ITM (1997) Improving Commercialisation Activities at Heriot-Watt University, Edinburgh, ITM, Heriot-Watt University Edinburgh.

ITM (1998) Commercialisation Project Summary 1997, internal document, Heriot-Watt University.

Jones-Evans, D. (1996) 'Technical entrepreneurship, strategy and experience', *International Small Business Journal*, **14**, 3, pp. 15–39.

Keeble, D. (1987) 'Entrepreneurship, high-technology industry and regional development in the United Kingdom: the case of the Cambridge Phenomenon', paper presented to the seminar 'Technology and territory: Innovation diffusion in the regional experience of Europe and the USA', Instituto Universitario Orientale, University of Naples, February.

Lawton Smith, H. (1990) 'Innovation and technical links: the case of advanced technology industry in Oxfordshire', *Area*, **22**, 9, pp. 125–135.

Lawton Smith, H. (1997) Barriers to technology Transfer: local impediments in Oxfordshire, Working Paper 67, ESRC Centre for Business Research, University of Cambridge.

Lindholm Dahlstrand, Å. (1999) 'Technology-based SMEs in the Göteborg Region: their origin and interaction with universities and large firms', *Regional Studies*, **33**, pp. 379–389.

McNicoll, I. (1995) *The Impact of the Scottish Higher Education Sector on the Economy of Scotland – Summary*, Glasgow, COSHEP.

Monck, C.S.P., Quintas, P., Porter, R.B., Storey, D.J. and Wynarczyk, P. (1988) *Science Parks and the Growth of High Technology Firms*, London, Croom Helm.

Morphet, C.S. (1987) 'Research, development and innovation in the segmented economy: spatial implications', pp. 45–62. In B. Van der Knaap and E. Wever (eds) *New Technology and Regional Development*, Beckenham, Croom Helm.

Oakey, R.P. (1985) 'British university science parks and high technology small firms: a comment on the potential for sustained industrial growth', *International Small Business Journal*, **4**, 1, pp. 58–67.

Oakey, R.P., Cooper, S.Y. and Biggar, J. (1993) 'Product marketing and sales in high-technology small firms', pp. 201–222. In P. Swann (ed.) *New Technologies and the Firm*, London, Routledge.

Office of Science and Technology (1999) Science Enterprise Challenge, http://www.dti.gov.uk/ost/ostbusiness/claysec.htm

Quinn, J.B., Anderson, P. and Finkelstein, S. (1996) 'Managing Professional Intellect: Making the Most of the Best', *Harvard Business Review*, March-April, pp. 71–80.

Scottish Council Development and Industry (1983) *Profit through Partnership: Industry-Academic Collaboration in Scotland*, Edinburgh, Scottish Council Development and Industry.

SE/RSE (1996) *Prosperity for Scotland: Commercialisation Enquiry Final Report*, Glasgow, Scottish Enterprise/Royal Society of Edinburgh.

Scottish Enterprise (1999) *The Network Strategy*, Glasgow, Scottish Enterprise.

Shanklin, W.L. and Ryans, J.K. (1988) 'Organising for high-tech marketing', pp. 487–498. In M.L. Tushman and W.L. Moore (eds) *Readings in the Management of Innovation*, 2nd edition, New York, Harper Collins.

SHEFC (1997) '*University Research in Scotland: Developing a Policy Framework*'. Report by the Scottish Universities Research Policy Conservation, Edinburgh.

Storper, M. (1995) 'The resurgence of regional economies, ten years later: the region as a nexus of untraded interdependencies', *European Urban and Regional Studies*, **2**, pp. 191–221.

Sweeny, G.P. (1987) *Innovation, Entrepreneurs and Regional Development*, London, Frances Pinter Publishers.

The British Council (1978) *Academic/Industrial Collaboration in Britain and Germany*, Proceedings of the *British-German Seminar on Academic Research and Industry*, Cologne, The British Council.

UKBI (1999) About UK Business Incubation, http://www.ukbi.co.uk/index.html.

UKSPA (1998) *UKSPA Annual Report 1998*, Birmingham, UKSPA.

UKSPA (2000) About UKSPA, http://www.ukspa.org.uk/htmlfiles/index1.htm.

Westhead, P. and Storey, D.J. (1994) *An Assessment of Firms Located On and Off Science Parks in the United Kingdom*, London, HMSO.

**ffrr**

# St·Matthe...
## Passio...

(J. S. BACH)

Complete recording by
**THE BACH CHOIR** and
**THE JACQUES ORCHESTRA**

| Dr. THORNTON LOFTHOUSE | .. | Harpsichord |
| Dr. OSBORNE PEASGOOD | .. | Organ |
| Dr. REGINALD JACQUES | .. | Conductor |

With the following artists:

| ELSIE SUDDABY | .. | Soprano |
| KATHLEEN FERRIER | .. | Contralto |
| ERIC GREENE | .. | Tenor |
| BRUCE BOYCE | .. | Bass |
| GORDON CLINTON | .. | Bass |
| HENRY CUMMINGS | .. | Bass |
| WILLIAM PARSONS | .. | Bass |

Side Nos.
(1-2) No. 1 Come ye daughters (Pts. 1 & 2).
(3) No. 1 Come ye daughters (Concl.).
No. 2/5 When Jesu had finished ; O blessed Jesu ;
Then assembled together ; Not upon the feast.
(4) Nos. 6/9 Now when Jesus was in Bethany ; To what
purpose is this waste ? When Jesus understood it ;
My Master and my Lord.
(5) No. 10 Grief for sin.
(6) No. 12 Break in grief.
(7) Nos. 13/17 Now the first day ; Where, where ? And
He said, Go into the city ; 'Tis I whose sin doth bind
... : And He answered and said.
...)/18 Then answered Judas ; Although

... had sung a hymn ;
... would I stand beside

...le farther ; The Saviour
... ; Gladly would I take.
... unto the disciples ; O
... ; Then cometh He to
... ★

◆ New issue this month

---

al Mendelssohn duets form an important
...

...prano) and

... (Contralto)

...t the Piano

...delssohn part songs. They are
...ning and have a lovely melodic
... No wonder they were popular
...e Victorian drawing rooms ! To
...ne with an ear for melody they are
... irresistible.

**...BEL BAILLIE (Soprano)**
...om...d by J. Francis and
...led...
...

---

## KATHLEEN FERRIE...
### (Contralto)
with PHYLLIS SPURR (Piano)

**AN DIE MUSIK**, Op. 88, No.
(Schubert)
**DER MUSENSOHN**, Op. 92, No.
(Schubert) .................

---

*24 JUNI 1949 — STADSSCHOUWBU...*

## ORFE...

Opera in drie bedrijven (vijf taferelen)

Muziek van

### CHRISTOPH WILLIBALD GLUCK

Tekst van
Raniero de' Calzabigi

PIERRE MONTEUX
NICOLAAS WIJNBERG

| ORFEO | | Mise en scène | |
| EURIDICE | | Choreographie | |
| AMOR | | .. KATHLEEN FERRIER |
| | | .GREET KOEMAN |
| | | LOUISE DE VRIES |

Joan Kalff en Cor Olthuis — Koor o.l.v. Henk van Wirdink — Ballet der Nederlandsche Opera; solisten Marsha S...
Divers vervaardigd o.l.v. W. L. Schäffer — Costuums uitgevoerd o.l.v. Zus van Os — Kapwerk: Fa. D. H. Michels

Pauze na het derde tafereel

Hun...
In sweet music...
Killing care, and grief o...
Fall asleep, or hearing die.

*Shakespeare*
(Henry VIII. III. 1)

---

## Decca
# MUSIC REVIEW

### JUNE, 1948

issued by
**THE DECCA RECORD CO., LTD., LONDON**

**KATHLEEN FERRIER**
(See page 2)

---

a mon cher Collaborateur
et bon ami
Joan Kalff
avec toute ma reconnaissance
et mon admiration sincère
*Pierre Monteux*

With happy memories
of a lovely festival,
*Kathleen Ferrier*

mi...
niet de ni ...
nisch ingevoegd in de ...
en Gluck waren niet ...
solistische ballet-episode...

January 1994.

To Melanie
From Andrew with love.
Hoping this provides some
inspiration for you.

# FERRIER
## - A Career Recorded

Paul Campion

WITH CONTRIBUTIONS BY DAME JANET BAKER
AND WINIFRED FERRIER

 *Julia MacRae*

LONDON   SYDNEY   AUCKLAND   JOHANNESBURG

First published in Great Britain 1992
by Julia MacRae
An imprint of the Random Century Group
20 Vauxhall Bridge Road, London SW1V 2SA

Random Century Australia (Pty) Ltd
20 Alfred Street, Milsons Point, Sydney, NSW 2061

Random Century New Zealand Ltd
PO Box 40–086, Glenfield, Auckland 10, New Zealand

Random Century South Africa (Pty) Ltd
PO Box 337, Bergvlei, 2012, South Africa


Designed by Douglas Martin

Typeset by 𝔽 Tek Art Limited, Croydon, Surrey
Printed and bound in Great Britain by
Butler and Tanner Ltd, Frome and London

FOR MY PARENTS

# Contents

LIST OF ILLUSTRATIONS ix

FOREWORD   Dame Janet Baker, DBE xi

THE KATHLEEN FERRIER CANCER RESEARCH FUND
Winifred Ferrier xiii

THE KATHLEEN FERRIER MEMORIAL SCHOLARSHIP
Winifred Ferrier xvi

INTRODUCTION and ACKNOWLEDGEMENTS xxi

PART ONE

| | | |
|---|---|---|
| Chapter One | January – June 1944 | 3 |
| Chapter Two | July – December 1944 | 5 |
| Chapter Three | January – June 1945 | 7 |
| Chapter Four | July – December 1945 | 8 |
| Chapter Five | January – June 1946 | 11 |
| Chapter Six | July – December 1946 | 14 |
| Chapter Seven | January – June 1947 | 19 |
| Chapter Eight | July – December 1947 | 30 |
| Chapter Nine | January – June 1948 | 36 |
| Chapter Ten | July – December 1948 | 40 |
| Chapter Eleven | January – June 1949 | 42 |
| Chapter Twelve | July – December 1949 | 47 |
| Chapter Thirteen | January – June 1950 | 62 |
| Chapter Fourteen | July – December 1950 | 69 |
| Chapter Fifteen | January – June 1951 | 72 |
| Chapter Sixteen | July – December 1951 | 76 |
| Chapter Seventeen | January – June 1952 | 83 |
| Chapter Eighteen | July – December 1952 | 92 |
| Chapter Nineteen | January – June 1953 | 100 |
| Chapter Twenty | The recordings that 'might have been' | 103 |
| Chapter Twenty-one | Kathleen Ferrier on film | 108 |

PART TWO   The Discography

Introduction 111

Disc List:   Issue Numbers and Dates UK and USA 113

Disc List:   Title by title, UK and USA 121

Appendices

Index of Composers 148

Bibliography 152

General Index 153

# Illustrations

(*between pages 68 and 69*)

1  Kathleen Ferrier at the Decca recording studio   (*Decca*)

2  With Dr Reginald Jacques   (*Kemsley House, Glasgow/Winifred Ferrier*)

3  Boyd Neel   (*Royal College of Music*)

4  Roy Henderson   (*John Vickers/Roy Henderson*)

5  Clemens Krauss   (*Fayer, Vienna/Decca*)

6  Sir John Barbirolli   (*Fox Photos/The Hulton-Deutsch Collection*)

7  Sir Malcolm Sargent   (*Auerbach/The Hulton-Deutsch Collection*)

8  Sir Adrian Boult   (*König/The Hulton-Deutsch Collection*)

9  Edmund Rubbra   (*Vaughan-Spencer/Boosey & Hawkes*)

10  Howard Ferguson   (*Dr Howard Ferguson*)

11  Sir Lennox Berkeley   (*BBC/Royal College of Music*)

12  William Wordsworth   (*Colin G Futcher/Jill Wordsworth*)

13  Jo Vincent   (*Paul Campion*)

14  John Newmark   (*Winifred Ferrier*)

15  *Messiah* at Bath Abbey: l to r: Alfred Hepworth, Eric Greene, William Parsons, KF, Cuthbert Bates, Elsie Suddaby, Henry Cummings, Dr Thornton Lofthouse   (*Bath Evening Chronicle*)

16  With Benjamin Britten   (*Particam Pictures, Amsterdam*)

17  Fritz Stiedry   (*Covent Garden Books*)

18  Rehearsing for the première of Britten's *The Rape of Lucretia*, Glyndebourne, 1946   (*Hulton-Deutsch Collection*)

19  Recording sheet from Decca session at Broadhurst Gardens, 1949   (*Decca*)

20  Recording sheet from KF's first test session, June 1944   (*EMI*)

21  *Orfeo*, Glyndebourne, 1947   (*Anefo, Amsterdam/Winifred Ferrier*)

22 Joan Taylor and KF   (*Joan Taylor*)

23 *Orfeo*, Amsterdam, with Greet Koeman   (*Anefo, Amsterdam*)

24 Lieder recital with Bruno Walter, Edinburgh Festival, 1949   (*Norward Inglis/Winifred Ferrier*)

25 KF with Bruno Walter   (*Hulton-Deutsch Collection*)

26 Owen Brannigan, KF, Reginald Goodall, Nancy Evans, Hans Oppenheim. Glyndebourne   (*Winifred Ferrier*)

27 KF, Renato Cellini, Ann Ayars, Zoë Vlachopoulos. Glyndebourne   (*Winifred Ferrier*)

28 KF with Phyllis Spurr   (*Winifred Ferrier*)

29 *Liebeslieder-Walzer* at the Edinburgh Festival, 1952, l to r: Irmgard Seefried, KF, Julius Patzak, Horst Günther, with Clifford Curzon and Hans Gal accompanying   (*Decca*)

30 Recital in Carlisle with Gerald Moore   (*Tassell/Winifred Ferrier*)

31 Kathleen Ferrier   (*Houston Rogers/Decca*)

*The endpaper montage is taken from programmes and catalogues with permission from Decca, EMI, BBC, Nederlands Theater Instituut.*

# Foreword   *Dame Janet Baker*

I was talking with a group of young singers the other day and asked them during our conversation what Kathleen Ferrier meant to them. One, a true contralto (rare bird!), immediately began to speak in the most passionate and vivid terms about her memories of being brought up with the sound of her mother's Ferrier records, and told us how totally overwhelmed she had been by Kathleen's glorious voice; she had decided to develop her own gift and to study the same repertoire as a direct result of Ferrier's artistry. It was fascinating to see the depth of feeling and the adoration this young student held for a performer who could only be known to her through the medium of recording but who, nevertheless, had been inspired by her to a marked degree.

There has been another indication during the past few months of the effect Kathleen Ferrier's work had on someone who did know her performances from personal experience, and who loved them so much that as a result of this devotion a truly enormous gift has been made to the memorial prize fund, a gift so magnificent that the prize has now become one of the most valuable in the world. Two reactions from people separated by a large gap in age, but which reflect unmistakably the power which this beloved performer has had, and still has, over the hearts of those who hear her.

Paul Campion's book sets out in the clearest terms to show us not only the extent and variation of Kathleen's recording career, but also makes it blindingly obvious to us the miracle she achieved in the very brief time she was allowed to develop it. We must just feel grateful to destiny, as in the case of Mozart, that she was spared to the world long enough for this legacy to be created. Although I never met her, I feel I knew her; I expect many of us share that. As a fellow Northerner, I like to imagine that if, as a young singer, I had ever shared the same platform with her, we would have had much in common. I'm quite sure we would have laughed a lot.

# The Kathleen Ferrier Cancer Research Fund   *Winifred Ferrier*

During the last two years of her life Kathleen had radiotherapy whenever it became necessary, under the care of Dr Gwen Hilton and her assistants at University College Hospital. Great pains were taken to ensure that Kathleen was able to continue singing and to do an amazing amount, despite the treatment.

She travelled the country giving recitals, taking part in oratorio and singing in Bach's *Mass in B Minor*, *St Matthew Passion*, the *Alto Rhapsody* and Chausson's *Poème de l'amour et de la mer*. In July 1951 she flew to Holland for performances of *Orfeo* with the Netherlands Opera. She sang in the Edinburgh Festivals of 1951 and 1952 and went to Belfast for a recital and to Dublin for a performance of *The Dream of Gerontius*. Most important of all, to her as to us, she made the prestigious recordings of *Das Lied von der Erde* and the *Rückert Lieder* with the Vienna Philharmonic Orchestra conducted by Bruno Walter, and the Bach and Handel arias with the London Philharmonic Orchestra under Sir Adrian Boult.

Kathleen was so grateful for all the skill and care lavished on her at University College Hospital that she intended to give a concert for the funds of the Radiotherapy Department. Unfortunately this was never possible. So, after her death, it was decided to establish a cancer fund in her name. An appeal was launched by Hamish Hamilton, Sir John Barbirolli, Sir Laurence Olivier, Dame Myra Hess, Sir Benjamin Ormerod and Dr Bruno Walter. The response was astounding. Amounts of money came in, large and small. The Hallé Orchestra gave a concert conducted jointly by Dr Bruno Walter and Sir John Barbirolli, and from this and many other sources the money to establish firmly a Kathleen Ferrier Cancer Fund at University College Hospital was raised.

Dr Nicholas Godlee, who now directs the Department, was trained initially by Dr Gwen Hilton and he has the same dedicated attitude to his patients. As well as adults, these include children from Great Ormond Street Hospital who are referred to University College Hospital if they need radiotherapy. He personally acknowledges donations sent to the Fund, some of them in memory of musical friends who have died. Money also comes from the royalties of some of Kathleen's recordings which have been discovered in broadcasts and tapes. The work of organising this and getting permission from all the people involved to donate their royalties has been done by a Decca Record Company executive. Permission has never been refused. Details of these records will be found in the relevant part of this book.

In 1983 doctors at University College Hospital arranged a Memorial Concert at the Barbican 'to commemorate this unique English singer'. A beautiful performance of *Messiah* was given and three of the soloists were Kathleen Ferrier Scholarship winners. All those concerned gave their services.

The programme contained a fascinating account of the work done in this very active centre and the article ended: 'For all this work we rely increasingly heavily on donations from charitable sources and all donations to the Kathleen Ferrier Cancer Fund will receive our grateful thanks.'

In 1987 the Trustees of the Fund and the Administrators of London University founded a Kathleen Ferrier Chair of Clinical Research. Dr R.L. Souhami was appointed as the first Professor. He writes:

> Since the Kathleen Ferrier Chair was first endowed in 1987 there have been many significant developments. The Chair was endowed with scientific and technical support and the team moved into new laboratories on the fifth floor of the Courtauld Institute in early 1988. These new laboratories have built up a team of researchers who have been examining the way in which anti-cancer drugs react with the essential constituent of the cell nucleus – DNA – and produce the anti-cancer effect. A detailed under-standing of the mechanism of action may lead to new and better drugs in the future. This work has gone very well and has attracted grants from the Cancer Research Campaign.
>
> At the same time, the Department has expanded with the appointment of two senior lecturers in Radiotherapy and Oncology and a further senior lecturer in Medical Oncology. This means that the Department of Cancer Medicine is now considerably larger than it was and its range of activities have greatly increased.
>
> A most exciting development has been the progressive amalgamation of the Middlesex and University College cancer departments on the Middlesex site. The first phase of the new building was opened in June 1990 and included a ten-bedded ward especially for the care of adolescents with cancer. This was the first such unit of its kind in the United Kingdom. The ward was officially opened by HRH The Duchess of York in November 1990. This unit which is under the direction of the Kathleen Ferrier Professor of Clinical Oncology, specializes in bone cancers. The success rate in treating these tumours in childhood and adolescence has increased greatly in recent years and the unit operates to the highest possible standards, attracting cases from all over England; many children also come from overseas to be treated. The second phase of development of the amalgamation is now

under way and will be completed by the beginning of 1992.

Other research interests in the Department have included studies on ways of approaching treatment of various forms of lung cancers with antibodies directed towards the tumour. We hope that this approach may help to increase the cure rate in some forms of lung cancer. This is the commonest form of cancer in adults and has been particularly resistant to treatment in recent years. The unit has a particular interest in lung cancer treatment and carries out very large-scale clinical trials of drug treatment and radiotherapy treatment in collaboration with colleagues in other hospitals in the South East of England, particularly at the London Chest Clinic and the Brompton Hospital.

It can be seen from this account that the establishment of a Kathleen Ferrier Chair has led to a considerable increase in the research and clinical activity within the departments of cancer medicine of both the Middlesex Hospital and University College Hospital. These exciting developments could not have come about without, of course, the endowments which led to the Chair being established in Kathleen Ferrier's name.

# The Kathleen Ferrier Memorial Scholarship  *Winifred Ferrier*

The prestigious Kathleen Ferrier Memorial Scholarship contest takes place every year in the spring. It is open to men and women singers who are British-born or are holders of British, Commonwealth, or Republic of Ireland passports. They must be over twenty-one years of age and traditionally must not have reached the age of twenty-six by the date of the final competition. In 1992, however, this was increased to twenty-nine.

The contest usually lasts for five days. During the first three, the adjudicators hear all the singers and decide on sixteen or so to sing again at the semi-final. From these, eight are usually selected to sing at the final contest. Then the adjudicators have the difficult task of deciding on the winners of the Scholarship and the Decca-Kathleen Ferrier Prize. Sometimes a third prize is awarded too.

Candidates have a wide choice of programme. For the preliminaries they choose two songs, one by a composer of the seventeenth or eighteenth century or an operatic or oratorio aria in its original key, and also a song written in the nineteenth or twentieth century in its original language. For the semi-final the contestants choose two songs from the same groups but they must be different from those in the preliminaries. For the final audition they sing three items, two from the original groups and one written by a living British composer – a condition imposed by the RVW Trust in return for a generous annual donation. Recently the Final has been held on a Friday evening instead of during the afternoon, and the singers have obviously enjoyed performing to a large and enthusiastic audience.

The competition has always been organised by the Secretary of The Royal Philharmonic Society and the dedicated work and expertise of these musicians has contributed largely to its success: D. Ritson Smith, Sylvia East and, from 1975, Shirley Barr.

The most difficult task has always been to find suitable adjudicators who are willing to spare the time from their busy lives, to listen and to judge the potential of so many young singers; over the years the number has varied between fifty and a hundred. For the five days of the contest a male and a female singer are joined by a critic, a conductor or a person involved in musical projects. For the final, two more outstanding musicians are required, making a panel of five, and many famous people have been glad to serve.

The Secretary, as administrator, and the Trustees meet regularly to discuss all the matters connected with the Scholarship including, of course, careful checks on the way that the funds are invested and used. Currently, the Trustees are Sheila Armstrong, Dame Janet Baker, Sir Nicholas Goodison, Roy Henderson, Geoffrey Parsons, John Shirley-Quirk, Paul Strang, Martin Williams and myself.

The Scholarship Final is always a great occasion with a remarkably high standard of singing for such young artists, and it is often very difficult to choose. Sometimes four or five prizes are deserved.

After the winners are announced, the adjudicators, the singers and their accompanists, relatives, friends and almost the whole audience surge into the Green Room. There are congratulations, greetings and comments from knowledgeable people and a way of getting sound advice and help. So, this is the way that the Scholarship has developed in the last thirty-six years.

All this stemmed from a letter in *The Times* in 1953 suggesting that there should be a musical memorial for Kathleen. It expressed the feelings of many people and was taken up enthusiastically by her colleagues and friends. They consulted The Royal Philharmonic Society, of which Kathleen was a Gold Medallist, and decided that a scholarship or scholarships should be founded in her name. An appeal for funds was launched by Sir John Barbirolli, Mr Hamish Hamilton, Mr Roy Henderson, Mr Gerald Moore and Sir Malcolm Sargent. From then on they all took a great interest in the development of the Scholarship, helping it in every way.

Hamish Hamilton became Chairman of Trustees and in September 1954 published a book called *Kathleen Ferrier: A Memoir*. Each of her friends wrote a chapter. Sir John Barbirolli's was entitled 'Kathleen . . . The Last Years', Benjamin Britten wrote of 'Three Premières', Roy Henderson's chapter was headed 'Per Ardua', Gerald Moore called his 'The Radiant Companion' and Bruno Walter wrote a moving 'Farewell'. The book was edited by Neville Cardus who wrote: 'To Mr Hamish Hamilton I am especially indebted. He has, so to say, been the book's conductor, always maintaining the ideal tempo for a publisher, never hurrying his executants along too quickly but taking care not to encourage any loitering by the way.' The book went into five impressions and all the proceeds from its sale were devoted to the Kathleen Ferrier Memorial Scholarship.

Hamish Hamilton was also instrumental in arranging for HRH The Duchess of Kent to become Patron. She attended the twenty-fifth anniversary final in 1980 and obviously enjoyed talking to the singers and their accompanists in the Green Room afterwards. She came again in 1988. Princess Alexandra attended the tenth anniversary final in 1965 and Princess Marina in 1968.

Gerald Moore was a wonderful help from the beginning. His knowledge of the musical world and his advice were invaluable. He often acted as adjudicator and Chairman of the panel, and in 1975 made a BBC Radio appeal for funds for the Scholarship which raised £1,610. He served as a Trustee until 1980.

Myers Foggin was also involved from the earliest days and he took over as Chairman of Trustees when Hamish Hamilton retired. Paul Strang became a Trustee in 1978 and took over as Chairman when Myers Foggin retired. He has taken a great interest in the financial affairs of the Scholarship and consulted with Roy Henderson who has been Honorary Treasurer for many years. Roy also acts as master of ceremonies at the competition final, introducing the members of the panel after they have chosen the winner of the Scholarship and of the Decca-Kathleen Ferrier Prize.

Dame Janet Baker has supported the Scholarship in many ways since she became a Trustee in 1978. She has often acted as adjudicator and Chairman of the panel and has given some excellent talks to the young singers. In 1990 The Royal Philharmonic Society awarded Dame Janet their Gold Medal. It was presented to her by Lady Barbirolli at the Royal Society of Arts and a concert was given in her honour. Asked by the organisers who she would like to perform at her concert, she chose winners of the Scholarship – Janice Watson, Stephen Gadd and Paul Clarke. Unfortunately Paul was indisposed and unable to appear but his place was taken by Jamie McDougall, a Scholarship finalist. After the interval, Alison Hudson joined them for a surprise performance of the *Liebeslieder-Waltzer*. Geoffrey Parsons and Stephen Betteridge accompanied them and all donated their services to the funds of the Musicians' Benevolent Fund.

From the beginning the Scholarship has been helped by Kathleen's friends and admirers. There have been donations, covenants and legacies but the expense of running it has increased every year and so has the demand for bigger prizes. It was a great help to have regular amounts from the RVW Trust. Then in 1978, the Decca Record Company introduced a Decca-Kathleen Ferrier Prize of £1,000, 'to match the Scholarship Award' which, that year, was £1,000. This prize ran for ten years and was then renewed for another five.

In 1986 Paul Strang had consultations with Mrs Lise Rueff Seligman who was interested in young singers and wished to support the competition. She generously offered to provide £2,000 per annum and said she did not mind how the extra prize money was used, so it was decided to increase the Scholarship Award to £5,000.

In 1992, thanks to an anonymous donor, it has been increased again, to £10,000.

Arrangements for the competition are vital to its success. Only the administrator and any voluntary helpers that she can recruit know how much time, care and hard work are required to enable young singers from many parts of Britain to take part. Entry forms and birth certificates must be checked, plans made for rehearsals with the accompanist if the singer is not bringing one, arrangements made for those living far away from London to sing as late as possible in the competition to avoid staying in London longer than necessary. Then there is the last minute preparation of the programme for the Final. The order of singing for this audition is drawn by ballot.

When everything works smoothly and the contestants feel that they are well cared for, they are free to concentrate all their energies on interpreting their songs. Their years of study are enhanced by inborn talent and imagination so they can convey to the audience the emotions expressed in the music.

The standard of singing varies somewhat from year to year. Sometimes there is an outstanding artist, sometimes two or three. Occasionally there is one of great distinction who takes part in the Final but who does not win a prize. Richard Fairman, in his article for *The Financial Times* of 30th April 1990, remarked on this when he wrote: 'Unfortunately, with all the prizes handed out, the cupboard was now bare and mezzo, Debra Stuart, had to go home empty-handed . . .'

In spite of these problems the adjudicators have awarded Scholarships and Decca-Kathleen Ferrier prizes to a large number of men and women now in the front rank of contemporary British singers. They include some from the Commonwealth: Victor Godfrey from Canada, Janice Chapman and Yvonne Kenny from Australia, Keith Lewis from New Zealand and Sandra Browne from Trinidad.

As new opera companies have grown, standards have become higher and singers have tackled more difficult works at an earlier age. Whereas some years ago most entrants were still at college, now some of them have appeared professionally in opera, oratorio and Lieder. The details are given in the account of their careers in the Scholarship programmes. It is also a splendid tribute to the British school of singing that they all quote the names of their teachers.

Today, the Scholarship is considered the most prestigious award of its kind in this country, an opinion based largely on the list of winners. It is impossible to keep track of all the work that these young singers are doing and invidious to choose outstanding ones. A chronological list of prizewinners is appended.

A notable aspect of the Kathleen Ferrier Memorial Scholarship has always been the warmth and dedication that Kathleen's memory has inspired in all those who have taken part in it. This has helped it to survive and to become an important part of British musical life. Long may it continue.

## Kathleen Ferrier Memorial Scholarship Winners

Joyce Barker, Elizabeth Simon (1956)
John Mitchinson, Neil Howlett (1957)
Maureen Jones, John Wakefield (1958)
Victor Godfrey, Elizabeth Vaughan (1959)
Elizabeth Harwood, Lorna Elias (1960)
Lorna Haywood, Audrey Deakin (1961)
Robert Bateman, Maureen Keetch (1962)
Janice Chapman, Ann Cooper (1963)
Alfreda Hodgson, Richard Angas (1964)
Sheila Armstrong, Margaret Price (1965)
Malvina Major, Hugh Sheena (1966)
William Elvin (1967) Gwynneth Griffiths (1968)
Della Jones, Brian Rayner Cook (1969)
Felicity Palmer (1970) Sandra Browne (1971)
Glyn Davenport (1972) Linda Esther Gray (1973)
Linda Finnie, Anthony Smith (1974)
Yvonne Kenny (1975) Keith Lewis (1976)
Lynda Russell (1977) Jacek Strauch (1978)
Alexander Garden (1979) Penelope Walker (1980)
Joan Rodgers (1981) Anne Dawson (1982)
Louise Jackson (1983) Peter Rose (1985)
Janice Close (1986) Janice Watson (1987)
Bryn Terfel Jones (1988) Paul Clarke (1989)
Stephen Gadd (1990) Mary Plazas (1991)

## Deca-Kathleen Ferrier Prize Winners

Jacek Strauch (1978) Lesley Garrett (1979)
Stewart Buchanan (1980) Brian Scott (1981)
Matthew Best (1982) Carol Smith (1983)
Susan Bullock (1984) Judith Howarth (1985)
Alastair Miles (1986) Elizabeth McCormack (1987)
Amanda Roocroft (1988) William Dazeley (1989)
Alison Hudson (1990) Jane Irwin (1991)

## Other Award Winners

THE BARONESS RAVENSDALE PRIZE
Helen Kucharek (1982) Ian Platt (1984)
Jane Webster (1986)
JURY'S PRIZE
Timothy Wilson (1985)
THIRD PRIZE
Bethan Dudley (1989) David Mattinson (1990) Gail Pearson (1991)

# Introduction

The first Kathleen Ferrier discography was published in *The Gramophone* in February 1954. Alec Robertson and Andrew Porter reviewed Kathleen's recording career and listed her records; at that time, of course, it was only records that were available. In the issue of January 1955 Andrew Porter corrected errors that had appeared in his earlier list and added some issues which had since been released.

In her biography of her sister, *The Life of Kathleen Ferrier*, Winifred Ferrier listed the works that Kathleen regularly performed and indicated which of them had been recorded; she did not include the many issues that have since been released, by both Decca and other companies, such as the Dutch performances of *The Rape of Lucretia, Orfeo ed Euridice, Kindertotenlieder* and Mahler's *Second Symphony*. These, and other broadcast performances that have been issued since Winifred's book, were included in a discography compiled by Maurice Leonard for his biography *Kathleen*, which was published in 1988; but even since then, yet more recordings have been found and released. There remain still a few which, until 1992, have not been issued commercially, and it has been the discovery of these, and some others still unpublished, that has made much of my research so rewarding.

After tracing a number of surviving broadcasts in the BBC Sound Archives, which may, with due notice, be heard at The British Library National Sound Archive (referred to under the relevant recording entries in the text as NSA), 29 Exhibition Road, London SW7 2AS, I realised that there might be other unpublished material, not only in the possession of broadcasting organisations for which Kathleen sang in a number of different countries, but also in private hands. So it proved, and a few unique recordings came to light; the Schubert songs accompanied by Britten; Mahler's *Third Symphony* conducted by Boult, *Bist du bei mir* in The Library of Congress in Washington, and a handful of others. It is very gratifying that Decca have decided to issue some of these on their new series of CDs and cassettes of Kathleen, to commemorate the eightieth anniversary of her birth.

The high regard in which Kathleen is still held nearly forty years after her death has been made very clear to me; correspondents ranging from some of the most famous musicologists and critics in the world, to record collectors who still proudly possess one or two of her original 78s, have expressed their admiration for her voice and artistry, and have all been keen to help me in my research. Their enthusiasm has been of great support.

This book is not intended to be a critical review of Kathleen's recorded legacy; it is, rather, a list of all extant recordings that I have traced, with details about the circumstances surrounding their making. It has been difficult sometimes to avoid expressing a personal preference for one version of a work over another, and in other ways judging the artistic rather than the factual aspects of Kathleen's recording career. I would only urge readers to listen to all the performances that they can find and make their own assessments. In one way I hope that this book is soon out of date; it would be good news indeed if its publication were to result in the tracing and issuing of yet more new material that I have not uncovered!

Several terms are used in the book which will require clarification.

1. 'Commercial recording' and 'recorded commercially' refer to recordings by Columbia and Decca which were made with the *intention* that they would be sold to the public, whether or not they were so sold. On the other hand, 'commercial issue' or 'issued commercially' refer to any recording that has been put on sale by any company, even if, when performed, there was no intention that it would be made generally available.

2. Up to about 1950, most records were recorded directly on to high polished wax discs (or 'waxes') at 78 rpm. A number was engraved on the ungrooved area towards the centre of the disc – 'the matrix number' – with a suffix which indicated the 'take' number that it represented. (When the same item was re-recorded it would usually bear the same matrix number, but the take suffix would be increased by one on each repeat performance.) The wax was then electroplated with a very thin layer of metal to create the matrix, or metalwork, and after the wax was stripped away, a negative version of the original recording remained. From the matrix, another metal disc was formed, called the mother, which was a positive version of the original recording. Yet another pressing, from the mother, created the stamper, which was finally used to make the black shellac records themselves. The same principles have been used over the last forty years to make 45 rpm and 33 rpm records as well.

With so many intricate processes, it is easy to see how recordings could become damaged before they even reached the pressing stage, and the importance of recording more than one wax of a particular item becomes clear. If the demand for a particular record was high, more than one stamper could be created using this process, and the output from the factory increased accordingly.

With the advent of tape recordings the situation becomes more complicated. In theory, an item might be recorded a number of times, and the best version would be transferred to a wax disc. If a satisfactory wax was made in this way, the matrix number would carry the suffix '1', even if it was not the first version to have been recorded on the original tape. All of Kathleen's recordings for Decca in 1950 (the sessions accompanied by John Newmark) and 1951 (the twelve British songs accompanied by Phyllis Spurr) are found to be 'take 1', which may lead to the conclusion that they were all originally recorded on tape. Even in Decca's archives there is no mention of second takes for any of these titles. The original matrix and take numbers can still be clearly seen on any of Kathleen's 78 rpm records, stamped into the run-off groove area near the label. In the listing of matrix and take numbers in the main text, the take number that was used for commercial issue is underlined; at least one copy of each of Kathleen's 78s has been checked to ascertain the take number, but it is possible that other takes have been used for commercial issue at some time.

During research I have sometimes come across different sets of facts, usually all from impeccable sources, that are mutually contradictory about one aspect or another of one of Kathleen's recordings. Some examples, among others, are the disputed date and conductor of the Dutch recording of *The Rape of Lucretia*; some of the dates of her Decca sessions between 1946 and 1952; the curiously complicated circumstances of the recording of Berkeley's *Four poems of St Teresa of Avila*, and the odd case of the two versions of each of the Bach cantatas recorded in 1949. Where I feel there is still real doubt as to the truth, that is made clear in the text; and when I choose one set of facts rather than another as being correct, then I at least mention the rejected alternative.

In general, musical works are referred to in the language in which they are sung; thus, there are details about both *St Matthew Passion* and *Matthäus-Passion*, and *Four serious songs* and *Vier ernste Gesänge*, as these works have been issued in both English and German. In some cases this does not apply, and a few works are referred to by their English title, irrespective of the sung language; *Rhapsody for contralto, male chorus and orchestra* (or *Alto Rhapsody*) and Bach's *Mass in B Minor* are examples.

Three aspects of the chronological numbering system I have used to identify Kathleen's recordings require explanation.

1.   Each 'item' has been allocated a number. An 'item' is a work or a piece of music that is complete in itself in the context of the recording. Hence, I consider both a complete peformance of, say, *St Matthew Passion*, and a short folk-song lasting less than two minutes both to be complete in themselves, and thus both to be an 'item'. When an excerpt from an item has been issued independently, it is referred to by the item number together with a distinguishing letter. So, the aria *Have mercy, Lord, on me* from the

Decca *St Matthew Passion* set is identified as No. 40e, as it is an excerpt from an item; but the same aria recorded by itself in February 1946 is considered to be an item in its own right, and is given its own item No. 26.

2. For every session at which an item was recorded it has been given a different item number, irrespective of the number of times it was recorded at the sessions, and irrespective of whether any of those takes were issued commercially. For example, the Brahms Lied *Gestillte Sehnsucht* was first recorded (two takes, neither issued) on 9th December 1947. Both those performances share the No. 46. It was again recorded (again, two takes, neither successful) on 22nd June 1948. Both those performances share the No. 54. It was recorded yet again (two takes) on 15th February 1949, and both those performances, one of which was issued, share the No. 71.

3. I have divided Kathleen's recording career into nineteen parts, each representing a six-month period, lasting either from January to June, or from July to December. The first recording in each part has been allocated a number ending either in 1 or 6, irrespective of the number of the last item in the previous six-month part. This has been done so that if and when more recordings are traced and inserted into the chronological listing, there will be minimal disruption to the numbers which follow. The built-in gaps between parts will act as a buffer when new items are entered. So although the final number in the present listing is No. 228, there are only 192 different items.

   Of those 192, 191 apply to Kathleen (No. 122, a solo for Elisabeth Schwarzkopf, has been included). Of the 191, 89 were recorded commercially, but only 80 of those were ever issued; the remaining 9 seem to have been destroyed, with no copies surviving. A further 86 items were issued commercially either complete or in part, and 16 more items in collections in different parts of the world remain unissued in any form.

Apart from an item number, the following information, where available, has been included for each entry.

1. The surname of the composer.
2. The names of the librettist, and the translator of the libretto into the sung language.
3. The title of the item, the name of any larger work from which it comes, and the opus number.
4. The language in which the item is sung.
5. The time, date and place of the recording.
6. The matrix and take number(s) to which that item number refers,

with the take number used for issue underlined.

7. The accompanist, conductor, orchestra, choir and other musicians who participated in the recording. Kathleen's name is always omitted here, her presence being understood.

8. In the case of a set of 78 rpm records, the form of presentation is usually shown, with straight and automatic record numbers and coupling order, matched to the appropriate matrix and take number.

9. Excerpts from an item (e.g. 88a or 120d) are shown after the details of the main item.

10. Question marks indicate that there is doubt about the accuracy of the information. See the relevant text for details.

At a recent check, it was discovered that Kathleen's recordings, in one quarter year alone, were distributed to the following countries: Australia, Belgium, Canada, Denmark, Germany, Ecuador, Taiwan, France, Greece, UK, Hong Kong, Eire, Israel, Italy, Japan, Korea, The Netherlands, Norway, Portugal, Spain, Sweden, Switzerland, South Africa and the USA; and there was one additional category – The Rest of the World. All those recordings were made in the space of a little over eight and a half years, between June 1944 and January 1953.

I hope that this book will be of interest to everyone who admires Kathleen Ferrier's singing. As well as enabling listeners to check immediately the details of every recording she made, it provides brief biographical information which helps to put those recordings into the larger context of her career. No British classical singer is remembered with such admiration worldwide as Kathleen; it is our good fortune still to be able to hear her, and to understand why.

During the preparation of this book, I have made every attempt to verify and double check every item of information; it is almost inevitable, however, that mistakes will have crept in at some stage, and for these I take full responsibility. Any information that readers have, that may clarify or correct what I have written, will be much appreciated.

It has been announced that several previously unissued items from the BBC Sound Archives will shortly be made available commercially as Compact Discs and tapes. It is not yet known whether any of Kathleen's unreleased BBC recordings will be included; consequently any relevant commercial release details are not given in this book, although the BBC's own Archives references are all quoted.

# Acknowledgements

So many people have helped me in the preparation of this book; special words of thanks must go to a particular few whom I have bothered frequently for over two years, and whose patience with me is astounding: Timothy Day, Curator of Western Art Music at The National Sound Archive, and the staff of the Listening Service; Ruth Edge of EMI Music Archives and her staff; Norma Jones of the Sound Library of the BBC Sound Archives; and John Parry of Decca International.

Others whose help has been invaluable in providing me with information and encouragement during my research are: André Achtien, Ann Ayars, Arthur Bannister, Lady Berkeley, Lady Bliss, Alan Blyth, Jesper Buhl, Director of Danacord Records, Bryan Crimp, formerly of EMI, Robert Dearling of The Guinness Book of Recorded Sound, Christopher Dyment, Nils Eriksen, Bjørn Granlund and Marit Grimstad of Norsk Rikskringkasting, Oslo, Norway, Dr Howard Ferguson, Walter Foster, Edward Greenfield, William Griffis, Keith Hardwick of EMI, The Earl of Harewood, Roy Henderson, Harald Henrysson of the Swedish National Radio Company, Luuk Hoekstra of The Netherlands Theatre Institute, Amsterdam, J.J. van Herpen of Hilversum, Barry Irving of *Gramophone*, Maurice Leonard, Michael Letchford, formerly of Decca, Derek Lewis, BBC Gramophone Librarian, Arthur Luke, Fred Maroth of Music and Arts Programs of America Inc., Edwin M. Matthias of The Library of Congress, Washington D.C., Don McCormick, Curator, Rodgers and Hammerstein Archives of Recorded Sound, New York Public Library, Bernice Mitchell, of Angel Records, New York, Christopher Pollard, Managing Editor of *Gramophone*, Geoff Pollock, L. Richman of Rococo Records Ltd, Gordon Rowley, Rosy Runciman, Archivist of Glyndebourne Festival Opera, Patrick Saul, Julia Spencer, John Steane, Joan Taylor, Jon Tolansky of the Music Performance Research Centre, Mrs Dr J. van Tongeren of Nederlands Omroepproduktie Bedrijf nv, Hilversum, Jeff Walden of the BBC Written Archives Centre, Caversham, Malcolm Walker, The Librarian and Pam Wheeler of the Britten-Pears Library, Aldeburgh, Suffolk, William Wilcox, Kenneth Wilkinson and Reg Williamson.

I offer my warm thanks to Julia MacRae, my publisher, and her team, for invaluable guidance during the preparation of this book; and to Dame Janet Baker, whose contribution of a Foreword I much appreciate.

Very many other people, I regret too numerous to mention individually, have taken time and trouble to reply to my letters and phone calls; although they were not able to provide me with new information, their interest and enthusiasm for my project have been very supportive. I thank them all.

Finally, my deepest gratitude is to Winifred Ferrier. She has made available to me Kathleen's diaries, correspondence, photograph albums and cuttings books. She has welcomed me in her home on many occasions, and recalled anecdotes and memories of events which took place forty years ago. Without her friendship and help this book could not have been written.

Paul Campion
December 1991

# Part One   *The Career*

# Chapter One   *January - June 1944*

Kathleen Ferrier's recording career was due to have begun earlier than it did. The archives show that, at 1pm on 19th May 1944, she was booked to record a Test Session, with Gerald Moore as her accompanist, at the EMI Studios in Abbey Road, North London. It is not known why the booking was postponed, nor what was to have been recorded on that occasion; but at 10.30 am on 30th June the two musicians *did* meet at Abbey Road, Studio 3, and made four titles.

Those four recordings were the only ones Kathleen ever made for HMV. The matrices used were given HMV numbers, not Columbia numbers; it was for Columbia that her first *issued* 78s were made. These test records were never issued as 78s, and were not released until December 1978, when they formed a substantial part of an EMI LP, *Great British Mezzo Sopranos and Contraltos*. That the matrices were preserved is probably due to the perception of Walter Legge, Artistic Director at EMI. Frequently, after the results of a Test Session had been heard, the metalwork was destroyed, but on the occasions when a special talent was recorded for the first time, Legge would insist that it be kept in the archives at Hayes. When compiling the LP on which these sides were first published, Bryan Crimp of EMI searched for the matrices, which were rumoured still to exist, and on finding them had vinyl pressings made for the transfer to LP. The four recordings give an indication of the repertoire that Kathleen was developing: Brahms songs (here sung in English, as much German music was at that time) were to play a very important part in her career. Among her surviving recordings, there are more works by Brahms than any other composer. Gluck's *What is life?* (also sung in English) was, in a way, to become Kathleen's theme song. Six versions of her singing this have survived, more than any other individual song or aria; but this, the earliest, is not typical; the two climactic top Fs are avoided, and the performance lacks tension and dramatic insight.

The final items from this session are the most interesting; they are two brief excerpts from Elgar's *The Dream of Gerontius*, both recorded on a single 12″ wax. Although the Angel was to become one of Kathleen's finest roles, and one in which she was greatly acclaimed, she never recorded any further music from the oratorio. The second excerpt, beginning *It is because* . . . stops suddenly, ending with the words . . . *the agony*, almost as if a silent signal had been given – 'Thank you, we'll let you know . . .'

These fragments may have been included in the session by EMI as a test for their forthcoming complete recording; at the time, Kathleen had never sung the work in public, and clearly it was felt at EMI that she was not yet ready to record it commercially. In the event, the oratorio *was* recorded under Malcolm Sargent in April 1945, with Gladys Ripley as the contralto soloist; and although in later years Kathleen sang other works by Elgar such as *The Apostles*, *The Kingdom*, *Sea Pictures*, and *The Music Makers*, she recorded none of his music apart from these frustratingly short passages from *The Dream of Gerontius*.

Recording during those June days of 1944 was a hazardous occupation. Earlier in the month, the first of the pilotless V1 weapons had been launched against Britain from occupied Europe, and to spend time in a soundproofed recording studio must have been an unnerving experience for any musician, so near to the centre of London. But the sound quality of these four test sides is good and clear, and almost entirely free from surface noise. Indeed, it is better than the dubbings from the shellac commercial pressings which seem to have been used for the reissues of Kathleen's 1944 and 1945 Columbias. The recording producer for this session was Walter Legge.

10.30 am on 30.6.44
EMI Studio 3, Abbey Road

1   GLUCK/Calzabigi (translated)
*What is life?* (*Orpheus and Euridice*)/English
Piano: Gerald Moore
Matrix 2EA 10249–1

2   BRAHMS/Reinick (translated)
*Constancy, Op. 3, No. 1*/English
Piano: Gerald Moore
Matrix 0EA 10250–1

3   BRAHMS/Traditional (translated)
*Feinsliebchen* (*Sweetheart*)/English
(No 12 of *49 Deutsche Volkslieder*)
Piano: Gerald Moore
Matrix 0EA 10251–1

4   ELGAR/Cardinal Newman
*My work is done . . . to . . . earth to Heaven* and *It is because . . . to
. . . the agony* (*The Dream of Gerontius Op. 38*)/English
Piano: Gerald Moore
Matrix 2EA 10252–1

# Chapter Two  *July - December 1944*

Another commercial Test Session was booked at Abbey Road, again with Moore, for 3.15 pm on 25th September. As Kathleen had already made four test sides in June, it is hard to imagine why it was thought necessary to undertake more. Indeed, the session may never have taken place; no recordings from it have survived, and apart from an official memo in EMI archives, no other reference has been traced.

Exactly three months to the day after Kathleen first visited Studio 3 she returned there to record what was to be her first published 78 rpm record. This time she was recorded on Columbia matrices, and all her commercial recordings were on that label until she transferred to Decca in February 1946.

Two excerpts from anthems by Maurice Greene (1696–1755), an English composer, had been selected for this session, which took place at 2.30 pm on 30th September, with Gerald Moore again at the piano. Kathleen had first met Moore in 1943: he was by then a most celebrated accompanist, who had for nearly twenty years worked with some of the finest singers and instrumentalists, and Kathleen was in some awe of him. They performed together a good deal over the next nine years, but their joint recordings, with one exception, are from Kathleen's short time as an EMI artist.

*The Gramophone* magazine, reviewing this record in November 1944, commented: 'This young singer has already won golden opinions and should gain another for having the courage to make her first appearance on records in little known music. Kathleen Ferrier possesses a sense of the value of words: being perhaps rather too near the microphone, her tone in the vigorous "*O praise the Lord*" has a little edge on it which does not really belong to the voice.' Subsequent reissues of the record have removed the artificial edge, and restored the true timbre of Kathleen's voice.

The recording producer for this session was Walter Legge:

2.30 pm on 30.9.44
EMI Studio 3, Abbey Road

6  GREENE (arranged by Roper)/The Bible
   *I will lay me down in peace* (from the anthem *O God of
   righteousness*)/English
   Piano: Gerald Moore
   Matrix CA 19599–1-2

7   GREENE (arranged by Roper)/The Bible
    *O praise the Lord* (from the anthem *Praise the Lord, O my soul*)/
    English
    Piano: Gerald Moore
    Matrix CA 19600–1-2

# Chapter Three  *January - June 1945*

After the critical approval of her first published record, Kathleen was invited to make more sides for Columbia early in 1945. The studio was booked for 6th March, when Kathleen and Gerald Moore were scheduled to record two Brahms songs, *Sapphic Ode* and *May Night*, both apparently in English: but the session was postponed, presumably at short notice, as EMI archives report that it was too late to stop Gerald Moore attending the studios. It is tempting to wonder if he still required his fee. The same Brahms items were rescheduled for 20th April 1945, but even then they were not recorded, as two Handel arias were substituted. *Sapphic Ode* was eventually recorded, but not until December 1949, for Decca, when it was sung in German. *May Night* never was.

The two arias that *were* performed are from Handel's opera *Ottone*, sung in a spurious English translation by Arthur Somervell; both featured regularly in her recitals at that time in her career. Winifred Ferrier remembers hearing the original copy of the 78 with Kathleen: 'She laughed at the way she had over-emphasised the words "Spring is coming" and said, "With some arm movements, it would make a nice little jazz number", and proceeded to show us how it would go!'

The recording producer for this session was Walter Legge.

> 2.30 pm on 20.4.45
> EMI Studio 3, Abbey Road

11   HANDEL/N. Haym (translated Arthur Somervell)
*Spring is coming (Ottone)*/English
Piano: Gerald Moore
Matrix CAX 9276–1-2

12   HANDEL/N. Haym (translated Arthur Somervell)
*Come to me, soothing sleep (Ottone)*/English
Piano: Gerald Moore
Matrix CAX 9277–1-2-3

# Chapter Four   *July - December 1945*

Kathleen was becoming increasingly disillusioned at Columbia, and did not enjoy a good relationship with Walter Legge. She decided to make no more solo records for the company, and asked Isobel Baillie to sing some duets with her, which Baillie agreed to do. Kathleen did not want to risk recording important solo material in her last session for Legge, knowing that Decca, the recording company she had decided to join, would give her the opportunity to sing some of her best concert and oratorio pieces.

Kathleen and Isobel Baillie first sang together in December 1941, in a performance of *Messiah*, but many years earlier than that, when Kathleen's principal interest had been the piano, she had acted as Baillie's accompanist at one of the soprano's recitals in the north of England. The two singers gave many performances together, and were much in demand as soloists in concerts and oratorios, but they were not close friends; mutual admiration, rather than affection, might fairly describe their working relationship.

Three duets by Purcell, three by Mendelssohn, and one traditional song were recorded in Studio 3 on 21st September 1945; in the event, two of the sides were never issued, and no copies of them appear to have survived. Although it is a duet, the recording sheet for *O wert thou in the cauld blast?* names Baillie only, with Moore as the accompanist; and, again according to the sheet, the duet *Turn ye to me* may have been sung unaccompanied, as Moore is not mentioned. Copies of the music of both songs were in Kathleen's collection, written in her own hand, perhaps prepared specifically for this session. Unless test pressings turn up, it cannot be confirmed exactly how the works were performed.

The Purcell duets are short: indeed, there is space for two of them on one side of a 10″ record. *Let us wander* was originally a duet for two sopranos with chorus entitled *We the spirits of the air*, and is performed here in an arrangement by Moffat. *Shepherd, leave decoying*, which follows *Let us wander* on the 78 side, is included in, but not listed on, the EMI Références CD which contains of most of Kathleen's EMI recordings. It is to be found at Index number 11 on CDH 761003 2, and follows *Let us wander*.

Of the issued Mendelssohn duets *I would that my love* is better known, but *Greeting* is no less fine. That makes all the more regrettable its omission from the above-mentioned CD of Kathleen's Columbia recordings. There is sufficient space for it, as the total time for the CD as issued is only 72′04. The duet had, however, previously been issued on LP in February 1967, as part of an EMI tribute to Gerald Moore at about the time of his retirement from the concert platform.

These two issued 10″ records with Baillie mark the end of Kathleen's contract with EMI, but they were not the last records she was to make for the company. As we shall see, in 1949 she was temporarily released by Decca to record Mahler's *Kindertotenlieder* with The Vienna Philharmonic under Bruno Walter, and that work, in due course, appeared on the Columbia label. The recording producer for this session was Walter Legge, and the balance engineer Arthur Clarke.

2.30 pm on 21.9.45
EMI Studio 3, Abbey Road

16   PURCELL/? Tate
*Sound the trumpet* (*Come ye sons of art away* – extract from *The Ode for Queen Mary*)/English
Piano: Gerald Moore, Soprano: Isobel Baillie
Matrix CA 19861–1-2

17   PURCELL /Dryden and Howard
*Let us wander* (*The Indian Queen*)/English
Piano: Gerald Moore, Soprano: Isobel Baillie
Matrix CA 19862–1-2

18   PURCELL/Dryden
*Shepherd, leave decoying* (*King Arthur*)/English
Piano: Gerald Moore, Soprano: Isobel Baillie
Matrix CA 19862–1-2

19   MENDELSSOHN /Heine (translated)
*I would that my love, Op. 63, No. 1*/English
Piano: Gerald Moore, Soprano: Isobel Baillie
Matrix CA 19863–1

20   MENDELSSOHN /Eichendorff (translated)
*Greeting, Op. 63, No. 3*/English
Piano: Gerald Moore, Soprano: Isobel Baillie
Matrix CA 19864–1-2

21   MENDELSSOHN /Burns
*O wert thou in the cauld blast? Op. 63, No. 5*/Scottish
Piano: Gerald Moore, Soprano: Isobel Baillie
?Sung as a solo by Isobel Baillie
Never issued/Destroyed
Matrix CA 19865–1

22   TRADITIONAL /*Turn ye to me*/English
     ?Piano: Gerald Moore, Soprano: Isobel Baillie
     Never issued/Destroyed
     Matrix CA 19866–1

The BBC Sound Archives contain a wealth of material, including some recordings of broadcasts going back over sixty years. The earliest of Kathleen's radio performances to have survived there is of an impressive work that she sang in November 1945 – *On the Field of Kulikovo* – by the Soviet composer Yuri Shaporin (1889–1966).

This Symphony Cantata, composed in 1938, has nine movements. There are solos for soprano, contralto, tenor and baritone, and a considerable amount of music for the large chorus. As recorded, the work lasts for just under an hour; Kathleen sings in two of the movements. To quote the spoken introduction: 'In simple, expressive music, mother and children weep for husband and father fallen in battle.' A beautiful woodwind introduction precedes the contralto's solo, with the men's chorus singing between verses. Kathleen also makes a contribution in the last movement, together with the other soloists and the chorus.

The choice of Albert Coates as conductor seems appropriate for this work. He was born in St Petersburg in 1882, and worked extensively in Germany before the First World War. He continued to conduct in Russia up to 1917, and returned occasionally after the Revolution. He died in 1953, two months after Kathleen.

The performance was broadcast simultaneously on the BBC Home Service and in the Soviet Union. Winifred Ferrier, who was present in the BBC's Maida Vale Studio, commented: 'There was no need to broadcast it to Russia: it was so loud that I'm sure it could have been heard from England!'

     7.45 pm–9.00 pm on 7.11.45
     BBC Maida Vale Studio 1, West London

23   SHAPORIN/From mystic poems by Block (English translation by
     D. Miller Craig)
     *On the Field of Kulikovo,* a Symphony Cantata/English
     Conductor: Albert Coates, Soprano: Laelia Finneberg, Tenor:
     Frank Titterton, Baritone: Roderick Jones
     BBC Symphony Orchestra: Leader Paul Beard
     BBC Choral Society, Chorus Master: Leslie Woodgate
     Never commercially issued/BBC Sound Archives Reference:
     Tape T 28115
     NSA Reference: NSA Tape T9184W+R

# Chapter Five   *January - June 1946*

In 1945 Kathleen had spoken of her unhappiness at Columbia to her teacher in London, the well-known baritone Roy Henderson; he suggested that she join Decca, to which company he was contracted. She did, and made her first record for Decca in February 1946. It is a sad irony that Kathleen and Henderson never recorded together as soloists; Henderson conducted Pergolesi's *Stabat Mater*, which was made in May 1946, but that was their only joint recording, despite the many public performances that they gave of oratorio during the 1940s. Another incentive for Kathleen to sign a contract with Decca was their assurance that they would include her in a complete recording of Handel's *Messiah*, a work she greatly loved. In the event, this *Messiah* project never came to fruition, and the only parts of the work that she recorded were the two arias which she sang during the last commercial session of her life in October 1952.

Kathleen's first session for Decca was rich indeed. She recorded the aria *Have mercy, Lord, on me* from Bach's *St Matthew Passion*, with the National Symphony Orchestra conducted by Malcolm Sargent. It was her first commercial recording with an orchestra.

Kathleen had been auditioned by Sargent in 1942, and he advised her to pursue her career in London rather than in the north of England. Through him, she had an introduction to Ibbs and Tillett, the concert agency, who continued to represent her throughout her life. She first sang under Sargent's baton in 1944, and as well as frequently appearing on concert platforms together, they recorded five published sides for Decca. (The 1949 performance of Brahms's *Four Serious songs* was not originally a Decca performance, but was taken from the BBC Sound Archives.) The Bach aria recorded on 6th February 1946 was probably regarded as a test for the complete *St Matthew Passion* that Decca were intending to record. Although it was given a 78 issue number, and was released at some stage, Decca archives do not reveal an issue date, and no review of the 78 has been traced in *The Gramophone*.

In 1954 the performance was issued as a 45 rpm record, and has since been transferred on to LP, cassette and CD. Clearly Kathleen and Decca were pleased enough by the results to make plans for the (almost) complete version of the *Passion*, the recording of which started in June 1947.

Kathleen's diary shows that *Laudamus Te* (from the *Mass in B Minor*) was also planned for the same session, but that idea was shelved before the recording took place; it was an aria that she never recorded commercially.

5.30 pm on 6.2.46
Kingsway Hall, London

26   J.S. BACH/The Bible (translated)
*Have mercy, Lord, on me* (Part 1) (*St. Matthew Passion* BWV 244)/
English
Matrix AR 10042–1–2
*Have mercy, Lord, on me*/(Part 2)
Matrix AR 10043-1-2
Conductor: Dr Malcolm Sargent, Solo violin: David McCallum
National Symphony Orchestra

Sargent was again the conductor when Kathleen revisited Kingsway Hall three weeks later to record arias by Handel and Gluck. These have remained extremely popular performances, but *What is life?* is certainly one of her best known recordings. This aria had already become one of her favourite recital pieces, and although five other versions by her survive, the Sargent version is by far the most celebrated, if not the most artistically distinguished.

6.00 pm on 27.2.46
Kingsway Hall, London

27   HANDEL/Salvi, altered by Haym (translated)
*Art thou troubled?* (*Rodelinda*)/English
Conductor: Dr Malcolm Sargent, London Symphony Orchestra
Matrix AR 10092–1–2

28   GLUCK/Calzabigi (translated)
*What is life?* (*Orpheus and Euridice*)/English
Conductor: Dr Malcolm Sargent, London Symphony Orchestra
Matrix AR 10093–1–2

By May 1946, Kathleen had already started preparing the title role in Britten's *The Rape of Lucretia*, which was to receive its world première at Glyndebourne in July. Time was found, however, to spend two days recording Pergolesi's *Stabat Mater*, in a version reorchestrated by Scott, conducted by Roy Henderson. For the *Stabat Mater* ten sides were needed, and Kathleen sang on six of them. Stylistically this version is 'unauthentic', but that it was recorded complete at all showed some courage on Decca's part. *Stabat Mater* was a favourite work of Henderson's during the war, as the chorus is for women's voices only; at that time it was difficult to find men who were free to sing. (In the original version, the 'choruses' are sung by the two soloists only.) He had conducted the work at two concerts at The National Gallery with the Nottingham

Oriana Choir and Joan Taylor, although it was Astra Desmond and not Kathleen who sang the contralto part on those occasions.

The sides which involved the chorus were recorded on 8th May, and those involving only the two soloists on 28th May. Roy Henderson remembers: 'The Oriana Choir travelled from Nottingham for a 10.15 am rehearsal (on 8th May) at Southwark Cathedral, followed by a lunchtime concert there, had a picnic lunch in the Cathedral grounds, and made their way to Broadhurst Gardens, West Hampstead, where the recording was made. I don't know what time they got back to Nottingham! They sang everything from memory. Joan Taylor was a pupil of mine at the Royal Academy of Music, so I had two pupils and my own small choir which I founded just to make music, and we had a lot of fun together.' Joan Taylor also recalls: 'The actual recording went well; it was always a joy to sing with Kathleen, as she was such a fine musician, and I felt we phrased and blended almost instinctively.'

Like many 78 sets of the time, this was issued in two formats: 'automatic coupling' and 'straight coupling'. The following layout illustrates how the two different couplings were presented.

Afternoon on 8.5.46 and 10.00 am on 28.5.46
Decca Studios, Broadhurst Gardens

29 Pergolesi
*Stabat Mater*, complete (orch. Scott)/Latin
Conductor: Roy Henderson, Soprano: Joan Taylor
The Boyd Neel String Orchestra, Nottingham Oriana Choir

| MATRIX/TAKE | DATE | AUTO RECORD NOS | STRAIGHT RECORD NOS | TITLE | SINGERS |
|---|---|---|---|---|---|
| AR 10287-1-2 | 8.5.46 | AK 1517 | K 1517 | *Stabat mater* | Chorus |
| AR 10288-1-2 | 8.5.46 | AK 1518 | K 1517 | *Cujus animam* | JT |
| | | | | *O quam tristis* | Chorus |
| AR 10289-1-2 | 28.5.46 | AK 1519 | K 1518 | *Quae moerebat* | KF |
| | | | | *Quis est homo* | JT |
| | | | | *Quis non posset* | KF/JT |
| AR 10290-1-2 | 8.5.46 | AK 1520 | K 1518 | *Pro peccatis* | Chorus |
| | | | | *Vidit suum* | JT |
| AR 10291-1-2 | 8.5.46 | AK 1521 | K 1519 | *Eia mater* | KF |
| | | | | *Fac ut* | Chorus |
| AR 10292-1-2 | 28.5.46 | AK 1521 | K 1519 | *Sancta mater* | KF/JT |
| AR 10293-1-2 | 28.5.46 | AK 1520 | K 1520 | *Sancta (contd)* | KF/JT |
| AR 10294-1-2 | 28.5.46 | AK 1519 | K 1520 | *Fac ut portem* | KF |
| AR 10295-1-2 | 28.5.46 | AK 1518 | K 1521 | *Inflammatus* | KF/JT |
| AR 10296-1-2 | 8.5.46 | AK 1517 | K 1521 | *Quando corpus* | Chorus |

# Chapter Six   *July - December 1946*

By September 1946, when Kathleen made her next recordings, she had already appeared in her operatic stage début as Lucretia. The first performances at Glyndebourne in July were followed by a tour of the English provinces and Edinburgh, and two weeks at Sadler's Wells Theatre in London.

To record two arias from Mendelssohn's *Elijah* must have proved something of a respite after so many performances of Britten's testing music. The oratorio was one in which Kathleen often sang; indeed, it was the work that had introduced her to Roy Henderson when they sang it together in 1942; it always remained a favourite with Kathleen as well as with audiences. The work has since gone out of fashion, and is now seldom heard in Britain.

Decca's archives give the date for this recording as 3rd September, but Kathleen's diary is marked very clearly on 2nd – 'Recording Elijah 3.30' – The recording venue cannot be confirmed; it was probably Decca's studios.

> 3.30 pm on 2.9.46
> ?Decca Studios, Broadhurst Gardens?

31   MENDELSSOHN/Paraphrase of Psalm 37, verses 1, 4 & 7
     *O rest in the Lord* (*Elijah, Op. 70*)/ English
     Conductor: Boyd Neel, The Boyd Neel Orchestra
     Matrix AR 10544–1–2

32   MENDELSSOHN/The Bible – Hosea vii, verse 13
     *Woe unto them* (*Elijah, Op. 70*)/ English
     Conductor: Boyd Neel, The Boyd Neel Orchestra
     Matrix AR 10545–1

Benjamin Britten first heard Kathleen sing in 1943, when she and Peter Pears were two of the soloists in a performance of *Messiah* in Westminster Abbey. He was impressed by the quality of her voice and her musicianship, and when he began composing *The Rape of Lucretia*, he felt sure she was the right singer to undertake the title role. At first Kathleen was apprehensive about the difficulties of the music, and equally concerned about making her stage début in such a modern work. At this point in her career, acting in opera did not come naturally to her, but nonetheless the opening night at Glyndebourne on 12th July was a critical (if not a great public) success. She appeared in many performances of the work in 1946 and 1947, but sang it very little after that; occasionally she included the Flower Song from Act 2 in recitals. Gluck's *Orfeo ed Euridice* was the only other opera that Kathleen sang in staged productions.

Two separate casts had been assembled to perform the opera at Glyndebourne and on the subsequent British tour. This was to avoid undue strain on singers who would otherwise be on stage virtually every evening, with some matinées, for a period of nine weeks. Kathleen was the Lucretia of what was called the 'first' cast, although both casts had superb singers, selected by Britten. Her opposite number in the 'second cast', was Nancy Evans, who became a good friend, and who later married Eric Crozier, the opera's producer. Whilst singers of one cast tended to stay together for performances, there were occasions when one from the other cast would appear instead, to replace his opposite number.

At the end of September 1946 Kathleen paid her first visit overseas, when she and the other participants in the Glyndebourne production of *The Rape of Lucretia* travelled to Holland to give performances in Amsterdam and The Hague. A performance from Stadsschouwburg (The Municipal Theatre) in Amsterdam was broadcast on 4th October, and excerpts have been released on a single LP. It was the first broadcast of the work, and featured the entire 'first cast'. When plans for releasing the complete performance were proposed in the early 1980s, permission could not be obtained from the Britten Estate, as it included scenes which the composer later revised; the Trustees did not feel it appropriate to allow the earlier versions to be made publicly available. Fortunately, the revised parts did not include any of Lucretia's music, so Kathleen's performance is heard complete on the published LP.

The broadcasting company archives (NOS) state that the recording was made on 5th October with the composer conducting. However, both Glyndebourne archives and a cutting from the Dutch radio programme listings for that week, which is in Kathleen's scrapbook, indicate that the performance was broadcast on 4th October. It seems unlikely that the opera would have been broadcast one night, and then recorded for sound archive purposes at the following night's performance. The naming of Britten as the conductor is also questionable; Glyndebourne archives show that he conducted only the first of the series of Dutch performances, on 2nd October, the remainder being shared between Reginald Goodall and Hans Oppenheim; it was Oppenheim who was in charge on the evening of the 4th, a fact confirmed by a theatre programme for that performance. Certainly, all performances were under the *supervision* of Britten, which does not mean that he conducted them all. Dutch archives show that he gave an interview on the same evening as the broadcast, but that does not necessarily mean that he also conducted on that occasion; indeed, *had* he conducted, he might well not have wished also to give an interview.

It is possible that the performance which Britten conducted was recorded, and not broadcast until 4th October, but that still does not account for the 5th being quoted as the recording date in the archives. With a work like *The Rape of Lucretia* there would have been considerable difficulties in recording on 78 rpm discs at a live performance, and then playing them back on the air at a later date, coping with the awkward side changes that the format dictated. It would have been easier to broadcast the first performance live, on 2nd October, and have done with it!

As well as giving what is probably the wrong date for the recording, the sleeve of the Educ Media record also gives the wrong date for the first performance of the opera (it was not 7th June 1946), and the accompanying libretto is not complete as is stated; several passages performed on the record are omitted from it. The orchestra is not that of The English Opera Group, which was not founded until well after this tour was completed, and, like the Dutch radio archives (from where the information surely originated) Britten, and not Oppenheim, is given as the conductor. The quality of sound on this recording is very variable; there is a good deal of surface noise, but that it has survived at all, and has been issued at least in part, is gratifying.

8.00 pm on ?4.10.46
Stadsschouwburg, Amsterdam

33   Britten/Ronald Duncan (after Obey's play *Le viol de Lucrèce*)
*The Rape of Lucretia, Op. 37*/English

Soprano: Joan Cross, Female Chorus
Soprano: Margaret Ritchie, Lucia
Mezzo: Anna Pollak, Bianca
Tenor: Peter Pears, Male Chorus
Baritone: Edmund Donlevy, Junius
Bass: Owen Brannigan, Collatinus
Bass: Otakar Kraus, Tarquinius
Conductor: ?Benjamin Britten/?Hans Oppenheim,
The Glyndebourne Opera Orchestra
Never issued complete, commercially/Dutch Radio Sound
Archives NOB: Reference EM-HM-0030

Representative excerpts have been issued from the complete
recording which is in NOS (Dutch Radio) Archives
33a Act 1 From *Rome is now ruled . . .* to *. . . Christ's own tears*
33b Act 1 From *My horse! My horse!* to *. . . Good night, Lucretia*
33c Act 2 From *She sleeps as a rose . . .* to *. . . Tarquinius is
drowned*
33d Act 2 From *Hush here she comes . . .* to *. . . Do you remember?*
33e Act 2 From *Lucretia, Lucretia, . . .* to *. . . It is all. It is all*

Of the five extracts, all except 33a include Kathleen

After the performances in Amsterdam, the second cast went to The
Hague, to continue the Dutch tour, while the first cast returned to
London. On 11th October the opera received its first British radio
broadcast on the Third Programme, given live from Camden Hippodrome, being used as a BBC studio. A letter in Glyndebourne archives
addressed to Rudolf Bing, General Manager of The Glyndebourne
Opera, confirms the arrangements that had been made for the rehearsal
(10.30 am–1.30 pm), and for the broadcast (Act 1: 7.15 pm and Act 2:
9.15 pm). The cast, with one exception, was that which had broadcast
in Amsterdam a week earlier; Frederick Sharp from the second cast
replaced Edmund Donlevy. Reginald Goodall was the conductor. In the
small orchestra were some well-known names from the immediate post-
war (and later) musical world, including Emanuel Hurwitz, Peter
Schidlof, Kenneth Essex, John Francis and Edward Downes, now a
celebrated conductor himself.

The broadcast was recorded off the air on acetate discs by George
Lascelles (now The Earl of Harewood), a friend of Britten's. Unfortunately not all the opera survives in this version, but the extant parts can
be heard at The National Sound Archive division of the British Library.
This provides the only general opportunity to hear some pages of the
original score that were subsequently revised by the composer.

One excerpt from Act 2 has been issued on a BBC tribute to Kathleen,
*The Singer and the Person* – but on the sleeve notes the date of the
broadcast has inadvertently been given as 4th October 1946. The sound
on this version of *The Rape of Lucretia* is markedly better than that of the
Amsterdam performance of the previous week.

In 1947, EMI made the first commercial recording of excerpts from
the opera, again conducted by Reginald Goodall, but because by this
time Kathleen was a Decca artist, she was unable to participate in it. It
has, however, preserved, among other interpretations, that of Nancy
Evans in the title role, Peter Pears as the Male Chorus (which he later
recorded complete for Decca when Dame Janet Baker sang Lucretia),
and that of Joan Cross as the Female Chorus.

7.15 pm–10.25 pm on 11.10.46
Camden Hippodrome, North London

34    BRITTEN/Ronald Duncan (after Obey's Play *Le viol de Lucrèce*)
*The Rape of Lucretia, Op. 37*/English
Soprano: Joan Cross, Female Chorus
Soprano: Margaret Ritchie, Lucia
Mezzo: Anna Pollak, Bianca
Tenor: Peter Pears, Male Chorus
Baritone: Frederick Sharp, Junius
Bass: Owen Brannigan, Collatinus
Bass: Otakar Kraus, Tarquinius
Conductor: Reginald Goodall, The Glyndebourne Opera
Orchestra

The surviving parts of this version are:
Act 1 From *Rome is now ruled . . .* to *. . . is love! Is love! Is love!*
Act 1 From *To the chaste Lucretia . . .* to *. . . Good night Lucretia*
Act 2 From *The prosperity of the Etruscans . . .* to *. . . know our knife*
Act 2 From *She sleeps as a rose . . .* to *. . . and wakes to kiss again*
Act 2 From *Oh! What a lovely day . . .* to *. . . to harness song to human tragedy* (The End)

In addition to the omissions indicated, other occasional words and phrases are also missing, due possibly to the difficulty of changing acetate discs during the recording of the broadcast.

Never issued commercially/BBC Sound Archives Reference:
Tape T 39584
NSA Reference: NSA Tape T9202W+R

34a From Act 2 *Lucretia! Lucretia! O never again must we two dare to part*
Bass: Owen Brannigan, Collatinus

# Chapter Seven    *January - June 1947*

Kathleen's reputation as a performer of German Lieder is far greater than her reputation as an opera singer. Few of her recitals were without at least one item by Schubert, Schumann or Brahms.

On 14th March 1947 she made her first recording of Schubert songs, with Phyllis Spurr as her accompanist. They first worked together in 1945, and over the next few years theirs became a very happy and successful musical association. Phyllis accompanied Kathleen on tours in Britain and Europe, and to Scandinavia in October 1949, including the broadcast recitals from Copenhagen and Oslo; they recorded together at several sessions in the Decca Studios at Broadhurst Gardens, not far from Kathleen's home in Frognal Mansions, Hampstead.

This record was the first of the many that Kathleen sang in German.

> 2.30 pm on 14.3.47
> Decca Studios, Broadhurst Gardens

> 36   SCHUBERT/Goethe
>       *Gretchen am Spinnrade, Op. 2, D118*/German
>       Piano: Phyllis Spurr
>       Matrix AR 11096–1–<u>2</u>

> 37   SCHUBERT/von Craigher
>       *Die junge Nonne, Op. 43, No. 1, D828*/German
>       Piano: Phyllis Spurr
>       Matrix AR 11097–<u>1</u>

Kathleen's success in *The Rape of Lucretia* at Glyndebourne led to an invitation to her to sing at Glyndebourne again in the summer of 1947, in a new production of Gluck's *Orfeo ed Euridice*. The difficulties that she encountered this time were not with the music, which she is quoted as saying 'lies in the fat of my voice', but with the conductor, Viennese-borne Fritz Stiedry. Stiedry was highly regarded; but, it seems, he was not easy to work with. During the rehearsals for *Orfeo*, he continually criticised Kathleen's acting, and changed words that she had spent hours learning. She had never previously sung in Italian, and Stiedry's attitude upset her badly. (She and the other members of the cast were fortunate in having as their Italian language coach Renato Cellini, who, in the 1950s, became a celebrated conductor himself.)

The two other leading singers who took part in this production were the Greek soprano Zoë Vlachopoulos, who spoke virtually no English except the then popular phrase 'Don't be vague, ask for Haig', advertising whisky, which she learnt from stage hands at Glyndebourne, and Ann Ayars. Ayars, a young American soprano, also partnered Kathleen in concert performances of *Orfeo ed Euridice* in New York in March 1950. She appeared in the Powell and Pressburger film *The Tales of Hoffmann*, conducted by Sir Thomas Beecham, in which Kathleen was also invited to take part, but declined.

The first night of the new production of *Orfeo* was a great success, and three days later the cast began to make a 'concise' recording at Kingsway Hall. Sessions on two further days were used to complete the fourteen sides of 78s which made up the set. Decca archives indicate that two takes were made of each side; on the published discs, however, one matrix (AR 11394) is clearly marked as a third take. The score is drastically cut (although the main arias are complete), but the sense of dramatic continuity is preserved. The original 78 rpm labels do not specify which musical numbers are found on which sides, but show simply, for example, *Act 2 continued*, or *Act 3 conclusion*. With the cuts as they are, it would have been virtually impossible to list each side's music and make sense of it. Stiedry's tempi in this set have often been criticised, particularly that of *Che farò*, which is taken much faster than was usual in the 1940s, although by the standards of some of today's performances, it seems he judged it about right. Whether the speed was part of his interpretation, or was dictated by the constraints imposed by the playing time of a 78 side, is unclear.

Until the discovery of the Dutch set of *Orfeo* in the 1970s, this 'concise' version was thought to be the most complete recording of Kathleen singing the title role, although yet another, less 'concise' version, recorded in 1950, has also been traced in New York.

The work was issued in both 'straight' and 'automatic' coupling systems. On reissues of this set, an orchestral section of side 4 has been omitted, as has the whole of side 7, with *The Dance of the Blessed Spirits*, and Euridice's solo with chorus; the chorus *Trionfi Amore* on side 13 has also been omitted, but the same chorus, at the very end of the opera, recorded on side 14, has been retained.

The listing below gives an indication of the music recorded on this set.

10.00 am–2.00 pm on 22.6.47, 10.00 am on 23.6.47, 10.00 am–
2.00pm on 29.6.47
Kingsway Hall, London

38   GLUCK/Calzabigi
*Orfeo ed Euridice*, Concise version/Italian
Soprano: Ann Ayars, Euridice
Soprano: Zoë Vlachopoulos, Amor
Conductor: Fritz Stiedry, Southern Philharmonic Orchestra,
Glyndebourne Festival Chorus

| SIDE NO. | MATRIX/TAKE | DATE | AUTO RECORD NOS | STRAIGHT RECORD NOS | TITLE | SINGERS |
|---|---|---|---|---|---|---|
| | | | | | *ACT 1* | |
| 1. | AR 11392-1-2 | 22.6.47 | AK 1656 | K 1656 | *Ah se intorno* | Chorus |
| | | | | | *Euridice!* | KF |
| | | | | | *Amici, quel lamento* | KF |
| 2. | AR 11393-1-2 | 22.6.47 | AK 1657 | K 1656 | *Ritornello* | Orchestra |
| | | | | | *Euridice!* | KF |
| | | | | | *Piango il mio ben* | KF |
| | | | | | *Io sapro* | KF |
| 3. | AR 11394-1-2--3 | 22.6.47 | AK 1658 | K 1657 | *Amore assisterà* | ZV |
| | | | | | *Della cetra* | ZV/KF |
| | | | | | *Ascolta* | ZV |
| | | | | | *Che disse!* | KF |
| | | | | | *ACT 2* | |
| 4. | AR 11395-1-2 | 22.6.47 | AK 1659 | K 1657 | *Chaconne* | Orchestra |
| | | | | | *Ballet* | Orchestra |
| 5. | AR 11396-1-2 | 22.6.47 | AK 1660 | K 1658 | *Chi mai dell'Erebo* | Chorus |
| | | | | | *Deh! Placatevi* | KF/Chorus |
| 6. | AR 11397-1-2 | 22.6.47 | AK 1661 | K 1658 | *Misero giovane* | Chorus |
| | | | | | *Mile pene* | KF/Chorus |
| | | | | | *Men tiranne* | KF/Chorus |
| 7. | AR 11398-1-2 | 23.6.47 | AK 1662 | K 1659 | *Dance of the Blessed Spirits* | Orchestra |
| | | | | | *E quest'asile* | AA/Chorus |
| 8. | AR 11399-1-2 | 23.6.47 | AK 1662 | K 1659 | *Che puro ciel!* | KF/Chorus |
| 9. | AR 11400-1-2 | 23.6.47 | AK 1661 | K 1660 | *Vieni a'regni* | Chorus |
| | | | | | *ACT 3* | |
| | | | | | *Ah vieni, o diletta* | KF/AA |
| | | | | | *Si, or il passo* | KF/AA |
| 10. | AR 11401-1-2 | 23.6.47 | AK 1660 | K 1660 | *Sol uno sguardo* | KF/AA |
| | | | | | *Tu tiran per* | KF/AA |

| SIDE NO. MATRIX/TAKE | DATE | AUTO RECORD NOS | STRAIGHT RECORD NOS | TITLE | SINGERS |
|---|---|---|---|---|---|
| 11. AR 11402-1-2 | 29.6.47 | AK 1659 | K 1661 | *Ah, potess'io* | AA |
| | | | | *Che fiero* | AA/KF |
| | | | | *Avezzo al contento/* | |
| | | | | *Qual dolor* | AA/KF |
| 12. AR 11403–1–2 | 29.6.47 | AK 1658 | K 1661 | *Ah! per me il duol* | KF/AA |
| | | | | *Qual pena* | KF/AA |
| | | | | *Che ho fatto* | KF |
| | | | | *Che farò* | KF |
| 13. AR 11404-1-2 | 29.6.47 | AK 1657 | K 1662 | *Ah! Finisca* | KF |
| | | | | *Non più!* | ZV/KF |
| | | | | *Frena, frena* | ZV/KF/AA |
| | | | | *Usciam di qua* | ZV |
| | | | | *Trionfi Amore* | KF/AA/ZV/ Chorus |
| 14. AR 11405-1-2 | 29.6.47 | AK 1656 | K 1662 | *Gaudio, gaudio* | KF/AA/ZV |
| | | | | *Trionfi Amore* | Chorus |

38a From Act 2 *Che puro ciel*

The day after the last session of *Orfeo ed Euridice* was the first day of one of Decca's major recording projects of the 78 era. The making of an almost complete *St Matthew Passion* took over eleven months, and eventually occupied forty-two sides of 12" discs. In the score, the *Passion* is divided into (coincidentally!) 78 numbers, comprising recitatives, arias, duets, choruses and chorales. In this Decca version the following numbers are omitted entirely:

    11.   Recitative for The Evangelist and Judas
    21.   Chorale
    65.   Recitative for Bass soloist
    66.   Aria for Bass soloist

and items 10, 26, 29, 32, 63 and 73 are reduced in length; some arias, for instance, are deprived of their full *da capo* repeat section, presumably because of the restrictions imposed by the comparatively short time for which a 12" 78 rpm side would play. Of Kathleen's arias, only her first – *Grief for sin* – is shortened in this way, which may explain why, at her last commercial session for Decca in 1952, this aria was again recorded, but on that occasion included the repeat.

The first part of the set to be made was a very abridged version of only fourteen sides, just a third of the work as finally issued. These excerpts needed the services of soprano, contralto, tenor and bass soloists, another bass in the recitatives, and a choir.

After the abridged set had been issued, recording was begun, in May 1948, on the remainder of the work, and it was issued 'complete' in three volumes of 78s, each containing seven records, incorporating the earlier sides in correct sequential order. This form of presentation must have been irksome to those who had purchased the abridged version and then wished to buy the full version, although apparently Decca were prepared to assist owners of the original seven discs in some way. Just how is not clear.

For the full version, the four original soloists, Elsie Suddaby, Kathleen Ferrier, Eric Greene and William Parsons were again used, to complete the full quota of recitatives and arias, and further singers were needed in some of the recitatives.

Establishing dates for the recording of individual sides is difficult, as evidence in Decca archives conflicts with some of the details noted in Kathleen's diary. For the abridged set, fourteen consecutive matrices were allocated, which appear to have been used in chronological order, which was not, however, sequence order of the work itself.

Decca's archives indicate that Kathleen recorded on both the dates which were used for the abridged version, 30th June and 4th July 1947, whilst her diary does not mention any session on 30th June (as it was the day after completing *Orfeo ed Euridice* she might well have required a day off), but mentions two sessions – from 2.00 pm to 5.00 pm and from 6.00 pm to 9.00 pm – on 4th July.

For the 1948 sessions, three sets of dates were needed, as detailed in Decca's archives: 3rd May; 8th May; and 7th, 8th, 9th, 10th and 11th June. On 3rd May Kathleen returned to London from a brief visit to Holland, arriving just in time to attend a recording session at Kingsway Hall from 6.00 pm to 9.00 pm at which she apparently recorded one side. In the archives, no differentiation is made between the set of five days in June; they are blocked together as a unit, but Kathleen's diary shows her participation in sessions from 6.00 pm to 9.00 pm on 9th June, and from 2.00 pm to 5.00 pm and from 6.00 pm to 9.00 pm on the 10th.

Twenty-six consecutive matrix numbers were used for the 1948 sessions, plus two completely out of sequence; Kathleen sang on these last two. The recording producer may have miscalculated how many sides would be required, and found himself short of matrix numbers towards the end! There was clearly an attempt to use these twenty-eight matrices in correct sequence of the work itself rather than chronologically, although it was not entirely successful. One curiosity apparent on the 78 set, but corrected on subsequent LP issues, concerns the bass aria, No. 51 – *Give, O give me back my Lord*. It was recorded, using one full side, for the abridged version on 4th July 1947, but when it came to 'filling in' round it in June 1948, the two previous items, Nos. 49 and

50, and the following item, No. 52, had to be recorded together on one side, putting No. 51 out of sequence.

Three labelling anomalies are apparent on the original 78s; only Eric Greene and the Bach Choir are named on the label for matrix AR 12287, although Gordon Clinton and Elsie Suddaby are both heard to sing a few words; their names were listed on Decca's session sheets for that matrix, but have subsequently been crossed through. And the choir do not sing at all on that side. The label for matrix AR 11425 credits Kathleen with singing on that side, although she does not, and the label for matrix AR 12290 credits Henry Cummings and not Gordon Clinton with singing Judas's few words, although Decca's session sheets give the latter's name. These errors may have been rectified on subsequent pressings of the set.

It is also interesting to note that on the abridged version take 1 is used of matrix numbers AR 11417 and AR 11418 (this latter being the first part of No. 47, Kathleen singing *Have mercy, Lord, on me*), but take 2 of both matrices is used on the complete version; these second takes were recorded at the 1947 sessions. It was necessary to record more than one take, since the metalwork was sometimes damaged in the delicate process involved in obtaining the stamper; should this happen, a back-up was needed, and the second take would be used instead. Decca's archives show that two takes were made for each side; there may have been more, however, as on some other recordings of Kathleen's, two takes have been similarly noted, but take three has been issued!

The forces assembled for this ambitious recording project were, apart from the four soloists already named, The Jacques Orchestra, The Bach Choir, Dr Osborne Peasgood at the organ, Dr Thornton Lofthouse at the harpsichord, Bruce Boyce, Henry Cummings and Gordon Clinton. The conductor was Dr Reginald Jacques. Boyce sang on two sides in 1947, but was either not available, or was not chosen to participate, the following year. As none of Jesus's words was recorded in 1947, Henry Cummings was not needed that year; his contributions to the set, and those of Gordon Clinton, are from 1948.

The work was sung in English, and both the artists involved, and the style of performance, are representative of a good standard *St Matthew Passion* of the time. In this recording, apart from the contralto's usual items, Kathleen also sings a phrase of recitative in No. 45 which in public performances is often allocated to another singer.

The abridged version was issued in both 'straight' and 'automatic' versions. Decca's recording sheets for the 1948 sessions show that 'straight' coupling was planned for the 'complete' set, although their advertising material states that it was available only as 'automatic'!

Winifred Ferrier, present at one of the sessions for this set of records, recalls the amount of time spent discussing how best to fit a particular section of music on to a 12″ wax: 'It wasn't easy to make records in those days, and getting it on to a disc took priority over interpretation sometimes!'

Dates given below are those found in Decca's archives.

## Abridged Version

30.6.47/2.00 pm–5.00 pm and 6.00 pm–9.00 pm on 4.7.47
Kingsway Hall, London

39  BACH (Revised by Elgar and Atkins)/The Bible, translated from the German by Troutbeck and Johnson
*St Matthew Passion*/BWV 244/English
Soprano: Elsie Suddaby, Tenor: Eric Greene (The Evangelist), Bass: William Parsons, Bass: Bruce Boyce, Conductor: Dr Reginald Jacques, The Jacques Orchestra, The Bach Choir, Organ: Dr Osborne Peasgood, Harpsichord: Dr Thornton Lofthouse

| MATRIX/TAKE | DATE | AUTO RECORD NOS | STRAIGHT RECORD NOS | MUSICAL NO. AND TITLE | SINGERS |
|---|---|---|---|---|---|
| AR 11424-1-2 | 4.7.47 | AK 1673 | K 1673 | 10 *Grief for sin* | KF |
| AR 11412-1-2 | 30.6.47 | AK 1674 | K 1673 | 12 *Break in grief* | ES |
| AR 11413-1-2 | 30.6.47 | AK 1675 | K 1674 | 19 *Jesus, Saviour* | ES |
| AR 11414-1-2 | 30.6.47 | AK 1676 | K 1674 | 25 *O grief!* | EG/Chorus |
| AR 11415-1-2 | 30.6.47 | AK 1677 | K 1675 | 26 *I would beside my Lord* | EG/Chorus |
| AR 11417-1-2 | 30.6.47 | AK 1678 | K 1675 | 44 *O Lord, who dares* | Chorus |
| | | | | 45 *Now Peter sat* | EG/ES/KF/BB |
| | | | | 46 *Surely* | EG/BB/ Chorus |
| AR 11418-1-2 | 30.6.47 | AK 1679 | K 1676 | 47 *Have mercy, Lord* (Part 1) | KF |
| AR 11419-1-2 | 30.6.47 | AK 1679 | K 1676 | 47 *Have mercy, Lord* (Part 2) | KF |
| | | | | 48 *Lamb of God* | Chorus |
| AR 11420-1-2 | 4.7.47 | AK 1678 | K 1677 | 51 *Give, o give* | WP |
| AR 11425-1-2 | 4.7.47 | AK 1677 | K 1677 | 53 *Commit thy way* | Chorus |
| | | | | 54 *Now at that feast* | ES/EG/BB/ Chorus |
| AR 11416-1-2 | 30.6.47 | AK 1676 | K 1678 | 70 *See ye! See* | KF/Chorus |
| AR 11421-1-2 | 4.7.47 | AK 1675 | K 1678 | 72 *Be near me, Lord* | Chorus |
| | | | | 73 *And behold, the veil* | EG/Chorus |

| MATRIX/TAKE | DATE | AUTO RECORD NOS | STRAIGHT RECORD NOS | MUSICAL NO. AND TITLE | SINGERS |
|---|---|---|---|---|---|
| AR 11422-1-2 | 4.7.47 | AK 1674 | K 1679 | 78 *In tears of grief* Chorus (Part 1) | |
| AR 11423-1-2 | 4.7.47 | AK 1673 | K 1679 | 78 *In tears of grief* Chorus (Part 2) | |

Details of the 1948 sessions are included here, rather than in Chapter Nine, a they comprise the major part of the project which commenced in June 1947.

## (Almost) Complete Version

6.00 pm–9.00 pm on 3.5.48/6.00 pm–9.00 pm on 8.5.48
7.6.48/8.6.48/6.00 pm–9.00 pm on 9.6.48
2.00 pm–5.00 pm and 6.00 pm-9.00 pm on 10.6.48/11.6.48
Kingsway Hall, London

40   BACH (revised by Elgar and Atkins)/The Bible, translated from the German by Troutbeck and Johnson
*St Matthew Passion*, BWV 244/English
Performers as in 39, plus: Bass: Gordon Clinton, Bass: Henry Cummings (Jesus)

| MATRIX/TAKE | DATE | AUTO RECORD NOS | MUSICAL NO. AND TITLE | SINGERS |
|---|---|---|---|---|
| | | | **VOLUME ONE** | |
| AR 12273-1-2 | .6.48 | AK 2001 | 1 *Come, ye daughters* Chorus (Part 1) | |
| AR 12274-1-2 | .6.48 | AK 2002 | 1 *Come, ye daughters* Chorus (Part 2) | |
| AR 12275-1-2 | .6.48 | AK 2003 | 1 *Come, ye daughters* Chorus (Part 3) | |
| | | | 2 *When Jesus* | EG/HC |
| | | | 3 *O blessed Jesu* | Chorus |
| | | | 4 *Then assembled* | EG |
| | | | 5 *Not upon the feast* | Chorus |
| AR 12276 1-2 | .6.48 | AK 2004 | 6 *Now when Jesus* | EG |
| | | | 7 *To what purpose* | Chorus |
| | | | 8 *When Jesus* | EG/HC |
| | | | 9 *My Master* | KF |
| AR 11424-1-2 | 4.7.47 | AK 2005 | 10 *Grief for sin* | KF |

| MATRIX/TAKE | DATE | AUTO RECORD NOS | MUSICAL NO. AND TITLE | SINGERS |
|---|---|---|---|---|
| AR 11412-1-2 | 30.6.47 | AK 2006 | 12 *Break in grief* | ES |
| AR 12277-1-2 | .6.48 | AK 2007 | 13 *Now the first* | EG |
| | | | 14 *Where wilt Thou* | Chorus |
| | | | 15 *And He said* | EG/HC |
| | | | 16 *'Tis I* | Chorus |
| | | | 17 *And He answered* (Part 1) | EG/HC |
| AR 12278-1-2 | .6.48 | AK 2007 | 17 *Then answered Judas* (Part 2) | EG/HC GC |
| | | | 18 *Although our eyes* | ES |
| AR 11413-1-2 | 30.6.47 | AK 2006 | 19 *Jesus, Saviour* | ES |
| AR 12279-1-2 | .6.48 | AK 2005 | 20 *And after* | EG/HC |
| | | | 22 *Peter answered* | EG/HC/GC |
| | | | 23 *Here would I stand* | Chorus |
| | | | 24 *Then cometh Jesus* | EG/HC |
| AR 11414-1-2 | 30.6.47 | AK 2004 | 25 *O grief!* | EG/Chorus |
| AR 11415-1-2 | 30.6.47 | AK 2003 | 26 *I would beside my Lord* | EG/Chorus |
| AR 12280-1-2 | .6.48 | AK 2002 | 27 *And He went* | EG/HC |
| | | | 28 *The Saviour, low* | WP |
| | | | 29 *Gladly would I* | WP |
| AR 12281-1-2 | .6.48 | AK 2001 | 30 *And He cometh* | EG/HC |
| | | | 31 *O Father* | Chorus |
| | | | 32 *Then cometh He* | EG/HC/GC |

## VOLUME TWO

| | | | | |
|---|---|---|---|---|
| AR 12282-1-2 | 8.5.48 | AK 2008 | 33 *Behold, my Saviour* (Part 1) | KF/ES/Chorus |
| AR 12283-1-2 | 8.5.48 | AK 2009 | 33 *Have lightnings* (Part 2) | Chorus |
| | | | 34 *And behold* | EG/HC |
| AR 12284-1-2 | .6.48 | AK 2010 | 35 *O Man* (Part 1) | Chorus |
| AR 12285-1-2 | .6.48 | AK 2011 | 35 *O Man* (Part 2) | Chorus |
| AR 12406-1-2 | 10.6.48 | AK 2012 | 36 *Ah! Now is my Saviour* (Part 1) | KF/Chorus |

| MATRIX/TAKE | DATE | AUTO RECORD NOS | MUSICAL NO. AND TITLE | SINGERS |
|---|---|---|---|---|
| AR 12407-1-2 | 10.6.48 | AK 2013 | 36 *Ah! Now is my Saviour* (Part 2) | KF |
| | | | 37 *And they that had* | EG |
| | | | 38 *How falsely* | Chorus |
| AR 12287-1-2 | .6.48 | AK 2014 | 39 *Yea, though* | EG/ES/GC |
| | | | 40 *He holds* | EG |
| | | | 41 *Endure, endure* (Part 1) | EG |
| AR 12288-1-2 | .6.48 | AK 2014 | 41 *Endure, endure* (Part 2) | EG |
| | | | 42 *And the High Priest* | EG/HC/GC Chorus |
| | | | 43 *Then did they spit* | EG/Chorus |
| AR 11417-1-2 | 30.6.47 | AK 2013 | 44 *O Lord, who dares* | Chorus |
| | | | 45 *Now Peter sat* | EG/ES/KF/BB |
| | | | 46 *Surely* | EG/BB/Chorus |
| AR 11418-1-2 | 30.6.47 | AK 2012 | 47 *Have mercy, Lord* (Part 1) | KF |
| AR 11419-1-2 | 30.6.47 | AK 2011 | 47 *Have mercy, Lord* (Part 2) | KF |
| | | | 48 *Lamb of God* | Chorus |
| AR 12297-1-2 | .6.48 | AK 2010 | 49 *When the morning* | EG/GC/Chorus |
| | | | 50 *And he cast down* | EG/GC |
| | | | 52 *And they took* | EG/HC/GC |
| AR 11420-1-2 | 4.7.47 | AK 2009 | 51 *Give, O give* | WP |
| AR 11425-1-2 | 4.7.47 | AK 2008 | 53 *Commit thy way* | Chorus |
| | | | 54 *Now at that feast* | ES/EG/BB/ Chorus |

## VOLUME THREE

| MATRIX/TAKE | DATE | AUTO RECORD NOS | MUSICAL NO. AND TITLE | SINGERS |
|---|---|---|---|---|
| AR 12289-1-2 | 3.5.48 | AK 2015 | 55 *O wondrous love* | Chorus |
| | | | 56 *The governor said* | EG/GC |
| | | | 57 *To all men* | ES |
| | | | 58 *For love* (Part 1) | ES |
| AR 12290-1-2 | 3.5.48 | AK 2016 | 58 *For love* (Part 2) | ES |
| | | | 59 *But they cried* | EG/GC/Chorus |
| AR 12291-1-2 | .6.48 | AK 2017 | 60 *O Gracious God!* | KF |
| | | | 61 *If my tears* (Part 1) | KF |

| MATRIX/TAKE | DATE | AUTO RECORD NOS | MUSICAL NO. AND TITLE | SINGERS |
|---|---|---|---|---|
| AR 12292-1-2 | .6.48 | AK 2018 | 61 *If my tears* (Part 2) | KF |
| AR 12293-1-2 | .6.48 | AK 2019 | 62 *Then the soldiers* | EG/Chorus |
| | | | 63 *O Sacred Head* | Chorus |
| | | | 64 *And after that* | EG |
| | | | 67 *And when they* (Part 1) | EG |
| AR 12286-1-2 | .6.48 | AK 2020 | 67 *And set up over* (Part 2) | EG/Chorus |
| | | | 68 *The thieves also* | EG |
| | | | 69 *Ah, Golgotha!* | KF |
| AR 11416-1-2 | 30.6.47 | AK 2021 | 70 *See ye! see* | KF/Chorus |
| AR 12294-1-2 | .6.48 | AK 2021 | 71 *Now from the sixth* | EG/HC/Chorus |
| AR 11421-1-2 | 4.7.47 | AK 2020 | 72 *Be near me, Lord* | Chorus |
| | | | 73 *And behold, the veil* | EG/Chorus |
| AR 12295-1-2 | .6.48 | AK 2019 | 74 *At evening* | WP |
| | | | 75 *Make thee clean* (Part 1) | WP |
| AR 12296-1-2 | .6.48 | AK 2018 | 75 *Make thee clean* (Part 2) | WP |
| AR 12298-1-2 | 3.5.48 | AK 2017 | 76 *And when Joseph* | EG/GC/Chorus |
| | | | 77 *And now the Lord* | ES/KF/EG/ WP/Chorus |
| AR 11422-1-2 | 4.7.47 | AK 2016 | 78 *In tears of grief* (Part 1) | Chorus |
| AR 11423-1-2 | 4.7.47 | AK 2015 | 78 *In tears of grief* (Part 2) | Chorus |

40a *Come, ye daughters*
40b *My Master and my Lord . . . Grief for sin*
40c *Behold, my Saviour . . . Have lightnings*
40d *Ah! Now is my Saviour gone*
40e *Have mercy, Lord, on me*
40f *Lamb of God*
40g *O Gracious God! . . . If my tears be unavailing*
40h *O Sacred Head*
40i *Ah, Golgotha! . . . See ye! See the Saviour's outstretched hands*
40j *Be near me, Lord*
40k *And now the Lord*
40l *In tears of grief*

# Chapter Eight   *July - December 1947*

As far as Kathleen's commercial recordings for Decca are concerned, the second half of 1947 was considerably less successful than the first; three sets of sessions resulted in only four published sides. Fortunately, some BBC broadcast material has been preserved from this period, although its sound quality is generally poor.

Brahms's *Vier ernste Gesänge* were favourite recital items of Kathleen's, which she learnt soon after first seeing them in the autumn of 1942. Three versions of Kathleen singing these songs survive; as she was dissatisfied with her performance on this occasion, these sides were never issued, but the two-record set *was* allocated commercial issue numbers, K 1742 and K 1743. It was not until nearly three years later that Kathleen recorded the work again in the Decca studio, on that occasion with John Newmark as the accompanist.

In his article on Kathleen's recordings in *The Gramophone* in February 1954, Andrew Porter wrote, 'Although this set is assigned . . . both English and American numbers, Kathleen Ferrier told me that she had no memory of having made it. It does not appear in the English Decca catalogue, and I have failed to trace any pressings of the records.' The reason for its non-appearance is understood, but it is surprising that Kathleen failed to recall the sessions.

> 2.30 pm on 7.10.47 and 2.30 pm on 8.10.47
> Decca Studios, Broadhurst Gardens

41   BRAHMS/The Bible
     *Vier ernste Gesänge, Op. 121*/German
     Piano: Phyllis Spurr

| MATRIX/TAKE | DATE | RECORD NOS | TITLE |
| --- | --- | --- | --- |
| AR 11613-1-2 | 7.10.47 | K 1742 | *Denn es gehet dem Menschen* |
| AR 11614-1-2 | 7.10.47 | K 1742 | *Ich wandte mich* |
| AR 11615-1-2 | 8.10.47 | K 1743 | *O Tod, wie bitter bist du* |
| AR 11616-1-2 | 8.10.47 | K 1743 | *Wenn ich mit Menschen* |

Never issued/Destroyed

As well as being extremely busy in all parts of the country singing in concerts, recitals and oratorios, Kathleen was also increasing the number of performances she gave on BBC radio. On 3rd November, she broadcast a recital which included works by four British composers,

Holst, Moeran, Jacobson and Rubbra. From this recital on the Third Programme, songs by Jacobson and Rubbra have survived. They were recorded off the air on acetate discs, which were lent to the National Sound Archive in 1980 by Alfred Lengnick and Co. Ltd, the publishing company, for dubbing on to tape, and are now in the NSA collection.

Maurice Jacobson, composer of *Song of Songs* (1946), first met Kathleen when he was adjudicator at the 1937 Carlisle Festival, at which she won both the piano and vocal classes. He accompanied her at many concerts during the war when they were touring for CEMA (Council for the Encouragement of Music and the Arts), and at her first London concert at The National Gallery in December 1942, less than a week after she moved to the capital.

Edmund Rubbra dedicated his *Three psalms* to Kathleen, and she first sang them on 24th January 1947, at the Church of St Bartholomew the Great in Smithfield, London. It was a later broadcast performance of the work (part of Kathleen's last radio recital) that was issued by Decca in 1975. As the rehearsal took place at the BBC's Maida Vale Studio 5, it seems likely that the broadcast was also made from there, although that has not been confirmed. The sound quality of these recordings is poor; the piano accompaniment is particularly heavy and badly balanced.

> 10.35–11.00 pm on 3.11.47
> ?BBC Maida Vale Studio 5, West London

42   JACOBSON/The Bible
*Song of songs*/English
Piano: Frederick Stone
Never commercially issued/BBC Sound Archives Reference:
Tape T 41797
NSA Reference: NSA Tape T9188W

43   RUBBRA
*Three psalms, Nos 6, 23 and 150, Op. 61*/English
*O Lord, rebuke me not/The Lord is my Shepherd/Praise ye the Lord*
Piano: Frederick Stone
Never commercially issued/BBC Sound Archives Reference:
Tape T 41797
NSA Reference: NSA Tape T4506W

The late summer and early autumn of 1947 saw Kathleen preparing for two performances which were to alter the course of her career. On 11th and 12th September she sang for the first time in Gustav Mahler's *Das Lied von der Erde*, under Bruno Walter, at the first Edinburgh

International Festival; the tenor soloist was her colleague and friend Peter Pears. Kathleen's introduction to Dr Walter led to an artistic association and a warm friendship that lasted until her death. Regrettably, no recording has survived from those 1947 Edinburgh performances; the earliest extant recording featuring both Kathleen and Bruno Walter is of Beethoven's *Ninth Symphony*, broadcast from London two months later on the BBC Home Service. The concert at The Royal Albert Hall also included Bruckner's *Te Deum*, but only the Symphony seems to have survived. It is the only recording which features both Kathleen and her partner of many oratorio performances, the well-loved tenor Heddle Nash; the other two soloists, Isobel Baillie and William Parsons, had both recorded commercially with Kathleen by this time. It is also the only surviving example of Kathleen singing music by Beethoven. The recorded sound is reasonable, but the issue of this disc by Educ Media many years later caused concern to Isobel Baillie, who felt little affection for the Symphony or the performance. Both the London Symphony and the London Philharmonic Orchestra have been credited by various sources with playing on this occasion. It was, in fact, the LPO, with the London Philharmonic Orchestra Choir.

> 7.30 pm–9.00 pm on 13.11.47
> The Royal Albert Hall, London

> 44   BEETHOVEN/Schiller
> *Symphony No. 9 in D Minor, Op, 125*/German
> Soprano: Isobel Baillie, Tenor: Heddle Nash, Bass: William
> Parsons, Conductor: Bruno Walter, London Philharmonic
> Orchestra, London Philharmonic Choir, Chorus Master:
> Frederick Jackson
> The recording is taken from a live BBC broadcast, a copy of
> which is in the archives of Swedish National Radio, but not in
> the BBC Sound Archives
> Swedish National Radio Company Archive Reference: LB 8194

Bruno Walter introduced Kathleen to Mahler's music, but it was Sir Adrian Boult who conducted the earliest surviving recording of her singing it. On 29th November 1947, the BBC Third Programme broadcast his *Third Symphony*, and a copy was made off the air on acetate discs by a listener. In 1981 this set was discovered in Manchester in a collection of about two hundred private recordings taken from the radio between October 1947 and April 1948. The performance of Mahler's *Third Symphony*, along with others from the same collection, is now in the possession of the Music Performance Research Centre, and is available for listening at the MPRC Studio at the Barbican Library in the City of London. In order to avoid clumsy side breaks, the unknown recorder used a double turntable so that the end of one disc would overlap the beginning of the next. This ensured that the performance was preserved complete, but did not account for the different aural characteristics of each recording machine; changes of sound quality are evident from one side to another. Although Kathleen made a number of broadcasts during the period covered by the 'Manchester' collection of private recordings, this set of discs is the only one which preserves her voice.

Neither Kathleen's diary nor *Radio Times* indicate which studio was used for this live broadcast; Sir Adrian Boult's 'Programme Book' (preserved among his papers at the BBC Written Archive Centre at Caversham) in which he noted details of all his concerts, confirms that it was from Maida Vale.

8.35 pm–9.45 pm on 29.11.47
BBC Maida Vale (Studio 1?), West London

45 MAHLER/Nietzsche
*Symphony No. 3 in D Minor*/German
Conductor: Sir Adrian Boult, BBC Symphony Orchestra,
Chesham Ladies Choir. 20 boys from the London Choir School
Chorus Master: Maurice Barnes
Never commercially issued/In The Music Performance Centre
Archive, Barbican Centre, London
Reference: MPRC ACQ 5

Kathleen and Phyllis Spurr paid another visit to Decca's own studios on 9th December. They were joined there by Max Gilbert, the viola player, and the three of them made their first (unsuccessful) attempts to record satisfactory takes of two Brahms songs. It proved extremely difficult for Kathleen and her accompanists to make versions which were suitable for publication. Further sessions were set aside in June 1948 and again in February 1949, and it was only on this last occasion that acceptable takes of both songs were obtained.

6.00 pm on 9.12.47
Decca Studios, Broadhurst Gardens

46 BRAHMS/Rückert
*Gestillte Sehnsucht, Op. 91, No. 1*/German
Piano: Phyllis Spurr, Viola: Max Gilbert
Matrix AR 11891–1–2
Never issued/Destroyed

47   BRAHMS/Geibel
     *Geistliches Wiegenlied, Op. 91, No. 2*/German
     Piano: Phyllis Spurr, Viola: Max Gilbert
     Matrix AR 11892–1–2
     Never issued/Destroyed

The only published recording that Kathleen made for Decca in the second half of 1947 was Brahms's *Alto Rhapsody* (or Brahms's 'Raspberry' as she affectionately referred to it). It was conducted by Viennese-born Clemens Krauss. This *Alto Rhapsody* was one recording that Kathleen felt did her justice. In an interview in *The Gramophone* published in March 1951, she said: 'Perhaps the best record I have made is the Brahms *Alto Rhapsody*. It was recorded in a large hall and my voice floated out naturally.' The reviewer in the same magazine felt, when the set was issued in June 1948, that: 'Miss Ferrier's performance is most beautiful and tender, although her voice is recorded too strongly throughout . . . but with all its defects of balance I think the recording is well worth getting for the sake of this artist's lovely performance.'

At the time of the recording Kathleen had been singing the *Rhapsody* regularly for over three years, and it continued to be a favourite work until almost the end of her career. Two other recordings, both from Scandinavia, have recently been found, and one of these has been released commercially, by Danacord. Of the three, this one for Decca is the slowest, lasting 15' 58".

Kathleen's diary shows that two sessions were booked at Kingsway Hall; the two 78 sides on which the soloist sings alone with the orchestra may have been recorded at one, and the work completed, with the men's chorus, at the other. Two takes were made of each side, and it is possible that with the need to rehearse the singers and the orchestra beforehand, two sessions would have been required to complete the work. This Decca two-record set was issued in both straight and automatic couplings in the following way.

6.30 pm on 18.12.47 and 10.00 am on 19.12.47
Kingsway Hall, London

48   BRAHMS/Goethe (from *Harzreise im Winter*)
     *Rhapsody for contralto, male chorus and orchestra, Op. 53*/German
     Conductor: Clemens Krauss, London Philharmonic Orchestra,
     London Philharmonic Choir (Men's Voices)

| SIDE NOS | MATRIX/TAKE | AUTO RECORD NOS | STRAIGHT RECORD NOS | TEXT | SINGERS |
|---|---|---|---|---|---|
| 1 | AR 11901-1-2 | AK 1847 | K 1847 | *Aber abseits* | KF |
| 2 | AR 11902-1-2 | AK 1848 | K 1847 | *Ach, wer heilet* | KF |
| 3 | AR 11903-1-2 | AK 1848 | K 1848 | *Ach, wer heilet* | KF/Chorus |
| 4 | AR 11904-1-2 | AK 1847 | K 1848 | *Öffne den umwölkten* | KF/Chorus |

# Chapter Nine   *January - June 1948*

On 1st January 1948 Kathleen, with her manager John Tillett, set sail for New York, where she began the first of her three visits to North America. After the success of *Das Lied von der Erde* in Edinburgh, Bruno Walter invited her to sing further performances with The New York Philharmonic Orchestra in Carnegie Hall. No sooner had she arrived in New York than she developed a cold which she feared might prevent her singing at all. All was well, however, and the performance on Sunday 18th January was broadcast over WCBS and the Columbia Broadcasting System. In the programme for these performances Kathleen was described, rather surprisingly, as a mezzo-soprano. The tenor soloist was Set Svanholm, who made his reputation principally as a Wagnerian singer, although he also sang some of the Italian repertory, and created the part of Peter Grimes in the Swedish première of Britten's opera.

It is with *Das Lied von der Erde* that the superb artistic partnership of Kathleen and Bruno Walter is mainly remembered. Apart from the Edinburgh performances in 1947, and the three in New York, they performed the work together at the Salzburg Festival in 1949, and in the famous recording made for Decca in Vienna in 1952. Walter was born in Berlin in 1876, and worked as Mahler's assistant in Vienna from 1901 to the composer's death in 1911. To him had fallen the honour and responsibility of conducting the first performance of *Das Lied von der Erde*, and he made the first commercial recording of it in 1936.

Rather to her disappointment, Kathleen did not receive total critical acclaim for her first New York performance of *Das Lied*, but after the broadcast of the second performance, the final concert was sold out. Several libraries in the United States hold incomplete copies of this performance, but The Rodgers and Hammerstein Archives of Recorded Sound in the New York Public Library have it in its entirety. The work is in six movements, six songs, three for tenor and three for contralto. From this recording, the contralto's second and third songs, *Von der Schönheit* and *Der Abschied*, have been issued as part of an American two-LP set, which also contains Mahler's *Second Symphony*, recorded in Amsterdam in 1951.

3.00 pm on 18.1.48
Carnegie Hall, New York

51  MAHLER/Translated from the Chinese by Bethge
*Das Lied von der Erde*/German
Tenor: Set Svanholm, Conductor: Bruno Walter, New York
Philharmonic Orchestra
A complete copy is in The Rodgers and Hammerstein Archives
in New York Public Library
Never commercially issued complete

51a *Von der Schönheit*
51b *Der Abschied*

A number of eminent British composers wrote works specifically for
Kathleen, and on 4th April 1948 she broadcast one such on the BBC
Third Programme: the first performance of Lennox Berkeley's *Four
poems of St Teresa of Avila*. Berkeley took as his text poems by the mystic
sixteenth-century Spanish Carmelite nun St Teresa, translated by
Arthur Symons.

When in 1978 the BBC was preparing the record *The Singer and the
Person* to commemorate the twenty-fifth anniversary of Kathleen's
death, Michael, son of Lennox Berkeley, found in his father's home
discs which were made around the time of the first broadcast of the
work. Although in poor condition, they were issued as part of the BBC
tribute, and provide the sole opportunity to hear the work performed
by its dedicatee.

A number of apparently contradictory 'facts' surround the broadcast
and the making of the discs owned by Sir Lennox. Kathleen's diary
shows that she attended two sets of rehearsals for the performance on
the afternoons of 3rd and 4th April; another entry shows 'Bond Street
Recording' for 4th April, a possible reference to the Aeolian Hall which
the BBC used as a studio. There seems no need to have recorded the
performance for broadcasting purposes, as it was being given live.
Perhaps the Aeolian Hall visit was specifically to record the discs later
given to the Berkeleys, which were not, therefore, made from the first
*broadcast*, but a few hours before it. However, the notes on the record
sleeve of *The Singer and the Person* state that the broadcast was given on
14th April, and Kathleen's diary also refers to this as being a broadcast
date. According to *Radio Times*, the work was broadcast on the 4th only,
and no mention is made of a repeat on the 14th. Coincidentally, a piano
work of Berkeley's is listed for a repeat performance on the 14th, having
been first broadcast on 5th April. Perhaps some confusion arose at the
BBC over which work of Berkeley's was being repeated, and Kathleen
was wrongly informed that it was hers.

Lady Berkeley's recollection is that the discs were of a rehearsal, possibly in the Aeolian Hall. There must remain a lot of doubt about the date and time of their origin, but in any case, it is known that Kathleen had supper at the home of the composer and his wife after the performance on the 4th. The première was a successful one. Lady Berkeley recalls: 'Lennox was thrilled that Kathleen was doing the songs and we were both devoted to her and had enormous admiration for her, both as a singer and a friend. My only regret is that the rehearsal discs which she gave us, which she had made privately, were not of a better quality, though the BBC did a marvellous job with them when they used them to issue as a recording'.

?6.40 pm–7.15 pm on 4.4.48
?BBC Studio, Aeolian Hall, Bond Street, London
?BBC Studio, Maida Vale, West London

52   BERKELEY/St Teresa of Avila, translated by Arthur Symons
     *Four poems of St Teresa of Avila, Op. 27*/English
     Conductor: Arnold Goldsborough, String Orchestra

On 3rd May, after returning from her visit to Holland, Kathleen recorded her first side of the 1948 *St Matthew Passion* sessions under Dr Reginald Jacques. Over the following seven weeks all of the additional twenty-eight sides were completed to add to the original fourteen from the previous year. Kathleen sang on a total of thirteen sides, five in 1947, and eight in 1948. (Details of dates and matrix numbers are given in Chapter Seven.)

For her next commercial session, Kathleen went to Kingsway Hall on 14th May (Decca archives give it as the 13th, but Kathleen's diary indicates that it was the later date), to record the popular aria *Ombra mai fu* from Handel's *Xerxes* – better, but innaccurately, known as Handel's *Largo*. Sir Malcolm Sargent and the London Symphony Orchestra accompanied three takes of the aria, none of which was thought sufficiently good to be issued; whether the preceding recitative *Frondi tenere . . .'* was included (as it was when the same forces gathered again five months later, and successfully recorded it) is not noted in Decca's archives.

2.30 pm on 14.5.48
Kingsway Hall, London

53   HANDEL/Adapted from a libretto by Minato
     *Frondi tenere*(?) *. . . Ombra mai fu* (*Xerxes*)/Italian
     Conductor: Sir Malcolm Sargent, London Symphony Orchestra
     Matrix AR 12344–1–2–3
     Never issued/Destroyed

Another fruitless session was held to try to record publishable versions of the two Brahms songs with viola, which had previously been attempted in December 1947. Phyllis Spurr and Max Gilbert were again the accompanists; just why the takes were thought unsatisfactory is not known.

2.30 pm on 22.6.48
Decca Studios, Broadhurst Gardens

54 BRAHMS/Rückert
*Gestillte Sehnsucht, Op. 91, No. 1*/German
Piano: Phyllis Spurr, Viola: Max Gilbert
Matrix AR 11891–3-4
Never issued/Destroyed

55 BRAHMS/Geibel
*Geistliches Wiegenlied, Op. 91, No. 2*/German
Piano: Phyllis Spurr, Viola: Max Gilbert
Matrix AR 11892–3-4
Never issued/Destroyed

# Chapter Ten   *July - December 1948*

If Christmas is said to arrive earlier every year, it arrived particularly early for Kathleen in 1948. On 6th August she recorded two popular Christmas songs with Boyd Neel and his String Orchestra, which were issued in October ready for the seasonal shoppers. On 31st August, the two songs were transferred from the original 10″ pressings to 12″ waxes, with matrix numbers DAR 12611 and DAR 12612, in which larger format they were issued in the United States.

> 2.30 pm on 6.8.48
> ?Decca Studios, Broadhurst Gardens

56  GRUBER(arr. Gideon Fagan)/Mohr
    *Silent night, holy night*/English
    Conductor: Boyd Neel, Boyd Neel String Orchestra
    Matrix DR 12581–1–2

57  TRADITIONAL(arr. Gideon Fagan)/Translated from Latin
    *O come all ye faithful*/English
    Conductor: Boyd Neel, Boyd Neel String Orchestra
    Matrix DR 12582–1–2

Kathleen was very proud of the fact that she took part in the first six Edinburgh Festivals – from 1947 to 1952 – and one item has survived from her 1948 appearances there. Parry's setting of *Love is a bable* was recorded by the BBC at a recital in Edinburgh's Freemasons' Hall on 26th August. The song was included among material used for a descriptive radio programme about the Festival, prepared on 6th October 1948 by John Keir Cross for the BBC Transcription Service, and it is still preserved in the BBC Sound Archives. Gerald Moore was the accompanist. No other items from the recital seem to have survived. *Love is a bable* was issued in 1979 on the BBC commemorative issue *The Singer and the Person*.

> 8.00 pm on 26.8.48
> Freemasons' Hall, Edinburgh

58  PARRY/Anon
    *Love is a bable, Op. 152, No. 3*
    Piano: Gerald Moore
    BBC Sound Archives References: Tape T 29270 and T 12556

On 7th October two more takes were made of the excerpt from Handel's *Xerxes*, which had previously been unsuccessfully recorded on 14th May. Fortunately, at the fifth attempt, a satisfactory version was obtained, and it was issued, unusually, with an aria by another performer on the other side – Richard Lewis singing *Where 'er you walk*, from the same composer's *Semele*. The preceding recitative is included, so it is more accurate to describe the performance in the way shown below, rather than as it appears on record labels.

7.30 pm on 7.10.48
Kingsway Hall, London

59  HANDEL/Adapted from a libretto by Minato
*Frondi tenere . . . Ombra mai fu (Xerxes)*/Italian
Conductor: Sir Malcolm Sargent, London Symphony Orchestra
Matrix AR 12344–4–5

# Chapter Eleven   *January - June 1949*

After a very small recorded output in 1948 (apart from the by now almost complete *St Matthew Passion*, Decca issued only three sides of Kathleen's from the whole year) 1949 proved to be most successful for Kathleen. Her sessions for Decca resulted in some excellent releases, and some of her broadcasts in both the UK and Europe have also been issued commercially.

A series of winter Promenade Concerts at the Royal Albert Hall included a performance of Brahms's *Four serious songs* in a special arrangement, with orchestral accompaniment, made by Malcolm Sargent. It was during the illness of his daughter Pamela, at whose bedside he spent many hours in 1944, that Sargent prepared his orchestration from Brahms's original piano version. Nancy Evans sang the first performance of this new version in Liverpool in August 1944, but to Kathleen went the privilege of giving the first radio broadcast, a little later the same month, sadly on the day following Pamela Sargent's death. Sargent's place on the podium on that occasion was taken by Julius Harrison; now, four years later, Kathleen broadcast them again, in English, and the recording made at the time by the BBC was held in their Sound Archives. This is the earliest of Kathleen's surviving broadcasts to have been issued by Decca: the royalties due to the estates of both Kathleen and Sir Malcolm have been donated to the Malcolm Sargent Cancer Fund for Children.

Kathleen's diary indicates that a rehearsal took place at 10.30 on the morning of the performance, and that the concert itself began at 7.30 pm; the *Four serious songs* were given in the second part of the concert, which was broadcast on the BBC Home Service.

> 7.30 pm–10.00 pm on 12.1.49
> The Royal Albert Hall, London

> 61   BRAHMS(arr. Sargent)/The Bible (English translation from the German by Paul England)
> *Four serious songs, Op. 121*/English
> Conductor: Sir Malcolm Sargent, BBC Symphony Orchestra
> BBC Sound Archives Reference: T 13261–3
> BBC Transcription Service Reference: TS 127021 (Side Number)

Less than a month later, Kathleen recorded seven folksongs, traditional airs, very different in their simplicity from so much that was in her repertory. In the UK only one 78 record resulted from the two sessions, one side of which is the celebrated *Blow the wind southerly*. This song is exceptional in more ways than one among Kathleen's recorded legacy; it is the only one sung unaccompanied (although on both 78 and subsequent releases, Phyllis Spurr is credited on the label with being the accompanist!), and it is the most frequently reissued of her recordings, on 45 rpm, 33 rpm 10″ and 12″ discs, tape cassettes, stereo 8 cartridges and, most recently, on Compact Disc.

On the reverse side of the original 78 record there are two items – *Ma bonny lad* and *The keel row*. Recording two songs on one side of a 78 was not unusual; Kathleen had already sung two duets with Isobel Baillie on one side of a Columbia 10″ in 1945, and was to record two Schumann songs on one side of a Decca 12″ wax in 1950, accompanied by John Newmark (although, in fact, this was never issued as a 78). The other four songs recorded at the sessions on 10th and 11th February were never issued on the UK as 78s, and made their first appearance in May 1951 on a 10″ Medium Play 33 rpm disc. All seven songs from these sessions were, however, issued on a set of three 78s in the United States, on the London label.

Decca archives show that two takes were made of *The lover's curse*, but the copy of the 78 from the American set in the BBC Gramophone Library is marked 'Take Three'! Matrix DR 13218 (Nos 63 and 64) appears to have been re-recorded on to a new matrix (DR 13218–*1A*), perhaps because of a technical flaw, or perhaps to combine the two songs, which may originally have been recorded on two separate waxes, on to one. John Culshaw, for many years a recording manager, and later musical director with Decca, was in charge of these sessions; he worked on other recordings with Kathleen too, but these, and the two days in October 1952, are the only sets of sessions that he specifically mentions in his autobiography *Putting the Record Straight*, published in 1981.

Kathleen's own view of her singing at these sessions was expressed in the interview with W.S. Meadmore of *The Gramophone* in the issue of March 1951: 'I think the folk songs I have recorded, particularly the unaccompanied *Blow the wind southerly*, and *The keel row*, are good.' Her opinion seems to be in accord with that of thousands of record buyers since.

The recording producer for these sessions was John Culshaw.

2.30 pm on 10.2.49
Decca Studios, Broadhurst Gardens

62   TRAD.Arr. W.G. Whittaker
     *Blow the wind southerly*/English
     Unaccompanied
     Matrix DR 13217–1–2

63  TRAD.Arr. W.G. Whittaker
    *Ma bonny lad*/Scottish
    Piano: Phyllis Spurr
    Matrix DR 13218–<u>1A</u>–1B

64  TRAD.Arr. W.G. Whittaker
    *The keel row*/English
    Piano: Phyllis Spurr
    Matrix DR 13218–<u>1A</u>–1B

65  TRAD.Arr. Grew/Johnson
    *Have you seen but a whyte lillie grow?*/English
    Piano: Phyllis Spurr
    Matrix DR 13219–<u>1</u>

    10.00 am on 11.2.49
    Decca Studios, Broadhurst Gardens

66  TRAD.Arr. Warlock
    *Willow, willow*/English
    Piano: Phillis Spurr
    Matrix DR 13220–<u>1</u>

67  TRAD.Arr. Hughes
    *The lover's curse*/English
    Piano: Phyllis Spurr
    Matrix DR 13221–1-2-<u>(3)</u>

68  TRAD.Arr. Hughes/W.B. Yeats
    *Down by the salley gardens*/English
    Piano: Phyllis Spurr
    Matrix DR 13222–<u>1</u>–2

Keen to record more sides before her departure for the United States on 18th February, Kathleen visited Decca's Studios on the 14th and 15th, again taking Phyllis Spurr as her accompanist. Three attempts to make an acceptable version of Schubert's *Der Musensohn* were all to no avail, but a first-time success was achieved with *An die Musik*. With Max Gilbert again playing viola, two more attempts were made to obtain satisfactory performances of the Brahms songs *Op. 91*, *Gestillte Sehnsucht* and *Geistliches Wiegenlied*; fortunately, those, too, were successful.

By this time Decca had allocated quite new matrix numbers to those songs, rather than continuing to increase the suffix on the original number first used in December 1947. Even so, there may have been some problems with the successful takes, as they appear to have been transferred to new matrices, both with the suffix 1A. On reissues, a curious addition is audible on *Geistliches Wiegenlied*, as a 'patch' lasting thirty-eight seconds has been inserted from a different pressing, perhaps to cover a fault on the record used to make the dubbing.

The Brahms songs were issued together on a 12″ 78 in December 1949, the month in which Kathleen and Phyllis recorded the published version of *Der Musensohn*, which was subsequently issued together with *An die Musik* in June 1950. It is extraordinary to think that Kathleen recorded only four of Schubert's songs commercially for Decca, although others have, of course, been issued from radio broadcasts.

2.30 pm on 14.2.49
Decca Studios, Broadhurst Gardens

69   Schubert/Goethe
*Der Musensohn, D 764 Op. 92, No. 1*/German
Piano: Phyllis Spurr
Matrix DR 13234–1-2-3
Never issued/Destroyed

70   Schubert/von Schober
*An die Musik, D 547, Op. 88, No. 4*/German
Piano: Phyllis Spurr
Matrix DR 13235–1–2

2.00 pm on 15.2.49
Decca Studios, Broadhurst Gardens

71   Brahms/Rückert
*Gestillte Sehnsucht, Op. 91, No. 1*/German
Piano: Phyllis Spurr, Viola: Max Gilbert
Matrix AR 13236–1A–2

72   Brahms/Geibel
*Geistliches Wiegenlied, Op. 91, No. 2*/German
Piano: Phyllis Spurr, Viola: Max Gilbert
Matrix AR 13237–1A–2-3

A tape of Kathleen, unique, off-stage and informal, exists, recorded at a party in New York at the home of the actor William Griffis. Although it has not proved possible to date the recording precisely, it seems to have been made during Kathleen's second visit to the United States, between late February and 26th May 1949; perhaps the later date is nearer the right one. The party seems to be a celebration of the successful conclusion of her American visit, and there is no doubt that everyone is having a hilarious time, being entertained by a very relaxed Kathleen.

Although the tape lasts only six minutes, Kathleen has time to sing from five songs – *Will o' the wisp, The Floral Dance, The Antelope Song, Sing, joyous bird* and *Annie Laurie*. She burlesques the overblown style employed by some singers when 'interpreting' such songs, and accompanies herself on the piano for each item. It is the only recording on which Kathleen can be heard playing this, her favourite instrument. Between songs she laughs and jokes with her friends, and tells them how, when accompanying her father in years past, she would unexpectedly change key, which always amused him very much! A short ciné film was made at this party, and to see her performing is as fascinating as to hear her (see Chapter Twenty-One). From this tape, *The Floral Dance* has been issued on the BBC tribute *The Singer and the Person*.

?May 1949/New York

73   *Kathleen Ferrier at a Party*
     NSA Reference: NSA Tape M7439W
     Never issued complete commercially/In a private collection

73a Moss
     *The Floral Dance*/English
     Piano: Kathleen Ferrier

# Chapter Twelve   *July - December 1949*

In the summer of 1949 Kathleen spent five weeks in The Netherlands, the culmination of which was the first performance of Benjamin Britten's new work, *Spring Symphony*. It was composed for The Boston Symphony Orchestra at the request of Serge Koussevitzky, who hoped to conduct the world première in the United States. However, that honour went instead to Eduard van Beinum in the Concertgebouw in Amsterdam, as part of the Holland Festival. Some sources give the date of the performance as 9th July, but others, including the Britten-Pears Library in Aldeburgh, confirm that it was, in fact, 14th July 1949.

*Spring Symphony* is composed for three soloists – soprano, contralto and tenor – mixed chorus, a separate chorus of boys' voices, and orchestra. The texts used are British poems, and include works from the thirteenth century (*Soomer is icoomen in* – anonymous) through to the twentieth, represented by W.H. Auden (*Out on the lawn I lie in bed*).

Kathleen did not start seriously learning the symphony until the first week of July, as she had been fully occupied with a new production of *Orfeo ed Euridice*, and many other concerts and recitals, but the first performance, with Jo Vincent and Peter Pears as the other soloists, went successfully. The presence of Field Marshal Montgomery, who was not, apparently, noted for his love of modern music, irritated Britten, as he feared that the reception given to the respected military leader might detract from the artistic acclaim the occasion deserved.

At least two private recordings were made of the broadcast of the première. One, belonging to Britten and Pears, was all but destroyed by sea water during the winter of 1953, when their home in Aldeburgh was flooded. The acetate discs still exist in the Britten-Pears Library, but almost nothing of the performance can be discerned from the unrelenting roar of the saline distortion. The other set, owned by Lord Harewood, was for many years feared lost, but in 1991 he rediscovered the discs in good condition, and donated them to The National Sound Archive in London. He was keen that the performance should be made publicly available both at the NSA and commercially. Subject to the necessary permissions being granted, Decca hope to issue the recording on CD in 1993. When issued, it will be the only complete recording of a work by Britten sung by Kathleen that has ever been commercially available.

14.7.49/Concertgebouw, Amsterdam

76  Britten/Various poets
   *Spring Symphony, Op. 44*/English

   Soprano: Jo Vincent, Tenor: Peter Pears, Dutch Radio Chorus
   and Boys Chorus, Concertgebouw Orchestra, Conductor:
   Eduard van Beinum
   Not yet commercially issued.
   NSA Reference: NSA Tape T 10543

The recital broadcast by the BBC, and recorded by the Transcription
Service, on 7th September 1949 from the Edinburgh International
Festival, is one of the best examples that survive of the way in which
Kathleen responded to a live audience. Like most singers, she was able
to interpret her material far more vividly in a public performance than
in the recording studio; interesting comparisons can be made between
versions of Lieder sung at this recital, and those made at other times
with only her accompanist and the microphone present.

With Bruno Walter at the piano (to modern ears, an unorthodox
accompanist), she sang as she never could in the cold atmosphere of a
studio, and held the audience in the Usher Hall enthralled. In the form
in which it has survived, the recording contains six Lieder by Schubert,
the song cycle *Frauenliebe und Leben* by Schumann, and four Lieder by
Brahms. *Radio Times* lists two further pieces by Brahms – *Wir wandelten*
and *Am Sonntag Morgen* –which, if performed, have not survived.

It was not until November 1975 that this recital was issued
commercially by Decca, taken from the original recordings in the BBC
archives; it required three sides of a double LP album, the fourth side
being devoted to another recital from BBC's archives, Kathleen's last
radio recording, from January 1953. Subsequent reissues of the
Edinburgh recording have omitted the later recital, enabling it to be
issued complete on one record, cassette and Compact Disc. Before
Decca's release, an earlier disc version of the performance was available
from the Bruno Walter Society in the United States, although this did
not include the short talk given by Kathleen, which is such an attractive
addition to Decca's version. *Frauenliebe und Leben* was released on yet
another American issue with a different coupling.

Kathleen recorded one of the Schubert Lieder commercially for Decca,
and three others survive in later BBC studio performances, but these
are the only extant versions of *Der Tod und das Mädchen* and *Du bist die
Ruh'*.

Schumann's *Frauenliebe und Leben* was commercially recorded with
John Newmark as accompanist in 1950 (Walter had made a previous
recording in the early 1940s with the soprano Lotte Lehmann). In the

1949 recording, Walter's style of playing seems unsubtle and heavy handed, but the evident rapport between singer and pianist gives this live performance from Edinburgh an energy that the studio recording lacks.

Kathleen recorded one of the Brahms Lieder commercially three months after the Edinburgh performance, with Phyllis Spurr; and another survives in an incomplete version from Denmark from October 1949, but neither *Immer leiser wird mein Schlummer* nor *Der Tod, das ist die kühle Nacht* was otherwise recorded. Like Kathleen's other 'live' recordings, this justly celebrated Edinburgh *Liederabend* shows how successfully she communicated with her audiences, and seemed to sing directly, and individually, to each listener. The order following is that of the original LP issue in 1975. According to *Radio Times*, *Du bist die Ruh'* was sung second in the programme, and *Der Vollmond strahlt* was sung after *Suleika 1*. The two missing (?) Brahms items were performed after *Der Tod, das ist die kühle Nacht*. On reissue in February 1986, *Frauenliebe und Leben* was placed at the end of the recital; the master tape in the BBC Sound Archives retains the original Third Programme announcements, although these have been omitted on the commercial release.

> 7.30 pm–9.00 pm on 7.9.49
> Usher Hall, Edinburgh
> All items, Piano: Bruno Walter.

77  SCHUBERT/Craigher
    *Die junge Nonne, D 828, Op. 43, No. 1*/German

78  SCHUBERT/Von Chézy
    *Der Vollmond strahlt* (Romance from *Rosamunde*), *D 797, Op. 26*/German

79  SCHUBERT/Platen
    *Du liebst mich nicht, D 756, Op. 59, No. 1*/German

80  SCHUBERT/Claudius
    *Der Tod und das Mädchen, D 531, Op. 7, No. 3*/German

81  SCHUBERT/Willemer adapted by Goethe
    *Suleika 1, D 720, Op. 14, No. 1*/German

82  SCHUBERT/Rückert
    *Du bist die Ruh', D 776, Op. 59, No. 3*/German

83   SCHUMANN/Chamisso
     *Frauenliebe und Leben, Op. 42 (Eight songs)*/German

84   BRAHMS/Lingg
     *Immer leiser wird mein Schlummer, Op. 105, No. 2*/German

85   BRAHMS/Heine
     *Der Tod, das ist die kühle Nacht, Op. 96, No. 1*/German

86   BRAHMS/Daumer
     *Botschaft, Op. 47, No.1*/German

87   BRAHMS/Wendish poem, German version by Wenzig
     *Von ewiger Liebe, Op. 43, No. 1*/German

   BBC Sound Archives Reference: T 14015–20
   BBC Transcription Service Reference: BBC TS 127021 (Side
   Number) *Du liebst mich nicht* only
   BBC Transcription Service Reference: BBC TS 101490 (Side
   Number)

Not all of Kathleen's surviving recordings are of her singing. There
are four brief examples of her speaking voice, of which the short talk,
given during the 1949 Edinburgh International Festival, is the only one
preserved by the BBC. Kathleen spoke several times on BBC radio, and
appeared on television on at least one occasion; but like so many
broadcasts which would now be considered of historical interest, most
were either not recorded at the time, or, if recorded, were not long saved
in the archives because of lack of space. This talk was broadcast on a
Scottish Home Service 'Arts Review' programme, entitled simply
'Edinburgh International Festival'. It was issued commercially by Decca
as an introduction to the Lieder recital with Bruno Walter, and an
extract was issued on *The Singer and the Person*.

Kathleen's speaking voice is as warm and rich as her singing voice.
She reveals a slight hesitation at some points, as if diffident about
speaking on the air, and an audible smile can be heard when she
mentions Bruno Walter's comments on her recital in New York.
Kathleen wrote the short talk herself; both its content and presentation
convey the amazement that she clearly felt in having achieved so much,
particularly overseas, in such a short time. One reference in the BBC
Sound Archives indicates that the talk was given on 8th September, and
another that it was on the 11th; an entry in Kathleen's diary '. . . 12.00
Broadcast' on the 11th surely confirms the date.

12.15–12.55 pm on 11.9.49
BBC Studio, Edinburgh

88 *What the Edinburgh Festival has meant to me*
Talk broadcast by the BBC
BBC Sound Archives Reference: LP 27264
NSA Reference: NSA Tape M7439W

88a Extract from talk

After working together at the Edinburgh Festival, Kathleen and Bruno Walter travelled to London to give two more concerts, and in Kingsway Hall on 4th October they realised one of their dearest artistic ambitions; to record together Mahler's *Kindertotenlieder*.

Walter had introduced Kathleen to the work in 1947, and she first performed it on BBC Radio on 25th November that year. Early in 1949 Kathleen asked Decca to release her temporarily from her contract, so that she might be 'lent' to American Columbia, the company for which Walter recorded, in order that this recording might be made. After their initial refusal, Kathleen wrote to Decca and told them in no uncertain terms how she felt about their decision. She emphasised that it would be good for Decca and good for her if she recorded with this very eminent, perhaps at that time *most* eminent, conductor of Mahler's music, and she also made clear her disappointment that the promised *Messiah* recording had never taken place. To be able to record *Kindertotenlieder* now would be more than sufficient compensation for that. So Decca agreed, and Kathleen made her first commercial recording with Walter; in 1952 the compliment was returned when American Columbia 'lent' Walter to Decca so that these two friends and devoted Mahlerians could record *Das Lied von der Erde* and three *Rückert Lieder*, again with the Vienna Philharmonic. After all that, however, there was a very long delay in releasing the recording in the UK. It appeared on a set of three 78s, and on a 10″ 33 rpm disc, in November 1952.

Kathleen wrote a letter home from the United States on 3rd February 1950 in which she referred to the recording. By that time she had been sent test pressings of the 78s: '. . . the first record is not the one to be published as I run out of breath in one phrase . . . I do hope you like the records – I was rather pleased with them myself, for once, but will probably change my mind when I hear them again.'

In his book *Walter Legge – A Discography*, published by Greenwood Press, Alan Sanders points out that matrix CAX 10624 (the first of the set) was transferred on to another wax, and allocated the number CAX 10624–1B. The recording sheets in EMI archives emphasise that there was a problem with a matrix of the first side, but do not specify its nature. *If* this is the side to which Kathleen referred in her letter, then the fault would still be audible on the newly made wax (which it is not); as this session was recorded on tape as well as disc (almost certainly the first of Kathleen's recordings at which the 'new' medium was used), it may be that the transfer was made from the tape of a different take of the first song. Another possibility is that the imperfect take that she had been sent was the *second* take on wax (which is known to have been made), and that the transfer to CAX 10624–1B was made for a technical rather than a vocal reason. EMI archives confirm that two other sides (CAX 10627 and 10629) were transferred from the tape source on to wax, and were both issued with the suffix 1A. Another factor which confuses the issue is the ambiguity of the meaning of 1A and 1B; these terms were also used when more than one wax was made of a given take, the number denoting the take number, and the suffix letter which turntable had been used. Recording 'double' in this way was frequently done in case a wax or matrix got damaged in processing; there would then be a spare back-up of the same performance. It is not entirely clear in the case of this recording just what 1A and 1B were intended to signify.

Whatever the truth or supposition about it, this *Kindertotenlieder* is preserved in excellent sound, and contains some wonderful singing and playing. It was the only recording that Kathleen made for Columbia after leaving that company for Decca in 1946; on 78s it was issued in Automatic Couplings only. For many years this was believed to be the only extant version of Kathleen singing the work, but in November 1987 Decca issued another, recorded at a live performance under Otto Klemperer, given in Amsterdam in July 1951.

The producer for this recording was Walter Legge, and the balance engineer Douglas Larter.

2.30 pm–5.30 pm on 4.10.49
Kingsway Hall, London

89   MAHLER/Rückert                •
*Kindertotenlieder*/German
Conductor: Bruno Walter, Vienna Philharmonic Orchestra

| SIDE | MATRIX/TAKE | AUTO RECORD NOS | TITLE |
|---|---|---|---|
| 1 | CAX 10624-1A-<u>1B</u>-2 | LX 8939 | *Nun will die Sonn'so hell aufgeh'n* |
| 2 | CAX 10625-<u>1</u>-2 | LX 8940 | *Nun seh'ich wohl, warum so dunkle* |
| 3 | CAX 10626-<u>1</u> | LX 8941 | *Wenn dein Mütterlein tritt zur Tur* |
| 4 | CAX 10627-<u>1A</u>-1B | LX 8941 | *Oft denk'ich, sie sind nur ausgegangen* |
| 5 | CAX 10628-<u>1</u>-2 | LX 8940 | *In diesem Wetter, in diesem Braus* (Pt 1) |
| 6 | CAX 10629-<u>1A</u>-1B | LX 8939 | *In diesem Wetter, in diesem Braus* (Pt 2) |

The day after *Kindertotenlieder* was recorded, Kathleen and Phyllis Spurr flew to Copenhagen on the first leg of a Scandinavian tour. Winifred Ferrier recalls that the plane was late arriving; with an orchestra and choir waiting to rehearse, Kathleen and her accompanist were given priority through customs, and driven at high speed to the concert hall to try to make up for lost time.

The following evening Kathleen sang Brahms's *Alto Rhapsody*, and two Lieder as encores, for a broadcast which was recorded. Unfortunately none of the three works has been satisfactorily preserved, but all have been issued commercially, in spite of their shortcomings. Despite the use of a double turntable so that long performances could be recorded complete, with overlapping sides, not all of *Alto Rhapsody* survived. Some discs had suffered damage, and there seemed to be no chance of assembling a complete version until a tape of the broadcast, recorded by Dr Bengt Andreas in Malmo, Sweden, was discovered. This enabled the engineers to fill in the gaps, but with the result that several times during the work the sound quality changes very noticeably. Apparently filters and digital processors were used to minimise the problem, but with only modest success. The completed performance takes 13' 23", compared with that conducted by Krauss at 15' 58", and Tuxen's, recorded in Oslo eight days after this one, at 12' 56". Both the Brahms songs, with Phyllis Spurr's accompaniment, are shorn of their opening bars. In the case of *Von ewiger Liebe*, thirty-two bars (approximately eighty seconds) are missing, comprising most of the first stanza; from *Wir wandelten*, three bars (of piano introduction only) are lost. Perhaps the sound engineer failed to position the recording head on to the wax in time, or maybe parts of the discs were irreparably damaged.

The performance of *Alto Rhapsody* is of particular importance, as it is the only surviving record of Kathleen singing under the conductorship of Fritz Busch. In 1950 he was to conduct *Alto Rhapsody* again, with Kathleen as soloist, at the Edinburgh Festival.

On the issued LP and CD, these performances are coupled with a 1950 performance of Beethoven's *Fifth Symphony* conducted by Wilhelm Furtwängler, also recorded in Copenhagen. Danacord, the issuing company, have donated funds from the sales of the recordings to cancer research. The recording engineer for Danish Radio was Frederic Heegaard.

8.00 pm on 6.10.49
Denmark's Radio Studio No. 1, Copenhagen

90 BRAHMS/Goethe (from *Harzreise im Winter*)
*Rhapsody for contralto, male chorus and orchestra, Op. 53*/German
Conductor: Fritz Busch, Danish Radio Symphony Orchestra,
Danish Radio Male Chorus

91   BRAHMS/Wendish poem, German version by Wenzig
     *Von ewiger Liebe, Op. 43, No. 1*/German
     Piano: Phyllis Spurr
     (Incomplete)

92   BRAHMS/Hungarian poem, German translation by Daumer
     *Wir wandelten, Op. 96, No. 2*/German
     Piano: Phyllis Spurr
     (Incomplete)

Another stop on the Scandinavian tour made by Kathleen and Phyllis
Spurr was in Oslo. Kathleen gave a further performance of the *Alto
Rhapsody* on 12th October, and, although not mentioned in her diary,
yet another was given for Norsk Rikskringkasting (Norwegian Radio)
on the 14th. This broadcast has survived in the archives of the radio
company, and is the finest of the three extant versions of the work. It
is in excellent sound, and has appreciably more pace than the version
recorded under Krauss in 1947. Kathleen seems in better voice than in
the Danish performance given the previous week, and the studio
audience applauds enthusiastically at the end. Despite its undoubted
technical and musical qualities, its commercial issue seems unlikely.

14.10.49/Studio of Norsk Rikskringkasting, Oslo

93   BRAHMS/Goethe (from *Harzreise im Winter*)
     *Rhapsody for contralto, male chorus and orchestra, Op. 53*/German
     Conductor: Erik Tuxen, Oslo Philharmonic Orchestra, Men of
     the Oslo Philharmonic Chorus
     Never commercially issued/In the archives of Norsk
     Rikskringkasting, Oslo, Norway
     Norsk Rikskringkasting Reference: Ark.Nr. 9189

Two days later, Kathleen was again in the Oslo broadcasting studios,
this time to give a recital with Phyllis Spurr. On tour she often
performed two contrasting programmes, and in Scandinavia in 1949 the
two consisted of: (a) Schubert, Schumann and Brahms – in fact, the very
programme that she performed at the Usher Hall, Edinburgh, the
previous month; and (b) a mixed recital consisting mainly of Handel,
Purcell, Wolf and Britten, with some other Italian and English songs.

It is part of this latter programme that has survived from the
performance on 16th October 1949. It seems that it was judiciously cut,
perhaps to fit a broadcasting schedule, but what remains provides an
opportunity to hear Kathleen sing seven songs she did not otherwise
record, and her only surviving performances of Wolf. After the concert,

the engineer replayed for Kathleen's 'benefit' the recording that had been made; as so often, she was very disappointed by her own efforts, and so it was consigned to a distant shelf in the archives. Seven years later, after her death, it was rediscovered and sent to Winifred Ferrier, so that she might hear and enjoy it. With the permission of Norsk Rikskringkasting, she in turn sent it to Decca, who issued it (with one omission) on a 12" LP in May 1957.

The surprising omission from this LP was *Mad Bess of Bedlam* by Purcell, in an arrangement by Benjamin Britten. It surely cannot have been for reasons of space on the disc, as the complete recital lasts only a little over thirty-four minutes. It was first released by Decca in April 1963, on a 45, coupled with two folk-songs accompanied by John Newmark. Even on the seven LP boxed set AKF 1–7 issued in 1973, *Mad Bess* does not appear on the same disc as the other items from the recital, and is not acknowledged as having been part of it originally. Only on the CD and cassette issued in 1992 has the whole recital been reassembled.

Kathleen sang very little Wolf, but *Verborgenheit* (*Secrecy*) was the song for which she was awarded the Gold Medal at the Millom Festival in 1938, although on that occasion it was performed in English. (The adjudicator commented '. . . her voice . . . makes me imagine I am being stroked'!)

The final item, given by Kathleen as an encore, is particularly intriguing. It is *Altar*, by Jensen, sung in Norwegian, which she learned just before the performance. She introduced the song with a few self-deprecatory words, which for some years were believed to be the only surviving example of her speaking voice. On some issues of *Altar*, this introduction is omitted. 'I should like to sing a song for you, if you will bear with some very bad Norwegian; it's a song called *Altar*, by Jensen.' The audience in the studio greets her performances with great enthusiasm.

Decca made 78 rpm matrices from the Norwegian source, but the recital was never released in 78 format. The order of items below is that given in the archives of Norsk Rikskringkasting, which is also the order in which the 78 matrices were prepared by Decca; the latest compilation places *Mad Bess* at the start of the recital.

16.10.49/Studio of Norsk Rikskringkasting, Oslo
On all items – Piano: Phyllis Spurr

94  PURCELL/Settle ?after Shakespeare
*Hark! The echoing air* (*The Fairy Queen*)/English
Matrix AR 22959

95  HANDEL/Adapted from Valerians, English version by
Albert G. Latham
*Like as the love-lorn turtle (Atalanta)*/English
Matrix AR 22960

96  HANDEL/English version by M.X. Hayes
*How changed the vision (Admeto)*/English
Matrix AR 22961

97  PURCELL(arr. Britten)/from *Choice Ayres and Songs to sing to the theorblute, or bass-viol*
*Mad Bess of Bedlam (From silent shades)*/English
Matrix AR 22962

98  WOLF/E. Mörike
*Verborgenheit, Mörike-Lieder No. 12*/German
Matrix AR 22963

99  WOLF/E. Mörike
*Der Gärtner, Mörike-Lieder No. 17*/German
Matrix AR 22964

100  WOLF/E. Mörike
*Auf ein altes Bild, Mörike-Leider No. 23*/German
Matrix AR 22965

101  WOLF/E. Mörike
*Auf einer Wanderung, Mörike-Lieder No. 15*/German
Matrix AR 22966

102  JENSEN/Moren
*Altar*/Norwegian
Preceded by a brief spoken introduction
Matrix AR 22967

From the archives of Norsk Rikskringkasting, Oslo, Norway
Norsk Rikskringkasting Reference: Ark.Nr. 9202

While Kathleen was travelling in Scandinavia, Decca began a project to record some (then) little known music by J.S. Bach, in commemoration of the two hundredth anniversary of his death in 1750. Two cantatas, Nos. 11 and 67, were planned for Kingsway Hall sessions under Dr Reginald Jacques. On 6th October, two of the soloists, William Herbert and William Parsons, with the Jacques Orchestra and the

Cantata Singers, recorded three 78 sides; on 1st November Kathleen recorded on three sides, Ena Mitchell sang her aria, and the two male soloists added further excerpts, making a set of three 12" 78s for cantata No. 11. Two days later, again with William Herbert and William Parsons but without Ena Mitchell, Kathleen recorded cantata No. 67 on four 12" 78 sides; the two cantatas were also issued on two separate 10" 33 rpm records.

Thanks to the perceptive listening of the reviewer in *The Gramophone*, however, it was not long before it was revealed that the 78 and 33 rpm versions are quite different performances. This is most clearly evident from the fact that on the 78s some of the numbers are shortened – Kathleen's solo *Ah, tarry yet, my dearest Saviour* is deprived of its middle section on the 78s, and the tempi of the two versions vary considerably; surprisingly, perhaps, it is on the 78s that they tend to be slower. The decorations of the harpsichord continuos differ, and, as final proof, if it were needed, in cantata No. 67 William Herbert sings the words 'Lord Jesus' in one version, but 'Christ Jesus' at the same point in the other.

Kenneth Wilkinson, the Chief Recording Engineer for Decca for many years, and the Assistant Engineer Arthur Bannister, both recall the sessions for these cantatas, and confirm that although Columbia used reel to reel tape at the *Kindertotenlieder* recording at the same venue on 4th October, Decca did not use tape at Kingsway Hall until 1951. It follows, therefore, that the differently issued versions of the cantatas are from different takes at the same sessions, both using 78 waxes as their origin. The job of making an LP in the days before tape masters was an arduous one, as they were dubbed direct from specially pressed 78 discs on to 33 rpm waxes. As one 78 on one turntable came to an end, the engineer had to ensure that the stylus of the next turntable was placed at the beginning of the next 78 at exactly the right moment, while the 33 rpm wax continued to rotate and record! Wilkinson and Bannister remember that the first Decca LP of Rimsky-Korsakov's *Scheherazade* took nearly two weeks to make in this way because, just as a successful wax was being completed a small error, perhaps on the last dubbing, would render the whole LP side useless. This must have been the method used to make the 33 rpm versions of the cantatas: Kathleen would have had to record the central part of her aria in Cantata 11 on to a 78 wax, so that could be slotted in to the LP version, even though it does not appear on the issued 78 set. Both of these works were issued by Decca on 33s in June 1950, but the 78s did not appear until September 1950 (No. 67) and March 1951 (No. 11). When the aria *Ah, tarry yet* was reissued on LP and cassette in September 1979, the full-length version was used; indeed, the full versions of both works have been used for all reissues since 1951. The 78 sets of the cantatas were issued only in 'auto' coupling. Cantata 67 has a choral version in

English of *Jesu, joy of man's desiring* as a filler on the 10″ 33 rpm disc.

Dr Reginald Jacques (1894–1969), the conductor, founded the Bach Choir and the Jacques Orchestra in London in 1931 and 1936 respectively. During the 1940s and early 1950s Kathleen often sang under his baton, and always tried to arrange performances with the Bach Choir, for which she had a special affection, in her heavy schedule. It was Dr Jacques who conducted her first important London *Messiah* in May 1943, in Westminster Abbey, with Baillie, Pears, and Parsons.

In the opinion of the reviewer in *The Gramophone*, BWV 11 was the first complete recording of a choral Bach cantata. The engineers for these sessions were Kenneth Wilkinson and Arthur Bannnister.

6.10.49 and 6.30 pm on 1.11.49
Kingsway Hall, London

103   BACH/The Bible, translated from the German
Cantata No. 11, *Praise our God*, BWV 11/English
(*Lobet Gott in seinem Reichen*)
Soprano: Ena Mitchell, Tenor: William Herbert,
Bass: William Parsons, Conductor: Dr Reginald Jacques,
Harpsichord Continuo: Dr Thornton Lofthouse,
The Jacques Orchestra, The Cantata Singers

| MATRIX/TAKE | DATE | AUTO RECORD NOS | TITLE | SINGERS |
|---|---|---|---|---|
| AR 14119-1 | 6.10.49 | AX 399 | *Praise our God* | Chorus |
| AR 14120-1 | 6.10.49 | AX 400 | *Praise Our God* (Contd) | Chorus |
| | | | *Then Jesus* | WH |
| | | | *My Saviour* | WP |
| AR 14121-1 | 1.11.49 | AX 401 | *Ah, tarry yet* | KF |
| AR 14122-1 | 1.11.49 | AX 401 | *Ah, tarry yet* (Contd) | KF |
| | | | *And behold* | WH |
| | | | *Now at thy feet* | Chorus |
| AR 14123-1 | 1.11.49 | AX 400 | *And while* | WH |
| | | | *Ye men* | WH/WP |
| | | | *Ah, Lord* | KF |
| | | | *Jesu all* | EM |
| AR 14124-1-2 | 6.10.49 | AX 399 | *When will* | Chorus |

104   BACH/The Bible, translated from the German
Cantata No.11, *Praise our God*, BWV 11/English
Artists as above
33 rpm Matrices DRL 258 and DRL 259

104a *Ah, tarry yet, my dearest Saviour*

6.30 pm on 3.11.49
Kingsway Hall, London

105  BACH/The Bible, translated from the German
Cantata No. 67, *Hold in affection Jesus Christ*, BWV 67/English
(*Halt in Gedaechtnis Jesum Christ*)
Tenor: William Herbert, Bass: William Parsons,
Conductor: Dr Reginald Jacques, Harpsichord Continuo:
Dr Thornton Lofthouse, Organ: Dr Osborne Peasgood,
The Jacques Orchestra, The Cantata Singers

| MATRIX/TAKE | AUTO RECORD NOS | TITLE | SINGERS |
|---|---|---|---|
| AR 14125-1 | AX 347 | *Hold in affection* | Chorus |
| AR 14126-1 | AX 348 | *Lord Jesus now* | WH |
| | | *Lord Jesus Thou* | KF |
| | | *Come all* | Chorus |
| AR 14127-1 | AX 348 | *And still* | KF |
| | | *Peace be unto you* | WP |
| AR 14128-1 | AX 347 | *Peace be unto you* (Contd) | WP |
| | | *Lord Christ* | Chorus |

106  BACH/The Bible, translated from the German.
Cantata No. 67, *Hold in affection Jesus Christ*, BWV 67/English
Artists as above
33 rpm Matrices DRL 260 and DRL 261

A few days before her departure to North America, on what was to be her last visit, Kathleen recorded for the BBC Third Programme a recital of music by Telemann and Bach. Three items were privately recorded from the broadcast of the programme, which took place on Boxing Day 1949, and two of them were issued by Decca in March 1985. The sound is of rather poor quality, but, as Kathleen never otherwise recorded the two songs, their survival and commercial release is gratifying. Fragments of the Telemann cantata from the same broadcast are believed still to be in a private collection, but have not been issued commercially. *Bist du bei mir* from this recital seems not to have survived.

6.00 pm–7.00 pm on 15.12.49
BBC Maida Vale Studio 5, West London

107   BACH
*Vergiss mein nicht*, BWV 505, No. 71 from *Geistliche Lieder und Arien*/German
Harpsichord: Millicent Silver

108   BACH
*Ach, dass nicht die letzte Stunde*, BWV 439, No. 1 from *Geistliche Lieder und Arien*/German
Harpsichord: Millicent Silver

109   TELEMANN
*Kleine Kantate von Wald und Au, for contralto, flute and continuo*/German
Flute: John Francis, Cello: George Roth, Harpsichord: Millicent Silver
Telemann never commercially issued/In a private collection

What turned out to be Kathleen's last visit to Decca's studio for nearly seven months took place on 19th December. She was due to remake Schubert's *Der Musensohn* which she had unsuccessfully recorded the previous February, and to record commercially two Brahms Lieder for the first time. Satisfactory takes were obtained of all three, and *Der Musensohn* was released as a 78 on the reverse side of *An die Musik*.

The two Brahms items were never issued as 78s, but made their first appearance on a 12" LP, LXT 2850, in November 1953, the month after Kathleen's death. It is difficult to see why it took four years to issue two such lovely performances. Perhaps the test pressings did not satisfy Kathleen, who may have hoped to remake them; she never did.

2.30 pm on 19.12.49
Decca Studios, Broadhurst Gardens

110   BRAHMS/Schmidt
*Sapphische Ode, Op. 94, No. 4*/German
Piano: Phyllis Spurr
Matrix DR 14418–1

111   BRAHMS/Daumer
*Botschaft, Op. 47, No. 1*/German
Piano: Phyllis Spurr
Matrix DR 14419–1

112 SCHUBERT/Goethe
*Der Musensohn, D764, Op. 92, No. 1*/German
Piano: Phyllis Spurr
Matrix DR 14420–1

# Chapter Thirteen *January - June 1950*

Four recordings have survived from Kathleen's last North American tour, which began on 26th December 1949. The first which can confidently be dated correctly is a performance of Brahms's *Four serious songs* in English, accompanied by her friend, occasional teacher, and correspondent, John Newmark.

Newmark first accompanied Kathleen earlier in 1949, on her second transatlantic visit; he responded to her plea for help when Arpad Sandor, her pianist, fell ill and was unable to continue with the tour. Although at the time of the emergency Newmark was accompanying George London, the Canadian bass-baritone, he was released from his contract, and flew to Chicago to continue where Sandor had left off and to share Kathleen's taxing itinerary. They worked very happily together during the remainder of her stay in North America, and Kathleen was keen to sing with him again on her next visit. After some initial difficulty over Newmark's obtaining a work permit for the United States (he was a Canadian citizen), their second tour was an even greater success. Early in 1950, Kathleen approached Decca with a view to his playing at some recording sessions in London during the summer, and in due course the arrangements were made. She was concerned about offending Phyllis Spurr, who had played on all her commercially made piano-accompanied records for Decca up to that time; but Phyllis seems not to have taken it amiss, and she later recorded again with Kathleen in December 1951.

Kathleen planned a further visit to North America in the autumn of 1951, and she and Newmark corresponded about her repertoire for the projected tour; sadly, it never took place, because of the onset of her illness.

Early in 1950 one of their first recitals was at the Town Hall, New York, given for The New Friends of Music; the tape of *Four serious songs* may have been taken from a radio broadcast.

8.1.50/Town Hall, New York

116 BRAHMS/The Bible, English translated from the German by Paul England
*Four serious songs, Op. 121*/English
Piano: John Newmark
Never commercially issued/ A tape in a private collection

Kathleen's tour took her to many parts of the United States and Canada. On 10th March she was interviewed on CBC radio in Montreal by, it is believed, Eric MacLean. She spoke about several aspects of her career and her plans for the future, replying thoughtfully and with good humour to his sometimes awkwardly phrased questions about the works of Benjamin Britten, particularly *The Rape of Lucretia* and *Spring Symphony*, and Chausson's *Poème de l'amour et de la mer* which she was still studying. (She was not to perform it in public until almost a year later, on 28th February 1951.) This is the last of the four surviving examples of Kathleen's speaking voice. An edited version of this interview was released by the BBC on their commemorative issue *The Singer and the Person* in 1979.

> 6.00 pm on 10.3.50
> CBC Studio, Montreal

117   Interview with Eric MacLean
      Never commercially issued complete/A tape in a private
      collection

117a Interview excerpts

A week after the interview in Montreal, Kathleen was back in New York to appear with Bruno Walter in a recital, and to sing in concert performances of Gluck's *Orfeo ed Euridice*, with Thomas Scherman conducting. These performances revived memories of Glyndebourne in 1947, as Ann Ayars, the Glyndebourne Euridice, was taking the part again. The concerts were sponsored by The Little Orchestra Society, which arranged to make a recording privately on acetates in the Town Hall. That recording is now in The Rodgers and Hammerstein Archives of Recorded Sound in New York Public Library, together with others made by The Little Orchestra Society at live performances. This concert performance seems to have been a cut version of the opera – though not cut as severely as Decca's 1947 recording – but it has not been possible to establish exactly what music was included and what was omitted.

> 17.3.50 Town Hall, New York

118   GLUCK/Calzabigi
      *Orfeo ed Euridice*, 'Complete version' (Cut)/Italian
      Soprano: Ann Ayars, Euridice
      Soprano: Louise Kinloch, Amor
      Conductor: Thomas Scherman, The Little Orchestra Society
      Never commercially issued/In The Rodgers and Hammerstein
      Archives of Recorded Sound, New York Public Library

There exists one further recording thought to have been made in the USA during Kathleen's 1950 tour which it has not yet been possible to date accurately.

1950 was the bicentenary of the death of J.S. Bach, and The Voice of America appears to have made a collection of performances of his works by different musicians. A recording of Kathleen singing *Bist du bei mir* from *The Anna Magdalena Song Book*, a favourite recital piece, survives in The Library of Congress Recorded Sound Collection in Washington DC, on a disc displaying the label:

The Voice of America

Bach Anniversary Concerts

Program No. 12

On the same disc is *Motet No. 6*, performed by the Collegiate Chorale, conducted by Robert Shaw. It seems likely that these performances, along with all the others in the series, were taken from Voice of America radio broadcasts; there is no reference in Kathleen's diary to a special Bach concert during the period of her American tour (26th December 1949–30th March 1950), and it has not been possible to ascertain any details other than that John Newmark was the accompanist. This performance was issued commercially for the first time in 1992.

?January–March 1950/?Voice of America Broadcast

119   BACH(attrib. Stölzel)
*Bist du bei mir . . . (The Anna Magdalena Song Book*, BWV 508)/
German
Piano: John Newmark
In the collection at the Library of Congress, Washington DC
Reference: Record NCP 1366

In June 1950, Vienna was a city occupied by Allied forces, with much of the destruction caused by advancing armies in 1945 still evident. It was here, as she revealed later, that Kathleen participated in one of the greatest musical experiences of her life.

The International Bach Festival brought to the city many fine musicians to commemorate the bicentenary of the composer's death; Kathleen was to sing in performances of three of his greatest works, *Matthäus-Passion, Mass in B Minor* and the *Magnificat*. The conductor was Herbert von Karajan, already a celebrated musical figure, who had conducted many German, Austrian and other European orchestras since well before the Second World War. Several of the singers who appeared on the platform with Kathleen in these performances had also already established successful international careers; they included Elisabeth Schwarzkopf, Irmgard Seefried, Paul Schoeffler and Otto Edelmann. The twenty-one-year-old bass-baritone Walter Berry was also making one of his earliest concert appearances in the same year as his début at The Vienna State Opera.

The Musikvereinssaal was the setting for the performances; broadcasts on Austrian Radio seem to have been the source for the complete recordings of *Matthäus-Passion* and the *B Minor Mass* which have survived, and were only in the late 1980s made generally available on LP and CD. In a letter sent home to London, Kathleen wrote how well rehearsals were progressing, and of Karajan's approval of her singing. Unfortunately their collaboration was limited to just a handful of performances in the summer of 1950.

The first work to be given was *Matthäus-Passion*. It was performed in German, the first time that Kathleen had sung it in the original language; as the only non-German speaking soloist she sounds very much at home. This was a more complete version than she had recorded in London for Decca in 1947 and 1948, and all her arias are sung with repeats, where appropriate. Not only has the full work been issued, but a CD of Kathleen's recitatives, arias and duets from this and the complete *Mass in B Minor* has also been released.

On the Foyer four-LP set of the *Passion*, there are errors in the accompanying booklet about the position of some side turns; despite that, all the music is there. Verona, on their release of the same performance on three CDs, go one better; the aria *Gerne will ich mich bequemen* for bass soloist is given one and a half times. The aria starts towards the end of the first CD, stops abruptly at the conclusion of its first section, and recommences from the beginning again at the start of the second CD. In addition to that, of eighteen cueing points on the first two CDs in the set, seven are incorrectly shown in the booklet, making it a real achievement to find some parts of the score at all. For a live recording of its period the sound is quite acceptable, and appreciably better than that of the *Mass in B Minor* from the same source.

6.00 pm on 9.6.50
Musikvereinssaal, Vienna

120   BACH/The Bible
*Matthäus-Passion*, BWV 244/German
Soprano: Irmgard Seefried
Tenor: Walther Ludwig, The Evangelist
Baritone: Paul Schoeffler, Jesus
Bass: Otto Edelmann
Bass: Erich Kaufmann, Petrus
Bass: Hardal Pröglhöf, Judas
Bass: Otto Wiener, Pilate
Bass-Baritone: Walter Berry, Pontifex

Soprano: Anny Felbermayer, Pilate's Wife
Soprano: Gisela Rathauscher, First Maiden
Soprano: Rosl Sterba, Second Maiden
Contralto: Magdalena Stowasser, First Witness
Tenor: Friedrich Uhl, Second Witness
Conductor: Herbert von Karajan, Vienna Symphony Orchestra,
Wiener Singverein, Organ: Alois Forer and Anton Heiler

120a *Du lieber Heiland du . . . Buss' und Reu'*
120b *So ist mein Jesus nun gefangen*/With Seefried and Chorus
120c *Ach, nun ist mein Jesus hin*
120d *Erbarme dich mein Gott*
120e *Erbarm'es Gott . . . Können Tränen meiner Wangen*
120f *Ach, Golgatha . . . Sehet, Jesus hat die Hand*/With Chorus

No recording of *Magnificat* appears to have survived, but both a rehearsal tape and the subsequent complete performance of the *Mass in B Minor* exist and have been issued commercially. Whilst rehearsals for the *Mass* were under way in the Musikvereinssaal, EMI were setting up their microphones to prepare for some commercial recordings. By good fortune, on the morning of either 13th or 14th June, Anthony Griffith, the sound engineer, was testing the recording machine as Kathleen and Elisabeth Schwarzkopf were preparing their solos and duets together. As a result, five items have survived on a tape in EMI archives. Of the five, two are Kathleen's solos, one is solo by Schwarzkopf, and two are duets. *Et in unum Dominum* lacks most of its orchestral introduction and part of the closing orchestral section, and *Agnus Dei* starts as Kathleen sings her first '. . . qui tollis', at bar 10, but the remainder are complete and preserve in excellent sound – far better than that on the published CD of the complete performance of 15th June – the radiance of the two voices, even though the time was 9.30 in the morning.

As in the complete performance, Schwarzkopf sings *Laudamus Te*, an aria which is sometimes sung by the alto; Kathleen sang it in many of her performances, but clearly on this occasion either Schwarzkopf or Karajan felt it would be more appropriately sung by the soprano. There is no other soprano solo in the *Mass*, so perhaps it was not unreasonable to allocate this to her. EMI issued *Laudamus Te* and the two duets for the first time to mark Schwarzkopf's 75th birthday in December 1990. Kathleen's two solos were first issued in December 1991 when they formed part of the CD version of EMI's *The Record of Singing, Volume 4*. They had not been part of the earlier LP version of the set.

Whilst EMI archives refer to the orchestra as the Vienna Philharmonic, Foyer and Verona issues of the complete *Mass* state that it was the Vienna Symphony; the latter name is that also used in reviews of the performance in *Weiner Zeitung* on 17th June. Both names may refer to the same body of musicians; if so, on this occasion they were called the Vienna Symphony.

The order of items below is not as they are sung in the *Mass*, but as they appear on EMI's master tape, which presumably reflects the order in which they were rehearsed.

> 9.30 am on 13 or 14.6.50
> Musikvereinssaal, Vienna
>
> BACH
> Excerpts from the *Mass in B Minor*, BWV 232/Latin

121  *Christe eleison*/Duet with Schwarzkopf
122  *Laudamus Te*/Solo for Schwarzkopf
123  *Qui sedes*/
124  *Agnus Dei* (Incomplete)/
125  *Et in unum Dominum* (Incomplete)/Duet with Schwarzkopf
   Conductor: Herbert von Karajan, Vienna Symphony Orchestra

It was the last performance in Vienna, that of the *Mass in B Minor* that so moved Kathleen; she praised the choir and orchestra, and later commented how their contributions had inspired the soloists. Elisabeth Schwarzkopf recalled in 1990 how, at one of the performances of the *Mass* (they also gave it together in Milan at the end of June), Karajan was seen to weep as Kathleen began the *Agnus Dei*, towards the end of the work. He was not, it seems, a man easily moved to tears. It was surely as a result of these performances that Kathleen was invited to record the *Mass* commercially for EMI in 1952, when Karajan again conducted, an invitation that for contractual and health reasons she had to decline.

Since its original release on a set of Foyer CDs, this version has been issued on the Verona label, also on CD. The booklet supplied with the Foyer version incorrectly states that the alto sings *Laudamus Te*. Whilst the sound quality is not up to the standard of the rehearsal tape, it is, nevertheless a most valuable set. The advantages of hearing Kathleen (and the other singers) live are hardly diminished by the allowances that have to be made. It clearly was a magnificent performance.

> 6.00 pm on 15.6.50
> Musikvereinssaal, Vienna

126  BACH
   *Mass in B Minor*, BWV 232/Latin
   Soprano: Elisabeth Schwarzkopf, Tenor: Walther Ludwig,

Baritone: Alfred Poell, Bass: Paul Schoeffler, Conductor: Herbert von Karajan, Vienna Symphony Orchestra, Wiener Singverein, Organ: Alois Forer and Anton Heiler, Harpsichord: Karl Pilss

126a *Christe eleison*/Duet with Schwarzkopf
126b *Qui sedes*
126c *Et in unum Dominum*/Duet with Schwarzkopf
126d *Agnus Dei*

1 Kathleen Ferrier at the Decca recording studio   ▷

△  3 Boyd Neel

△ . 4 Roy Henderson

△  5 Clemens Krauss
▽  7 Sir Malcolm Sargent

△  6 Sir John Barbirolli
▽  8 Sir Adrian Boult

△  9  Edmund Rubbra

△  10  Howard Ferguson

▽  11  Sir Lennox Berkeley

▽  12  William Wordsworth

△ 13 Jo Vincent

△ 14 John Newmark

△ 15 *Messiah* at Bath Abbey: l to r: Alfred Hepworth, Eric Greene, William Parsons, KF, Cuthbert Bates, Elsie Suddaby, Henry Cummings, Dr Thornton Lofthouse

△ 16 With Benjamin Britten

◁ 17 Fritz Stiedry

18 Rehearsing for the première of Britten's *The Rape of Lucretia*, ▷
Glyndebourne, 1946

DEPARTMENTAL MEMO.

FROM:- WEST HAMPSTEAD.
TO:   Mr.Axtmann.
      Mr. Sarton.
      Mr. Norris.
      Mr. Kelly.
      Miss Harris.
      Mr. Hoy.
      Mrs Sleet.
      Lord Halsbury.
      Mr.Schwarz.

REF:_ ACH/F/
DATE:- 14th February, 1949.

KATHLEEN FERRIER.
Piano Acc: PHYLLIS SPURR.

DR.13234-1-2-3  Time.2.15.   DER MUSENSOHN.(Schubert)
*M 38122*

DR.13235-1      "  3.05.    AN DIE MUSICK. (Schubert)
*M 632* -2      "  3.00.
*71144.*

15th Feb. 1949.

KATHLEEN FERRIER - Contralto.
MAX GILBERT - Viola.
PHYLLIS SPURR - Pianoforte.

*Sung in German*

AR.13236-1A  Time.5.04.   GESTILLTE SEHNSUCHT. Op.91. (Brahms)  Simrock Edition.
      -2        "  5.05.   (Longing at Rest)
*T.5647*
*K.2289*
*K.23025*
AR.13237-1      "  5.00    GEISTLICHES WIEGENLIED. Op.91 (Brahms)
      -2        "  5.00    (Cradle Song of the Virgin)
      -3        "  4.58.

A.C. HADDY.
RECORDING STUDIOS.

19  Recording sheet from Decca session at Broadhurst Gardens, 1949

# THE GRAMOPHONE CO. LTD., HAYES, MIDDX.

## TECHNICAL RECORDING DEPARTMENT.

The following Selection was made on **30th June 1944** at **Abbey Rd.**

| | |
|---|---|
| Matrix No. (and Recording Mark.) | Red Form No. _____ |
| | Listed Record No. _____ |
| Size ... ... ... ... | **12"** |
| | Date Issued _____ |
| Category ... ... ... | **Vocal — COMMERCIAL TEST** |
| | Wear Test Report _____ |
| Title ... ... ... ... | **MissKathleen Ferrier** |
| | **with Gerald Moore at the Piano** |
| Artist ... ... ... ... | |
| (In the case of Dance Band or similar recording state if with vocal refrain.) | |
| Subject to Artist's Royalty | **2EA 10249 –1 Have I lost thee"Orfeo"** |
| (If more than one artist, state names and proportion payable to each.) | **(Gluck)** |
| | **2EA 10252 –1 Angel's Address "Gerontius"** |
| Language of Text ... ... | **(Newman/Elgar)** |
| †Accompaniment (see footnote) | **OEA 10250 –1 Constancy (Brahms)** |
| (State name of Orchestra or Accompanist.) | |
| | **OEA 10251 –1 Feinsliebchen (Brahms)** |
| †Conductor (see footnote) | |
| Name of Author ... ... | |
| Name of Composer ... | |
| Name of Arranger ... | |
| Country of first publication | |
| Year of publication ... ... | |
| Publisher of { British ... ... | |
| Sheet Music { Foreign ... ... | |
| If unpublished, name and address of Copyright Owner | |

†A typewritten asterisk (*) indicates that artist's name given here is to appear in label copy and printed matter. IF NO ASTERISK NAME TO BE OMITTED.

REF-6125

20 Recording sheet from KF's first test session, June 1944

△  22 Joan Taylor and KF

△  23 *Orfeo*, Amsterdam, with Greet Koeman

△ 24 Lieder recital with Bruno Walter, Edinburgh Festival, 1949

▽ 25 KF with Bruno Walter

△ 26 Owen Brannigan, KF, Reginald Goodall, Nancy Evans, Hans Oppenheim.
Glyndebourne

▽ 27 KF, Renato Cellini, Ann Ayars, Zoë Vlachopoulos.
Glyndebourne

▽  28  KF with Phyllis Spurr

▽  29  *Liebeslieder-Walzer* at the Edinburgh Festival, 1952, l to r:
Irmgard Seefried, KF, Julius Patzak, Horst Günther, with
Clifford Curzon and Hans Gal accompanying

Kathleen Ferrier
DECCA
RECORDING ARTIST

# Chapter Fourteen  *July - December 1950*

Kathleen's arrangements for John Newmark's visit to London in July went as planned, and together they recorded six works – two major groups of Lieder and four short songs. Kathleen wrote to Newmark earlier in the year expressing her delight at obtaining for him Decca's top terms – three pounds a day living expenses, and ten pounds for each double-sided 78 rpm disc recorded. Accompanists, it seems, were not remunerated on a royalty basis, but received a once-for-all payment. These recordings with Newmark were the only commercial ones that Kathleen made for Decca during the whole of 1950, and were the last occasions on which she worked with Newmark.

Of the works recorded, only *Vier ernste Gesänge* and the two Scottish folk-songs were issued as 78s, although 78 matrices were made for all of the sides; Decca had recently issued another version of Schumann's cycle on 78s, with the contralto Astra Desmond, accompanied by Phyllis Spurr, which may explain their apparent reluctance to issue Kathleen's performance in that format. It was, however, released on a 12″ LP in January 1951. *Frauenliebe und Leben* is a more thoughtful, less spontaneous performance than that rather eccentrically accompanied by Bruno Walter ten months earlier, but the sound quality is far better on the later version. The two short Schumann Lieder were both recorded on one wax, but that is not apparent from their first release – on a 10″ 33 – in 1954. It seems likely that they were recorded to become the sixth side of the possible (but unissued) set of three 12″ 78s of *Frauenliebe und Leben*.

The recording of *Vier ernste Gesänge* is the only one of the three surviving versions of Kathleen singing the work which is in German, and both the others are public performances. As in the case of *Frauenliebe und Leben*, the interpretive advantages of hearing her singing in front of a live audience must be weighed against the better quality of sound of the Decca studio version. The two 78 record set of *Vier ernste Gesänge* was issued in automatic coupling only, but was not released in that format until October 1951, ten months after its appearance on LP, coupled with *Frauenliebe und Leben*.

The two charming Scottish songs were recorded, Newmark admits, as a special favour to him from Kathleen. Beautifully sung (and accompanied) they have never gained the popularity of some of Kathleen's other folk-song records. *Ca' the Yowes* was selected by EMI to represent Kathleen's art in their impressive project, *The Record of Singing*, of which Volume 4 was reviewed in *Gramophone* in April 1989.

Decca's archives indicate that these recordings took place over three days: 12th, 14th and 17th July. Once again, Kathleen's diary yields different information; it mentions 12th, 13th, 14th, 17th, and 18th. It seems unlikely that these twelve sides would have taken five days to record, so some of the sessions may have been cancelled. The dates below are from Decca, the times from the diary.

2.30 pm on 12.7.50
Decca Studios, Broadhurst Gardens

131   SCHUMANN/Chamisso
*Frauenliebe und Leben, Op. 42* (eight songs)/German
*Seit ich ihn gesehen*/Matrix AR 15209–1

*Er, der Herrlichste von allen/Ich kann's nicht fassen, nichtglaube/*
Matrix AR 15210-1

*Du Ring an meinem Finger/Helft mir, ihr Schwestern*
Matrix AR 15211-1
Piano: John Newmark

6.30 pm on 14.7.50
Decca Studios, Broadhurst Gardens

*Süsser Freund, du blickest/An meinem Hertzen, an meiner Brust/*
Matrix AR 15212–1

*Nun hast du mir den ersten Schmerz getan*/Matrix AR 15213–1
Piano: John Newmark

132   SCHUMANN/Rückert
*Widmung, Op. 25, No. 1*/German
Piano: John Newmark
Matrix AR 15214–1

133   SCHUMANN/Rückert
*Volksliedchen, Op. 51, No. 2*/German
Piano: John Newmark
Matrix AR 15214–1

2.30 pm on 17.7.50
Decca Studios, Broadhurst Gardens

134　BRAHMS/The Bible
*Vier ernste Gesänge, Op. 121*/German

| SIDE NO. | TITLE | AUTO COUPLING | MATRIX NOS |
|---|---|---|---|
| 1 | *Denn es gehet dem Menschen* | AX 563 | AR 15219-1 |
| 2 | *Ich wandte mich* | AX 564 | AR 15220-1 |
| 3 | *O Tod, wie bitter bist du* | AX 564 | AR 15221-1 |
| 4 | *Wenn ich mit Menschen* | AX 563 | AR 15222-1 |

Piano: John Newmark

135　TRAD(arr. Roberton)
*The fidgety bairn*/Scottish
Piano: John Newmark
Matrix DR 15223–1

136　TRAD Scots tune (arr. Jacobson)/Burns
*Ca' the yowes*/Scottish
Piano: John Newmark
Matrix DR 15224–1

# Chapter Fifteen   *January – June 1951*

1951 was an unkind year to Kathleen. In January she braved bad weather and flew to Holland for performances of *Orfeo ed Euridice*, and after recitals in Paris and Zurich arrived in Rome, only to receive a telegram from Winifred saying that their father was seriously ill, and was not expected to live. She decided that it would be better not to return to London, but to continue with her tour of Italy, and it is from one of her engagements shortly after her father's death that the enigmatic recording of a recital seems to originate.

In their catalogue, Rococo Records describe this recording of Kathleen's as a 'live performance' recital in Italy. Kathleen visited Italy twice only; for the first time in June 1950 when she sang Bach's *B Minor Mass* under Karajan at La Scala, Milan, after the successful performance in Vienna, and now again at the end of January and early February 1951. That appears to limit the possible periods for the recital to two, and there is no trace of her having performed anything other than the *B Minor Mass* on the earlier occasion.

Kathleen gave a recital in Rome on 2nd February, and her diary confirms that it included all the items on the Rococo disc, as well as four additional songs, but there is no indication that it was broadcast or recorded. However, in Milan on 6th February, Kathleen pre-recorded a programme for Italian Radio, and although it has not been possible to confirm what was sung on that occasion, it seems likely that it would be much the same as her Rome performance. A letter from Ibbs and Tillett, her agents in London, found among Kathleen's papers, gives the schedule for this Italian tour, and the accompanist named is Giorgio Favaretto, contracted to play for most performances. The possibility that the pre-recorded discs (or possibly tapes by that time) survived after they were broadcast, and found their way into Rococo's catalogue, seems a strong one; and whilst it cannot be confirmed as the source of this intriguing recital, the Milan Radio studio does seem to be the most likely venue. The lack of audience noise or applause strengthens the possibility of a studio recording rather than a public performance. The broadcast date has not been traced.

Five of the twelve items of Rococo's (later Rodolphe's) issue were never otherwise recorded by Kathleen; another five survive in only one other version, *Love is a bable* in two others, and *Che farò* in five. The sound quality, for the standards of the day, is adequate; the piano accompaniment is not sympathetically recorded, but the value of having preserved five otherwise unrecorded items is more important than any minor technical shortcomings. *The Spanish lady* was included by the BBC on their record and cassette *The Singer and the Person*.

　?6.2.51/?RAI Studios, Milan
　?All with Giorgio Favaretto, Piano

141　HANDEL/Congreve
　　*Where 'er you walk (Semele)*/English

142　HANDEL/Adapted from Valerians/English version by Albert G. Latham
　　*Like as the love-lorn turtle (Atalanta)*/English

143　PURCELL/Settle (?) After Shakespeare
　　*Hark! The echoing air (The Fairy Queen)*/English

144　MONTEVERDI/Rinuccini
　　*Lasciatemi morire (Arianna)*/Italian

145　LOTTI
　　*Pur dicesti (Arminio)*/Italian

146　GLUCK/Calzabigi
　　*Ah diletta, Euridice . . . Che farò senza Euridice? (Orfeo ed Euridice)*/Italian

147　SCHUBERT/Rückert
　　*Lachen und Weinen, D 777, Op. 59, No. 4*/German

148　BRAHMS/Anon
　　*Sonntag, Op. 47, No. 3*/German

149　PARRY/Anon
　　*Love is a bable, Op. 152, No. 3*/English

150　STANFORD/M. O'Neill
　　*The fairy lough, Op. 77, No. 2*/English

151　TRAD. Scots tune (arr. Jacobson)/Burns
　　*Ca' the yowes*/Scottish

152　TRAD./Traditional
　　*The Spanish lady*/English

It is to Sir John Barbirolli that the credit must go for encouraging Kathleen to learn Chausson's *Poème de l'amour et de la mer*. By 1951 Barbirolli and Kathleen were old friends, although their musical association did not start off entirely happily in December 1944, when they had performed Elgar's *Sea Pictures* together in Sheffield. After Bruno Walter, Kathleen came to recognise Barbirolli as the greatest musical influence in her life. They spent much time together. Sir John, his wife Evelyn (a celebrated oboeist) and Kathleen would play chamber music for hours, relaxing in Kathleen's Frognal flat, or the Barbirollis' home. Sir John had conducted many performances of Kathleen's since 1944, and became concerned that her voice was not being used to its full potential. He felt there was a danger that it would gradually darken in timbre and lose the colour and freshness that had always been its radiant feature. The voice's range deserved to be extended, its higher notes nurtured.

Kathleen spent over a year preparing to sing *Poème de l'amour et de la mer*. Not only was its style entirely different from anything she had learnt so far, but so was the language. Up to that time she had sung nothing in French, and she sought help from Pierre Bernac, the French baritone, with both the linguistic and musical problems of the work. To Kathleen, the discovery of the beauty of the music of Chausson was as much a milestone as had been her introduction to Mahler. It revealed not just the work of another composer, but an entirely new repertoire, one which she was not given the time to explore more fully.

Kathleen gave her first performance of the work on 28th February 1951, and nine days later she sang it again on a BBC Third Programme broadcast from Manchester, with Sir John Barbirolli, of course, conducting the Hallé Orchestra. The programme also included works by Rossini, Fauré and Duruflé, but the Chausson was Kathleen's only contribution on that occasion. At the request of the conductor, a recording was made of Kathleen's performance on shellac discs, which years later came into the possession of Mr Ian Cosens, who lived at Sowerby Bridge, West Yorkshire. Realising their musical and historical value, he contacted Winifred Ferrier, who in turn sent a tape dubbing to Decca, so that the technicians might assess the feasibility of issuing the performance commercially. Despite imperfect and very faded sound quality, the decision was taken to release the work on LP and cassette, and Winifred travelled to Sowerby Bridge to collect the precious discs. Sadly, by this time Mr Cosens had succumbed to cancer, and he never knew that his initiative had led to the commercial release of his set of 78s. Apart from flawed sound, much improved by Decca's engineers, the performance lacks five (non-vocal) bars, Nos 129–133; it was issued just thirty-four years after being recorded, in March 1985. Unfortunately, along with a number of other Decca releases of Kathleen's recordings, it is accompanied by inaccurate sleeve notes, which give incorrect information about her early family life. The CD version was first released in 1992.

This recording is the only one published of Kathleen performing with Sir John Barbirolli, and is the only one of her singing in French.

8.00–8.50 pm on 9.3.51
Milton Hall, Deansgate, Manchester

153   CHAUSSON/Bouchor
*Poème de l'amour et de la mer, Op. 19*/French
Conductor: Sir John Barbirolli, Hallé Orchestra

Just a few days after this broadcast, Kathleen discovered the truth that she had for so long feared, and began her two-and-a-half-year fight against cancer.

# Chapter Sixteen   *July – December 1951*

After an operation in April 1951, it was over two months before Kathleen sang in public again. In the middle of the summer, she flew to take part in the Holland Festival, and gave performances of *Orfeo ed Euridice*, Mahler's *Kindertotenlieder* and *Second Symphony* with Otto Klemperer, and Bach's *B Minor Mass* under the Romanian composer and conductor, Georges Enesco. By good fortune, recordings of all these works have survived from the month of July; Kathleen's arrival at Schiphol Airport was filmed for a Dutch newsreel, and is the second of the only two examples traced of her appearing on film.

When *Orfeo ed Euridice* was first issued by EMI in the UK in April 1978, it was believed to have originated from one of the performances that Kathleen gave in Amsterdam in January 1951; however, recently traced Dutch archive material (KRO Radio Station) gives 10th July as the correct date, and seems likely to be accurate. Three performances were given of the opera that month; one was in The Hague on the 3rd, and the two in Amsterdam were on the 4th and 10th.

The original 78s of this performance were transferred in 1965 on to reel to reel tape, and it was in this form that it was rediscovered in the archives of the NOS (Dutch Broadcasting Corporation) in the 1970s by Klaas Posthuma, the producer and technical supervisor of the release. Permission then had to be obtained from both KRO and NOS before it could be published. Royalties from the EMI issues of this performance are donated to The Kathleen Ferrier Memorial Scholarship Fund in London, which finances an annual competition and awards grants to young singers.

The difference in Kathleen's interpretation between the Glynde-bourne recording of 1947 and this one is astonishing. Here can be heard a fully formed characterisation, a passionate, and at times tragic hero. Kathleen's Italian had also greatly improved since the earlier version, and she really convinces that she is not just a concert singer on stage, but a fine singing actress. Against that, certain disadvantages are very evident, unavoidable in the recording of a staged performance. The sound is good, but not of studio standard, the other singers competent but certainly not excellent, and the *corps de ballet* and chorus decidedly heavy-footed. Greet Koeman (Euridice) and Nel Duval (Amor) were sisters, who often sang with the former Netherlands Opera, and appeared with Kathleen in both the January and the July performances of *Orfeo*. Charles Bruck, a pupil of Pierre Monteux (who had conducted the original production with Kathleen in 1949), was the principal conductor of the former Netherlands Opera during the early 1950s; another recording of him conducting *Orfeo*, made several years after this one, with the Belgian mezzo-soprano Rita Gorr, has also been issued in recent years.

Many words have been written about the different versions that exist of *Orfeo ed Euridice*; suffice it to say here that this performance contains much more music than the 'concise' version from Glyndebourne, but not as much as some more recent recordings of the work. Four excerpts have been issued by EMI on CD, but it seems unlikely that the complete version will appear from that company in that format; it has, however, appeared complete on a Verona Record Company CD set.

The producer for the EMI issue of this recording was Klaas. A. Posthuma, and the transfer engineer Maarten Proost.

> 8.30 pm on 10.7.51
> Stadsschouwburg, Amsterdam

156 Gluck/Calzabigi
  *Orfeo ed Euridice*/Italian
  Soprano: Euridice, Greet Koeman
  Soprano: Amor, Nel Duval
  Conductor: Charles Bruck, Orchestra and Chorus of the former
  Netherlands Opera
  From a recording made available by courtesy of
  Nederlandse Omroep Stitching and Katholieke Radio Omroep
  Dutch Radio Sound Archives NOB Reference: EM–HM–0719

  156a *Chiamo il mio ben cosi*/Act 1
  156b *Deh! Placatevi con me*/Act 2
  156c *Che puro ciel!*/Act 2
  156d *Che ho fatto, ohimè – Che farò senza Euridice?*/Act 3
  156e *Ah, più non m'ode – Che farò senza Euridice?*/Act 3

Kathleen's second Holland Festival performance which was recorded, and remained for years in Dutch Radio archives, was a concert in the Concertgebouw, Amsterdam, given on 12th July. It commemorated the death forty years earlier (on 18th May 1911) of Gustav Mahler, and was conducted by Dr Otto Klemperer, whom the composer had known well, and had encouraged in his musical career. Working with Klemperer was a very different experience from working with Walter, and Kathleen wrote some time after this concert: 'I hate to work with Klemperer . . . I find he shouts like a madman . . . just to try to impress – though why he should think it impresses I can't think. Perhaps his Mahler comes off sometimes, because he wastes no time nor sentiment

– but ohh!!! Whattaman.' On 12th July 1951 Klemperer's Mahler certainly did come off, and Kathleen, the other singers, and the Concertgebouw Orchestra give their best for him.

The programme on that evening opened with Mozart's *Masonic Funeral Music*, after which Kathleen sang *Kindertotenlieder*. After the interval the *Resurrection Symphony* was performed, with Kathleen and Jo Vincent as the two soloists. The whole performance was broadcast by KRO and the two latter items, at least, were recorded on 78 rpm discs. The Symphony was the first to be issued by Decca, in September 1982, on two LPs, and equivalent cassettes. The sound is clear, with a wide dynamic range, everything from solo singing to the loudest orchestral tuttis being admirably recorded; there is, though, a small amount of surface noise from the original discs, to which the ears can soon become attuned, and easily 'listen through' to the music. For some years before Decca's issue, the Symphony had been available on an Educ Media LP set, together with two extracts from Kathleen's 1948 New York performance of *Das Lied von der Erde*.

More recently, the fourth movement, *Urlicht*, a short solo for contralto (also used by Mahler in *Das Knaben Wunderhorn*) has been issued on a Verona CD, together with excerpts from the Vienna Festival performances of Bach recorded in 1950; and Verona have also issued the Symphony complete on one CD, but sold together with another, of Dietrich Fischer-Dieskau singing Mahler's *Lieder eines fahrenden Gesellen* under Wilhelm Furtwängler. Decca's CD version of the performance was issued in 1990, on a single disc, and whilst its sound quality is far better than that on Verona, it has had the concert hall atmosphere removed between the first and second, and second and third movements. On Verona, the feel of a live performance is maintained; the strings re-tune, and the audience shuffles, but not distractingly. It all sounds more natural. Perhaps the two versions were based on different tapes (made from the same master discs), one of which had been 'tidied up'.

*Kindertotenlieder* was issued as one side of a Decca LP and cassette in November 1987, but is not in as good quality sound as the Symphony. The original discs have become worn and scratched over the years, and whilst this is a valuable performance to hear, a different reading from Bruno Walter's recorded in 1949, and has the benefit of being a public performance, in clarity of orchestral detail it leaves a good deal to be desired. There are no plans at present to reconstruct the original concert and issue both Mahler works together on CD.

8.15 pm on 12.7.51
Concertgebouw, Amsterdam

157 MAHLER/Rückert
*Kindertotenlieder*/German
Conductor: Otto Klemperer, Concertgebouw Orchestra
Amsterdam
A recording in the archives of Katholieke Radio Omroep

158 MAHLER/Klopstock and Mahler
*Symphony No. 2 in C Minor, The Resurrection*/German
Soprano: Jo Vincent, Conductor: Otto Klemperer,
Concertgebouw Orchestra, Amsterdam Toonkunstkoor
A recording made available by courtesy of Nederlandse Omroep
Stichting and Katholieke Radio Omroep
Dutch Radio Sound Archives NOB References: EM–HM–0753,
EM–HM–0878 and EM–HM–0908

158a *Urlicht*/Fourth movement

Whilst still in Holland, Kathleen sang the *B Minor Mass* with Georges
Enesco conducting, and almost immediately on her return to London
sang the same work twice more with him for the BBC. The performance
on 17th July was broadcast at 7.55 pm on the Third Programme, and the
following evening the same forces gave another on the Home Service
at 7.50 pm; both were from the Concert Hall at Broadcasting House,
London. By an amazing chance, a complete recording of the earlier
performance was discovered in the late 1980s, lying in a box with some
other discs, in a corner of Bush House, London, home of the BBC World
Service. On 6th July 1990 the BBC broadcast it again in their Radio 3
series *Mining the Archive*, probably the first time for nearly thirty-eight
years that it had been heard on the air in the UK.

Comparisons with Karajan's performance in Vienna in 1950 show
how much more 'traditionally' Enesco took his Bach. His tempi are
slower, the pulse of the work less marked. In *Et in unum Dominum* he
takes 5' 19" compared with Karajan's 4' 37", and *Qui sedes* is 5' 53" where
Karajan takes 5' 13", and Boult, 5' 25". The recording provides an
illustration of the approach to Bach's music prevalent in the 1950s,
before the 'authentic' style of performance had gained popularity. It
illustrates, too, how Kathleen sang *Laudamus Te*, of which no other
recording exists. Schwarzkopf had sung it in Vienna, and it was not
included in Kathleen's recital of Bach arias recorded under Boult in
1952, although two other numbers from this Mass were; and, despite a
plan to record it at her first session for Decca back in 1946, it was not,
after all, made on that occasion.

*The Listener's* critic commented on Enesco's 'careful regard for Bach's orchestration, which showed how unpleasant it can sound to modern ears.' How much more 'unpleasant' might that critic find a performance in the 1990s! Alan Blyth, the eminent music critic, believes that this performance, together with the Dutch *The Rape of Lucretia* and the Dutch *Orfeo ed Euridice*, reproduces most faithfully the sound of Kathleen's voice as he recalls hearing it in the 1940s and 1950s. Because they were all live performances, they reveal the directness and spontaneity that did not come naturally to her in the cold atmosphere of the recording studio.

The other singers in this performance were the Belgian soprano Suzanne Danco, Peter Pears, and the basses Bruce Boyce and Norman Walker. BBC archives have revealed the fees paid to the artists. Danco received 120 guineas, Kathleen 80 guineas and Peter Pears 25!

> 7.55–10.35 pm on 17.7.51
> The Concert Hall, Broadcasting House, London

159  BACH
> *Mass in B Minor*, BWV 232/Latin
> Soprano: Suzanne Danco, Tenor: Peter Pears, Bass: Bruce Boyce,
> Bass: Norman Walker, Conductor: Georges Enesco, Boyd Neel
> Orchestra, BBC Chorus, Harpsichord: George Malcolm,
> Chorus Master: Leslie Woodgate
> Never commercially issued/BBC Sound Archives Reference:
> T 80775
> NSA Reference: NSA Tape B 6063

In December 1951, Kathleen paid her first visits to Decca's studios for nearly seventeen months, to record twelve British songs, including six composed or arranged by Roger Quilter. She had particular cause to remember with affection one song from those six, *To Daisies*, with which she had won the Silver Bowl in the 1937 Carlisle Festival – having accepted a shilling bet that she would not enter both Piano and Voice Classes, she delighted herself, and surprised most of her friends, by winning both! The judges of the Voice Class were Yeoman Dodds and Maurice Jacobson: the latter became a good friend and colleague, working with Kathleen on CEMA tours during the early days of the Second World War, and acting as her accompanist at her first London engagement.

It is possible that these 1951 sessions were the first for Decca at which Kathleen recorded directly on to reel to reel tape rather than wax discs, although the exact date when this 'new' system began cannot be established; in any case, waxes were at some stage made of all twelve songs, including those which never appeared as 78s. Only seven songs were issued as 78s, on six 10" sides (explained by that fact that one side of record M 681 contains both *The stuttering lovers* and *I will walk with my love*), the remainder appearing first on a 10" 33 rpm record in 1952; ironically, although *To Daisies* was issued as a 78, it was the only one of the twelve songs not to be published on that early 10" 33 disc. The whole output of the three sessions gives the impression of being a sequel to the 1949 recordings of folk-songs, and on the CD issue of April 1988 all nineteen are presented, together with the two Scottish songs accompanied by John Newmark.

These were the last piano accompanied commercial sessions that Kathleen attended for Decca, and the last at which Phyllis Spurr accompanied her. With the exception of the first of the recordings (*O waly, waly*), none of the songs from these sessions exist in other versions by Kathleen; they are sung with a direct simplicity that defies the word 'interpretation', and both serious and humorous songs reveal something of those qualities that she herself possessed.

Kathleen's diary confirms the times and dates of the recording sessions, and Decca's archives show how the songs were divided up over the sessions.

2.00–5.00 pm on 10.12.51
Decca Studios, Broadhurst Gardens

160   Collected Sharp (arr. Britten)/Traditional
      *O waly, waly*/English
      Piano: Phyllis Spurr
      Matrix DR 16592–1

161   Trad. (arr. Hughes)/Traditional
      *I have a bonnet trimmed with blue*/English
      Piano: Phyllis Spurr
      Matrix DR 16593–1

162   Trad. (arr. Sharp)/Traditional
      *My boy Willie*/English
      Piano: Phyllis Spurr
      Matrix DR 16593–1

163   Trad. (arr. Hughes)/Traditional
      *I will walk with my love*/English
      Piano: Phyllis Spurr
      Matrix DR 16594–1

164   TRAD. (arr. Hughes)/Traditional
      *The stuttering lovers*/English
      Piano: Phyllis Spurr
      Matrix DR 16594–1

165   QUILTER/Tennyson
      *Now sleeps the crimson petal, Op. 3, No. 2*/English
      Piano: Phyllis Spurr
      Matrix DR 16595–1

      2.00–5.00 pm on 11.12.51
      Decca Studios, Broadhurst Gardens

166   HUGHES, adapted Gray/Traditional
      *I know where I'm going*/English
      Piano: Phyllis Spurr
      Matrix DR 16601–1

167   QUILTER/Anon
      *The fair house of joy, Op. 12, No. 7*/English
      Piano: Phyllis Spurr
      Matrix DR 16602–1

168   QUILTER/Herrick
      *To daisies, Op. 8, No. 3*/English
      Piano: Phyllis Spurr
      Matrix DR 16603–1

      2.00–5.00 pm on 12.12.51
      Decca Studios, Broadhurst Gardens

169   TRAD. (arr. Quilter)/Percy's Reliques
      *Over the mountains*/English
      Piano: Phyllis Spurr
      Matrix DR 16604–1

170   TRAD. (arr. Quilter)/Burns
      *Ye banks and ye braes*/Scottish
      Piano: Phyllis Spurr
      Matrix DR 16605–1

171   TRAD. (arr. Quilter)/Jonson
      *Drink to me only with thine eyes*/English
      Piano: Phyllis Spurr
      Matrix DR 16606–1

The Victoria and Albert Museum in South Kensington was the setting for the first London performance of Benjamin Britten's canticle *Abraham and Isaac*, which he had composed for, and dedicated to, Kathleen and Peter Pears.

After a tour organised in aid of The English Opera Group (which had been founded early in 1947 by Britten, Eric Crozier and John Piper, respectively the composer, producer and designer of the first production of *The Rape of Lucretia*), Britten, Ferrier and Pears came to London to give what Britten later described as 'the happiest of concerts', and to record a broadcast for the BBC. The recording contained most of the items that had been performed on the tour, including Lieder by Schubert, duets by Purcell and Morley, arias by Handel and Lotti, and the first broadcast performance of *Abraham and Isaac*. The sixty-minute recital was due to be given on the Third Programme on 6th February, two days after it had been recorded at the BBC's Maida Vale Studios; but on that day the country was grieving at the passing of King George the Sixth, who had died in the morning's early hours. Radio schedules were altered, and solemn music was broadcast instead, as a mark of mourning. *Abraham and Isaac* did not receive its first broadcast after all.

It was not until 13th May 1952 that the recording was eventually played on the Third Programme, and, some months afterwards the BBC's copy of the recital was destroyed. Despite continuing rumours that *Abraham and Isaac* has survived, so far nothing has come to light; it seems very sad that her performance of this 'sweet piece – simple and very moving', as Kathleen described it, should have gone forever.

Despite that loss, six items from the recital have survived, recorded at home on acetate discs by Geoff Pollock, an avid collector of 'off the air' recordings, then living in north-west London; by Schubert, three of the Lieder are sung by Pears and three by Kathleen, and all of them are accompanied on the piano by Britten, making these probably the only extant recordings of Britten and Kathleen performing together. *Ganymed* does not exist in any other performance of Kathleen's, and is thus a particularly important discovery; both *Du liebst mich nicht* and *Lachen und Weinen* have survived in other versions, the former from the 1949 Edinburgh International Festival, and the latter from Kathleen's Italian recital of 1951, but it is the special combination of accompanist and singer that makes these performances so important. Regrettably, *Du liebst mich nicht* is incomplete, shorn of its last twelve bars. Despite that, these three Lieder have been issued by Decca on cassette and CD, in a new compilation released in 1992, although those sung by Pears have not been included.

> 3.30–5.00 pm on 4.2.52
> BBC Maida Vale Studio 2, West London

176   SCHUBERT/Goethe
*Ganymed, D 544, Op, 19, No. 3*/German
Piano: Benjamin Britten

177   SCHUBERT/Platen
*Du liebst mich nicht, D 756, Op. 59, No. 1*/German
Piano: Benjamin Britten
(Incomplete)

178   SCHUBERT/Rückert
*Lachen und Weinen, D 777, Op. 59, No. 4*/German
Piano: Benjamin Britten

Kathleen recorded more works by Brahms than any other composer. She was constantly adding to her repertoire, thanks largely to the advice of Bruno Walter, and continued to develop her interpretive powers throughout her career. The BBC recital broadcast on 2nd April 1952 is the last surviving example of her singing solo Lieder by Brahms – The *Liebeslieder-Walzer* and *Vocal Quartets* were still to follow in September – and she otherwise recorded only one out of the five extant items.

The Third Programme recital consisted of six Brahms Lieder, and chamber music by Dvořák. Private recordings (some of which have since been placed in the BBC's archives), were made of parts of the broadcast by, among others Geoff Pollock. The recital was given live from the Concert Hall at Broadcasting House, and Mr Pollock recorded four of the Lieder complete. The fifth, *Wir wandelten*, is, ironically, without its first sixteen bars; this was one of the pieces that Kathleen gave as an encore in Denmark in October 1949, on the record of which the opening bars are also missing, so no quite complete recording of it sung by Kathleen has survived. The third work sung in the recital is missing altogether; *Radio Times* shows that *Der Tod, das ist die kühle Nacht* was scheduled to be performed, and probably it was, but it seems not to have been captured by any of the recorders that evening. The four complete Lieder have only been issued once – on *The Singer and the Person*, the BBC's own recorded tribute to Kathleen; the sound quality is acceptable, but not as good as the BBC's own archive material from the same period.

*Ruhe Süssliebchen in Schatten* is the ninth of fifteen romances from *Die schöne Magelone*, Op. 33; *Auf dem See* is Op. 59, No. 2, and not the Lied of the same name to words by Reinhold (Op. 106, No. 2) as shown on the record sleeve notes. Kathleen's diary tells of a rehearsal in the Concert Hall between 8.00 and 9.00 pm, before the broadcast began at 10.00 pm. Frederick Stone, for thirty years a pianist with the BBC, who broadcast frequently with Kathleen, gives his reliable support. The sequence of items below is that given for the performance in *Radio Times*.

10.00–11.25 pm on 2.4.52
The Concert Hall, Broadcasting House, London

179  BRAHMS/Tieck
*Ruhe Süssliebchen in Schatten* (from *Die schöne Magelone*) *Op. 33, No. 9*/German
Piano: Frederick Stone
BBC Sound Archives Reference: LP 27264
NSA Reference: NSA Tape M548W

180  BRAHMS/Simrock
*Auf dem See, Op. 59, No. 2*/German
Piano: Frederick Stone
BBC Sound Archives Reference: LP 27264
NSA Reference: NSA Tape M548W

181  BRAHMS/Daumer
*Wir wandelten, Op. 96, No. 2*/German
Piano: Frederick Stone
(Incomplete)
Never commercially issued/A tape in a private collection

182  BRAHMS/Heine
*Es schauen die Blumen, Op. 96, No. 3*/German
Piano: Frederick Stone
BBC Sound Archives Reference: LP 27264
NSA Reference: NSA Tape M548W

183  BRAHMS/Halm
*Der Jäger, Op. 95, No. 4*/German
Piano: Frederick Stone
BBC Sound Archives Reference: LP 27264
NSA Reference: NSA Tape M548W

'Heavenly birthday party mit cake!' was Kathleen's diary entry on 22nd April. She spent her fortieth birthday in the company of her good friends the Barbirollis; the day was memorable not only for Sir John's surprise party for her, but also for a broadcast of *Das Lied von der Erde* which she, Sir John, and the tenor Richard Lewis gave in the evening on the BBC Third Programme.

Gordon Rowley spent the evening of 22nd April 1952 in his lodgings in Hertford, experimenting with his new Mark 1 Ferrograph tape recorder, and he decided to find some worthwhile music to record from the radio, as a change from the lighthearted *Goon Show*. He thought he would see what was on the BBC Third Programme. Fortunately the tape that he made still exists, and is highly prized. Mr Rowley wrote to Maurice Leonard, Kathleen's biographer, in 1988, on reading that only one example of her singing under the baton of Sir John Barbirolli had survived – Chausson's *Poème de l'amour et de la mer* – and reported the existence of a second – *Das Lied von der Erde*. Regrettably there seems no likelihood that it will ever be issued, as Decca's superb version under Walter is still one of their most enduring classical recordings. The fees payable to the Musicians' Union on the release of an orchestral or choral work, even one recorded as long ago as forty years, seem to make the issue of a second Ferrier version in the UK an unviable commercial proposition.

Despite a slightly brittle start to the first song, *Das Trinklied*, where the tape has deteriorated, and occasional aural blemishes (caused, according to Mr Rowley, by the passing of trains on the adjacent railway line), the performance has survived nearly forty years very well, with both Kathleen and Richard Lewis in excellent voice. Certainly there is a sense of strain in parts of the sixth song, *Der Abschied*, which can also be heard on Kathleen's commercial recording under Walter made only three weeks later in Vienna, but the tension that this vocal quality adds to the performance as a whole is entirely appropriate for the text and the music; had her voice been lighter and less rich she might more comfortably have overcome the difficulties that *Der Abschied* poses. The performance contains minor vocal imperfections – the occasional frog in the throat that Kathleen so dreaded when broadcasting – but it has a spontaneity that can sometimes be edited out of commercial issues.

Rehearsals for the broadcast took place at Milton Hall in Deansgate, Manchester at 11.00 am, and the live broadcast began at 7.30 pm.

> 7.30–8.45 pm on 22.4.52
> Milton Hall, Deansgate, Manchester

184    MAHLER/Translated from the Chinese by Bethge
*Das Lied von der Erde*/German
Tenor: Richard Lewis, Conductor: Sir John Barbirolli, Hallé Orchestra
Never commercially issued/A tape in a private collection

Kathleen's visit to Vienna in May 1952 was a far less joyful one than that of June 1950. True, she was to fulfil an ambition that she had cherished for at least two years (one which seemed doomed before it had even been planned), but much of the time she was in pain, and only reluctantly did her doctor allow her to travel.

Since recording *Kindertotenlieder* with Bruno Walter in 1949, her greatest ambition had been to work with him on *Das Lied von der Erde*, but contractual agreements again got in the way. Decca had 'lent' Kathleen to American Columbia in 1949, but the compliment was not easily returned. As early as August 1950 Walter wrote pessimistically to Kathleen about his attempts to get a reciprocal release to record with Decca, despite the apparent fairness of such an arrangement.

> I am afraid that my efforts to free myself for a recording of *Das Lied von der Erde* with you will not be successful. The Columbia people seem extremely reluctant to commit themselves, and although they have not given a definitely negative answer, my impression is not a very favourable one ... I made a most urgent appeal to reciprocate the courtesy of Decca having permitted you to make the *Kindertotenlieder* with us. I shall certainly continue my efforts, but I did not want to keep you waiting for an answer any longer.

Just what finally persuaded Columbia to relent is not clear, but had they not done so, this classic recording, which has become a standard beside which newer versions have frequently been compared, would never have been made.

Commentators have often remarked on the tragic aspects of Kathleen's recording of *Das Lied von der Erde*, and with hindsight it is easy to impose on it more sombre overtones than it deserves. It is only fair to appreciate that at the time the recording was made, although she was clearly far from well, Kathleen was optimistic about her future. In Winifred's view, Kathleen was convinced right into 1953 that the treatment she was receiving would ensure a complete cure of her cancer. The quality of the interpretation, particularly of her third song *Der Abschied* (by far the longest of the six of which the work consists), can only be fairly assessed on its musical merits, and should not be overshadowed by other unduly emotional considerations.

Details of the sessions for the recording of *Das Lied von der Erde* and the three *Rückert Lieder* have not survived in Decca's archives, so estimating the dates and schedules in Vienna necessitates a large amount of informed guesswork. Kathleen left London by plane on 13th May, and work in the Grosser Musikvereinssaal began the next day, most, if not all, of which was taken up with tests before the recording proper began. As tape was being used, it was possible to record, hear a playback immediately, and then establish the optimum balance levels between soloists and orchestra. So the main sessions for *Das Lied* probably took place on the two days following the tests, 15th and 16th May.

Walter conducted two public performances of *Das Lied von der Erde* with Kathleen, in the Musikvereinssaal at 3.00 pm on the 17th, and at 11.00 am on 18th May (these are the only two dates and times noted in Kathleen's diary for the whole of her stay in Vienna); recording would not have continued on those days. According to Bernadine Hammond, Kathleen's secretary and companion, on the day after the morning concert the participants went to the studio to hear the edited tape. As they were leaving this playback Kathleen called to the engineers that she would see them tomorrow – 'You haven't seen the last of me yet, boys' – which leaves only 20th May, the known last day of recording, for the *Rückert Lieder* sessions.

The substantial contributions of the tenor soloist, Julius Patzak, were probably recorded at different sessions, but on the same days, as Kathleen's. As the two soloists never sing together, but perform alternate songs, it is quite possible that as far as the recording was concerned, they met only at the final playback.

Victor Olof of Decca, whom Kathleen had known for a number of years (in a letter to John Newmark in 1950 she refers to him as Decca's musical adviser) was the producer in charge of the sessions, and he naturally felt some responsibility for her while she was in Vienna. In his biography of Kathleen, Maurice Leonard describes the difficulties that she had in completing the *Rückert Lieder* on the last day of recording. She was in some pain, and technical problems persisted. Miss Hammond recalled years later how, at the last session, Victor Olof despaired of securing a complete version of *Um Mitternacht*. Several takes were made, none of which proved satisfactory, and, with very little time left before the Musikvereinssaal had to be vacated, Kathleen was able to record one more version, which proved to be technically and musically ideal.

When the two-record set of *Das Lied von der Erde* and the *Rückert Lieder* was first issued, there was some criticism of the flawed sound of the celeste at the end of *Der Abschied*; these comments angered Olof, for the celeste was insignificant compared to the moving and inspired singing of Kathleen. He felt it was better to keep the take as it was, rather than try again and risk losing the interpretation.

On 21st May Kathleen and Walter left Vienna. They parted at Zurich airport where they both had to change planes, and they never met again. *Das Lied von der Erde* which had been the first work they performed together in public, also proved to be the last.

As originally issued, *Das Lied von der Erde* required three sides of 12″ Long Playing record to accommodate its sixty minutes' running time, so the three of Mahler's five Lieder to words by Friedrich Rückert were used to fill the fourth side. In September 1954 the Lieder were released together on a 10" 33 rpm record, and in 1969 on a Decca 'Ace of Clubs' LP, as a pairing with Strauss's *Vier letzte Lieder* sung by Lisa della Casa. It would have been ideal if Kathleen had also recorded the other two Lieder – *Liebst du um Schönheit* and *Blicke mir nicht in die Lieder* and thus completed the set, but there is no indication that such a course was ever intended for these Viennese sessions.

Although neither *Das Lied von der Erde* nor the *Rückert Lieder* were ever issued by Decca on 78s, matrices were made; the prefix 'V' indicates that the recording was made in Vienna, but the sequence of matrix numbers does not necessarily indicate the order of recording. These Mahler works are the only commercial recordings that Kathleen made outside London, although, of course, performances from other cities have since been issued by Decca and other companies. The recording producer for all these sessions was Victor Olof.

?15 and 16.5.52/Grosser Musikvereinssaal, Vienna

185   MAHLER/Translated from the Chinese by Bethge
      *Das Lied von der Erde*/German

> *Das Trinklied vom Jammer der Erde*/Patzak/Matrix Nos. VAR 252-3
> *Der Einsame im Herbst*/Ferrier/Matrix Nos. VAR 254-5
> *Von der Jugend*/Patzak/Matrix No. VAR 256
> *Von der Schönheit*/Ferrier/Matrix Nos. VAR 257-8
> *Der Trunkene im Frühling*/Patzak/Matrix No. VAR 259
> *Der Abschied*/Ferrier/Matrix Nos. VAR 260-66
> Tenor: Julius Patzak, Conductor: Bruno Walter, Vienna
> Philharmonic Orchestra

The order of the works below is that in which it is believed they were recorded.

?20.5.52/Grosser Musikvereinssaal, Vienna

186   MAHLER/Rückert
      *Ich bin der Welt abhanden gekommen*/German
      Conductor: Bruno Walter, Vienna Philharmonic Orchestra
      Matrix No. VAR 269

187   MAHLER/Rückert
      *Ich atmet einen linden Duft*/German
      Conductor: Bruno Walter, Vienna Philharmonic Orchestra
      Matrix Nos. VAR 270-1

188   MAHLER/Rückert
      *Um Mitternacht*/German
      Conductor: Bruno Walter, Vienna Philharmonic Orchestra
      Matrix Nos. VAR 267-8

The song recital broadcast on 5th June 1952 was the first non-commercial recording of Kathleen's that Decca issued. It was also the first from which the royalties were given to the Cancer Fund at University College Hospital, which had been opened in her name. It was originally released complete (ten songs) in June 1954 on a 10″ 33 rpm record, and was reissued in the same format, but with a different record number, in October 1959. Kathleen recorded only one of the songs from the recital commercially, but two others (*The fairy lough* and *Love is a bable*) survive from other radio broadcasts. *O waly, waly* was part of Decca's own recital recording made in December 1951. This later version was included on only the first two commercial issues of the broadcast; subsequently it was omitted, perhaps as it was felt that Decca's own was a better recorded performance. It has at last been reinstated, on cassette and CD, in Decca's British Music series.

Some major British composers and folk-song arrangers are represented. Kathleen's only recordings of Vaughan Williams (who greatly admired her), and Frank Bridge (a teacher of Benjamin Britten), are included, as well as two songs composed by (rather than arranged by) Peter Warlock. Two of Britten's arrangements of folk-songs are listed in *Radio Times* as being the final items of this recital, but time was obviously found to add *Kitty my love*, arranged by Hughes, as a delightful conclusion. Perhaps the broadcast was under-running by one minute fifteen seconds.

Kathleen would remember with affection *Silent Noon*, as it was with that song that she won the Gold Cup at the Workington Festival in 1938. The adjudicator on that occasion was Dr J.E. Hutchinson, who, the following year, became her first professional singing teacher. He provided her with a really sound vocal technique, and introduced her to the repertoire that was the basis of her first success in the early days of the Second World War.

This short recital was broadcast live from the BBC Concert Hall, on the Home Service.

      7.30–8.00 pm on 5.6.52
      The Concert Hall, Broadcasting House, London

189   STANFORD/M. O'Neill
      *The fairy lough, Op. 77, No. 2*/English
      Piano: Frederick Stone

190 STANFORD/W.M. Letts
*A soft day, Op. 140, No. 3*/English
Piano: Frederick Stone

191 PARRY/Anon
*Love is a bable, Op. 152, No. 3*/English
Piano: Frederick Stone

192 VAUGHAN WILLIAMS /D.G. Rosetti
*Silent noon*/English
Piano: Frederick Stone

193 BRIDGE/Tennyson
*Go not, happy day*/English
Piano: Frederick Stone

194 WARLOCK/J. Fletcher
*Sleep*/English
Piano: Frederick Stone

195 WARLOCK/Shakespeare
*Pretty ring time* (From *As You Like It*)/English
Piano: Frederick Stone

196 Coll. SHARP (arr. Britten)/Traditional
*O waly, waly*/English
Piano: Frederick Stone

197 TRAD. (arr. Britten)/Traditional
*Come you not from Newcastle?*/English
Piano: Frederick Stone

198 TRAD. (arr. Hughes)/Traditional
*Kitty my love*/English
Piano: Frederick Stone

For the entire recital: BBC Sound Archives Reference: T 29656
NSA Reference: NSA Tape T 9188R

# Chapter Eighteen  *July - December 1952*

Kathleen was booked to appear in four concerts at the 1952 Edinburgh International Festival; she had not sung in public since early June, and was eagerly looking forward to performing again with Barbirolli and van Beinum in three of her favourite works. However, one evening at the Usher Hall was being devoted to music that she had not sung before: Brahms's *Three Vocal Quartets,* and his more famous *Liebeslieder Walzer.* In both of these works she was joined by the soprano Irmgard Seefried, Julius Patzak, and the baritone Horst Günther, who took over at short notice from the indisposed Frederick Dalberg. The pianists Clifford Curzon and Hans Gal were the accompanists, and the programme was completed by Curzon and Gal playing Schubert piano music. The concert was a terrific success, and, fortunately, parts of the broadcast were recorded privately by at least three listeners to the BBC Third Programme; one of them was Alan Blyth, the author and music critic, and another Geoff Pollock, who had already recorded Schubert and Brahms Lieder earlier in the year.

When Decca were planning to release the public performance of *Kindertotenlieder* conducted by Klemperer, recorded in the Concertgebouw, Amsterdam in July 1951, they hoped to find a work for the second side of the LP and tape in which no other conductor had participated. This meant either searching for another Klemperer performance (and as he was contracted to EMI that itself might cause further complications), or finding a work in which no conductor took part. It was then that the tapes of *Liebeslieder Walzer* were traced, and one in particular was selected as the source for the issued recording. As the work needs no conductor, simply four singers and two pianists, it filled the requirements as a partner to *Kindertotenlieder* admirably, and its lilting charm acts as a delightful contrast to the gravity of the Mahler. In addition, Number 15 from a later set of vocal waltzes – *Neue Liebeslieder* – was also performed, and has been included with the Opus 52 on the issued recording. Permission to publish the recording had, of course, to be obtained from the performers, or their estates, and their royalty payments went to assist the Kathleen Ferrier Cancer Fund at University College Hospital.

Apart from the issued *Liebeslieder Walzer*, at least one recording has survived of the lesser known *Three Vocal Quartets* which were performed in the first half of the programme. Brahms set words by three German writers for his Opus 64; seldom performed, the work is less immediately attractive than the *Walzer*, and there are no plans at present to issue the performance.

8.00–8.55 pm and 9.10–9.40 pm on 2.9.52
Usher Hall, Edinburgh

201 BRAHMS
*Three Vocal Quartets, Op. 64*/German
*An die Heimat*/Sternau
*Der Abend*/Schiller
*Fragen*/Daumer
Soprano: Irmgard Seefried, Tenor: Julius Patzak, Baritone: Horst
Günther, Piano: Hans Gal
Never commercially issued/A tape in a private collection

202 BRAHMS/Polydora
*Liebeslieder Walzer* (18 vocal waltzes), *Op. 52*/German
Soprano: Irmgard Seefried, Tenor: Julius Patzak, Baritone: Horst
Günther, Piano Duet: Clifford Curzon and Hans Gal

203 BRAHMS/Polydora
*Zum Schluss*, No. 15 from *Neue Liebeslieder, Op. 65*/German
Soprano: Irmgard Seefried, Tenor: Julius Patzak, Baritone: Horst
Günther, Piano Duet: Clifford Curzon and Hans Gal

Kathleen and Dame Myra Hess had been friends for nearly ten years
– ever since Kathleen's first London concert at the National Gallery –
and although they never recorded together, on 29th September 1952
they shared a BBC Third Programme recital, broadcast live from Maida
Vale Studios. Accompanied by Frederick Stone, Kathleen sang five
Schubert Lieder; interspersed with them, Dame Myra played solo piano
music by Schubert and Schumann. Two of Kathleen's contributions
have been issued by the BBC, on *The Singer and the Person* album in 1979,
but the remaining three (other versions of which had by that time
already been issued by Decca) remain unpublished, and probably
unheard on the air for nearly forty years.

Kathleen repeated three items which were recorded at the 1949
Edinburgh International Festival recital with Bruno Walter, *Suleika 1*,
*Der Vollmond strahlt* and *Die junge Nonne*. She had also made this last
title for Decca in 1947. The two otherwise unrecorded items were
*Rastlose Liebe, Op. 5, No. 1*, and *Wasserfluth*, the sixth of the twenty-four
songs that comprise *Winterreise, Op. 89*. Kathleen never sang complete
performances of *Winterreise*; indeed, until the 1980s it was very seldom
sung by women, but it is interesting that she chose to perform this
extract from it. Was she, perhaps, considering the whole work as a
recital piece? These performances were recorded by the BBC and
retained in their own archives; the sound quality is good, which makes
it the more regrettable that they have not had wider circulation.

Rehearsals were held at Maida Vale at 8.15 pm, before the broadcast began at 10.25 pm.

> 10.25–11.15 pm on 29.9.52
> BBC Maida Vale Studio 2, West London

204   SCHUBERT/Willemer adapted by Goethe
*Suleika 1, D 720, Op. 14, No. 1*/German
Piano: Frederick Stone

205   SCHUBERT/Von Chézy
*Der Vollmond strahlt* (Romance from *Rosamunde*), *D 797, Op. 26*/
German
Piano: Frederick Stone

206   SCHUBERT/Goethe
*Rastlose Liebe, D 138, Op. 5, No. 1*/German
Piano: Frederick Stone

207   SCHUBERT/Müller
*Wasserfluth* (from *Winterreise*), *D 911, Op. 89, No. 6*/German
Piano: Frederick Stone

208   SCHUBERT/Craigher
*Die junge Nonne, D 828, Op. 43, No. 1*/German
Piano: Frederick Stone

> BBC Sound Archives Reference: LP 27264
> NSA Reference: NSA Tape T9188W

Kathleen's last sessions for Decca were on 7th and 8th October 1952, in Kingsway Hall, London, where her first recording for them had also taken place nearly seven years earlier. With the London Philharmonic Orchestra under Sir Adrian Boult she recorded four arias by Bach and four by Handel.

It was on 7th October that the Bach arias were taped. Kathleen's diary shows that there were originally plans to record the short Cantata No. 53 – *Schlage doch gewünschte Stunde* (sometimes attributed to Bach, but now believed to be by G.M. Hoffmann) on this day. That diary entry was then crossed out, leaving two arias from the *Mass in B Minor*, *Grief for sin* from the *St Matthew Passion*, and *It is finished* (but performed under the title *All is fulfilled*) from the *St John Passion*. For many years, these excerpts from the *Mass* were generally believed to be the sole surviving examples of Kathleen singing from the work, and they still remain the only ones published by Decca.

*Grief for sin* was sung in its full version, with da capo repeat; the same aria performed in Decca's 1947/1948 set under Dr Jacques was given without repeat, and its re-recording at this 1952 session may have been due to Kathleen's wish to make a complete version. Unfortunately, the recitative *My Master and my Lord* which precedes it was not recorded. Kathleen recorded no other music from *St John Passion*; she sang the complete work occasionally during her career, but less often than either the *B Minor Mass* or *St Matthew Passion*. In this performance she uses the words 'All is fulfilled' throughout the aria, reverting only for the final two phrases to 'It is finished', the title she had given it in her diary.

During two sessions on 8th October, Kathleen recorded four arias by Handel, none of which survives in other versions. *Messiah* is represented by two arias. Ever since signing her first contract with Decca, Kathleen had hoped to record a complete version of the work. Indeed, they had promised such a recording as an incentive to her in 1946, but it never took place, much to her disappointment; as a final irony, Decca did record a complete version in 1953, during the period of her final illness, in which she would undoubtedly have sung had she been well enough. It, too, was conducted by Sir Adrian Boult, and the young Norma Procter sang the alto part.

Although Kathleen recorded Bach's *Grief for sin* in its full version on the previous day, *He was despised* was sung without its powerful middle section – *He gave His back to the smiters*. This omission robs the aria of much of its dramatic impact, and the contrast of moods is entirely lost. Whether she usually, or ever, included that section in her public performances is in doubt; but beautiful though the recording is, it would have been more effective if sung complete.

The other two arias by Handel, *Father of Heaven* from *Judas Maccabaeus* and *Return, O God of Hosts!* from *Samson* are less familiar than those from *Messiah*, and show Kathleen's skill at sculpting a musical line in slow, rather sombre music. Apart from *O Thou that tellest*, the overall impression that this recital leaves on the listener is of sombre interpretations of Baroque music, sung in the traditional, undecorated style which was then customary.

Decca hoped that Sir John Barbirolli would be available to conduct these sessions; he was at the time contracted to EMI, and correspondence about his possible release survives in record company archives. Clearly the decision-makers at EMI did not feel in any way inclined to 'lend' him for these sessions; ironically, however, at about the same time, the possibility of Kathleen's being 'lent' to EMI was under discussion, for new recordings of Beethoven's *Ninth Symphony*, probably with Toscanini, and the *Mass in B Minor* with Karajan. Even if her final illness had not prevented it, it seems unlikely that she would have been released by Decca, albeit in exchange for Sir John Barbirolli.

So it was, then, that Sir Adrian Boult took charge of these sessions, for the only commercial recordings that he made with Kathleen. John Culshaw, who had supervised some of Kathleen's previous recordings, was producer, and he wrote most movingly in his autobiography *Putting the Record Straight* about these sessions. He recalled that on 8th October Kathleen was expecting a phone call from the hospital to give her the results of tests that had been carried out a few days earlier. When she returned from the telephone, having been given the message, she smiled warmly and said, 'They say I'm all right, luv. They've just phoned to say I'm all right.' But it was not really so. Exactly a year later she died in University College Hospital.

Kathleen's career ended too soon for any of her recordings to have been made in genuine stereophonic sound; but in the late 1950s almost every new issue on 33 rpm records was available in both mono and stereo versions, and Decca decided to release the eight arias from these sessions in a new stereophonic format. Adding new orchestral backgrounds to existing recordings was not a new technique. It had been tried in the 1920s and 1930s when several pre-electric records of Caruso and Tetrazzini had been 'enhanced' by the addition of an electrically recorded orchestral or organ accompaniment; but Decca's plan was subtler, and more effective, than those early attempts.

Early in 1960, the London Philharmonic Orchestra and Sir Adrian Boult met again in Kingsway Hall to re-record the accompaniments to the arias in stereophonic sound. Boult, on the podium, had a loudspeaker relaying the original recording at a very low volume so that he could maintain exactly the right speeds, and after what must have been very much trial and error, completely new, fully synchronised accompaniments were successfully taped. These were then superimposed on to the original tracks, so that Kathleen would appear to be singing from the centre of a stereophonic spread. The very high and low frequencies were removed from the original tape, in order to reduce the contribution of the original orchestra, but unfortunately that also altered the tonal quality of Kathleen's voice; there is some loss of the warmth that most of her records convey so well. The effect is, rather, of Kathleen singing through a hole in the centre of the orchestra.

Two of the arias have important parts for solo instrumental accompaniments. Ambrose Gauntlet who plays the viola de gamba in *All is fulfilled* suffers less from the new format than Michael Dobson, player of the oboe d'amore in *Qui sedes*. While the soloist is playing with the orchestra only, he seems to be performing in the remake, but while he is supporting Kathleen's voice, the original accompaniment appears to have been retained; this leads to a change in prominence of the instrument, exaggerated by the different aural qualities of the two recordings. It is not clear whether these instrumentalists participated in the original recording sessions, or the remake, or both, but there must have been many players in the LPO who were present in 1952 and also in 1960. Heard today, the effect of this stereophonic enhancement is surely less impressive than it was in 1960; at that time stereo records were still something of a novelty, and the technical skill that went to creating these new versions was greatly admired.

The new performances were released by Decca in September 1960, and most subsequent reissues were in the stereo format until December 1985, when the arias made their first appearance on CD. For that version, and its companion issues on LP and cassette released in 1986, the original mono tapes were used; the clarity of the digitally remastered sound may have revealed too much of the earlier orchestral performance underneath than was acceptable. These are the only recordings of Kathleen's to have been re-created in real stereo: indeed, there appear not to have been any other attempts at all to enhance mono originals in this way. This method of genuine stereophonic re-recording should not be confused with the electronic enhancement, which was used on some issues of Kathleen's recordings (and many others as well), which were originally made monophonically. Electronic stereo gives a broader spread to the sound of a recording, but not the directional quality that is a feature of true stereo.

78 rpm matrices were made of every item from the original sessions, although none of the arias was ever issued as a 78 record. Their first appearance in the UK was on a 12″ Long Playing record, issued in February 1953, the month of Kathleen's last public appearance. The order below is that in which it is believed the recordings were made. The recording producer for these sessions was John Culshaw.

2.00–5.00 pm and 6.00–9.00 pm on 7.10.52
Kingsway Hall, London

209   BACH/The Bible (translated from the German)
*Grief for sin (St Matthew Passion,* BWV 244)/English
Conductor: Sir Adrian Boult, London Philharmonic Orchestra,
Harpsichord continuo: Basil Lam
Matrices AR 17234/5

210   BACH/Translated from the German
*All is fulfilled (St John Passion,* BWV 245)/English
Conductor: Sir Adrian Boult, London Philharmonic Orchestra,
Viola da gamba: Ambrose Gauntlet, Harpsichord continuo: Basil Lam
Matrix AR 17236

211   BACH
*Qui sedes (Mass in B Minor*, BWV 232)/Latin
Conductor: Sir Adrian Boult, London Philharmonic Orchestra,
Oboe d'amore: Michael Dobson, Harpsichord continuo: Basil
Lam
Matrix AR 17237

212   BACH
*Agnus Dei (Mass in B Minor*, BWV 232)/Latin
Conductor: Sir Adrian Boult, London Philharmonic Orchestra,
Harpsichord continuo: Basil Lam
Matrix AR 17238


10.00 am–1.00 pm and 2.00–5.00 pm on 8.10.52
Kingsway Hall, London

213   HANDEL/The Bible, arranged Jennens
*O Thou, that tellest good tidings to Zion (Messiah)*/English
Conductor: Sir Adrian Boult, London Philharmonic Orchestra,
Harpsichord continuo: Basil Lam
Matrix AR 17228

214   HANDEL/The Bible, arranged Morell
*Father of Heaven (Judas Maccabaeus)*/English
Conductor: Sir Adrian Boult, London Philharmonic Orchestra,
Harpsichord continuo: Basil Lam
Matrices AR 17231/2

215   HANDEL/The Bible, arranged Jennens
*He was despised(Messiah)*/English
Conductor: Sir Adrian Boult, London Philharmonic Orchestra,
Harpsichord continuo: Basil Lam
Matrices AR 17229/30

216   HANDEL/Hamilton, after Milton
*Return, O God of Hosts (Samson)*/English
Conductor: Sir Adrian Boult, London Philharmonic Orchestra,
Harpsichord continuo: Basil Lam
Matrix AR 17233

19.2.60 and 13.5.60
Kingsway Hall, London
Re-created versions of the above works, with stereophonically
recorded accompaniments
Conductor: Sir Adrian Boult, London Philharmonic Orchestra

217   BACH
*Grief for sin*

218   BACH
*All is fulfilled*

219   BACH
*Qui sedes*

220   BACH
*Agnus Dei*

221   HANDEL
*O Thou, that tellest good tidings to Zion*

222   HANDEL
*Father of Heaven*

223   HANDEL
*He was despised*

224   HANDEL
*Return, O God of Hosts*

# Chapter Nineteen   *January - June 1953*

In January 1953 Kathleen began rehearsing the new production of *Orpheus and Euridice* which, at Sir John Barbirolli's instigation, was being mounted specially for her at Covent Garden. The two performances she gave, of the four that were planned, were her last public appearances. Her last new recital for the BBC also dates from January, although it was not broadcast until 4th April on the Third Programme. The recording was kept in the BBC Sound Archives, and was first issued commercially by Decca in November 1975. It provided the fourth side of the double LP set of which the first three sides were the 1949 Edinburgh Festival recital.

The twenty-four minute broadcast consisted of modern music by three living British composers: Howard Ferguson, William Wordsworth and Edmund Rubbra. Howard Ferguson's *Discovery*, composed in 1952, consists of five songs to texts by Denton Welch, from his anthology *A Last Sheaf*; Wordsworth's three songs, *Opus 5*, were composed in 1935, and Rubbra's *Three Psalms Opus 61*, in 1946. Kathleen's first broadcast of *Three psalms* was recorded off the air in 1947, but this later performance enjoys far better sound, and a more sympathetically caught, if not ideal, piano accompaniment. It seems fitting that Kathleen should have been the dedicatee of the last music she recorded.

Dr Ferguson recalled working with Kathleen on his songs:

> She sang my *Discovery* most beautifully, with all the warmth, understanding and musicality that was so typical of her performances. One very poignant memory remains of the rehearsal at which I played through the cycle with Kathleen at her Frognal flat. The macabre third song, *Jane Allen*, is about a mad housemaid who, after finishing her work, drank a cup of Indian tea, then dropped a letter in a tree. It ends, 'And this is what the letter said: "When you get this, I'll be dead".' I knew only too well how ill Kathleen then was; and when she turned to me at the end of the song and said very simply, 'Poor soul', I had the greatest difficulty in not bursting into tears.

Unfortunately, Ernest Lush, for many years one of the BBC's highly regarded in-house accompanists, suffers from the then-prevalent practice of giving the pianist too backward a balance, but he offers good support to Kathleen's singing of the music of all three composers.

*Radio Times* lists the order of performance of the songs in *Discovery* differently from that in which Decca have issued it. The apparent order of the broadcast puts *Dreams Melting* at the beginning, leaving the title song to be the final one. Wordsworth's three songs are set to poems by Stephen Phillips, Rupert Brooke and Wilfred Gibson; although that order is the one in which *Radio Times* lists their performance, it is not the sequence in which Decca have issued them. The Brooke and Gibson songs' positions are exchanged. As a result of a misprint in the manuscript of *The Clouds*, at one point Kathleen sang an F sharp in error. She apologised afterwards to the composer, but he later acknowledged that 'It sounds quite good as sung!'

None of the works from this recital has achieved great popularity since this recording was made; it is typical of Kathleen that she sang them with the same conviction and perception as anything grander or better loved from her repertoire. Her diary reveals that she and Ernest Lush rehearsed at Maida Vale Studios between 2.00 and 3.00 pm on 12th January, and that the recording was made between 3.00 pm and 4.00 pm. Its first broadcast was between 6.50 and 7.20 pm on 4th April, nearly twelve weeks later. The order below is that indicated in *Radio Times* for the broadcast.

> 3.00–4.00 pm on 12.1.53
> BBC Maida Vale Studio 5, West London

226  FERGUSON/Denton Welch (from *A Last Sheaf*)
     *Discovery, Op. 13*/English
     *Dreams melting/The freedom of the City/Babylon/Jane Allen/Discovery*
     Piano: Ernest Lush

227  WORDSWORTH/*Three Songs, Op. 5*/English
     *Red Skies* Stephen Phillips/*Clouds* Rupert Brooke/*The Wind*
     Wilfred Gibson
     Piano: Ernest Lush

228  RUBBRA/The Bible
     *Three Psalms, Nos 6, 23 and 150, Op. 61*
     *O Lord, rebuke me not/The Lord is my Shepherd/Praise ye The Lord*
     Piano: Ernest Lush

     For the entire recital: BBC Sound Archives Reference:
     Tape T 20487–9
     NSA Reference: NSA Tape M4420W

Praise ye the Lord.
Praise God in His sanctuary:
Praise Him in the firmament of His power.
Praise Him for His mighty acts:
Praise Him according to His excellent greatness.
Praise Him with the sound of the trumpet:
Praise Him with the psaltery and harp.
Praise Him with the timbrel and dance:
Praise Him with stringed instruments and organs.
Praise Him upon the loud cymbals:
Praise Him upon the high sounding cymbals.
Let ev'ry thing that hath breath praise the Lord.
Praise ye the Lord.

# Chapter Twenty  *The recordings that 'might have been'*

The recordings of Kathleen Ferrier that 'might have been' fall into three distinct categories:

I Those which are known to have been made, commercially, by broadcasting organisations or privately, but which seem not to have survived.
II Those which were planned to be made, but which never were.
III Those of works which were particularly important in her repertoire, but which were apparently never even contemplated.

  I The main text includes commercial recordings for EMI and Decca which were made, but which were destroyed before issue. These are:

No. 21: *O wert thou in the cauld blast?*/Mendelssohn
No. 22: *Turn ye to me*/Traditional
No. 41: *Vier ernste Gesänge*/Brahms
No. 46: *Gestillte Sehnsucht*/Brahms
No. 47: *Geistliches Wiegenlied*/Brahms
No. 53: *Frondi tenere (?) . . . Ombra mai fu*/Handel
No. 54: *Gestillte Sehnsucht*/Brahms
No. 55: *Geistliches Wiegenlied*/Brahms
No. 69: *Der Musensohn*/Schubert

and presumably all takes, other than those which were used for commercial issue, recorded between 1944 and 1952.

Of Kathleen's broadcasts, two can be confirmed as having been recorded and kept, for a short time at least, in the BBC's archives. One is that pre-recorded on 15th December 1949 (Nos 107–109) and broadcast eleven days later, although the source for the issued items seems not to be the BBC copy itself, but off-the-air acetates. The other recording is that which included Britten's *Abraham and Isaac*, made on 4th February 1952. The complete programme for that broadcast was:

| 1. (Tenor) | Recit. *Ah! che pur troppo è vero* | Handel, realised |
| | Aria *Col partir la bella Chlori* | Britten |
| 2. (Contralto) | Aria *Pur dicesti* | Lotti, realised Britten |

| | | | |
|---|---|---|---|
| 3. (Duets) | *Sweet nymph, come to thy lover* | | |
| | *I go before, my darling* | Morley | |
| 4. (Duet) | *Corydon and Mopsa's Dialogue* | Purcell, realised | |
| | *(The Fairy Queen)* | Britten | |
| 5. (Lieder- | *Ganymed* | | |
| Contralto) | *Du liebst mich nicht* | | |
| | *Lachen und Weinen* | | |
| (Lieder- | *Vom Mitleiden Maria* | | |
| Tenor) | *Der zürnenden Diana* | | |
| | *Liebesbotschaft* | Schubert | |
| 6. (Duet) | *Abraham and Isaac* – a canticle | | |
| | from the Chester Miracle | | |
| | Play for contralto, tenor and | | |
| | piano | Op. 51 Britten | |

It is very likely that other programmes were recorded by broadcasting organisations, either in advance of their scheduled broadcast date (as in the case of Nos 226–228) or on the occasion of a live broadcast (such as Nos 23, 33, 61, 159 et al.), but, unlike these, were not kept for long in the archives.

Undoubtedly amateur radio enthusiasts recorded some of Kathleen's broadcasts, either on acetate discs, or, from the early 1950s, on tape. A number of surviving recordings have, of course, been preserved in this way, such as Nos 176–178, 179–183, and 184.

A set of amateur recordings of Kathleen was made in the 1940s by a pupil at Rugby School, on the occasion of a recital there; when she heard the results later, she declared that they sounded better than her commercial versions of the same pieces; these have not been traced, and it is not known whether they have survived.

II Several references are made in the text to recordings which either a recording company or Kathleen herself, hoped, expected, or was asked to make. Some others, not mentioned, have been traced, and are also included in the list below: details of them are taken from Kathleen's diary.

| | | | |
|---|---|---|---|
| 1. *Sapphic Ode* | Brahms | 6.3.45 | Abbey Road |
| 2. *May Night* | Brahms | 6.3.45 | Abbey Road |
| 3. *Sapphic Ode* | Brahms | 20.4.45 | Abbey Road |
| 4. *May Night* | Brahms | 20.4.45 | Abbey Road |
| 5. *Laudamus Te* | Bach | 6.2.46 | Kingsway Hall |
| 6. *Schlage doch gewünschte Stunde* | Bach? | | |
| | Hoffmann? 7.10.52 | | Kingsway Hall |

| | | | |
|---|---|---|---|
| 7. *Mass in B Minor* | Bach | .11.52 | Vienna and London |
| 8. *Symphony No. 9* | Beethoven | .53? | New York? |
| 9. *Four serious songs* | Brahms ) | | |
| 10. *Rhapsody for alto, male chorus and orchestra* | Brahms ) | ) 5-7.1.53 | Kingsway Hall |
| 11. *Abraham and Isaac* | Britten ) | | Hamilton |
| 12. *Corydon and Mopsa's Dialogue* | Purcell ) | 28-29.5.53 | Terrace |
| 13. *Canzonets* | Morley ) | | St John's Wood |

The two sets of sessions for 1953 are particularly interesting. No doubt Kathleen and Decca were keen to record two of her favourite works for Long Playing records, and arranged four three-hour sessions at Kingsway Hall on three days in January, just before rehearsals began for *Orpheus* at Covent Garden. *Four serious songs* must have been planned in the orchestral version, as the performance recorded with John Newmark's piano accompaniment was not yet two and a half years old; and Kingsway Hall would be an unlikely venue for recording a piano accompanied session.

Kathleen's recording of *Alto Rhapsody*, with Krauss, was five years old, and suffered from three side changes in its 78 version. A new version, recorded on tape rather than wax, would probably be an improvement on it. No conductor or orchestra is mentioned in connection with these sessions, which are all marked 'Cancelled' in Kathleen's diary.

A bizarre newspaper cutting from October 1953 has been found which, whilst deeply regretting Kathleen's death, also announces that '. . . the last two recordings she made will be in the shops in about two weeks' time. They are four of Brahms's songs, and his *Alto Rhapsody*'. Odd indeed, as it was already over nine months since they had *not* been recorded. What was issued in November 1953 was the first LP of the Krauss *Alto Rhapsody*, coupled with the two *Songs with viola, Op. 91, Sapphische Ode* and *Botschaft* – the first release of the latter two in any format.

The more famous, and more deeply regretted, instance of pre-advertising was the announcement, in *The Gramophone*'s May 1953 edition, of the release of a 12" LP, number LXT 2789, which contained duets by Purcell, Morley and Benjamin Britten. The two days in May marked 'Recording' in Kathleen's diary were surely those booked to tape the duets, which included *Abraham and Isaac*. After Kathleen was taken ill at Covent Garden in February, Decca arranged to record at her new flat in Hamilton Terrace, St John's Wood. Arthur Bannister, Decca's Recording Engineer, remembers being sent there in advance to test the acoustics of Kathleen's room;

it seemed to promise well. Before the recording could be made, however, she suffered a serious relapse, and was rushed back into hospital. The record was never made, and in November's issue of *The Gramophone* Decca had to publish a notice of regret that it would not, after all, be possible to issue it.

It was then that Britten remembered the recording that had been made for the BBC broadcast in February 1952; that could be used for commercial release instead. But on investigation it was found that it had gone, presumably destroyed in the normal course of events, after being broadcast once or twice again. Perhaps, somewhere, a copy of *Abraham and Isaac* is still in a collection, waiting to be found and enjoyed. This, surely, of all the recordings 'that might have been' is the most keenly missed.

There is no evidence that Kathleen was ever actually invited to take part in Decca's complete *Messiah*, recorded in the autumn of 1953; when arrangements were being made for the sessions, she was probably already in hospital, and it may have been felt that it would be better not to mention it to her at that stage, after she had waited over seven years to participate in it.

III Of the many works in Kathleen's repertoire that she did not record, nor ever planned to, a handful stand out that really should have been made. Apart from the two fragments from *The Dream of Gerontius* (No. 4), nothing by Elgar was ever recorded. A complete version of that work, preferably with Barbirolli conducting, would have preserved her moving interpretation of the Angel; but, as in the case of Bruno Walter, borrowing and lending musicians between companies was an almost insuperable problem, and Barbirolli was contracted at that time to EMI. Although Kathleen never cared for Elgar's *Sea Pictures*, that, too, could have made a fine recording. She preferred *The Apostles* and *The Kingdom* in which she occasionally sang, but from which she left nothing.

Kathleen sang songs by twentieth-century British composers, such as Holst, Moeran, Michael Head, Bax, Scott, and Delius, of which not a note was recorded; and others by Vaughan Williams and Stanford, who are represented by only one and two pieces respectively which have survived. She also performed music from earlier centuries, by Boyce, Byrd and Carey, of which we have nothing. During 1951 and 1952 Kathleen was studying songs by Fauré, but probably never sang them in public, let alone recorded them.

Although three major Bach recordings have come to light in recent years, (Nos 120, 126 and 159) nothing remains of Kathleen's interpretations of his *Christmas Oratorio* or *Magnificat*, and but one aria from *St John Passion*. We can hear only a few arias from operas by Handel; she sang many others in her recitals. She recorded none of his oratorios or operas in complete performances, although an excerpt each from *Judas Maccabaeus* and *Samson* was made in October 1952.

Kathleen's repertoire of German Lieder was growing year by year, especially those by Brahms and Schubert; some of the more popular ones from her repertoire that she never recorded are *Mainacht, Minnelied, Heimkehr, Heidenröslein, Erlkönig,* and *An Sylvia*. The list could be longer.

After the exciting discoveries in recent years of some of Kathleen's broadcasts, it is hoped that others will still be found, and issued commercially; there is still so much that might have been.

# Chapter Twenty-One   *Kathleen Ferrier on film*

Only two fragments of Kathleen on film have been traced during research. The earlier, which cannot be accurately dated, was taken at the party in New York, probably early in 1949, at which the tape *Kathleen Ferrier at a Party* (No. 73) was also recorded. During its approximately six minutes' running time, it shows Kathleen at the piano, playing and singing, guying the performances of other singers who take simple songs too seriously. Although it was taken at the same party as the tape, the two are not synchronised. From a remark heard on the tape it can be assumed that someone forgot to turn on the tape while the film was running, and instead of acting as a true sound track to the film, it is another performance of probably the same material. On the BBC film *Blow the wind southerly*, first shown in 1968 to commemorate the fifteenth anniversary of Kathleen's death, the 'soundtrack' was put to the film, and conveyed an impression of Kathleen performing her 'cabaret' repertoire. Other shots in the film show guests, including Ann Ayars the soprano, and general party scenes.

On 1st July 1951 Kathleen flew to Schiphol Airport near Amsterdam, at the start of her visit to the Holland Festival. The newsreel camera filmed the arrival of three celebrities: Tamara Toumanova, the ballerina; Walt Disney, who also gave a short interview, and Kathleen. She is seen coming down the steps from the plane, smiling broadly, and talking to Peter Diamand, Director of the Holland Festival; behind her is Bernadine Hammond, her companion, who had travelled with her since the onset of her illness the previous March. The film of Kathleen lasts just twelve seconds.

Nothing seems to survive of Kathleen performing on stage or in the concert hall, and no trace of any recorded television appearances has been found.

# Part Two   *The Discography*

# Introduction

□ *78 rpm 10"*          ◇ *45 rpm 7"*          ○ *33 rpm 10"*
■ *78 rpm 12"*                                 ● *33 rpm 12"*

\* *Compact Disc*      •• *Tape Cassette*      ⋮ *Stereo 8 Cartridge*

This list of Kathleen Ferrier's issued recordings includes all major British and USA releases, recorded in Europe for Columbia and Decca. In addition, a number of issues from other companies are listed, most of which are taken from live broadcast performances in various countries. Of these latter, those which have been fairly widely available in the UK are included in the British listing (e.g. on labels such as Rococo, Rodolphe, Danacord, Foyer and Verona), whilst those which were issued in the United States are included in the USA lists (e.g. The Bruno Walter Society and Educational Media).

British issues are followed by a date in brackets, which is the date of release. If a release date has not been traced, the date preceded by 'R' is the month of review in *The Gramophone*. In some cases a date has had to be estimated (e.g. recordings from foreign companies); it may not be accurate, but will indicate an approximate year; and in others, no guess at an issue date has been attempted.

Under the title of each item the British issues are shown first, in the following order: 78s (10" and 12"), 45s, 33s (10" and 12"), CDs, Cassette Tapes and Stereo 9 Cartridges marked with the symbols shown above. After the rule ——————————— the USA issues are listed in the same order.

Kathleen's early Columbia records were never issued as 78s in the USA, but they have appeared there on LPs and CDs; some of her early Decca 78s were issued in the USA by American Decca on the same number as in Britain, so these numbers have not been duplicated in the American lists.

When her records (including several 78s) were issued on the London and other affiliated labels from the late 1940s, they were given entirely different numbers from their British counterpart, and these are listed below. Eight of Kathleen's recordings were issued both in the original monaural version, and in a stereo re-creation which was added to the original tapes in 1960. The two versions (Nos 209–216 for the original mono, and 217–224 for the stereo remake) are kept distinctly separate from one another, so that the reader may see which issues are in which version. Not all issues since 1960 have been in the stereo re-creation.

Both in Britain and the USA a number of recordings have been issued which have been subjected to an 'electronic stereo enhancement' process. This is not to be confused with the genuine stereo accompaniments added to Nos 209–216, which created Nos 217–224. Issues subjected to the electronic process have not been listed separately.

The recordings Kathleen made between 1944 and 1953, which have been issued by EMI and Decca, have been released in many countries of the world, often with catalogue numbers different from those given here. Only those numbers issued in the United Kingdom and the USA are shown below.

# Disc List – *Issue Numbers and Dates, UK and USA*

## 78 rpm Records
### BRITISH ISSUES

*Columbia*

□ DB 2152 (11.44)  ■ DX 1194 (6 .45)
□ DB 2194 (11.45)  ■ LX 8939–41 (11.52)
□ DB 2201 ( 1.46)

*Decca*

□ M 622 (10.48)   ■  K 1465 (Untraced)
□ M 652 ( 6.50)   ■  K 1466 ( 7.46)
□ M 657 ( 9.50)   ■  K 1517–21 (R  7.47)
□ M 679 ( 2.52)   ■ AK 1517–21 (R  7.47)
□ M 680 ( 9.52)   ■  K 1556 (10.46)
□ M 681 (10.52)   ■  K 1632 ( 8.47)
                  ■  K 1656–62 (R 12.47)
□ F 9300 (12.49)  ■ AK 1656–62 (R 12.47)
                  ■  K 1673–9 (R  1.48)
                  ■ AK 1673–9 (R  1.48)
                  ■  K 1847–8 ( 6.48)
                  ■ AK 1847-8 ( 6.48)
                  ■ AK 2001-21 (11.48)
                  ■  K 2135 ( 5.49)
                  ■  K 2289 (12.49)

                  ■ AX 347–8 ( 9.50)
                  ■ AX 399–401 ( 3.51)
                  ■ AX 563–4 (10.51)

### USA ISSUES

*London*

□ R 10102   ■ T 5052
□ R 10103   ■ T 5349
□ R 10104   ■ T 5434
            ■ T 5435
            ■ T 5647

## 45 rpm Records
### BRITISH ISSUES

*Columbia*

◇ SED 5526 (10.55)
◇ SED 5530 ( 3.56)

◇ SCD 2143 (11.60)

*Decca*

◇ 45–71034 (12.54)
◇ 45–71035 (12.54)
◇ 45–71036 (12.54)
◇ 45–71037 (12.54)
◇ 45–71038 (12.54)

*Decca*

◇ 45–71039 (12.54)
◇ 45–71072 ( 4.55)
◇ 45–71108 (12.55)
◇ 45–71112 ( 5.56)
◇ 45–71130 ( 6.56)
◇ 45–71135 ( 4.56)
◇ 45–71138 ( 6.56)
◇ 45–71139 ( 6.56)

◇ CEP 518 (12.57)
◇ CEP 550 ( 7.58)
◇ CEP 569 (11.58)
◇ CEP 587 ( 3.59)
◇ CEP 663 ( 7.60)
◇ CEP 719 ( 3.62)
◇ CEP 720 ( 3.62)
◇ CEP 721 ( 3.62)
◇ CEP 722 ( 3.62)
◇ CEP 723 ( 3.62)
◇ CEP 724 ( 3.62)
◇ CEP 725 ( 3.62)
◇ CEP 726 ( 3.62)
◇ CEP 5508 ( 4.63)

# Re–created Stereo 45 rpm records

*Decca*

◇ SEC 5099 (10.61)

## USA ISSUES

*London*

◇ 45–40166
◇ D 18060

# 33 rpm Records

## BRITISH ISSUES

*Columbia*

○ 33C 1009 (11.52)

*HMV*

● HLM 7002 ( 3.72)
● HLM 7145 (12.78)
  (Great British Mezzo–Sopranos and
  Contraltos)

● HQM 1072 ( 2.67)

HMV

*Rococo*

• 5265

• RLS 725 ( 4.78) (Two–record
  set – Orfeo ed Euridice)

• EX 7697431 ( 4.89) (Eight records –
  The Record of Singing Volume 4)

*Rodolphe*

• RP 12407

*Danacord*

• DACO 114 (1985)

*BBC Artium*

• REGL 368 (R 12.79)
  (Kathleen Ferrier –
  The singer and the person)

*Foyer*

• FO 1046 (1986) (Four–record set –
  Matthäus–Passion)

*Decca*

○ LW 5072 (12.53)
○ LW 5076 ( 1.54)
○ LW 5083 ( 1.54)
○ LW 5089 ( 2.54)
○ LW 5094 ( 3.54)
○ LW 5098 ( 3.54)
○ LW 5123 ( 9.54)
○ LW 5225 ( 3.56)
○ LW 5353 (10.59)

*Decca*

• LXT 2556 ( 1.51)
• LXT 2721 ( 9.52)
• LXT 2722 ( 9.52)
• LXT 2757 ( 1.53)
• LXT 2850 (11.53)
• LXT 2893 ( 2.54)
• LXT 5324 ( 5.57)
• LXT 5382 (11.57)
• LXT 5576 (10.60)
• LXT 6278 ( 4.67)
  (Part of Vienna
  Philharmonic Festival
  boxed set)

*Decca*

• 6 BB 197–8 (11.75) (Two records –
  Edinburgh Festival recital & last
  broadcast recital)

• D 42 D 3 ( 4.77) (Three–record set –
  St Matthew Passion)

• D 264 D 2 ( 9.82) (Two–record set
  Mahler's Second Symphony)

○ LX 3006 ( 6.50)
○ LX 3007 ( 6.50)
○ LX 3040 ( 5.51)
○ LX 3098 (11.52)
○ LX 3133 ( 6.54)

○ BR 3052 ( 6.60)

• LXT 6907 (10.78)
• LXT 6934 ( 9.79)

• ACL 52 ( 9.59)
• ACL 109–11 (11.60)
  (Three records –
  St Matthew Passion)

• 414 095–1DH ( 3.85)
• 414 194–1DM ( 5.86)
• 414 611–1DG ( 2.86)
• 414 623–1DG ( 6.86)
• 417 182–1DM ( 5.86)
• 417 466–1DM ( 1.87)
• 417 634–1DM (11.87)

• ACL 293 (11.66)
• ACL 305 ( 9.68)
• ACL 306 ( 9.68)
• ACL 307 ( 9.68)
• ACL 308 (10.68)
• ACL 309 (10.68)
• ACL 310 (10.68)
• ACL 318 ( 6.69)

• ECS 562 (10.70)
• ECS 2178 (11.77)

• PA 172 (10.71)

• DPA 623–4 (12.78) (Two–record set
  – Favourite composers – Schumann)

• DPA 627–8 (12.79) (Two–record set –
  The music of England)

*Decca*

*Decca*

- AKF 1–7 (10.73)
  (Seven-record set)
  N.B. AKF 4 is in
  Re-created Stereo

- SPA 205 (  3.72)
- SPA 316 (12.73)
- SPA 355 (  7.74)
- SPA 433 (  9.75)
- SPA 524 (  6.78)

## Re-created stereo 33 rpm Records

*Decca*

- SXL 2234 (  9.60)

- DPA 551–2 (  9.76)
  (Two-record set –
  Favourite composers – Handel)
- SDD 286 (10.71)

- SDD M 432–4 (  9.74) (Three-record set –
  Festival of Sacred Music)

*Decca*

- AKF 4 (10.73)

- SPA 297 (12.73)
- SPA 322 (  9.74)
- SPA 448 (  8.76)
- SPA 531 (10.78)
- SPA 566 (  9.80)
- SPA 588 (  4.81)

## USA ISSUES

*London*

○ LD 9066
○ LD 9088
○ LD 9096
○ LD 9097
○ LD 9098
○ LD 9099
○ LD 9137
○ LD 9229

*London*

- LLP 271
- LLP 625–6
- LLP 688
- LLP 845
- LLP 903
- LLP 924
- LLP 1529
- LLP 1670
-     5020
-     5069–70
-     5083
-     5092
-     5098
-     5103
-     5258
-     5291
-     5411

○ LPS 48
○ LPS 104
○ LPS 160
○ LPS 161
○ LPS 538
○ LPS 1032

- 414 095–1LH
- 414 194–1LJ
- 414 611–1LJ
- 414 623–1LJ
- 417 466–1LJ

*London*
- STS 15200
- STS 15201
- STS 15202

- 2-LONDON A–4212
  (Two-record set – Das Lied von der
  Erde and Three Rückert Lieder)

*American Columbia*

○ Masterworks ML 2187

● Masterworks ML 4980

*Richmond*
- R 23182
- R 23183
- R 23184
- R 23185
- R 23186
- R 23187
- R 23206

- 3–RICHMOND A 43001
  (Three-record set – St Matthew
  Passion)

*Bruno Walter Society*
*(Educ Media)*

- IGI 369

- IGI 374 (Two-record set –
  Mahler's Second Symphony and
  two songs from Das Lied von
  der Erde)

- BWS 707

- BWS 742

- DIS 3700

*CBS Odyssey*

- 2-Odyssey 32 26 0016
  (Two-record set – Kindertotenlieder
  and Mahler's Fifth Symphony)

*Capitol Seraphim*

- Seraphim M 60044
- Seraphim M 60203

- IH-6150 (Eight records – The Record of
  Singing Volume 4)

*Arabesque*

- Arabesque 8070

# Compact Discs
## BRITISH ISSUES

*EMI*

★ CDH 7 61003–2 ( 1.88)
★ CMS 7 63790–2 (11.90)
 (Limited Edition 5-CD set – Schwarzkopf)
★ CDM 7 63655-2 (12.90)
★ CHS 7 69741-2 (12.91)

*Decca*

★ 414 194–2DH (10.84)
★ 414 611–2DH ( 4.88)
★ 414 623–2DH (12.85)
★ 417 192–2DH ( 4.88)
★ 421 299–2DH ( 4.88)

*EMI*

(The Record of Singing Volume 4)

*Foyer*

★ 3 CF 2013 (1988) (Three-CD set – Matthäus-Passion)

★ 2 CF 2022 (1988) (Two-CD set – Mass in B Minor)

*Decca*

★ 425 970–2DM (11.90)
★ 425 995–2DM ( Spring 92)
★ 430 061–2LM (11.90)
★ 430 096–2DWO ( 9.90)
★ 433 468–2DM ( 4.92)
★ 433 469–2DM ( Spring 92)
★ 433 470–2DM ( Spring 92)
★ 433 471–2DM ( Spring 92)
★ 433 472–2DM ( Spring 92)
★ 433 473–2DM ( Spring 92)
★ 433 474–2DM ( Spring 92)
★ 433 475–2DM ( Spring 92)
★ 433 476–2DM ( Spring 92)
★ 433 477–2DM ( Spring 92)

*Danacord*

★ DACO CD 301 (1986)

*Verona*

★ 27016–7 (1989) (Two-CD set – Orfeo ed Euridice)

★ 27062–3 (1990) (Two-CD set – Mahler's Second Symphony & Lieder eines fahrenden Gesellen with Fischer-Dieskau)

★ 27070–2 (1989) (Three-CD set – Matthäus-Passion)

★ 27073–4 (1989) (Two-CD set – Mass in B Minor)

★ 27076 (1990)

# USA ISSUES

*London*

★ 414 194-2LH
★ 425 970-2LM
★ 425 995-2LM
★ 433 468-2LM
★ 433 469-2LM
★ 433 470-2LM
★ 433 471-2LM
★ 433 472-2LM
★ 433 473-2LM
★ 433 474-2LM
★ 433 475-2LM
★ 433 476-2LM
★ 433 477-2LM

*Angel*

★ CDH–61003
★ CDM–63655

# Tape Cassettes
## BRITISH ISSUES

*EMI*

•• EG 7 63655-4 (12.90)

*Decca*

••KACC 309 (11.73)

••KCSP 172 ( 6.72)
••KCSP 205 ( 5.72)
••KCSP 316 ( 1.74)
••KCSP 355 ( 8.74)
••KCSP 433 ( 9.75)
••KCSP 524 ( 6.78)

••K 264 K22 ( 9.82)
(Two tapes – Mahler's
Second Symphony)

••K MON2 7050 ( 2.78)

*BBC Artium*

•• ZCF 368 (R 12.79)

*Decca*

••KDPC 623–4 (12.78) (Two tapes
– Favourite composers –
Schumann)
••KDPC 627–8 (12.79) Two tapes –
music of England

••K 160 K54 ( 9.79)
(Set of four Cassettes – Nos 160
K1–4)
NB Cassette 160 K2 is in Re-
created stereo
••KECC 2178 (11.77)

••KLXTC 6934 ( 9.79)

*Rodolphe*

•• RPK 22407

*Decca*

••414 095–4DH ( 3.85)
••414 611–4DG ( 2.86)
••414 194–4DM ( 5.86)
••414 623–4DG ( 6.86)
••417 182–4DM ( 5.86)
••417 466–4DM ( 1.87)
••417 634–4DM (11.87)
••430 096–4DWO ( 9.90)
••430 061–4LM (11.90)
••433 468–4DM ( 4.92)
••433 469–4DM ( 4.92)
••433 470–4DM ( 4.92)
••433 471–4DM ( 4.92)
••433 472–4DM ( 4.92)
••433 473–4DM ( 4.92)
••433 474–4DM ( 4.92)
••433 475–4DM ( 4.92)
••433 476–4DM ( 4.92)
••433 477–4DM ( 4.92)

# Re-created Stereo Tape Cassettes

*Decca*

••KCSP 297 (11.73)
••KCSP 322 ( 8.74)

••KCSP 448 ( 8.76)
••KCSP 531 (10.78)
••KCSP 566 ( 9.80)
••KCSP 588 ( 4.81)

*Decca*

••KDPC 551–2 ( 9.76) (Two tapes
– Favourite composers Handel)

••KSDC 286 (11.73)
••160 K2 ( 9.79)

*Decca*

••411 887–4DN ( 9.84)
••414 047–4DN ( 1.85)

••414 048–4DN ( 1.85)
••421 175–4DC ( 2.88)

## USA ISSUES

*London*

••414 095–4LH
••414 194–4LJ
••414 611–4LJ
••414 623–4LJ
••417 466–4LJ
••433 469–4LM

*Arabesque*

••Arabesque 9070

## Stereo 8 Cartridges

*Decca*

- ECSP 172 ( 9.73)
- ECSP 205 (11.72)
- ECSP 316 ( 1.74)
- ECSP 355 ( 8.74)

## Re-created Stereo – Stereo 8 Cartridges

- ECSP 322 ( 8.74)

# Disc List – *Title by Title, UK and USA*

1  WHAT IS LIFE?

● HLM 7145

2  CONSTANCY

● HLM 7145

3  FEINSLIEBCHEN

● HLM 7145

4  MY WORK IS DONE . . . IT IS BECAUSE . . .

● HLM 7145

6  I WILL LAY ME DOWN IN PEACE

| □ DB 2152 | ◇ SED 5530 | ● HLM 7002 | ★ CDH 7 61003–2 |
|---|---|---|---|
| | | ● M 60203 | ★ CDH–61003 |

7  O PRAISE THE LORD

| □ DB 2152 | ◇ SED 5530 | ● HLM 7002 | ★ CDH 7 61003–2 |
|---|---|---|---|
| | | ● M 60203 | ★ CDH–61003 |

11  SPRING IS COMING

| ■ DX 1194 | ◇ SED 5526 ◇ SCD 2143 | ● HLM 7002 | ★ CDH 7 61003–2 |
|---|---|---|---|
| | | ● M 60203 | ★ CDH-61003 |

12  COME TO ME, SOOTHING SLEEP

| ■ DX 1194 | ◇ SED 5526 ◇ SCD 2143 | ● HLM 7002 | ★ CDH 7 61003–2 |
|---|---|---|---|
| | | ● M 60203 | ★ CDH–61003 |

16  SOUND THE TRUMPET

| □ DB 2201 | ◇ SED 5530 | ● HLM 7002 | ★ CDH 7 61003–2 |
|---|---|---|---|
| | | ● M 60203 | ★ CDH–61003 |

17  LET US WANDER

| □ DB 2201 | ◇ SED 5530 | ● HLM 7002 | ★ CDH 7 61003–2 |
|---|---|---|---|
| | | ● M 60203 | ★ CDH–61003 |

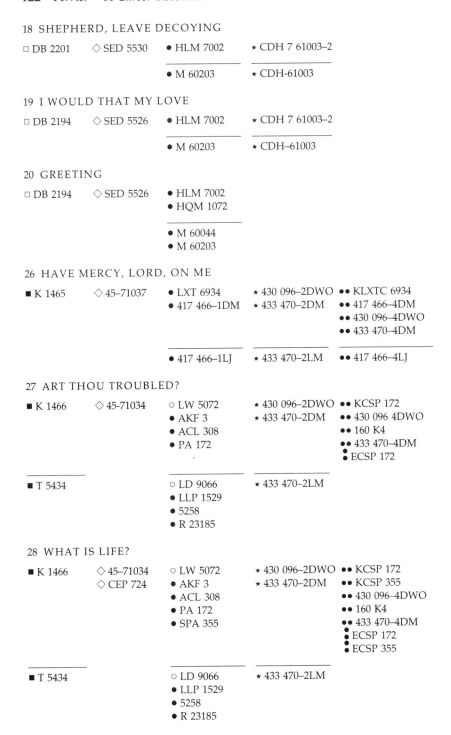

18 SHEPHERD, LEAVE DECOYING

□ DB 2201    ◇ SED 5530    ● HLM 7002    ★ CDH 7 61003–2

                            ● M 60203      ★ CDH-61003

19 I WOULD THAT MY LOVE

□ DB 2194    ◇ SED 5526    ● HLM 7002    ★ CDH 7 61003–2

                            ● M 60203      ★ CDH–61003

20 GREETING

□ DB 2194    ◇ SED 5526    ● HLM 7002
                            ● HQM 1072

                            ● M 60044
                            ● M 60203

26 HAVE MERCY, LORD, ON ME

■ K 1465    ◇ 45–71037    ● LXT 6934       ★ 430 096–2DWO   ●● KLXTC 6934
                          ● 417 466–1DM    ★ 433 470–2DM    ●● 417 466–4DM
                                                            ●● 430 096–4DWO
                                                            ●● 433 470–4DM

                          ● 417 466–1LJ    ★ 433 470–2LM    ●● 417 466–4LJ

27 ART THOU TROUBLED?

■ K 1466    ◇ 45-71034    ○ LW 5072        ★ 430 096–2DWO   ●● KCSP 172
                          ● AKF 3          ★ 433 470–2DM    ●● 430 096 4DWO
                          ● ACL 308                         ●● 160 K4
                          ● PA 172                          ●● 433 470–4DM
                            .                               ● ECSP 172

■ T 5434                  ○ LD 9066         ★ 433 470–2LM
                          ● LLP 1529
                          ● 5258
                          ● R 23185

28 WHAT IS LIFE?

■ K 1466    ◇ 45–71034    ○ LW 5072        ★ 430 096–2DWO   ●● KCSP 172
            ◇ CEP 724     ● AKF 3          ★ 433 470–2DM    ●● KCSP 355
                          ● ACL 308                         ●● 430 096–4DWO
                          ● PA 172                          ●● 160 K4
                          ● SPA 355                         ●● 433 470–4DM
                                                            ● ECSP 172
                                                            ● ECSP 355

■ T 5434                  ○ LD 9066         ★ 433 470–2LM
                          ● LLP 1529
                          ● 5258
                          ● R 23185

## 29 STABAT MATER

| ■ K 1517–21 | | ● LXT 6907 | ★ 433 470–2DM | ●● 417 466–4DM |
| ■ AK 1517–21 | | ● 417 466–1DM | | ●● 433 470–4DM |
| | | ● 417 466–1LJ | ★ 433 470–2LM | ●● 417 466–4LJ |

## 31 O REST IN THE LORD

| ■ K 1556 | ◇ 45–71039 | ○ LW 5072 | ★ 430 096–2DWO | ●● KCSP 316 |
| | ◇ CEP 724 | ● AKF 3 | ★ 433 470–2DM | ●● KCSP 433 |
| | | ● ACL 308 | | ●● 430 096–4DWO |
| | | ● SPA 316 | | ●● 160 K4 |
| | | ● SPA 433 | | ●● 433 470–4DM |
| | | | | ● ECSP 316 |
| | ◇ D 18060 | ○ LD 9066 | ★ 433 470–2LM | |
| | | ● LLP 1529 | | |
| | | ● 5258 | | |
| | | ● R 23185 | | |

## 32 WOE UNTO THEM

| ■ K 1556 | ◇ 45–71112 | ● AKF 3 | ★ 430 096–2DWO | ●● 430 096–4DWO |
| | ◇ CEP 724 | ● ACL 308 | ★ 433 470–2DM | ●● 433 470–4DM |
| | | ● R 23185 | ★ 433 470–2LM | |

## 33a ROME IS NOW RULED

## 33b MY HORSE! MY HORSE!

## 33c SHE SLEEPS AS A ROSE

## 33d HUSH HERE SHE COMES

## 33e LUCRETIA, LUCRETIA

| | | ● IGI 369 | | |

## 34a LUCRETIA, LUCRETIA, O NEVER AGAIN MUST WE TWO DARE TO PART

| | | ● REGL 368 | | ●● ZCF 368 |
| | | ● Arabesque 8070 | | ●● Arabesque 9070 |

## 36 GRETCHEN AM SPINNRADE

| ■ K 1632 | ◇ CEP 663 | ○ LW 5098 | ★ 430 096–2DWO | ●● 430 096–4DWO |
| | | ● AKF 6 | ★ 433 471–2DM | ●● 160 K4 |
| | | ● ACL 307 | | ●● 433 471-4DM |
| ■ T 5435 | | ○ LD 9099 | ★ 433 471–2LM | |
| | | ● LLP 1529 | | |
| | | ● 5258 | | |
| | | ● R 23184 | | |

## 37  DIE JUNGE NONNE

| ■ K 1632 | ◇ CEP 663 | ○ LW 5098 | ★ 430 096–2DWO | ●● 430 096–4DWO |
| | | ● AKF 6 | ★ 433 471–2DM | ●● 433 471–4DM |
| | | ● ACL 307 | | |

| ■ T 5435 | | ○ LD 9099 | ★ 433 471–2LM |
| | | ● LLP 1529 | |
| | | ● 5258 | |
| | | ● R 23184 | |

## 38  ORFEO ED EURIDICE – CONCISE

| ■ K 1656–62 | ● LXT 2893 | ★ 433 468–2DM | ●● 417 182–4DM |
| ■ AK 1656–62 | ● ACL 293 | | ●● 433 468–4DM |
| | ● 417 182–1DM | | |

| | ● LLP 924 | ★ 433 468–2LM |
| | ● 5103 | |

## 38a  CHE PURO CIEL

| ■ K 1659 | ○ LW 5225 | ●● KCSP 172 |
| ■ AK 1662 | ● PA 172 | ●● ECSP 172 |

| | ○ LD 9229 | |

## 39  ST MATTHEW PASSION – ABRIDGED

■ K 1673–9    (For excerpts, see under 40)
■ AK 1673–9

## 40  ST MATTHEW PASSION – (ALMOST) COMPLETE

| ■ AK 2001–21 | ● ACL 109–11 |
| | ● D 42 D3 |

| | ● 3-RICHMOND A 43001 |

## 40a  COME, YE DAUGHTERS

| ■AK 2001-2–3 | ★ 433 469–2DM | ●● 433 469–4DM |

| | ★ 433 469–2LM | ●● 433 469–4LM |

## 40b  MY MASTER AND MY LORD . . . GRIEF FOR SIN

| ■ AK 2004–5 | ● ACL 308 | ★ 433 469–2DM | ●● 433 469–4DM |
| ■ K 1673 (Aria only) | | | |
| ■ AK 1673 (Aria only) | | | |

| | ● R 23185 | ★ 433 469–2LM | ●● 433 469–4LM |

## 40c  BEHOLD, MY SAVIOUR . . . HAVE LIGHTNINGS

| ■ AK 2008–9 | ★ 433 469–2DM | ●● 433 469–4DM |

| | ★ 433 469–2LM | ●● 433 469–4LM |

### 40d AH! NOW IS MY SAVIOUR GONE

| | | | |
|---|---|---|---|
| ■ AK 2012–3 | ● AKF 3<br>● ACL 308 | ★ 433 469–2DM | ●● 433 469–4DM |
| | ● R 23185 | ★ 433 469–2LM | ●● 433 469–4LM |

### 40e HAVE MERCY, LORD, ON ME

| | | | |
|---|---|---|---|
| ■ AK 2012–1<br>■ K 1676<br>■ AK 1676 | ● AKF 3<br>● ACL 308<br>● PA 172 | ★ 433 469–2DM | ●● KCSP 172<br>●● 433 469–4DM<br>⦂ ECSP 172 |
| | ● R 23185 | ★ 433 469–2LM | ●● 433 469–4LM |

### 40f LAMB OF GOD

| | | | |
|---|---|---|---|
| ■ K 1676<br>■ AK 1679<br>■ AK 2011 | | ★ 433 469–2DM | ●● 433 469–4DM |
| | | ★ 433 469–2LM | ●● 433 469–4LM |

### 40g O GRACIOUS GOD! . . . IF MY TEARS BE UNAVAILING

| | | | |
|---|---|---|---|
| ■ AK 2017–8 | ● AKF 3<br>● ACL 308 | ★ 433 469–2DM | ●● 433 469–4DM |
| | ● R 23185 | ★ 433 469–2LM | ●● 433 469–4LM |

### 40h O SACRED HEAD

| | | | |
|---|---|---|---|
| ■ AK 2019 | | ★ 433 469–2DM | ●● 433 469–4DM |
| | | ★ 433 469–2LM | ●● 433 469–4LM |

### 40i AH, GOLGOTHA! . . . SEE THE SAVIOUR'S OUTSTRETCHED HANDS

| | | | |
|---|---|---|---|
| ■ AK 2020–1<br>■ K 1678 (Aria only)<br>■ AK 1676 (Aria only) | ● AKF 3<br>● ACL 308 | ★ 433 469–2DM | ●● 433 469–4DM |
| | ● R 23185 | ★ 433 469–2LM | ●● 433 469–4LM |

### 40j BE NEAR ME, LORD

| | | | |
|---|---|---|---|
| ■ K 1678<br>■ AK 1675<br>■ AK 2020 | | ★ 433 469–2DM | ●● 433 469–4DM |
| | | ★ 433 469–2LM | ●● 433 469–4LM |

### 40k AND NOW THE LORD

| | | | |
|---|---|---|---|
| ■ AK 2017 | | ★ 433 469–2DM | ●● 433 469–4DM |
| | | ★ 433 469–2LM | ●● 433 469–4LM |

## 401 IN TEARS OF GRIEF

■ K 1679                                    ★ 433 469–2DM        •• 433 469–4DM
■ AK 1674–3
■ AK 2016–5

                                           ★ 433 469–2LM        •• 433 469–4LM

## 44 BEETHOVEN'S NINTH SYMPHONY

                                • BWS 742

## 48 ALTO RHAPSODY

■ K 1847–8     ◇ CEP 569     • LXT 2850      ★ 421 299–2DH        •• 433 477–4DM
■ AK 1847–8                  • AKF 5          ★ 433 477–2DM
                             • ACL 306

                             • LLP 903        ★ 433 477–2LM
                             • 5098
                             • R 23183
                             • STS 15201

## 51a VON DER SCHÖNHEIT

## 51b DER ABSCHIED

                                • IGI 374

## 52 FOUR POEMS OF ST TERESA OF AVILA

                                • REGL 368                        •• ZCF 368

                                • Arabesque 8070                  •• Arabesque 9070

## 56 SILENT NIGHT, HOLY NIGHT

□ M 622        ◇ 45–71036    • LXT 6934      ★ 433 473–2DM        •• KLXTC 6934
               ◇ CEP 518     • PA 172                             •• KCSP 172
                                                                  •• 433 473–4DM
                                                                  ● ECSP 172

■ T 5052       ◇ 45–40166                     ★ 433 473–2LM

## 57 O COME ALL YE FAITHFUL

□ M 622        ◇ 45–71036    • LXT 6934      ★ 433 473–2DM        •• KLXTC 6934
               ◇ CEP 518                                          •• 433 473–4DM

■ T 5052       ◇ 45–40166                     ★ 433 473–2LM

## 58 LOVE IS A BABLE

                                • REGL 368                        •• ZCF 368

                                • Arabesque 8070                  •• Arabesque 9070

## 59 FRONDI TENERE . . . OMBRA MAI FU

| ■ K 2135 | ◇ 45–71039 | ○ LW 5072 | ★ 430 096–2DWO | ●● 430 096–4DWO |
|---|---|---|---|---|
| | ◇ CEP 724 | ● AKF 3 | ★ 433 470–2DM | ●● 433 470–4DM |
| | | ● ACL 308 | | |

| ■ T 5349 | ◇ D 18060 | ○ LD 9066 | ★ 433 470–2LM |
|---|---|---|---|
| | | ○ LPS 104 | |
| | | ● LLP 1529 | |
| | | ● 5258 | |
| | | ● R 23185 | |

## 61 FOUR SERIOUS SONGS

| | ● LXT 6934 | ★ 433 472–2DM | ●● KLXTC 6934 |
|---|---|---|---|
| | ● 414 095–1DH | | ●● 414 095–4DH |
| | | | ●● 433 472–4DM |

| | ● 414 095–1LH | ★ 433 472–2LM | ●● 414 095–4LH |
|---|---|---|---|

## 62 BLOW THE WIND SOUTHERLY

| □ F 9300 | ◇ 45–71135 | ○ LX 3040 | ★ 417 192–2DH | ●● KACC 309 |
|---|---|---|---|---|
| | ◇ CEP 725 | ○ LW 5225 | ★ 430 096–2DWO | ●● KCSP 172 |
| | | ○ BR 3052 | ★ 433 475–2DM | ●● KCSP 205 |
| | | ● AKF 1 | | ●● KECC 2178 |
| | | ● ACL 309 | | ●● KDPC 627 |
| | | ● PA 172 | | ●● 430 096–4DWO |
| | | ● SPA 205 | | ●● 160 K4 |
| | | ● DPA 627 | | ●● 433 475–4DM |
| | | ● ECS 2178 | | ⦙ ECSP 172 |
| | | | | ⦙ ECSP 205 |

| □ R 10102 | | ○ LD 9229 | ★ 433 475–2LM |
|---|---|---|---|
| | | ○ LPS 48 | |
| | | ● 5411 | |
| | | ● R 23186 | |

## 63 MA BONNY LAD

| □ F9300 | ◇ 45–71135 | ○ LX 3040 | ★ 417 192–2DH | ●● KACC 309 |
|---|---|---|---|---|
| | ◇ CEP 725 | ○ BR 3052 | ★ 430 096–2DWO | ●● KCSP 172 |
| | | ● AKF 1 | ★ 433 475–2DM | ●● 430 096–4DWO |
| | | ● ACL 309 | | ●● 160 K4 |
| | | ● PA 172 | | ●● 433 475–4DM |
| | | | | ⦙ ECSP 172 |

| □ R 10102 | | ○ LPS 48 | ★ 433 475–2LM |
|---|---|---|---|
| | | ● 5411 | |
| | | ● R 23186 | |

## 64  THE KEEL ROW

| □ F 9300 | ◇ 45–71135 | ○ LX 3040 | ★ 417 192–2DH | ●● KACC 309 |
|---|---|---|---|---|
| | | ● AKF 1 | ★ 430 096–2DWO | ●● KCSP 172 |
| | | ● ACL 309 | ★ 433 475–2DM | ●● KDPC 627 |
| | | ● PA 172 | | ●● 430 096–4DWO |
| | | ● DPA 627 | | ●● 160 K4 |
| | | | | ●● 433 475–4DM |
| | | | | ● ECSP 172 |

| □ R 10102 | | ○ LPS 48 | ★ 433 475–2LM | |
|---|---|---|---|---|
| | | ● 5411 | | |
| | | ● R 23186 | | |

## 65  HAVE YOU SEEN BUT A WHYTE LILLIE GROW?

| | ◇ CEP 725 | ○ LX 3040 | ★ 417 192–2DH | ●● KACC 309 |
|---|---|---|---|---|
| | | ○ BR 3052 | ★ 433 475–2DM | ●● 433 475–4DM |
| | | ● AKF 1 | | |
| | | ● ACL 309 | | |

| □ R 10103 | | ○ LPS 48 | ★ 433 475–2LM | |
|---|---|---|---|---|
| | | ● 5411 | | |
| | | ● R 23186 | | |

## 66  WILLOW, WILLOW

| | ◇ CEP 725 | ○ LX 3040 | ★ 417 192–2DH | ●● KACC 309 |
|---|---|---|---|---|
| | | ○ BR 3052 | ★ 433 475–2DM | ●● 160 K4 |
| | | ● AKF 1 | | ●● 433 475–4DM |
| | | ● ACL 309 | | |

| □ R 10103 | | ○ LPS 48 | ★ 433 475–2LM | |
|---|---|---|---|---|
| | | ● 5411 | | |
| | | ● R 23186 | | |

## 67  THE LOVER'S CURSE

| | | ○ LX 3040 | ★ 417 192–2DH | ●● KACC 309 |
|---|---|---|---|---|
| | | ○ BR 3052 | ★ 433 475–2DM | ●● 160 K4 |
| | | ● AKF 1 | | ●● 433 475–4DM |
| | | ● ACL 309 | | |

| □ R 10104 | | ○ LPS 48 | ★ 433 475–2LM | |
|---|---|---|---|---|
| | | ● 5411 | | |
| | | ● R 23186 | | |

## 68  DOWN BY THE SALLEY GARDENS

| | ◇ 45–71135 | ○ LX 3040 | ★ 417 192–2DH | ●● KACC 309 |
|---|---|---|---|---|
| | ◇ CEP 518 | ○ BR 3052 | ★ 433 475–2DM | ●● 433 475–4DM |
| | ◇ CEP 725 | ● AKF 1 | | |
| | | ● ACL 309 | | |

| □ R 10104 | | ○ LPS 48 | ★ 433 475–2LM | |
|---|---|---|---|---|
| | | ● 5411 | | |
| | | ● R 23186 | | |

70  AN DIE MUSIK

| □ M 652 | ◇ CEP 663 | ○ LW 5098 | ★ 430 096–2DWO | ●● KCSP 172 |
| | ◇ CEP 719 | ● AKF 6 | ★ 433 471–2DM | ●● 430 096–4DWO |
| | | ● ACL 307 | | ●● 160 K4 |
| | | ● PA 172 | | ●● 433 471–4DM |
| | | ● SPA 524 | | ● ECSP 172 |

| | | ○ LD 9099 | ★ 433 471–2LM | |
| | | ● LLP 1529 | | |
| | | ● 5258 | | |
| | | ● R 23184 | | |

71  GESTILLTE SEHNSUCHT

| ■ K 2289 | ◇ CEP 720 | ● LXT 2850 | ★ 421 299–2DH | ●● 433 477–4DM |
| | | ● AKF 5 | ★ 433 477–2DM | |
| | | ● ACL 306 | | |

| ■ T 5647 | | ● LLP 903 | ★ 433 477–2LM | |
| | | ● 5098 | | |
| | | ● R 23183 | | |

72  GEISTLICHES WIEGENLIED

| ■ K 2289 | ◇ CEP 720 | ● LXT 2850 | ★ 421 299–2DH | ●● 433 477–4DM |
| | | ● AKF 5 | ★ 433 477–2DM | |
| | | ● ACL 306 | | |

| ■ T 5647 | | ● LLP 903 | ★ 433 477–2LM | |
| | | ● 5098 | | |
| | | ● R 23183 | | |

73a  THE FLORAL DANCE

| | | ● REGL 368 | | ●● ZCF 368 |

| | | ● Arabesque 8070 | | ●● Arabesque 9070 |

77–87  DIE JUNGE NONNE

    DER VOLLMOND STRAHLT

    DU LIEBST MICH NICHT

    DER TOD UND DAS MÄDCHEN

    SULEIKA 1

    DU BIST DIE RUH'

    FRAUENLIEBE UND LEBEN

    IMMER LEISER WIRD MEIN SCHLUMMER

    DER TOD, DAS IST DIE KÜHLE NACHT

    BOTSCHAFT

VON EWIGER LIEBE

| | | |
|---|---|---|
| ● 6BB 197–8 | ★ 414 611–2DH | ●● 414 611–4DG |
| ● 414 611–1DG | ★ 433 476–2DM | ●● 160 K3 |
| | | ●● 433 476–4DM |

| | | |
|---|---|---|
| ● 414 611–1LJ | ★ 433 476–2LM | ●● 414 611–4LJ |
| ● BWS 707 | | |

83 FRAUENLIEBE UND LEBEN ONLY

● DIS 3700

88 WHAT THE EDINBURGH FESTIVAL HAS MEANT TO ME

| | | |
|---|---|---|
| ● 6BB 197 | ★ 414 611–2DH | ●● 414 611–4DG |
| ● 414 611–1DG | ★ 433 476–2DM | ●● 433 476–4DM |

| | | |
|---|---|---|
| ● 414 611–1LJ | ★ 433 476–2LM | ●● 414 611–4LJ |

88a EXTRACT FROM TALK

| | |
|---|---|
| ● REGL 368 | ●● ZCF 368 |

| | |
|---|---|
| ● Arabesque 8070 | ●● Arabesque 9070 |

89 KINDERTOTENLIEDER

■ LX 8939–41

| | |
|---|---|
| ○ 33C 1009 | ★ CDH 7 61003–2 |
| ● HLM 7002 | |

| | |
|---|---|
| ○ ML 2187 | ★ CDH–61003 |
| ● ML 4980 | |
| ● M 60203 | |
| ● 32 26 0016 | |

90–92 ALTO RHAPSODY

VON EWIGER LIEBE

WIR WANDELTEN

| | |
|---|---|
| ● DACO 114 | ★ DACO CD 301 |

94 HARK! THE ECHOING AIR

| | | |
|---|---|---|
| ● LXT 5324 | ★ 433 473–2DM | ●● 433 473–4DM |
| ● AKF 2 | | |
| ● ACL 310 | | |

| | |
|---|---|
| ● LLP 1670 | ★ 433 473–2LM |
| ● 5291 | |
| ● R 23187 | |

95  LIKE AS THE LOVE-LORN TURTLE

        ◇ CEP 587    ● LXT 5324    ★ 433 473–2DM    ●● 433 473–4DM
                        ● AKF 2
                        ● ACL 310

                        ● LLP 1670    ★ 433 473–2LM
                        ● 5291
                        ● R 23187

96  HOW CHANGED THE VISION

                        ● LXT 5324    ★ 433 473–2DM    ●● 433 473–4DM
                        ● AKF 2
                        ● ACL 310

                        ● LLP 1670    ★ 433 473–2LM
                        ● 5291
                        ● R 23187

97  MAD BESS OF BEDLAM

        ◇ CEP 5508    ● AKF 3    ★ 433 473–2DM    ●● 433 473–4DM
                        ● ACL 310

                        ● R 23187    ★ 433 473–2LM

98  VERBORGENHEIT

                        ● LXT 5324    ★ 433 473–2DM    ●● 433 473–4DM
                        ● AKF 2
                        ● ACL 307

                        ● LLP 1670    ★ 433 473–2LM
                        ● 5291
                        ● R 23184

99  DER GÄRTNER

                        ● LXT 5324    ★ 433 473–2DM    ●● 433 473–4DM
                        ● AKF 2
                        ● ACL 307

                        ● LLP 1670    ★ 433 473–2LM
                        ● 5291
                        ● R 23184

100  AUF EIN ALTES BILD

        ◇ CEP 587    ● LXT 5324    ★ 433 473–2DM    ●● 433 473–4DM
                        ● AKF 2
                        ● ACL 307

                        ● LLP 1670    ★ 433 473–2LM
                        ● 5291
                        ● R 23184

**101 AUF EINER WANDERUNG**

| | | |
|---|---|---|
| ● LXT 5324 | ★ 433 473–2DM | ●● 433 473–4DM |
| ● AKF 2 | | |
| ● ACL 307 | | |
| | | |
| ● LLP 1670 | ★ 433 473–2LM | |
| ● 5291 | | |
| ● R 23184 | | |

**102 ALTAR**

◇ CEP 587

| | | |
|---|---|---|
| ● LXT 5324 | ★ 433 473–2DM | ●● KCSP 172 |
| ● AKF 2 | | ●● 433 473–4DM |
| ● PA 172 | | • ECSP 172 |
| | | |
| ● LLP 1670 | ★ 433 473–2LM | |
| ● 5291 | | |

**103 CANTATA NO. 11 (78 rpm VERSION)**

■ AX 399–401

**104 CANTATA NO. 11 (33 rpm VERSION)**

| | |
|---|---|
| ○ LX 3006 | ●● 417 466–4DM |
| ● ACL 52 | |
| ● ECS 562 | |
| ● 417 466–1DM | |
| | |
| ○ LPS 160 | ●● 417 466–4LJ |
| ● LLP 845 | |
| ● 5092 | |
| ● R 23206 | |
| ● 417 466–1LJ | |

**104a AH, TARRY YET, MY DEAREST SAVIOUR**

| | | |
|---|---|---|
| ● LXT 6934 | ★ 433 470–2DM | ●● KLXTC 6934 |
| | | ●● 433 470–4DM |
| | ★ 433 470–2LM | |

**105 CANTATA NO. 67 (78 rpm VERSION)**

■ AX 347–8

**106 CANTATA NO. 67 (33 rpm VERSION)**

| |
|---|
| ○ LX 3007 |
| ● ACL 52 |
| ● ECS 562 |
| |
| ○ LPS 161 |
| ● 5092 |
| ● R 23206 |

107  VERGISS MEIN NICHT

| | | |
|---|---|---|
| • 414 095–1DH | ★ 433 473–2DM | •• 414 095–4DH |
| | | •• 433 473–4DM |
| • 414 095–1LH | ★ 433 473–2LM | •• 414 095–4LH |

108  ACH, DASS NICHT DIE LETZTE STUNDE

| | | |
|---|---|---|
| • 414 095–1DH | ★ 433 473–2DM | •• 414 095–4DH |
| | | •• 433 473–4DM |
| • 414 095–1LH | ★ 433 473–2LM | •• 414 095–4LH |

110  SAPPHISCHE ODE

| | | | |
|---|---|---|---|
| ◇ 45–71130 | • LXT 2850 | ★ 430 096–2DWO | •• KCSP 172 |
| ◇ CEP 719 | • AKF 5 | ★ 433 471–2DM | •• 430 096–4DWO |
| | • ACL 306 | | •• 433 471–4DM |
| | • PA 172 | | • ECSP 172 |
| | • LLP 903 | ★ 433 471–2LM | |
| | • 5098 | | |
| | • R 23183 | | |

111  BOTSCHAFT

| | | | |
|---|---|---|---|
| ◇ 45–71130 | • LXT 2850 | ★ 430 096–2DWO | •• 430 096–4DWO |
| ◇ CEP 719 | • AKF 5 | ★ 433 471–2DM | •• 433 471–4DM |
| | • ACL 306 | | |
| | • LLP 903 | ★ 433 471–2LM | |
| | • 5098 | | |
| | • R 23183 | | |

112  DER MUSENSOHN

| | | | | |
|---|---|---|---|---|
| □ M 652 | ◇ CEP 719 | ○ LW 5098 | ★ 430 096–2DWO | •• KCSP 172 |
| | ◇ CEP 663 | • AKF 6 | ★ 433 471–2DM | •• KCSP 524 |
| | | • ACL 307 | | •• 430 096–4DWO |
| | | • PA 172 | | •• 160 K4 |
| | | • SPA 524 | | •• 433 471–4DM |
| | | | | • ECSP 172 |
| | | ○ LD 9099 | ★ 433 471–2LM | |
| | | • LLP 1529 | | |
| | | • 5258 | | |
| | | • R 23184 | | |

117a  INTERVIEW EXCERPTS

| | |
|---|---|
| • REGL 368 | •• ZCF 368 |
| • Arabesque 8070 | •• Arabesque 9070 |

119  BIST DU BEI MIR

⋆ 433 473–2DM    •• 433 473–4DM

⋆ 433 473–2LM

120  MATTHÄUS–PASSION

● FO 1046    ⋆ Foyer 3CF 2013
⋆ Verona CD 27070–2

120a  DU LIEBER HEILAND DU . . . BUSS UND REU

120b  SO IST MEIN JESUS NUN GEFANGEN

120c  ACH, NUN IST MEIN JESUS HIN

120d  ERBARME DICH, MEIN GOTT

120e  ERBARM' ES GOTT . . . KÖNNEN TRÄNEN

120f  ACH GOLGATHA . . .  SEHET, JESUS HAT DIE HAND

⋆ Verona CD 27076

121  CHRISTE ELEISON

⋆ CDM 7 63655–2    •• EG 763655–4
⋆ CMS 7 63790–2

⋆ CDM–63655

122  LAUDAMUS TE

⋆ CDM 7 63655–2 •• EG 763655–4
⋆ CMS 7 63790–2

⋆ CDM–63655

123  QUI SEDES

124  AGNUS DEI

⋆ CHS 7 69741–2

125  ET IN UNUM DOMINUM

⋆ CDM 7 63655–2 •• EG 763655–4
⋆ CMS 7 63790–2

⋆ CDM–63655

126  MASS IN B MINOR

⋆ Foyer 2CF 2022
⋆ Verona CD 27073–4

126a  CHRISTE ELEISON

126b  QUI SEDES

126c  ET IN UNUM DOMINUM

126d  AGNUS DEI

⋆ Verona CD 27076

131  FRAUENLIEBE UND LEBEN

| | | | |
|---|---|---|---|
| | ○ LW 5089 | ⋆ 433 471–2DM | •• KDPC 624 |
| | • LXT 2556 | | •• 433 471–4DM |
| | • AKF 6 | | |
| | • ACL 307 | | |
| | • DPA 624 | | |
| | ○ LD 9098 | ⋆ 433 471–2LM | |
| | • LLP 271 | | |
| | • 5020 | | |
| | • R 23184 | | |

132  WIDMUNG

| | | | |
|---|---|---|---|
| ◇ 45–71130 | ○ LW 5098 | ⋆ 433 471–2DM | •• 433 471–4DM |
| ◇ CEP 719 | • AKF 6 | | |
| | • ACL 307 | | |
| | ○ LD 9099 | ⋆ 433 471–2LM | |
| | • LLP 1529 | | |
| | • 5258 | | |
| | • R 23184 | | |

133  VOLKSLIEDCHEN

| | | | |
|---|---|---|---|
| ◇ 45–71130 | ○ LW 5098 | ⋆ 433 471–2DM | •• 433 471–4DM |
| ◇ CEP 719 | • AKF 6 | | |
| | • ACL 307 | | |
| | ○ LD 9099 | ⋆ 433 471–2LM | |
| | • LLP 1529 | | |
| | • 5258 | | |
| | • R 23184 | | |

134  VIER ERNSTE GESÄNGE

| | | | |
|---|---|---|---|
| ■ AX 563–4 | ○ LW 5094 | ⋆ 421 299–2DH | •• 433 477–4DM |
| | • LXT 2556 | ⋆ 433 477–2DM | |
| | • AKF 5 | | |
| | • ACL 306 | | |
| | ○ LD 9097 | ⋆ 433 477–2LM | |
| | • LLP 271 | | |
| | • 5020 | | |
| | • R 23183 | | |

135  THE FIDGETY BAIRN

| □ M 657 | ◇ CEP 5508 | ● AKF 1<br>● ACL 309 | ★ 417 192–2DH<br>★ 433 475–2DM | ●● KACC 309<br>●● 433 475–4DM |
|---|---|---|---|---|
| | | ● R 23186 | ★ 433 475–2LM | |

136  CA' THE YOWES

| □ M 657 | ◇ 45–71072<br>◇ CEP 5508 | ● AKF 1<br>● ACL 309<br>● EX 7697431 | ★ 417 192–2DH<br>★ 433 475–2DM | ●● KACC 309<br>●● 160 K4<br>●● 433 475–4DM |
|---|---|---|---|---|
| | | ● R 23186<br>● IH–6150 | ★ 433 475–2LM | |

141–151  WHERE 'ER YOU WALK

LIKE AS THE LOVE-LORN TURTLE

HARK! THE ECHOING AIR

LASCIATEMI MORIRE

PUR DICESTI

EURIDICE . . . CHE FARÒ?

LACHEN UND WEINEN

SONNTAG

LOVE IS A BABLE

THE FAIRY LOUGH

CA' THE YOWES

| ● Rococo 5265<br>● RP 12407 | ●● RPK 22407 |
|---|---|

152  THE SPANISH LADY

| ● Rococo 5265<br>● RP 12407<br>● REGL 368 | ●● RPK 22407<br>●● ZCF 368 |
|---|---|
| ● Arabesque 8070 | ●● Arabesque 9070 |

153  POÈME DE L'AMOUR ET DE LA MER

| ● 414 095–1DH | ★ 433 472–2DM | ●● 414 095–4DH<br>●● 433 472–4DM |
|---|---|---|
| ● 414 095–1LH | ★ 433 472–2LM | ●● 414 095–4LH |

156  ORFEO ED EURIDICE

| ● RLS 725 | ★ Verona CD 27016–7 |
|---|---|

156a  CHIAMO IL MIO BEN

156b  DEH! PLACATEVI CON ME

156c  CHE PURO CIEL

156d  CHE HO FATTO . . . CHE FARÒ?

|  |  |
|---|---|
| ★ CDH 7 61003–2 |  |
| ★ CDH–61003 |  |

156e  AH PIÙ NON M'ODE . . . CHE FARÒ?

| ● REGL 368 | ●● ZCF 368 |
|---|---|
| ● Arabesque 8070 | ●● Arabesque 9070 |

157  KINDERTOTENLIEDER

| ● 417 634–1DM | ★ 425 995–2DM | ●● 417 634–4DM |
|---|---|---|
|  | ★ 425 995–2LM |  |

158  MAHLER'S SECOND SYMPHONY

| ● D 264 D2 | ★ Verona CD 27062 | ●● K 264 K2 |
|---|---|---|
|  | ★ 425 970–2DM |  |
| ● IGI 374 | ★ 425 970–2LM |  |

158a  URLICHT

| ★ Verona CD 27076 |
|---|

160  O WALY, WALY

| ◇ 45–71072 | ○ LX 3098 | ★ 417 192–2DH | ●● KACC 309 |
|---|---|---|---|
| ◇ CEP 726 | ● BR 3052 | ★ 433 475–2DM | ●● 433 475–4DM |
|  | ● AKF 1 |  |  |
|  | ● ACL 309 |  |  |
|  | ○ LPS 538 | ★ 433 475–2LM |  |
|  | ● 5411 |  |  |
|  | ● R 23186 |  |  |

161  I HAVE A BONNET

| ◇ 45–71108 | ○ LX 3098 | ★ 417 192–2DH | ●● KACC 309 |
|---|---|---|---|
|  | ● AKF 1 | ★ 433 475–2DM | ●● 433 475–4DM |
|  | ● ACL 309 |  |  |
|  | ○ LPS 538 | ★ 433 475–2LM |  |
|  | ● 5411 |  |  |
|  | ● R 23186 |  |  |

162  MY BOY WILLIE

| | | ◇ 45–71108 | ○ LX 3098 | ★ 417 192–2DH | •• KACC 309 |
| | | | • AKF 1 | ★ 433 475–2DM | •• 433 475–4DM |
| | | | • ACL 309 | | |
| | | | ○ LPS 538 | ★ 433 475–2LM | |
| | | | • 5411 | | |
| | | | • R 23186 | | |

163  I WILL WALK WITH MY LOVE

| □ M 681 | ◇ 45–71108 | ○ LX 3098 | ★ 417 192–2DH | •• KACC 309 |
| | ◇ CEP 725 | ○ BR 3052 | ★ 433 475–2DM | •• 433 475–4DM |
| | | • AKF 1 | | |
| | | • ACL 309 | | |
| | | ○ LPS 538 | ★ 433 475–2LM | |
| | | • 5411 | | |
| | | • R 23186 | | |

164  THE STUTTERING LOVERS

| □ M 681 | ◇ 45–71108 | ○ LX 3098 | ★ 417 192–2DH | •• KACC 309 |
| | | • AKF 1 | ★ 433 475–2DM | •• 433 475–4DM |
| | | • ACL 309 | | |
| | | ○ LPS 538 | ★ 433 475–2LM | |
| | | • 5411 | | |
| | | • R 23186 | | |

165  NOW SLEEPS THE CRIMSON PETAL

| □ M 680 | ◇ 45–71139 | ○ LX 3098 | ★ 417 192–2DH | •• KACC 309 |
| | ◇ CEP 726 | ○ BR 3052 | ★ 433 475–2DM | •• 433 475–4DM |
| | | • AKF 1 | | |
| | | • ACL 309 | | |
| | | ○ LPS 538 | ★ 433 475–2LM | |
| | | • 5411 | | |
| | | • R 23186 | | |

166  I KNOW WHERE I'M GOING

| □ M 681 | ◇ CEP 726 | ○ LX 3098 | ★ 417 192–2DH | •• KACC 309 |
| | | ○ BR 3052 | ★ 433 475–2DM | •• 433 475–4DM |
| | | • AKF 1 | | |
| | | • ACL 309 | | |
| | | ○ LPS 538 | ★ 433 475–2LM | |
| | | • 5411 | | |
| | | • R 23186 | | |

167  THE FAIR HOUSE OF JOY

    ◇ 45–71139    ○ LX 3098    ★ 417 192–2DH    ●● KACC 309
                    ● AKF 1      ★ 433 475–2DM    ●● 433 475–4DM
                    ● ACL 309

                    ○ LPS 538    ★ 433 475–2LM
                    ● 5411
                    ● R 23186

168  TO DAISIES

□ M 680    ◇ 45–71139    ● AKF 1    ★ 417 192–2DH    ●● KACC 309
                    ● ACL 309  ★ 433 475–2DM    ●● 433 475–4DM

                    ● R 23186  ★ 433 475–2LM

169  OVER THE MOUNTAINS

    ◇ 45–71139    ○ LX 3098    ★ 417 192–2DH    ●● KACC 309
                    ● AKF 1      ★ 433 475–2DM    ●● 433 475–4DM
                    ● ACL 309

                    ○ LPS 538    ★ 433 475–2LM
                    ● 5411
                    ● R 23186

170  YE BANKS AND YE BRAES

□ M 679    ◇ 45–71035    ○ LX 3098    ★ 417 192–2DH    ●● KACC 309
         ◇ CEP 518    ○ BR 3052    ★ 433 475–2DM    ●● 160 K4
        ◇ CEP 726    ● AKF 1                  ●● 433 475–4DM
                    ● ACL 309

                    ○ LPS 538    ★ 433 475–2LM
                    ● 5411
                    ● R 23186

171  DRINK TO ME ONLY

□ M 679    ◇ 45–71035    ○ LX 3098    ★ 417 192–2DH    ●● KACC 309
         ◇ CEP 518    ○ BR 3052    ★ 433 475–2DM    ●● 160 K4
        ◇ CEP 726    ● AKF 1                  ●● 433 475–4DM
                    ● ACL 309

                    ○ LPS 538    ★ 433 475–2LM
                    ● 5411
                    ● R 23186

176  GANYMED

                              ★ 433 471–2DM    ●● 433 471–4DM

                              ★ 433 471–2LM

177  DU LIEBST MICH NICHT

                                 ★ 433 471–2DM     •• 433 471–4DM

                                 ★ 433 471–2LM

178  LACHEN UND WEINEN

                                 ★ 433 471–2DM     •• 433 471–4DM

                                 ★ 433 471–2LM

179  RUHE SÜSSLIEBCHEN IN SCHATTEN

                        • REGL 368                       •• ZCF 368

                        • Arabesque 8070           •• Arabesque 9070

180  AUF DEM SEE

                        • REGL 368                       •• ZCF 368

                        • Arabesque 8070           •• Arabesque 9070

182  ES SCHAUEN DIE BLUMEN

                        • REGL 368                       •• ZCF 368

                        • Arabesque 8070           •• Arabesque 9070

183  DER JÄGER

                        • REGL 368                       •• ZCF 368

                        • Arabesque 8070           •• Arabesque 9070

185  DAS LIED VON DER ERDE

| | | | |
|---|---|---|---|
| • LXT 2721–2 | ★ 414 194–2DH | •• KMON 2 7050 | |
| • LXT 5576 | | •• 414 194–4DM | |
| • LXT 6278 | | •• 160 K1 | |
| • AKF 7 | | | |
| • ACL 305 | | | |
| • 414 194–1DM | | | |
| • LLP 625–6 | ★ 414 194–2LH | •• 414 194–4LJ | |
| • 5069–70 | | | |
| • R 23182 | | | |
| • STS 15200 | | | |
| • 2-London A-4212 | | | |
| • 414 194–1LJ | | | |

186 ICH BIN DER WELT ABHANDEN GEKOMMEN

| | | |
|---|---|---|
| ○ LW 5123 | ⋆ 421 299–2DH | •• KMON 2 7050 |
| • LXT 2721 | ⋆ 433 477–2DM | •• 160 K1 |
| • AKF 6 | | •• 433 477–4DM |
| • ACL 318 | | |

| | |
|---|---|
| ○ LD 9137 | ⋆ 433 477–2LM |
| • LLP 625 | |
| • 5069 | |
| • STS 15202 | |
| • 2-London A-4212 | |

187 ICH ATMET' EINEN LINDEN DUFT

| | | |
|---|---|---|
| ○ LW 5123 | ⋆ 421 299–2DH | •• KMON 2 7050 |
| • LXT 2721 | ⋆ 433 477–2DM | •• 160 K1 |
| • AKF 6 | | •• 433 477–4DM |
| • ACL 318 | | |

| | |
|---|---|
| ○ LD 9137 | ⋆ 433 477–2LM |
| • LLP 625 | |
| • 5069 | |
| • STS 15202 | |
| • 2-London A-4212 | |

188 UM MITTERNACHT

| | | |
|---|---|---|
| ○ LW 5123 | ⋆ 421 299–2DH | •• KMON 2 7050 |
| ○ LW 5225 | ⋆ 430 096–2DWO | •• KCSP 172 |
| • LXT 2721 | ⋆ 433 477–2DM | •• 430 096–4DWO |
| • AKF 6 | | •• 160 K1 |
| • ACL 318 | | •• 433 477–4DM |
| • PA 172 | | • ECSP 172 |

| | |
|---|---|
| ○ LD 9137 | ⋆ 433 477–2LM |
| ○ LD 9229 | |
| • LLP 625 | |
| • 5069 | |
| • STS 15202 | |
| • 2-London A-4212 | |

189 THE FAIRY LOUGH

| | | |
|---|---|---|
| ○ LX 3133 | ⋆ 430 061–2LM | •• 430 061–4LM |
| ○ LW 5353 | ⋆ 433 473–2DM | •• 160 K4 |
| • AKF 2 | | •• 433 473–4DM |
| • ACL 310 | | |

| | |
|---|---|
| ○ LPS 1032 | ⋆ 433 473–2LM |
| • R 23187 | |

## 190 A SOFT DAY

| | | |
|---|---|---|
| ○ LX 3133 | ★ 430 061–2LM | ●● 430 061–4LM |
| ○ LW 5353 | ★ 433 473–2DM | ●● 433 473–4DM |
| ● AKF 2 | | |
| ● ACL 310 | | |
| ○ LPS 1032 | ★ 433 473–2LM | |
| ● R 23187 | | |

## 191 LOVE IS A BABLE

| | | |
|---|---|---|
| ○ LX 3133 | ★ 430 061–2LM | ●● 430 061–4LM |
| ○ LW 5353 | ★ 433 473–2DM | ●● 433 473–4DM |
| ● AKF 2 | | |
| ● ACL 310 | | |
| ○ LPS 1032 | ★ 433 473–2LM | |
| ● R 23187 | | |

## 192 SILENT NOON

| | | |
|---|---|---|
| ○ LX 3133 | ★ 430 061–2LM | ●● 430 061–4LM |
| ○ LW 5353 | ★ 433 473–2DM | ●● 160 K4 |
| ● AKF 2 | | ●● 433 473–4DM |
| ● ACL 310 | | |
| ○ LPS 1032 | ★ 433 473–2LM | |
| ● R 23187 | | |

## 193 GO NOT, HAPPY DAY

| | | |
|---|---|---|
| ○ LX 3133 | ★ 430 061–2LM | ●● KCSP 172 |
| ○ LW 5353 | ★ 430 096–2DWO | ●● 430 061–4LM |
| ● AKF 2 | ★ 433 473–2DM | ●● 430 096–4DWO |
| ● ACL 310 | | ●● 160 K4 |
| ● PA 172 | | ●● 433 473–4DM |
| | | ● ECSP 172 |
| ○ LPS 1032 | ★ 433 473–2LM | |
| ● R 23187 | | |

## 194 SLEEP

| | | |
|---|---|---|
| ○ LX 3133 | ★ 430 061–2LM | ●● 430 061–4LM |
| ○ LW 5353 | ★ 433 473–2DM | ●● 433 473–4DM |
| ● AKF 2 | | |
| ● ACL 310 | | |
| ○ LPS 1032 | ★ 433 473–2LM | |
| ● R 23187 | | |

195  PRETTY RING TIME

|  | | |
|---|---|---|
| ○ LX 3133 | ⋆ 430 061–2LM | •• 430 061–4LM |
| ○ LW 5353 | ⋆ 433 473–2DM | •• 433 473–4DM |
| ● AKF 2 | | |
| ● ACL 310 | | |

|  | |
|---|---|
| ○ LPS 1032 | ⋆ 433 473–2LM |
| ● R 23187 | |

196  O WALY, WALY

|  | | |
|---|---|---|
| ○ LX 3133 | ⋆ 430 061–2LM | •• 430 061–4LM |
| ○ LW 5353 | ⋆ 433 473–2DM | •• 433 473–4DM |

|  | |
|---|---|
| ○ LPS 1032 | ⋆ 433 473–2LM |

197  COME YOU NOT FROM NEWCASTLE?

|  | | |
|---|---|---|
| ○ LX 3133 | ⋆ 430 061–2LM | •• KCSP 172 |
| ○ LW 5353 | ⋆ 430 096–2DWO | •• 430 061–4LM |
| ● AKF 2 | ⋆ 433 473–2DM | •• 430 096–4DWO |
| ● ACL 310 | | •• 160 K4 |
| ● PA 172 | | •• 433 473–4DM |
| | | ⦂ ECSP 172 |

|  | |
|---|---|
| ○ LPS 1032 | ⋆ 433 473–2LM |
| ● R 23187 | |

198  KITTY MY LOVE

|  | | |
|---|---|---|
| ○ LX 3133 | ⋆ 430 061–2LM | •• KCSP 172 |
| ○ LW 5353 | ⋆ 430 096–2DWO | •• 430 061–4LM |
| ● AKF 2 | ⋆ 433 473–2DM | •• 430 096–4DWO |
| ● ACL 310 | | •• 160 K4 |
| ● PA 172 | | •• 433 473–4DM |
| | | ⦂ ESCP 172 |

|  | |
|---|---|
| ○ LPS 1032 | ⋆ 433 473–2LM |
| ● R 23187 | |

202  LIEBESLIEDER WALTZER

|  | | |
|---|---|---|
| ● 417 634–1DM | ⋆ 425 995–2DM | •• 417 634–4DM |

|  | |
|---|---|
| | ⋆ 425 995–2LM |

203  ZUM SCHLUSS

|  | | |
|---|---|---|
| ● 417 634–1DM | ⋆ 425 995–2DM | •• 417 634–4DM |

|  | |
|---|---|
| | ⋆ 425 995–2LM |

**206 RASTLOSE LIEBE**

| | | |
|---|---|---|
| ● REGL 368 | | ●● ZCF 368 |
| ● Arabesque 8070 | | ●● Arabesque 9070 |

**207 WASSERFLUTH**

| | | |
|---|---|---|
| ● REGL 368 | | ●● ZCF 368 |
| ● Arabesque 8070 | | ●● Arabesque 9070 |

**209 GRIEF FOR SIN**

◇ CEP 721

| ○ LW 5083 | ★ 414 623–2DH | ●● 414 623–4DG |
|---|---|---|
| ● LXT 2757 | ★ 433 474–2DM | ●● 433 474–4DM |
| ● LXT 5382 | | |
| ● 414 623–1DG | | |
| ○ LD 9096 | ★ 433 474–2LM | ●● 414 623–4LJ |
| ● LLP 688 | | |
| ● 5083 | | |
| ● 414 623–1LJ | | |

**210 ALL IS FULFILLED**

◇ 45–71112
◇ CEP 721

| ○ LW 5083 | ★ 414 623–2DH | ●● 414 623–4DG |
|---|---|---|
| ● LXT 2757 | ★ 433 474–2DM | ●● 433 474–4DM |
| ● LXT 5382 | | |
| ● 414 623–1DG | | |
| ○ LD 9096 | ★ 433 474–2LM | ●● 414 623–4LJ |
| ● LLP 688 | | |
| ● 5083 | | |
| ● 414 623–1LJ | | |

**211 QUI SEDES**

◇ 45–71138
◇ CEP 722

| ○ LW 5083 | ★ 414 623–2DH | ●● 414 623–4DG |
|---|---|---|
| ● LXT 2757 | ★ 433 474–2DM | ●● 433 474–4DM |
| ● LXT 5382 | | |
| ● 414 623–1DG | | |
| ○ LD 9096 | ★ 433 474–2LM | ●● 414 623–4LJ |
| ● LLP 688 | | |
| ● 5083 | | |
| ● 414 623–1LJ | | |

**212 AGNUS DEI**

◇ 45–71138
◇ CEP 722

| ○ LW 5083 | ★ 414 623–2DH | ●● 414 623–4DG |
|---|---|---|
| ● LXT 2757 | ★ 433 474–2DM | ●● 433 474–4DM |
| ● LXT 5382 | | |
| ● 414 623–1DG | | |
| ○ LD 9096 | ★ 433 474–2LM | ●● 414 623–4LJ |
| ● LLP 688 | | |
| ● 5083 | | |
| ● 414 623–1LJ | | |

213 O THOU THAT TELLEST GOOD TIDINGS TO ZION

| ◇ 45–71038 | ○ LW 5076 | ★ 414 623–2DH | •• 414 623–4DG |
| ◇ CEP 550 | ● LXT 2757 | ★ 433 474–2DM | •• 433 474–4DM |
| | ● LXT 5382 | | |
| | ● 414 623–1DG | | |

| | ○ LD 9088 | ★ 433 474–2LM | •• 414 623–4LJ |
| | ● LLP 688 | | |
| | ● 5083 | | |
| | ● 414 623–1LJ | | |

214 FATHER OF HEAVEN

| ◇ CEP 723 | ○ LW 5076 | ★ 414 623–2DH | •• 414 623–4DG |
| | ● LXT 2757 | ★ 433 474–2DM | •• 433 474–4DM |
| | ● LXT 5382 | | |
| | ● 414 623–1DG | | |

| | ○ LD 9088 | ★ 433 474–2LM | •• 414 623–4LJ |
| | ● LLP 688 | | |
| | ● 5083 | | |
| | ● 414 623–1LJ | | |

215 HE WAS DESPISED

| ◇ CEP 550 | ○ LW 5076 | ★ 414 623–2DH | •• KCSP 172 |
| | ○ LW 5225 | ★ 433 474–2DM | •• 414 623–4DG |
| | ● LXT 2757 | | •• 433 474–4DM |
| | ● LXT 5382 | | ‖ ECSP 172 |
| | ● PA 172 | | |
| | ● 414 623–1DG | | |

| | ○ LD 9088 | ★ 433 474–2LM | •• 414 623–4LJ |
| | ○ LD 9229 | | |
| | ● LLP 688 | | |
| | ● 5083 | | |
| | ● 414 623–1LJ | | |

216 RETURN, O GOD OF HOSTS

| ◇ 45–71038 | ○ LW 5076 | ★ 414 623–2DH | •• 414 623–4DG |
| ◇ CEP 723 | ● LXT 2757 | ★ 433 474–2DM | •• 433 474–4DM |
| | ● LXT 5382 | | |
| | ● 414 623–1DG | | |

| | ○ LD 9088 | ★ 433 474–2LM | •• 414 623–4LJ |
| | ● LLP 688 | | |
| | ● 5083 | | |
| | ● 414 623–1LJ | | |

217 GRIEF FOR SIN (Re-created Stereo)

| | ● SXL 2234 | | •• KSDC 286 |
| | ● SDD 286 | | •• KCSP 531 |
| | ● AKF 4 | | •• 160 K2 |
| | ● SPA 531 | | |

218  ALL IS FULFILLED (Re-created Stereo)

| | |
|---|---|
| ● SXL 2234 | ●● KSCD 286 |
| ● SDD 286 | ●● KCSP 531 |
| ● AKF 4 | ●● 160 K2 |
| ● SPA 531 | |

219  QUI SEDES (Re-created Stereo)

| | |
|---|---|
| ● SXL 2234 | ●● KSCD 286 |
| ● SDD 286 | ●● KCSP 531 |
| ● AKF 4 | ●● 160 K2 |
| ● SPA 531 | |

220  AGNUS DEI (Re-created Stereo)

| | |
|---|---|
| ● SXL 2234 | ●● KSDC 286 |
| ● SDD 286 | ●● KCSP 322 |
| ● SPA 322 | ●● KCSP 531 |
| ● AKF 4 | ●● 414 047–4DN |
| ● SPA 531 | ●● 160 K2 |
| | ● ECSP 322 |

221  O THOU, THAT TELLEST GOOD TIDINGS TO ZION (Re-created Stereo)

| | | |
|---|---|---|
| ◇ SEC 5099 | ● SXL 2234 | ●● KSDC 286 |
| | ● SDD 286 | ●● KCSP 297 |
| | ● SPA 297 | ●● KDPC 552 |
| | ● AKF 4 | ●● KCSP 531 |
| | ● SPA 531 | ●● 160 K2 |
| | ● DPA 552 | |

222  FATHER OF HEAVEN (Re-created Stereo)

| | |
|---|---|
| ● SXL 2234 | ●● KSDC 286 |
| ● SDD 286 | ●● KCSP 566 |
| ● AKF 4 | ●● KCSP 531 |
| ● SPA 531 | ●● 421 175–4DC |
| ● SDDM 433 | ●● 160 K2 |
| ● SPA 566 | |

223  HE WAS DESPISED (Re-created Stereo)

| | | |
|---|---|---|
| ◇ SEC 5099 | ● SXL 2234 | ●● KSDC 286 |
| | ● SDD 286 | ●● KCSP 448 |
| | ● AKF 4 | ●● KCSP 531 |
| | ● SPA 531 | ●● 411 887–4DN |
| | ● SPA 448 | ●● 414 048–4DN |
| | | ●● 160 K2 |

224  RETURN, O GOD OF HOSTS (Re-created Stereo)

| | |
|---|---|
| ● SXL 2234 | ●● KSDC 286 |
| ● SDD 286 | ●● KCSP 531 |
| ● AKF 4 | ●● 106 K2 |
| ● SPA 531 | |

226–228  DISCOVERY

THREE SONGS

THREE PSALMS

● 6BB 198       ★ 430 061–2LM    ●● 430 061–4LM
                ★ 433 472–2DM    ●● 433 472–4DM

                ★ 433 472–2LM

# Index – *Composers*

(The reference numbers shown are those for the items in the discography, and are not page numbers.)

Bach, Johann (1685–1750)
  *The Anna Magdalena Songbook Bist du bei mir (attrib. Stölzel?), BWV 508,* 119
  *Cantata No. 11: Praise our God; BWV 11,* 103, 104
  *Cantata no 67: Hold in affection Jesus Christ, BWV 67,* 105, 106
  *Geistliche Lieder und Arien: Vergiss mein nicht, no 71, BWV 505,* 107
  *Ach, dass nicht die letzte Stunde, no 1, BWV 439,* 108
  *Mass in B Minor, BWV 232:*
    Complete, 126, 159
    *Christe Eleison,* 121
    *Laudamus Te* (Schwarzkopf), 122
    *Qui sedes,* 123, 211, 219
    *Et in unum Dominum,* 125
    *Agnus Dei,* 124, 212, 220
  *Matthäus-Passion, BWV 244:*
    Complete version, 120
  *St Matthew Passion, BWV 244:*
    Abridged version, 39
    Complete version (cut), 40
    *Grief for sin,* 209, 217
    *Have mercy, Lord, on me,* 26
  *St John Passion, BWV 245:*
    *All is fulfilled,* 210, 218

Beethoven, Ludwig van (1770–1827)
  *Symphony no 9 in D Minor, op 125,* 44

Berkeley, Sir Lennox (1903–1990)
  *Four Poems of St Teresa of Avila, op 27,* 52

Brahms, Johannes (1833–1897)
  *Auf dem See, op 59, no 2,* 180
  Botschaft, op 47, no 1, 86, 111
  *Constancy, op 3, no 1,* 2
  *Der Jäger, op 95, no 4,* 183
  *Der Tod, das ist die kühle Nacht, op 96, no 1,* 85
  *49 Deutsche Volkslieder:*
    *Feinsliebchen (Sweetheart) no 12,* 3
  *Es schauen die Blumen, op 96, no 3,* 182
  *Gestillte Sehnsucht, op 91, no 1,* 46, 54, 71
  *Geistliches Wiegenlied, op 91, no 2,* 47, 55, 72
  *Immer leiser wird mein Schlummer, op 105, no 2,* 84
  *Liebeslieder-Walzer, op 52,* 202
  *Neue Liebeslieder, op 65, no 15:*
    *Zum schluss,* 203
  *Rhapsody for contralto, male chorus and orchestra, op 53,* 48, 90, 93
  *Sapphische Ode, op 94, no 4,* 110
  *Die schöne Magelone:*
    *Ruhe Süssliebchen in Schatten, op 33, no 9,* 179
  *Sonntag, op 47, no 3,* 148
  *Three vocal quartets, op 64:* 201
  *Four serious songs, op 121,* 61, 116
  *Vier ernste Gesänge, op 121,* 41, 134
  *Von ewiger Liebe, op 43, no 1,* 87, 91
  *Wir wandelten, op 96, no 2,* 92, 181

Bridge, Frank (1879–1941)
  *Go not, happy day,* 193

Britten, Benjamin (1913–1976)
  *The Rape of Lucretia, op 37:*
    Complete, 33
    Incomplete, 34
  *Spring Symphony, op 44,* 76

Chausson, Ernest, (1855–1899)
 *Poème de l'amour et de la mer, op 19,*
  153

Elgar, Sir Edward (1857–1934)
 *The Dream of Gerontius op 38:*
  My work is done . . ., 4
  It is because . . ., 4

Ferguson, Dr Howard (b.1908)
 *Discovery, op 13:* 226

Gluck, Christoph (1714–1787)
 *Orfeo ed Euridice:*
  Concise version, 38
  Complete version (cut), 118
  Complete version, 156
  What is life? 1, 28
  Euridice . . . Che farò? 146

Greene, Maurice (1696–1755)
 *O God of righteousness:*
  I will lay me down in peace, 6
 *Praise the Lord, O my Soul:*
  O Praise the Lord, 7

Gruber, Franz (1787–1863)
 Arr. Gideon Fagan
 *Silent night, holy night,* 56

Handel, George (1685–1759)
 *Admeto:*
  How changed the vision, 96
 *Atalanta:*
  Like as the love-lorn turtle, 95, 142
 *Judas Maccabaeus:*
  Father of Heaven, 214, 222
 *Messiah:*
  O Thou, that tellest good tidings to
  Zion, 213, 221
  He was despised, 215, 223
 *Ottone:*
  Come to me soothing sleep, 12
  Spring is coming, 11
 *Rodelinda:*
  Art thou troubled? 27
 *Samson:*
  Return, O God of Hosts, 216, 224

*Semele:*
  Where 'er you walk, 141
 *Xerxes:*
  Frondi tenere . . . Ombra mai fu,
  53, 59

Hughes, Herbert (1882–1937),
  adapted Gray
 *I know where I'm going,* 116

Jacobson, Maurice (1896–1976)
 *Song of Songs,* 42

Jensen, L.I. (1894–1969)
 *Altar,* 102

Lotti, Antonio (c.1667–1740)
 *Arminio:*
  Pur dicesti, 145

Mahler, Gustav (1860–1911)
 *Das Lied von der Erde,* 51, 184, 185
 *Rückert Lieder:*
  Ich atmet' einen linden Duft, 187
  Ich bin der Welt abhanden
  gekommen, 186
 *Um Mitternacht,* 188
 *Kindertotenlieder,* 89, 157
 *Symphony no 2 in C Minor,* 158
 *Symphony no 3 in D Minor,* 45

Mendelssohn, Felix (1805–1847)
 *Elijah, op 70:*
  O rest in The Lord, 31
  Woe unto them, 32
 *I would that my love, op 63, no 1,* 19
 *Greeting, op 63, no 3,* 20
 *O wert thou in the cauld blast? op 63,*
  no 5, 21

Monteverdi, Claudio (1567–1643)
 *Arianna:*
  Lasciatemi morire, 144

Moss, Katie (1881–1947)
 *The Floral Dance,* 73a

Parry, Sir Charles H. (1848–1918)
    *Love is a bable, op 152, no 3*, 58, 149, 191

Pergolesi, Giovanni (1710–1736)
    *Stabat Mater*, 29

Purcell, Henry (1659–1695)
    Arr. Britten
    *Choice Ayres and Songs:*
        *Mad Bess of Bedlam (From silent shades)*, 97
    *Come ye sons of art away:*
        *Sound the trumpet*, 16
    *The Fairy Queen:*
        *Hark! The echoing air*, 94, 143
    *The Indian Queen:*
        *Let us wander*, 17
    *King Arthur:*
        *Shepherd, leave decoying*, 18

Quilter, Roger (1877–1953)
    *Now sleeps the crimson petal, op 3, no 2*, 165
    *The fair house of joy, op 12, no 7*, 167
    *To daisies, op 8, no 3*, 168

Rubbra, Edmund (1901–1986)
    *Three Psalms, op 61:* 43, 228

Schubert, Franz (1797–1828)
    *An die Musik, op 88, no 4, D 547*, 70
    *Der Musensohn, op 92, no 1, D 764*, 69, 112
    *Der Tod und das Mädchen, op 7, no 3, D 531*, 80
    *Die junge Nonne, op 43, no 1, D 828*, 37, 77, 208
    *Du bist die Ruh', op 59, no 3, D 776*, 82
    *Du liebst mich nicht, op 59, no 1, D 756*, 79, 177
    *Ganymed, op 19, no 3, D 544*, 176
    *Gretchen am Spinnrade, op 2, D 118*, 36
    *Lachen und Weinen, op 59, no 4, D 777*, 147, 178
    *Rastlose Liebe, op 5, no 1, D 138*, 206

*Rosamunde:*
    *Der Vollmond strahlt, op 26, D 797*, 78, 205
*Suleika 1, op 14, no 1, D 720*, 81, 204
*Winterreise:*
    *Wasserfluth, op 89, no 6, D 911*, 207

Schumann, Robert (1810–1856)
    *Frauenliebe und Leben, op 42*, 83, 131
    *Volksliedchen, op 51, no 2*, 133
    *Widmung, op 25, no 1*, 132

Shaporin, Yury (1887–1966)
    *On the Field of Kulikovo*, 23

Stanford, Sir Charles (1852–1924)
    *A soft day, op 140, no 3*, 190
    *The fairy lough, op 77, no 2*, 150, 189

Telemann, Georg (1681–1767)
    *Kleine Kantate von Wald und Au, for contralto, flute and continuo*, 109

TRAD.
    Arr. Fagan
        *O come all ye faithful*, 57
    Arr. Britten
        *Come you not from Newcastle?*, 197
    Arr. Grew
        *Have you seen but a whyte lillie grow?*, 65
    Arr. Hughes
        *Down by the salley gardens*, 68
        *I have a bonnet trimmed with blue*, 161
        *I will walk with my love*, 163
        *Kitty my love*, 198
        *The lover's curse*, 67
        *The stuttering lovers*, 164
    Arr. Jacobson
        *Ca' the yowes*, 136, 151
    Arr. Quilter
        *Drink to me only with thine eyes*, 171
        *Over the mountains*, 169
        *Ye banks and ye braes*, 170

Arr. Roberton
  *The fidgety bairn*, 135
Arr. Sharp
  *My boy Willie*, 162
Coll. Sharp, Arr. Britten
  *O waly, waly*, 160, 196
Arr. Warlock
  *Willow, willow*, 66
Arr. Whittaker
  *Blow the wind southerly*, 62
  *Ma bonny lad*, 63
  *The keel row*, 64
  *The Spanish lady*, 152
  *Turn ye to me*, 22

Vaughan Williams, Ralph (1872–1958)
  *Silent noon*, 192

Warlock, Peter (Philip Heseltine)
  (1894–1930)
  *Pretty ring time*, 195
  *Sleep* 194

Wolf, Hugo (1860–1903)
  *Auf eine altes Bild, Mörike-Lieder, no
  23*, 100
  *Auf einer Wanderung, Mörike-Lieder,
  no 15*, 101
  *Der Gärtner, Mörike-Lieder, no 17*, 99
  *Verborgenheit, Mörike-Lieder, no 12*, 98

Wordsworth, William (1908–1988)
  *Three Songs, op 5:* 227

*Postscript*

Just before going to press a further discovery was made of privately recorded acetate discs of Kathleen. They date from 27th June 1947, when the BBC broadcast a live performance of *Orfeo ed Euridice* on the Third Programme, direct from Glyndebourne. The discs contain excerpts from Act 2 and Act 3 of the opera. All the vocal music also features on the Decca commercial recording made the same month, and the interpretation naturally is very similar. The sound quality is poor, and the voices and orchestra sound distant, but these fragments are the only surviving example of Kathleen actually singing at Glyndebourne. Whether any more of the broadcast was recorded is not known. These are the only discs that have been traced.

Side 1.  Act 2  *Deh placatevi con me* . . . up to . . . *al mio cor.* with Chorus

Side 2.  Act 2  Orchestra only (1′ 45″) *Che puro ciel* (first part)

Side 3.  Act 2  *Che puro ciel* (concluded), with Chorus
                *Ballet music* – Orchestra

Side 4.  Act 3  *Vieni, vieni con me o cara,* with Ann Ayars. *A dovessi* . . . up
                to . . . *oscuro fassi gia.* Ann Ayars

                Conductor Fritz Stiedry
                Southern Philharmonic Orchestra
                Glyndebourne Festival Chorus

# Selected Bibliography

Blyth, Alan (ed.) (1979) *Opera on Record, Vol. 1*, Hutchinson.
Blyth, Alan (ed.) (1983) *Opera on Record, Vol. 2*, Hutchinson.
Blyth, Alan (ed.) (1986) *Song on Record, Vol. 1*, Cambridge University Press.
Blyth, Alan (ed.) (1988) *Song on Record, Vol. 2*, Cambridge University Press.
Blyth, Alan (ed.) (1991) *Choral Music on Record*, Cambridge University Press.
Culshaw, John (1981) *Putting the Record Straight*, Secker and Warburg.
Ferrier, Winifred (1955) *The Life of Kathleen Ferrier*, Hamish Hamilton.
Leonard, Maurice (1988) *Kathleen*, Hutchinson.
Sanders, Alan (comp.) (1984) *Walter Legge – A Discography*, Greenwood Press.
Steane, John (1974) *The Grand Tradition*, Duckworth.

# General Index

Andreas, Dr Bengt 53
Ayars, Ann 20, 21, 63, 108

Bach, Johann Sebastian 104, 105, 106
Baillie, Isobel 8, 9, 10, 32, 43, 58
Baker, Dame Janet 17
Bannister, Arthur 57, 58, 105
Barbirolli, Sir John 74, 75, 86, 92, 95, 100, 106
Barbirolli, Lady Evelyn 74, 75, 86, 92
Bax, Sir Arnold 106
Beard, Paul 10
Beecham, Sir Thomas 20
Beethoven, Ludwig van 105
Beinum, Eduard van 47, 48, 92
Berkeley, Lady 38
Bernac, Pierre 74
Berry, Walter 64
Bing, Rudolf 17
Blyth, Alan 80, 92
Boult, Sir Adrian 32, 33, 79, 94, 95, 96, 97, 98, 99
Boyce, Bruce 24, 25, 28, 80
Boyce, William 24, 25, 28, 80
Brahms, Johannes 7, 11, 19, 103, 104, 105, 107
Brannigan, Owen 16, 18
Britten, Benjamin 12, 14, 16, 36, 54, 55, 63, 83, 84, 103, 104, 105, 106
Bruck, Charles 76, 77
Bruckner, Anton 32
Busch, Fritz 53
Byrd, William 106

Carey, Henry 106
Casa, Lisa della 89
Cellini, Renato 19
Chausson, Ernest 63, 86
Clarke, Arthur 9
Clinton, Gordon 24, 26, 27, 28, 29
Coates, Albert, 10
Cosens, Ian 74
Crimp, Bryan 3

Cross, Joan 16, 17, 18
Cross, John Keir 40
Crozier, Eric 15, 83
Culshaw, John 43, 96, 97
Cummings, Henry 24, 26, 27, 29
Curzon, Clifford 92, 93

Dalberg, Frederick 92
Danco, Suzanne 80
Delius, Frederick 106
Desmond, Astra 13, 69
Diamand, Peter 108
Disney, Walt 108
Dobson, Michael 96, 98
Dodds, Yeoman 80
Donlevy, Edmund 16, 17
Downes, Edward 17
Duval, Nel 76, 77
Dvorak, Anton 84

Edelmann, Otto 64, 65
Elgar, Sir Edward 74, 106
Enesco, Georges 76, 79, 80
Essex, Kenneth 17
Evans, Nancy 15, 17, 42

Fauré, Gabriel 106
Favaretto, Giorgio 72, 73
Felbermayer, Anny 66
Ferrier, Winifred 7, 10, 24, 53, 55, 72, 74, 87
Finneberg, Laelia 10
Fischer-Dieskau, Dietrich 78
Forer, Alois 66, 68
Francis, John 17, 60
Furtwängler, Wilhelm 53, 78

Gal, Hans 92, 93
Gauntlet, Ambrose 96, 97
Gilbert, Max 33, 34, 39, 44, 45
Gluck, Christoph 15
Goldsborough, Arnold 38
Goodall, Reginald 15, 17, 18

Gorr, Rita 77
Greene, Eric 23, 24, 25, 26, 27, 28, 29
Griffis, William 45
Griffith, Anthony 66
Günther, Horst 92, 93

Hammond, Bernadine 88, 108
Handel, George 11, 83, 103, 107
Harewood, The Earl of 17, 47
Harrison, Julius 42
Head, Michael 106
Heegaard, Frederic 53
Heiler, Anton 66, 68
Henderson, Roy 11, 12, 13, 14
Herbert, William 56, 57, 58, 59
Hess, Dame Myra 93
Holst, Gustav 31, 106
Hurwitz, Emanuel 17
Hutchinson, Dr J E 90

Ibbs and Tillett 11, 72

Jacobson, Maurice 80
Jacques, Dr Reginald 24, 25, 38, 56,
   58, 59, 95
Jones, Roderick 10

Karajan, Herbert von 64, 65, 66, 67,
   68, 72, 79, 95
Kaufmann, Erich 65
Kinloch, Louise 63
Klemperer, Otto 52, 76, 77, 78, 79, 92
Koeman, Greet 76, 77
Koussevitsky, Serge 47
Kraus, Otakar 16, 18
Krauss, Clemens 34, 53, 54, 105

Lam, Basil 97, 98
Larter, Douglas 52
Lascelles, Viscount, *See* Harewood
Legge, Walter, 3, 4, 5, 7, 8, 9, 51, 52
Lehmann, Lotte 48
Lengnick, Alfred & Co. 31
Leonard, Maurice 86, 88
Lewis, Richard 41, 86
Lofthouse, Dr. Thornton 24, 25, 58,
   59
London, George 62

Lotti, Antonio 83, 103
Ludwig, Walther 65, 67
Lush, Ernest 100, 101

Maclean, Eric 63
Mahler, Gustav 31, 74, 76, 92
Malcolm, George 80
McCallum, David 12
Mendelssohn, Felix 103
Mitchell, Ena 57, 58
Moeran, Ernest 31, 106
Monteux, Pierre 76
Montgomery, Field Marshall 47
Moore, Gerald 3, 4, 5, 6, 7, 8, 9, 10, 40
Morley, Thomas 83, 104, 105

Nash, Heddle 32
Neel, Boyd 14, 40
Newmark, John 30, 43, 48, 55, 62, 64,
   69, 70, 71, 81, 88, 105

Olof, Victor 88, 89
Oppenheim, Hans 15, 16

Parsons, William 23, 25, 27, 28, 29,
   32, 56, 57, 58, 59
Patzak, Julius 88, 89, 92, 93
Pears, Peter 14, 16, 17, 18, 32, 47, 48,
   58, 80, 83, 84
Peasgood, Dr Osborne 24, 25, 59
Pergolesi, Giovanni 11
Pilss, Karl 68
Piper, John 83
Poell, Alfred 68
Pollak, Anna 16, 18
Pollock, Geoff 83, 84, 92
Porter, Andrew 30
Posthuma, Klaas 76, 77
Procter, Norma 95
Pröglhöf, Hardal 65
Proost, Marten 77
Purcell, Henry 83, 104, 105

Rathauscher, Gisela 66
Ripley, Gladys 4
Ritchie, Margaret 16, 18
Roth, George 60
Rowley, Gordon 86

Sanders, Alan 51
Sandor, Arpad 62
Sargent, Malcolm 4, 11, 12, 38, 41, 42
Scherman, Thomas 63
Schidlof, Peter 17
Schoeffler, Paul 64, 68
Schubert, Franz 54, 92, 103, 104, 107
Schumann, Robert 19, 54, 93
Schwarzkopf, Elisabeth 64, 66, 67, 68, 79
Scott, Cyril 106
Seefried, Irmgard 64, 65, 92, 93
Sharp, Frederick 17, 18
Shaw, Robert 64
Silver, Millicent 60
Spurr, Phyllis 19, 30, 33, 34, 39, 43, 44, 45, 49, 53, 54, 55, 56, 60, 61, 62, 69, 81, 82
Stanford, Sir Charles 106
Sterba, Rosl 66
Stiedry, Fritz 19, 20, 21
Stone, Frederick 31, 85, 90, 91, 93, 94
Stowasser, Magdalena 66

Strauss, Richard 89
Suddaby, Elsie 23, 24, 25, 27, 28, 29
Svanholm, Set 36, 37

Taylor, Joan 13
Tillett, John 36
Titterton, Frank 10
Toscanini, Arturo 95
Toumanova, Tamara 108
Tuxen, Erik 53, 54

Uhl, Friedrich 66

Vaughan Williams, Ralph 106
Vincent, Jo 47, 48, 78, 79
Vlachopoulos, Zoë 20, 21

Walker, Norman 80
Walter, Bruno 9, 31, 32, 36, 37, 48, 49, 50, 51, 52, 63, 69, 74, 78, 84, 86, 87, 88, 89, 90, 93, 106
Wiener, Otto 65
Wilkinson, Kenneth 57, 58